CW00761992

Gustav Stein

The Gymnasium of the Horse

XENOPHON PRESS

Gustav Steinbrecht

The Gymnasium of the Horse

Revised for the First Time, Completed and Published

By

Leibstallmeister Paul Plinzner

Continued on the Basis of New Scientific Discoveries
And Practical Experiences
By
Hans von Heydebreck Colonel (retired)

With a Foreword
By
William C. Steinkraus

Translated from German
By
Helen K. Gibble

XENOPHON PRESS 2011
Franktown, Virginia

Xenophon Press Library

Another Horsemanship, Jean-Claude Racinet, 1994

Baucher and His School, General Decarpentry 2011

Dressage in the French Tradition, Dom Diogo de Bragança 2011

École de Cavalerie Part II (School of Horsemanship), François Robichon de la Guérinière 1992

Healing Hands, Dominique Giniaux, DVM 1998

Methodical Dressage of the Riding Horse, and Dressage of the Outdoor Horse, Faverot de Kerbrech 2010

Racinet Explains Baucher, Jean-Claude Racinet 1997

System of the Art of Riding, Louis Seeger 2012

The Écuyere of the Nineteenth Century in the Circus, Hilda Nelson 2001

The Gymnasium of the Horse, Gustav Steinbrecht 1995

The Handbook of Jumping Essentials, François Lemaire de Ruffieu 1997

The Maneige Royal, Antoine de Pluvinel 2010

Total Horsemanship, Jean-Claude Racinet 1999

What the Horses have Told me, Dominique Giniaux, DVM 1996

Available at **www.XenophonPress.com**

Copyright © 1995 by Xenophon Press

Copyright © 2011 by Xenophon Press LLC

Translated from the German 10th Edition, 1978, Copyright 1995 by Xenophon Press. All rights reserved. No part of this work may be reproduced or transmitted in any form or by any means, electronic or mechanical, including photocopying, or by any information storage or retrieval system except by a written permission from the publisher.

Published by Xenophon Press LLC

7518 Bayside Road, Franktown, Virginia 23354-2106, U.S.A.

ISBN-10 933316259
ISBN-13 9780933316256

Front cover picture: Sketch by Leonardo da Vinci

FOREWORD

This foreword may require a word of explanation if not apology, for some readers may find it passing strange that a landmark of the dressage literature should be introduced by someone usually identified exclusively with show jumping. Please note, however, that there is an immediate precedent in the 1935 (Fourth) German edition of the present work, on which this translation is based, for it bears a "Geleit für den Nachdruck" (A Preface for the Reprint) by the great German show jumping star (later a celebrated course designer) Col. H. H. "Mickey" Brinckmann. Given this precedent, I hope it is not entirely inappropriate for another show jumper to add a few words, especially one who has had a long and enduring interest in dressage, and may even qualify as a dressage person himself, through marriage. And after all, a horse is a horse and a rider a rider; the insights of the great trainers are all largely inter-disciplinary, and applicable to almost anything on four legs, once the concepts are understood.

Even so, the communication of equestrian concepts is sometimes more easily said than done, especially when foreign languages are involved. German can be a language of great precision, but effortless readability is not ordinarily cited as one of its strong points, even by Germans; preserving clarity of expression without sinking into a maze of convolutions is something even gifted translators often failed to achieve. Translating a text like Steinbrecht's from German into coherent English requires not only a thorough command of both languages, but also a horseman's instinct for the true intended meaning, and Helen Gibble has earned the thanks of all English-speaking riders for having accomplished so skillfully so demanding a task.

There can be no doubt that translation difficulties have presented a serious barrier to the appearance in English of Steinbrecht's monumental **Gymnasium des Pferdes**, an event that has had to wait for more than a century notwithstanding the book's unquestionable excellence. This deficiency has been especially regrettable in countries like ours that aspire to improving their competitive results in Olympic dressage, for there is undoubtedly a strong reciprocal relationship between a nation's standard of proficiency in any activity and the existence of a sound and comprehensive literature on the subject in the native language; neither is likely to exist without the other. We have done very well in English with respect to skiing, golf and even corporate takeovers, but pickings in dressage, especially of the foreign literature in translation, have been distinctly slim for a very long time. And until recently, we have paid the price.

This is rather ironic, for the very first serious book on riding, Grisone's **Gli Ordini di Cavalcare** of 1550 took only ten years to be translated into English (by Thomas Blundeville). For the next four hundred years or so, however, the rate of publication of major dressage tests in English (either original or in translation) rarely exceeded three or four per century, the German literature in particular being almost entirely ignored. The 1956 publication of Seunig's **Horsemanship** was a real breakthrough, and since then the situation has gotten much better. However, the number of masterpieces in print in English is still hardly so great that we could have continued to ignore indefinitely the absence of Steinbrecht's **Gymnasium**.

Who was the author of this book the Germans consider worthy of ranking with Xenophon, Pluvinel, Newcastle, and Guérinière? The simple answer is that he was someone who devoted his entire life to horse and who, just before his death, arranged for the publication of what he had learned. But more particularly, Gustav Steinbrecht was born in 1808 in Amfurt, Saxony, the son of a village pastor. Not being suited for the church, he studied veterinary medicine in Berlin, but soon found himself drawn to the manège at Moabit of the celebrated dressage trainer Louis Seeger, where he stayed for eight years, long enough to become an accomplished écuyer and win the hand of Seeger's niece. In 1834 he took over the direction of a private manège in Magdeburg, where he remained for eight more years before returning to Berlin to work again with Seeger, now at the height of his fame. In 1849 he became director of the "Seegerhof" and began transcribing the notes which were eventually to become the heart of the **Gymnasium**. A decade later he acquired his own manège in Dessau, but when his wife found that city too confining he returned once again to Berlin in 1865, where he continued to train horses almost until his death in February, 1885. By then, fortunately for us, he had entrusted the completion of his manuscript to a devoted pupil and disciple, Paul Plinzner, who saw it through to publication in the fall of the same year. Since then the **Gymnasium** has proven an enduring monument to its author, having gone through innumerable printings of four separate editions, and provided a constant source of inspiration and enlightenment for generation after generation of German-speaking horsemen.

Today it stands a cornerstone of the equestrian literature, a work of truly remarkable coherence, comprehensiveness, and depth of understanding; its careful study cannot help but repay the thoughtful horseman many times over. This being the case, all of us who have had to make do without a translation until now owe yet another debt of gratitude to the intrepid dressage publisher Ivan Bezugloff, who has succeeded where so many have failed in finally getting this marvelous work into print in English. I fervently hope that it finds the wide audience it so richly deserves, for I must confess to being one of those who have long urged Ivan to undertake it. I hope you agree that it was worth the wait.

William Steinkraus

December 1994
Noroton, Connecticut

A Preface for the Reprint

Rarely has the reissuance of a book been expected with such patience as this long-planned reprint of our masterwork about the art of riding.

The **Gymnasium of the Horse** lives not only as a book; the brilliance of its spirit renews itself over time. No false doctrine, not even the most recent one about the so-called "instant training," will endure in the face of the pure clarity of Steinbrecht's principles.

Although the circle of trainers and riders is small in whose γυμνασιον the classical rules of the art of riding are being adhered to, it is large enough to remain directive in practical equestrian life and for its evaluation.

Across the turn of the century there is a straight path from Steinbrecht's **Gymnasium of the Horse** over the old and new riding rules of the cavalry and Hans von Heydebreck's **Deutsche Dressurprüfung** [German Dressage Test] to the training guidelines of the Federation for Breeding and Testing of German Horses {HDP} and thus in most recent times, the successful activities of the Training Division of the HDP and especially of the Association of German Judges.

Here in the **Gymnasium** we are in the middle. Only those who untiringly search for the truth of equestrianism will find confirmation in practice of the discoveries described in Heydebreck's epilogue as the healthiest and most reliable foundations because they are constructed according to the laws of nature "on which any true art must be based."

Habent sua fata libelli. This old Roman saying arises in view of the strange fate of our instruction manual: In five generations the ideas of Steinbrecht have been passed on in direct succession from master to student and have been put to use in the saddle. Together they built on the heritage that we now place into the hands of our young riders and their teachers. On the hundredth anniversary of the birth of Hans von Heydebreck we appreciate with them the timeless work that he has developed to its present perfection. The genial combination of Steinbrecht's "pure" teaching with the progressive development of scientific equestrian research opens for us on the basis of classical dressage a multifaceted gymnastic methodology. We gain from it new experiences about the relationship of the "military school" to working at the posting trot, to riding cross-country and to modern gymnastic exercises for jumping.

Thus we confirm the accuracy of the thesis that even future discoveries will be unable to change Steinbrecht's system because its principles have been gleaned from nature.

Hans Heinrich Brinckmann

Warendorf, June 1966

Preface by the Publisher of the First Edition

What the γυμνασιον was for the young Greek, the institution in which he developed the gifts of his body to the fullest and the greatest harmony through daily exercises, that is the *riding arena* for the horse. In the arena we do horse gymnastics where we develop the horse's muscle structure through a system of stages of ever-increasing exercises that follow one another in a logical sequence to enable the muscles to easily put the skeleton into the carriage it requires for service under saddle, to keep it in this carriage continuously and without force, and to move with strength and agility. The mathematical order, the logical clarity, and, in a way, the irrefutable truth of the art of riding is not expressed as clearly in any other recent work as it is in the unfortunately much too little known and read book by *Louis Seeger*, **System der Reitkunst** [System of the Art of Riding]. This genial master who was a student of the famous *Weyrotter* of Vienna, was fortunate to himself have a student who in a long and extremely active life undauntedly practiced and expanded his teachings. I speak of the unfortunately now deceased Gustav Steinbrecht who was known and highly esteemed in large circles of the equestrian world. To this man, whose reputation is so firmly established that it is superfluous to say anything further in his praise - which would also definitely be in contradiction to his unassuming ways - the publisher of the present work owes everything that he was able to accomplish in the art of riding. Every happy hour I spent in the saddle I owe to the generous teachings available to me for years without limits. Now he has also become the cause of my spending so many a pleasurable evening at my desk in theoretical work for our art.

Three years ago, my esteemed master handed me a collection of thoughts which he had set down on paper from the plethora of his rich experiences at the time, for use as I saw fit. I found such a treasure of convincing truths in these utterances that exposed the essence of the art of riding in such a precise manner that I believed I should not deprive the riding public of them. Unfortunately Steinbrecht's health had already been undermined to such an extent because of the hard work that he performed all of his life and he had to avoid any strenuous mental activity. With a heavy heart I had to give up my attempts of urging him to complete these fragments and, since he had given me unlimited power, I had the choice of either publishing the fragments or independently completing them, as best as I was able to, into a complete whole. Since I believed to have entered into my mentor's mind, I undertook the latter to the best of my abilities under the circumstances to pass on to the world after me the overall results of a life which, with unusual talents, had been dedicated completely and exclusively to the noble equestrian art.

The kind reader will find similarities with Louis Seeger in the basic ideas of the present work, which is only natural because of the relationship between Steinbrecht and Seeger. If, on the other hand, differences in the views of the two masters also become evident this should not surprise anyone since a man of Steinbrecht's talents could impossibly pass through life without putting the stamp of his individuality on his work. I am not impartial and must therefore leave it to the reader's judgment if I state my view that I found Steinbrecht's method the most practical anywhere. He always shows us attainable goals and a path to these goals that cannot be missed. While Seeger wrote his book in a cold, strictly scientific style, so that it became known much less than it deserved, the warm tone of the Steinbrecht notes that were produced from the full passion for the subject and taken directly from practical life touches me with particular sympathy, and I have attempted to retain his style as much as possible.

If therefore the present work is written throughout in a popular, easily understood way, so that the kind reader can take it up just like any other entertaining book, it is nevertheless not intended for the layman. It is actually not what one understands as a guideline for training horses, a lesson plan so to speak for working the horse. Instead it attempts to immovably set the goals of the equestrian art, to show what means the horse's nature gives us to attain these goals, and to explain how a system of gymnastic exercises that we call the training of horses can be assembled through appropriate use of these means. By always directing the reader toward the essence of dressage, which becomes clear at any time, on the one hand, in view of the purpose of such dressage and, on the other hand, in view of the nature of the horse, the arrangement of the details of the work are always left to the reader's own discretion in the conviction that his true understanding of the matter will be his best guide.

Although the kind reader himself will feel very clearly which parts of the present work originate from me personally, it is nevertheless my duty to expressly confess that the last three chapters about the canter, the piaffe and the passage and about the airs above the ground, as well as the conclusion, have come exclusively from my pen, while I made only insignificant changes in the remaining, major part of Steinbrecht's work. If thus, in the course of the text of this work, the first person singular is used, this refers to the undersigned in the last three chapters, in the remainder of the book to Steinbrecht. By asking the kind reader's indulgence for my contribution to the work in which I tried to follow the spirit of my master to the best of my ability, I can only wish that the reader will reap the same benefits from reading Steinbrecht's own statements that I gained to the richest degree from editing them.

Potsdam, December 1884.

Paul Plinzner

Introduction to the Fourth Edition

Since the publication of the first edition of the **Gymnasium** precisely fifty years have passed and yet the principles laid out in this work continue to be applicable. It has therefore also become increasingly popular during the last decades, particularly since the German Riding Rules for the Army of the Deutsche Reich were based on the Steinbrecht principles. It remains the undisputed merit of the late Leibstallmeister Plinzner to have made Steinbrecht's teachings accessible to us after the latter's death on the basis of documentation he left behind. Most of all it must be pointed out that in the last three chapters of the **Gymnasium**, which were written exclusively by him, Plinzner was able to catch Steinbrecht's spirit and thus present a uniform system.

So far, the **Gymnasium** has undergone three editions published by Leibstallmeister Plinzner, the last one appearing in the year 1900. Now that edition is also out of print and the present publishing house decided on a new edition. I was requested to edit this new edition which I agreed to do with even more pleasure since it was Plinzner's desire, as stated in the foreword to the Third Edition, that one of his students, of which I was one, to whom he was privileged to transfer Steinbrecht's teachings continue the work in the same spirit and fill existing gaps.

Although I have been one of the most ardent defenders of the Steinbrecht system, having introduced it not only in the Riding Rules, in the preparation of which I was allowed to participate together with some other members of a committee established for that purpose, and have also promoted these unexcelled equestrian principles in the spoken and written word for recognition and distribution, I was aware of the high demands that I would have to meet in editing it. On the one hand, it is my opinion that there is no other work on riding in all the world that reveals so clearly the great truths of the art of riding and delves as deeply into the essence of gymnastic horse training than Steinbrecht's **Gymnasium**. On the other hand, however, it postulates some theses which no longer withstand modern scientific research and are even contradictory somewhat to important major principles laid down at other locations in the work. One example is the repeated statement that a horse in lateral flexion moving on a straight line always puts more weight on the inside hind leg than on the outside hind leg. In the conclusion drawn from that statement the author contradicts himself and the principles that he established in the definition of the term balance. This had to be examined carefully in the new edition.

If I therefore changed the existing text there as well as at some other points, this should in no way diminish or reduce the merit of the former imperial Leibstallmeister for this important work. To the contrary, I am particularly pleased to take the opportunity to give him the recognition he deserves to the highest degree here in the same way as I have done elsewhere in verbal and written communications. Under his direction I worked at the Royal Stables for three years and learned such an infinite amount that I will be grateful to him, my highly esteemed instructor, for the rest of my life. Even after my return to the practical life of a soldier I always stayed in close equestrian contact with him and exchanged thoughts in friendship. Later our opinions diverged in some points. The reason for this was mainly that Plinzner, in view of the special demands of his responsible position, began to adapt Steinbrecht's equestrian principles and teachings according to his own experiences to the specific requirements of that position. For me any deviation from Steinbrecht's teachings, which were my equestrian bible, was always a sin against the holy spirit of riding.

However, this divergence in our views about riding has fortunately not clouded our close personal relationship even though shortly before the war, soon after the German Riding Rules had been published, in which, as already mentioned, I participated and which were entirely based on Steinbrecht's major principles of dressage training, there were some public polemics, not initiated by me, that temporarily clouded this relationship somewhat. Yet, this dispute never interfered with my admiration for my former instructor and equestrian friend. Substantive differences in the opinion of experts, I am deeply convinced, should never have such repercussions. That is the reason that I here again take the opportunity to thank the late Leibstallmeister in the name of the entire equestrian world that he was instrumental in relating to us the golden rules of the greatest German riding master, Steinbrecht, in his **Gymnasium**. I want to thank him personally once more as well. Plinzner has made these teachings clear to me in practice and has thus enhanced and deepened my equestrian knowledge and expertise. He awakened in me an understanding for the essence of the art of riding and made me its most faithful disciple. The more practical experience I have gained, the more relentlessly I have espoused Steinbrecht's basic views.

There is no standing still in the world, development continues in all areas. In the teaching of riding, not only has stop-action photography given us new knowledge about the sequence of movements of the horse, through more recent scientific research we have also gained new insights into the various body parts of the horse, particularly the participation of its muscles and joints in motion. In the present new edition of the **Gymnasium** obvious gaps in the system have been closed in Steinbrecht's sense and some erroneous views in the rider's language, which perhaps had crept in only inadvertently, have been corrected.

For the kind reader's understanding I would like to point out that in the chapters that Plinzner indicated as being authored by Steinbrecht, that is, up to the lateral movements inclusively, almost only stylistic changes have been made and my deviating opinions have been expressed in footnotes to the text. Additions have been made to the last sections authored by Plinzner, mainly the chapter on the canter, and a few changes have been made. Those I explained in remarks in which I refer to the earlier wording.

The subject matter has also been arranged in a somewhat different way in that I combined the actual haute école movements in a large chapter and preceded them with a separate chapter about the "Lower Level Movements." This chapter briefly discusses the perfection of the three basic paces required to obtain classical collection up to the school walk, the school trot, and the school canter. A few explanatory words have been added to the halts and rein-back - both were somewhat short-changed in the earlier editions.

In addition, the statements about the work between the pillars have been shortened somewhat since, according to modern interpretation of academic riding as still practiced at the Spanish Riding School in Vienna, this inanimate tool has lost greatly in significance as a training aid. Instructions about developing the haute école leaps have also been omitted since, in my opinion, any classical trainer who justifiably attempts to involve himself with these movements that are presently useful only for exhibition purposes, no longer needs special instruction.

Moreover, further scientific research about the activity and interaction of the muscles moving the horse's limbs and the resulting consequences for appropriate gymnastic exercises for these muscles provided new revelations about the training methods to be employed, as this has also happened in the field of human gymnastics due to anatomical and physiological research so that the gymnastic development of the human body has continuously been perfected. However, even future discoveries will not change anything in the basics of the Steinbrecht system. His principles, which he took from nature, have become increasingly more popular everywhere, not only in Germany, in other countries as well. It has been my endeavor all through my life to prepare the way for them, to promote them, and to thus benefit the art of riding. These thoughts and desires were also what guided me during the work on this new edition.

Omitted has been the former conclusion which in some part no longer suits modern conditions.

In an epilogue I have attempted to set down the most important thoughts of the old "Conclusion" and to once more emphatically illuminate everything said there and elsewhere about the practical use of dressage training, including classical dressage, and about the need for academic riding schools in view of the present state of riding in general. Since World War I, I have spoken and fought for this concept verbally and in writing and believe to be justified in some way to conclude my work in Steinbrecht's sense by adding the urgent admonition that the German riding world must have such a cultural center where the equestrian art is nurtured.

May it be created before it is too late and may it use as its motto Steinbrecht's golden rule:
"Ride Your Horse Forward and Set It Straight"
for the advantage and benefit of German riding.

In closing, I must give especially heartfelt thanks once more, as often before, to my dear friend and equestrian partisan, General von Josipovich, for the support he gave me. He has again been faithfully at my side with his advice and has furthered my work particularly by making available to me his copy of the **Gymnasium** in which he had made numerous marginal comments. These conclusive explanations have been a great help to me because they have given me additional important insights.

Completed in July of 1935.

Hans von Heydebreck, Colonel (ret.)

CONTENTS

A. The Rider's Seat and Aids

1. The Seat

Before we turn to the actual object of this book, the *working of the horse*, it is necessary for us to agree on the means that we have available to accomplish this task. I do not refer to the external tools which we use during our work: the bridle, saddle, spurs, whip, lunge line, pillars. These will not be covered in separate chapters, but will be mentioned only occasionally. I mean, rather, the use that man can make of his own body for the purpose of working the horse. This use of his limbs will be appropriate and successful only if it is based in every respect on a detailed understanding of the nature of the horse and on a precise knowledge of its anatomy. Understood in this way, the means for working the horse are mainly the appropriate, *natural* seat on the horse and then, as a result of such a seat, the correct *use of the limbs* to influence the horse.

It cannot, of course, be my intention to repeat the generally known rules for the rider's seat. Instead, I merely want to briefly illuminate those points which I think are essential for the seat as a means for dressage training.

A deep-rooted prejudice has established a so-called "normal" seat for the rider, that is, a body position to be presented by the mounted rider once and for all. I believe, the fact that this "normal" seat is demonstrated to the student right at the beginning and is practiced with great discipline is the main reason why many young people are frightened away from the arena and from the systematic study of the art of riding. Instead, they prefer the unrestrained and exclusive riding of hunts and steeplechases, although with suitable instruction they might have become higher-level dressage riders.

A "normal" seat on the horse, even if in the majority of cases this means only a posture that is correct, does not exist at all because the rider sits the horse correctly only if his center of gravity, or rather the line of the center of gravity of his body, coincides with that of the horse. Only then is he in complete harmony with his horse and only then does he become one with it. Since, however, the center of gravity of the horse can be displaced in various ways, depending on its changing position and carriage, the rider's position must change accordingly every time. It is the privilege of the fine, well-educated rider to feel at once where the horse's center of gravity lies, to bring himself into harmony with it, and to then displace the horse's center of gravity so that the horse will carry itself in such a way that it produces the rider's beautiful, light, and unrestrained seat.

There are but a few riders of whom one can say that the horse increases in value one hundred percent when they are in the saddle. If the rider cannot adjust his position according to that of the horse, or is unable to correctly shape the horse's carriage according to his own, the result will always be a caricature. The Englishman on his horse, with loose reins, short stirrups, and a hunched back, is not a beautiful sight, yet he is a natural one and cannot therefore be called a caricature. The wretched Sunday rider, however, with his stretched-out legs, hollow back, and arms tight against his body, on his tired nag, is the most ridiculous sight in the world, and thus the object of much derision.

The so-called "normal" seat becomes a beautiful and elegant seat only if the horse, after having been put into the correct balance, puts its rider into this seat itself. Such a picture is then truly one of harmony, and no man will appear more to advantage anywhere than if he can present himself on his horse in such a way. Whoever understands that beauty and lightness of seat do not depend only on the posture of the rider, but just as much on the correct carriage and the regular gaits of the horse, will find it quite natural that I recommend directing the student, as soon as he has become somewhat secure, to work on his horse's carriage, although this might once in a while occur at the expense of his normal position.

For the beginning rider, the most important teacher of a correct seat must always be the horse. A good seat (natural, supple, soft) has enormous importance not only for the rider in general, but especially for the rider who later on wishes to train a horse. This importance will be encountered again and again in every chapter of this book. There can be nothing more wrong than to put the student on a worn-out and disabled, bent-out-of-shape and difficult nag, to force him on this caricature of a riding horse into the so-called "normal" seat, and then demand that, with this type of gymnastics, he should begin to develop a love for, much less a feeling for, the horse.

The old masters put their students on completely trained dressage horses, initially between the pillars, without stirrups or reins. No other instruction was required than to sit down uninhibitedly the way it felt good, to spread the seat bones well, and to let the legs hang down naturally. Then, in the orderly, cadenced movements of the piaffe, the student began to feel the horse so that a transition could be made to the pesade and to leaps in which the rider then learned to maintain his seat by softly following the movements of the horse. Thus prepared, the student was then put on the lunge line, also on a dressage horse and, again without stirrups or reins, he practiced on a moving horse that which he had learned previously in place between the pillars: to softly follow all movements of the horse or, in other words, to be in *balance*, which is much more the basis for a good and secure seat than the so highly touted firm grip of the legs.

With such schooling, including occasional brief reminders by the instructor, the beautiful lines of the seat would come quite naturally. The student is able to enjoy his work right from the start, giving him a foundation for his whole life for that which is most important in riding and particularly in schooling horses: the *fine feel for the horse*.

It needs no explanation that training recruits this way is hardly possible in the army, but the young person who wants to study the art of riding in an expert manner should not be trained in any other way. If one hears the general complaint today that we no longer have any good trainers to whom we can entrust a young horse without worry, that is the natural result of the fact that there no longer exist any academic riding schools where dressage horses are trained, to later become the true teachers of the riding student.

When the student has learned the natural seat on the normally trained horse, it will be necessary to teach him, as well, the deviations from this seat as required for a horse that is green or only lightly schooled. For this purpose, he should also occasionally ride such horses, and it should be pointed out to him how he can remain in *harmony* with them as well by correctly distributing his weight; that is, how he can retain his balance while always being able to grip with his legs to secure his seat during particularly rough and violent movements.

The main rule for this balanced seat, which is based on the correct displacement of the center of gravity, is that the rider's straight spine must always be perpendicular to that of the horse; that is, it must form two right angles with it. According to this principle, we see the race rider lean far forward with his upper body so as to increase the speed of his mount whereas, if his body were leaning back or even in an upright position, he would not be able to follow the movements of the horse. We also see the well-trained military horse under its upright rider perform the most intricate turns and movements, always in regular gaits with a lightness, willingness, and endurance which will inevitably arouse interest in the layman for such a beautiful and seemingly easy art. In this position of the horse, its center of gravity falls approximately in the middle between forehand and hindquarters, and its spine is horizontal; thus the vertical position of the rider. Finally, we see the dressage horse with its hind legs put well under, its haunches bent, and its croup lowered, performing its graceful, yet powerful, movements on and above the ground. The rider guides it with a slightly reclining upper body and with a security and accuracy as if the horse's four legs were his own. In these movements, the horse's center of gravity is vertically[1] above its hindquarters, and its spine is sloped downward from front to back.

By observing the above-mentioned principle regarding the coincidence or, more correctly, precise vertical congruence of the centers of gravity of man and horse, the rider can make it infinitely easier for the horse to carry his weight, not directly, but in effect. That is the reason why horses not only perform twice as well under a good rider as under a poor one, but also why they remain useful many years longer, although the poor rider perhaps puts less weight in the saddle. It is also the reason why any dead weight is such an impediment to movement and is therefore avoided as much as possible in the race horse. The same principle explains how the equilibrist, standing still, can balance two or even three men of his own size and weight and can even move under their enormous weight. In their lifeless state, even one of these men would perhaps be a heavy load for him.

If then, as we have seen, the rider's seat is dependent mainly on the carriage of the horse, and is correct only if the rider unequivocally accommodates himself to this carriage, there does exist, of course, a significant influence on his outline, and that is the saddle which serves as his support. The stiff, stereotypical, so-called "normal" seat - the shape of which I may assume to be known to the reader of this book - had its origin in a time in which saddles very much facilitated an erect carriage of the body by their padded seats, high back rests, and thick knee rolls so that, on the well-trained dressage horses of that time, the rider's position could easily appear natural and graceful.

In our cavalry, this is also the prescribed seat, and can be practiced as such since it is practically evoked by the Hungarian or stock saddle.

Once, however, the stock saddle has been replaced in the army by a saddle that comes closer to the shape of the English saddle, the present "normal" seat will have to be relinquished, and this will be a great advantage for riding purposes and even more for working a horse. The stock saddle is not of advantage for working a horse since it permits only a crotch seat and more or less prevents the finer aids of balance and weight distribution from becoming effective. Moreover, its hollow position on the horse's back removes the rider too far from the horse. Therefore, all non-commissioned officers should be schooled on saddles similar to the English saddle until they attain a highly perfected, balanced seat, and then they should be asked to train young horses. They would then become much better trainers for these young horses and better teachers for their troops, and would be able to serve 10 to 15 years longer with healthy and agile bodies.[2]

Just as many other exercises, if done regularly and appropriately, serve to keep a man's limbs supple, agile, and strong, riding, as the most perfect of all physical exercises, must also serve this purpose - and does so, as experience has shown, in those cases where it is done correctly. If, therefore, professional riders, or people of another profession requiring much and extended riding, seem to be stiff and worn out before their time, this is either the result of other adverse influences or of a forced, unnatural seat that has needlessly worn away their strength. With correct, natural balance, one can spend the greater portion of one's life on a horse and still appear youthful and fresh into an advanced age. A cramped, stiff seat must have a much more disadvantageous effect on the rider's body since our present-day English saddles do not make it the least bit easier for such a rider. Except for the seat and stirrups, such a saddle does not provide a comfortable support for the rider. The always practical English-man has gradually evolved this saddle from the heavy German dressage saddle, not only to make it easier for his horses during strenuous competitive rides and hunts but also to be immediately free of the saddle in case of a fall. He knows that under such conditions bone fractures and other injuries are caused more often from being crushed by the horse than from contact with the ground.

While the English saddle has advantages for hunting and steeplechase riding as well as for military and dressage riding, its usefulness is augmented in the latter discipline in that it facilitates, even demands, a finely balanced seat from the rider and thus, although making the task more difficult for him, causes the rider to endeavor to advance the art to a higher degree of perfection. While the old masters, on their dressage saddles, knew how to advance the art of riding to a high level under greater expenditures of time and strength on the part of horse and rider, we, if we reach that same level with our lighter, more agile, and nobler horses, will have produced a more perfect art since we have attained this goal with nothing but simple, natural means.

Aware of the danger that I might bore the reader, I continue to refer to the fact that everything stiff and forced in the rider's position must be avoided and that the rider must understand what is necessary for a correct position and why.

A back that is braced too much curves the spine forward, just as a back that is relaxed too much curves it toward the rear and has the same disadvantages, only in the opposite direction. For some students it is very difficult to find the middle ground between these two extremes, but almost everything else depends on it. *The spine is like the trunk from which all limbs branch out and to which all organs are attached.* The activity of the organs and the forcefulness of the limbs must also be a function of the position of this trunk. When the student is doing seat exercises, both extremes should once in a while be produced intentionally in order to make him experience the feeling of the natural, straight position. This will also be of great help to him when, later, while training his horse in dressage, he will often require these two extreme positions as aids to bring his center of gravity into coincidence with that of his horse. Pulling back the shoulders is necessary, not only to free the chest cavity so that the precious organs in it are not constricted but also to give the upper arms their quiet, natural, straight-down position and a secure support from the small of the back. However, pulling the shoulders up should be avoided since that not only restricts the freedom of the arms but would also impart a somewhat forced appearance to the entire upper body.

Next to the correct position of the spine, the flat position of the thigh is the major point in the entire theme of the correct seat. The correct position of this limb produces steadiness of the hips, broadens the seat area, and secures the rider's position by permitting him to close his legs in cases where balance alone might be insufficient, without in any way interfering with the horse.

Although the lower legs are less important for a correct seat[3], they are the main source of the driving aids and the correct position of the stirrups. Since, for this purpose, the lower legs must be agile and elastic in the ankle joints, it is quite wrong to force the student to acquire the habit of carrying the lower legs in a stiff and immobile way by making him stretch the knee joints and raise his toes excessively. Stiff lower legs will, later on, neither hold the stirrups correctly on the feet nor enable the rider to give correct aids with calves and spurs. The only reason for raising the toes is to put the heels down so that the still inexperienced student will not worry his horse by inadvertently touching it with the spurs. As soon as the rider's position is secure, with proper balance and closing of the thighs, he can let his lower legs hang down quite softly and naturally.

In order to be able to resist or, rather, counteract the strong influences exerted on his seat by the horse's movements, the rider must be flexible in the hips and be able to easily and nimbly turn his upper body from the hips. To attain such skill, the student should frequently be made to intentionally lose his balance toward one side or the other during seat exercises without stirrups and then, when too much of his weight hangs toward that side, regain the correct seat merely by swinging his hips, without any support from hands or legs.

At this point, I would like to refer to a brochure by Count Denes Szechenyi, who – in the correct realization of the importance of, and the basic requirements for, a natural, balanced seat – likewise recommends doing seat exercises on the lunge without stirrups or reins. He even suggests playing ball in this position. This will certainly produce more enthusiastic and sensitive riders than will forcing them into the stiff "normal" seat.

The fine arts produce true beauty only if they stay within the confines of nature. Any digression beyond these boundaries is punished by distortions and caricatures and, although fashion sometimes sees beauty in such aberrations, they have nothing in common with true art. I close this important chapter by asking each rider who truly wants to earn this title to let each of his limbs find its resting point, and thus steadiness, by letting it hang under its own weight, and to put no force or stiffness in his overall posture. Any such effort would require the expenditure of forces and thus would not only be very tiring, but would also rob the limbs of their elasticity and agility and have an inhibiting influence on the freedom of movement of the horse.

The rider should act artificially in the form of an exertion of force only if the aids require it; as soon as the horse has accepted these aids, the rider should return to the rest position and follow the movement of the horse by appropriately positioning his body. If we look at the groups of Greek riders at their ancient Olympic games, we are enraptured by the grace and loveliness expressed in every position of rider and horse. Would the old masters of sculpture, who for centuries have been ideals that have never since been attained, have been able to create such beauty if they had not had the models embodied before them?

ENDNOTES:

[1] The center of gravity lies vertically above the hind legs only in the so-called schools above the ground; in the other dressage movements, for example the piaffe and passage, the center of gravity has been moved back only to the extent that it falls approximately on a perpendicular drawn through the point of contact between the last dorsal vertebra and the first lumbar vertebra. (Hanz von Heydebreck)

[2] In the meantime, the stock saddle has been replaced by the army saddle which has a shape closer to the English saddle. If the advantages of this change as predicted here by Steinbrecht have unfortunately not come about to their full extent, the reason for this is that the army is simply of the opinion that the stiff seat of the grenadier is indispensable for reasons of discipline. It should be hoped, however, that it will become the increasingly accepted knowledge that the discipline of mounted troops is far more a function of well moving horses than of stiffly sitting riders, and that therefore a natural seat which furthers this way of going of the horses will be permitted. (Paul Plinzner)
Unfortunately, the shape of the army saddle still does not completely meet the requirements placed on a saddle that promotes a natural, unconstrained seat. (Hans von Heydebreck)

[3] As will be discussed in greater detail in the chapter about "The Driving Aids," lower legs that lie softly against the horse's body increase the area of contact between rider and horse and thus also ensure that the upper body remains in balance. The rider must therefore attempt, by softly gripping around the barrel-shaped body of his horse, to be in touch with the horse on the most intimate level. This brings him "deep into the saddle" and enables him to remain "in the saddle" in all gaits, that is to "sit the horse." (Hans von Heydebreck)

2. The Aids

The young horse must first learn the art of understanding its rider and must be made familiar with the aids before it can be expected to be obedient. Its response to the aids is therefore based primarily on systematic familiarization; with increasing practice it learns to pay attention to the aids and submits to their constraints. If it is treated correctly, the horse thus gradually arrives at willing obedience. Resistance will be the exception. It should also be noted that the resistance a horse offers against the rider's aids are usually based on sensitivity or fear which are augmented further by harsh aids. Therefore initial demands must be moderate and all actions that could produce resistance should be avoided until the horse submits to the rider's will as a matter of course.

Aids are the rider's influences on his horse with which he conveys his will. They are the language through which he communicates with his horse. Although the horse's obedience to the aids is ultimately the result of the respect the horse has of the pain that the rider might inflict on it as punishment in the case of disobedience, this must not lead to the conclusion that strong aids ensure obedience. Depending on the strength of the action, we distinguish *finer* and *stronger aids*. But, once these aids are increased to the point that they generate pain, they cease being aids and become punishment. It is almost unbelievable how receptive the completely trained horse finally becomes for fine aids so that it appears miraculous to the layman if such a horse works under its skilled rider without any perceptible aids and with the utmost of energy and accuracy, as if the animal were reading the rider's mind. In observing the threatening spur upon the slightest resistance, the horse follows the softest, hardly discernible pressure of the leg to let its body take on the most artificial positions and bends, and it willingly follows the finest pressure of a finger on the rider's hand to perform the most difficult turns.

The aids are separated into *driving aids, restraining aids,* and *supporting aids.*

(a) The Driving Aids

Among the driving aids, those that the rider is able to give with his lower legs are of the greatest importance because they are the most effective and the most natural. We see a farmer keeping his horse moving with dangling legs by using his heels on the horse's ribs to make it go faster. These aids from the lower legs are again broken down into aids given with the spurs, the calves, and the knees.

Correct and thorough work with the *spurs* is the only way to make a horse supple and active through and through.[1] Without absolute obedience to the spurs it is impossible to determine the position of the horse, to arbitrarily move its center of gravity, or to determine the direction and cadence of its movement. All this depends on the action of the hind legs, whether they move the weight more forcefully forward or carry it with elasticity. All forward movement starts in the hind legs and can be truly mastered only by the spurs. If individual, ticklish horses refuse to accept the spurs and yet in the end perform their movements from heels without spurs but with the aid of the whip that is not proof for the indispensability of the spurs. The obedience of such horses in spite of all their sensitivity to the legs will be rather questionable as soon as the long training whip is no longer hovering nearby as a threatening ghost.

A horse that is completely obedient to the spurs moves forward from the uniform pressure of both legs. If at the same time the hands prevent it from moving forward it will collect itself; that is, its hind legs will step under more. The more the horse does this, the more weight is put on the hind legs. This then causes the joints of the hind legs to bend and is called "lowering the haunches." If one leg acts stronger than the other, the horse moves away from that leg and takes on a lateral position; if the counter-action of the other leg prevents it from doing so, however, it bends in the rib cage and is thus capable of performing the most difficult turns. Such obedience is the result of earlier spur actions during dressage training, and the fear of a repetition of these influences keeps the horse always attentive and willing.

The rider can use the spurs in various ways, and we want to turn now to the different gradations of their use.

The *jab with the spur* is the strongest and most emphatic influence with the spurs. It gives the horse a momentary, intense pain and, by injuring the skin, causes infection and swelling of the parts involved so that, for some time, the sensitivity at that point is even greater. I speak of course of spurs that really deserve their name and are equipped with five- to six-point rowels. Rowels with very many fine and very pointed tips are not good since they injure without drawing blood and therefore often produce unpleasant edemas.[2]

Lazy horses and those that are reluctant to use their power are driven into lively action by a jab with the spurs; and any stubbornness, resistance, or mischievousness is punished with the spurs. The rider must give the jab forcefully and decisively, but more from the ankle joints than from the knees. He must raise his heel slightly and thus point the spur toward the horse so that, at the moment of contact with the horse, the stirrup hits against the heel. It is very wrong for the rider to swing out his legs; that is, to initially move his lower legs forward to produce more impetus from the greater distance traversed by his swinging legs. On the one hand, this will give away his intention in advance, and the horse will certainly interfere more or less with the execution of the jab; on the other hand, the rider relinquishes his secure leg position so that he will be unable to grip tightly with his knees at the moment when he urgently needs to do so to be able to resist violent and uncontrolled movements on the part of the horse. But even for the most violent and repeated spur jabs, all activity must be limited entirely to movements of the lower legs, up to the knees. Any visible participation of the arms or the upper body is annoying and bad manners.

Before the jab is performed, the spur must be directed toward that part of the body which is to be hit, since its effect is very different depending upon whether the jab is directed toward the ribs or more toward the flanks. The more forward a jab is to be, the more the foot must first be directed outwardly, originating mainly from the ankle joint, so that the flat position of thigh and knee, which produces the grip, is not adversely influenced. Such grip is that much more necessary in such a case since, at the most important moment, right after the jab has been performed, the support of the stirrup is no longer available as it flies against the heel.

The *prick with the spur* is no punishment but an aid. It differs essentially from the jab in that the rider retains his support in the stirrups. He needs this support when he uses the spur just as much as a painter needs the maulstick to make his hand secure and yet light in guiding the brush. The rider first places his lower leg against the horse's body, then pulls up his heel with his toes supported in the stirrup so that the spur is about one-half to one inch away from the part on which it is to act. From that distance, the prick is made. Riders with long lower legs must take the stirrup onto the tip of their toes in order to be able to raise their heel. They must often try to shorten their legs by bending their knees more.[3] The spur prick serves as a vivid reminder of the spur if the horse seems to be inattentive or negligent in its response to the soft aids from the calves.

A *flat touch with the spur*, where not the rowel but the inside of the neck of the spur touches the horse's side, as well as the even more subtle aid where the spur merely approaches to the point where it barely touches the hair, are finer gradations of the above-described aid. They, therefore, serve the same purpose, depending on the temperament, sensitivity, and good will of the horse. The more subtle the intended aid, the more support must be given by the stirrup to give the foot a point of rest from which it can reliably direct the spur. This holding of the stirrup with the heel raised slightly is again a finer degree of the spur aids under discussion. For a very attentive and obedient horse it is threat enough to produce greater activity. This aid, which I will call the "threatening leg position," must be considered the most subtle spur aid of all.

The *spur pressure* is a continuation of the leg pressure. With a simultaneously restraining hand, it is the most intensive means to get a horse away from the reins. The horse is held in front and thus prevented from escaping forward from a painful tickling of the spur. It can do nothing else but become light in the hands by pushing itself together and yielding the previously resistant poll.

To use spur pressure, as for all spur aids, the rider must position his foot, supported in the stirrup, so that the spur touches the intended point and presses against the horse's body with a force determined precisely by the horse's temperament and sensitivity. This pressure must be reduced or cease completely the more the horse yields and becomes light in the hand.

Just as the threatening leg position must be considered the lightest spur aid, so is the spur pressure the strongest such aid and it must, therefore, be used with the greatest moderation since its misuse can easily produce resistance and even complete unresponsiveness. Most of all, the intensity of the spur pressure must be in precisely the correct relationship to the restraining effect of the hands. Only then will the intended result of moving away from the hand be realized and, exactly at the moment when this result has been attained, both aids must cease and hands and legs must return to the previously employed, more passive behavior. With the required consequence in this procedure, spur pressure will soon become superfluous, and the mere pressure of the leg in the above-described threatening position (or, at most, an occasional reminder by a slight prick with the spur) will suffice to keep the horse light in the hand. It should, in any case, always be the rider's endeavor to use the spur aids as lightly as possible since exaggerated and rough use of the spurs at best dulls the horse and makes it insensitive.

While the spur aids mainly aid the activity of the hind legs and are intended to produce a stimulating, electrifying effect in the horse, the *calf aids* are like steady barriers within which the hindquarters must work. For that reason, the rider should always have his lower legs in contact with the horse. This contact will establish itself automatically if he lets his legs hang naturally; he should not try to find such contact through an artificial position of his legs. The soft contact of the calves from a natural position of the legs serves the horse as a guideline for the sequence of its hind legs while it enables the rider to evaluate the horse's movement with more certainty.

The area of contact between the rider and his horse is not only the basis on which he must keep the weight of his upper body in equilibrium, but it is also, simultaneously, the means which inform him of the horse's movement. The correct and quick recognition of the effect the horse's movement has on us is the so extremely important characteristic which we attribute to the *tactful rider* or call the *mark of a sensitive rider*. The greater the areas are which connect horse and rider, the more reliable will be such a perception. The rider is unable to observe visually the placement of his horse's feet, at least not without jeopardizing his position. He is here like the blind person who, with a high development of his sense of touch, must try to replace the missing eyesight in the best possible way. The strangest examples teach us how well these unfortunates are able to do this. As the blind person touches the object before him very softly and lightly with his fingertips in order not to interfere with the work of the sensitive nerve ends by too much pressure, so it is the rider's first obligation to keep soft and natural those parts of his body with which he feels his horse. If his seat meets this requirement, he will soon feel the movement of the horse's legs and will be able to distinguish each individual one; he will thus have the means at his disposal with which to control them as if they were his own. How much a stiff and forced posture interferes with the fine feeling of a rider is evident in many an old practical horseman who, in spite of many years of work and practice, is still in doubt about the position of his horse's feet and must assure himself visually with ridiculous behavior.

[13]

From this quiet, rather passive contact of his calves, the rider must often change to greater activity of the same. This is done partly by increased pressure and partly by moving the lower legs further back towards the horse's flanks. In both cases, the effect is reinforced even more if, with greater force in the stirrups, the calves are tensioned and thus their contact becomes more noticeable. Generally, the calves act by a quiet, continuous pressure which is increased as required and is used sometimes more in front, sometimes further toward the flanks, to keep the horse in its bend and the hind legs strictly on the prescribed lines. But it is also possible to produce a driving force by exerting more pressure with the legs while they drop against the horse's body in the rhythm of its movement.

As easy as these aids seem to be, their manifold gradations and the need to give them at the proper time are very difficult and require, most of all, complete independence of the lower leg from the thigh. They are therefore the privilege of such riders who have acquired a secure, balanced seat and do not need their legs to maintain it. This is the reason why poor and mediocre riders cannot get along with finely and thoroughly schooled horses; their heavy seat and their hard leg position unsettles such horses and will often inadvertently force such riders into gaits which they cannot handle and which they do not understand.

After the calf aids, the next lighter leg aid is the *knee pressure*. As the final point of closing the legs, the rider should always have available such knee pressure since he requires it at times when he must resist greatly or must give a strong aid. As a driving aid, however, the knee pressure is one of the most subtle aids that is understood only by perfectly trained dressage horses. Even with horses which already move in balance, knee pressure still acts on the forward portion of the rib cage which is quite unyielding and which is not so sensitive that the horse would be caused to move forward. If, however, the horse has its haunches well under itself, it will push its hindquarters forward and in between the rider's open legs so that the rider's knees come to rest behind the stirrup leathers and against the more sensitive portion of the rib cage where they will be able to produce an effective, forward driving pressure. It is therefore completely unreasonable to demand a driving effect from knee pressure on green or only poorly trained horses since this is an aid which belongs only to the most refined dressage training.

This completes the discussion of the driving aids given by the rider with his legs, and we will now proceed to those influences additionally available to him, namely the *whip*, the *long training whip*, and the *click of the tongue*.

Although the *crop*, like sharp spurs[4], has almost become old-fashioned, it still provides the same good service in training the young horse and in presenting the well-ridden horse as it did for the work of the old masters. The pointed crop of old, a slender, flexible hazelnut or birch shoot, was ever present, since its elegant carriage and correct use was a major feature of riding etiquette. It provided the rider with an opportunity to properly place his unoccupied right hand and to simultaneously accustom it to carrying a sword or other weapon while the left, or rein, hand alone took care of guiding the horse. Additionally, the rider used the whip to augment his other aids in many upper level dressage movements in that he applied it to ask the horse to pull up his fore or hind legs or to extend them. To do this, he placed the whip on the horse's shoulder, under its belly, or on its croup.

We, too, cannot do without this instrument because the student, as long as he is unable to use his spurs securely and correctly, needs the whip to wake up lazy horses. The trainer must use it as an aid for the green horse to gradually invoke respect and obedience to the spurs. The spurs produce a stinging pain which often causes young horses to stop, to strike out against them, or to fight them in some other way. The whip, however, as the most natural instrument of punishment, is noted by every creature and is therefore the sole and sufficient scepter of the coachman, the herdsman, and even the bear and tiger tamer.

The rider carries the crop in his right hand, either with the tip pointing upward so that it is inclined slightly toward the horse's left ear as required by a correct position of the hand, or he carries it tip down so that it hangs down behind his right leg. In the tip-up position, he is able, with raised elbow, to reach over his left hand and touch the left side of the horse from the shoulder to the hind leg, and thus support the aids of the left leg. And, in this position, the horse is urged on gently and in a friendly manner by a twitter of the tip of the crop. With the tip downward, the right side of the horse is easy to reach, and thus the activity of the right leg can be supported.

When using the whip as punishment, it is better to use the tip-up position since the so-called hunting lash is most easily performed this way, where the crop is swung in a forceful manner from the right to the left around the horse's body. First, the hand must be raised to the level of the face, then the arm is extended toward the right side, and the lash is performed strongly and quickly from the shoulder and wrist. If the arm is first extended and then raised, the horse sees the movement and will bring the prompt punishment to naught, more or less, by premature flight.

The whip plays a particularly important role in the preparation of a horse that is to be ridden in a side-saddle where the whip must replace some of the leg aids. It is therefore important to become skillful in its use and to know the different effects of its various applications. In order to be able to securely and promptly hit individual parts of the horse, the crop must not be too long and the tip not too flexible, while the thick end must not lie uncomfortably in the hand due to its excessive size.

The *long training whip* is also a driving aid, but mainly for working the very green horse on the lunge, for very lazy horses, or for correcting ruined or stubborn horses that do not want to submit to the rider's punishment. The *chambriere*[5] of the old masters played a very important role in the training and even in the presentation of airs above the ground since it was not always possible for the rider to control the heavy and colossal horses of that time in such collected and powerful movements with only conventional aids. Our lighter, more noble and fiery horses of the present generally do not need such reinforcement to bring out a display of power. For us, the long training whip is more a device for punishment than a tool for giving aids.

Finally, as regards *voice aids*, for reasons of good behavior, such aids must be avoided if possible in the presence of other riders or must be used very discreetly. Such aids would easily irritate other horses, and a strange concert would result if a dozen riders were simultaneously talking to their horses with clicking tongues. Nevertheless, the usefulness of voice aids cannot be denied, and the trainer may apply them here and there when quietly schooling a young horse.

By nature, the horse is a mentally very talented creature whose intelligence is shaped considerably by its association with humans, so that it can be made very receptive to impressions coming from the human voice. The timid horse should, therefore, be made confident by friendly, soft talk; the hot horse can be calmed with cajoling words; an encouraging shout can help the hesitant horse to take an obstacle more willingly; and a threatening word may perhaps divert an obstinate horse from a spiteful act. Yet, the effectiveness of such aids is always conditional only, because no horse will lower its haunches or take on a bent position upon a mere word. The click of the tongue is the most common of the voice aids. It serves to enliven the horse and has the great advantage that the rider need not change the direction and position of his body, which is often of great importance in upper level dressage movements.

ENDNOTES:

[1] There is no doubt that the spur is the best aid for the fully educated, sensitive rider to control the horse. However, experience has shown that unexperienced riders create immense disadvantages and great difficulties for themselves by the incorrect use of the spurs, primarily if they use the spurs on lazy horses, without knowing the effect of their action. I therefore believe it is necessary to examine in detail which mechanical effect the spur exerts on the horse.

Any soft contact with the spur, namely a sharp spur, acts on the horse like the sting of an insect and initiates the same, natural counteraction: the horse briefly lifts its hind leg on that side, as if it were to chase away a nasty originator of this painful action. In addition, it will usually pull in the threatened side and turn its head and neck in that direction in order to use its mouth as a defense as well. Such an aid can therefore never be a driving aid; to the contrary, it can only be restraining. Consequently, its use for suspicious, sensitive horses can only be a disadvantage. It is usually the inexperienced rider who employ this aid in such cases, while they are unable to utilize the advantages resulting from it under other circumstances. It should be obvious that horses whose hind legs stick to the ground for too long a time, that is, horses that drag their feet, can be caused to move their feet in a more lively manner if the spurs are used softly, at the correct time, in the cadence of the movement. In addition, the rider will use such an aid to advantage in order to realize a lateral bend and will also be able to get horses that are stiff in neck and poll to yield more quickly. If, however, forward movement is to be brought about simultaneously, other aids must support the action. First of all, the legs, by keeping in contact with the horse's body and exerting pressure, will cause the hind legs to push off forcefully, and the rider will lean back a little with his upper body to press the joints of the hind legs together and to thus get them to spring off energetically.

Only a jab with the spur can have a truly driving effect; and this will usually be done with both spurs together, particularly if it is to be a punishment. The spur is used on one side only if a horse resists one leg. Since misuse of the spurs produces great disadvantages, practical utility riding will generally be limited to using the spurs only as reinforcement of the leg aids to make them more impressive, or as a punishment. In dressage riding, the spur will always retain its decisive significance since its electrifying effects on the springs of the hindquarters cannot be replaced by any other aid. Also, a rider equipped with perfect equestrian tact will be able to reap great benefits from the above described different spur aids, particularly for difficult horses. The beginner, however, will usually use them at the wrong moment on suspicious and tense horses that hold back, and thus will easily produce

[17]

disobedience and resistance. (Hans von Heydebreck)

[2] Such injuries from spurs must be avoided under all circumstances. They usually occur from incorrect use of the spurs or because the rowel becomes jammed, which happens particularly during the shedding season. In connection with this, I urgently warn against the use of sharp spurs. (Hans von Heydebreck)

[3] To avoid such a disadvantageous change in the position of the legs, riders with long legs should fasten the spurs a bit higher, while otherwise spurs generally belong directly above the heel seam. (Hans von Heydebreck)

[4] See footnote 1.

[5] Translator's note: a long whip for working horses in hand.

(b) The Restraining Aids

Forward is the motto in the equestrian art, as anywhere else in the world. It is therefore necessary for the rider to have more means at his disposal to drive the horse forward than to restrain it. The restraining aids are limited solely to the action of the hands, that give such aids, by means of various bits, to the mouth, chin, or nose of the horse. Although the rider's appropriate posture and weight distribution may have a reinforcing effect for the hand aids, they cannot replace the influence of the hands, just as the correct follow-up of the rider's weight can very much support the driving aids, but never completely replace them. I will talk later in greater detail about this support of the actual aids by body position and weight distribution and will now discuss the actions of the hands.

If, in connection with riding, mention is made generally of only one *rein hand*, this of course means the left hand, which holds the curb reins, the major reins. However, guiding a horse with the left hand alone requires a completely trained horse that is capable of responding to the curb only. The old masters, who had time and means for such thorough work, knew only the curb as the bit for the well-ridden horse and placed their little finger between its two reins. For preparing the green horse, they used the cavesson. Today, since we have once and for all added the bridoon and its two reins to the curb bit, we admit right from the start that we do not intend to, or are not able to, work our horses to such perfection that they can be mastered under all circumstances with only the curb reins in the left hand. By admitting this, we ask for almost the impossible if we want to guide our horses, that are trained for military duty, strictly with the same hand movements as the masters did with their dressage horses. Because of the differences in our bits, and primarily the less perfect carriage of our horses, we must also modify the hand aids just as we must adapt our seat to the changed conformation of our present-day horses and to the English saddle.

The rein hand not only determines the direction in which the horse is to move but also the tempo of its various gaits. It is therefore the main tool with which the rider speaks to his horse and communicates his will to it. The skill of the hands can justifiably be considered a measure of the rider's total skill. It is completely erroneous to believe that good hands could be an isolated favorable characteristic of some riders. Rather, they are the result of a perfect seat and fine feeling.[1] If mobility and dexterity of the hands were equivalent to light and skillful hands on a horse, all magicians, pianists, and other such artists would automatically be imbued with this trait. Yet, in practice, we find that this is certainly not the case, and even very tender women's hands can badly mistreat the mouth of a horse by sheer clumsiness. But we may see a rider with a fist that may have become sinewy and thick from heavy toil exercise his fine and sensitive horse with such assurance and skill that it is evident that the horse likes to work under him. We often hear the statement that somebody is not a particularly good rider, but has very good hands; or, vice versa, that he is a very good rider, but has just one fault: heavy hands. This is an obvious contradiction because whoever has really good hands on a horse is a master of the art of riding, even if his posture and his manners on a horse give the layman the impression of a lack of equestrian polish. A person who really has bad hands can never be a rider in the true sense of the word, no matter how firm his seat, how much courage and elegance of appearance he displays. His fault is the product of a lack of feel for, and understanding of, the horse.

The influence of the hands becomes a guiding aid only by correct coaction and interaction with the aids of the legs and seat. The correctness of these guiding aids depends on the correct length of the reins which, in turn, can be obtained only from the correct contact of the horse with the bit; this is the much-discussed and described *contact* of the horse. The reins are the connecting means between the rider's hand and the horse's mouth. Shortening of the reins causes the bit to press on the bars and thus has an effect on the mouth which, in the correctly trained horse, propagates through the entire spine down to the last joint in the hind legs.

According to the laws of physics, the speed and reliability of the messages through the reins should be greater the tighter the reins are held. But, since they act on a very sensitive organic part, excessive pressure of the bit will cause the horse to either escape the resulting pain, or the responsiveness to such bit action will be lost because the nerves in the part subjected to pressure lose their sensitivity. Either the horse escapes "behind the bit" by avoiding contact, and thus the influence of the reins, by incorrectly positioning or arbitrarily moving its head and neck, or it has "lost its mouth," that is, it has a "dead mouth." It then uses the rider's hands as a support for the weight of its forehand as a fifth leg, so to speak. Both faults cancel out the guiding action of the reins and both are produced by hard hands.

[20]

Just as with the driving aids, where the legs should always have a natural, soft *contact* with the horse's body in order to guide the hindquarters, the reins as the guide for the forehand should also always be held with soft tension. This produces a light but steady seat of the bit on the bars, and that is called the contact the horse establishes with the rider's hands. It tells the horse the direction to take, and the rider is not only able to quickly and reliably express his will, but he also has one more connection with which to evaluate position and movement of his horse.

Some writers have attempted to set a standard for this contact and also describe it in physical terms. They prescribe that the opposition the hand experiences from the horse's mouth should be approximately equivalent to the resistance of soft butter that is cut with a thread or which is felt if a certain weight is pulled on a thread. Such comparisons are useless, however, since every horse in its individuality will produce its own particular type of contact just as its gaits will be different as a function of its unique conformation. Horses having fine, sharp bars, a light forehand, and a lively temperament will generally tend to take on a lighter contact and perhaps can never be forced into a firm one. On the other hand, horses with the opposite conformation will more or less have an opposite tendency. The understanding trainer will not fight such natural particularities, but will try to handle them by suitable selection of bits and mainly by the skillful use of his hands.

Even with one and the same horse, the contact will be different depending on its state of training. The more forward its center of gravity, the stronger must be the contact since, in this position, the horse requires more support from the hands than guidance. Correct bends and turns are then out of the question. To the same degree as the centers of gravity of horse and rider, which must always be vertically above one another, are displaced toward the back, the finer must be the contact. The lightest bit pressure possible on the bars will then increase their sensitivity and enable the horse to discern and obey the softest movements of the rider's hands.

There are three gradations in the degree of contact, namely, the *light contact*, the *soft contact*, and the *firm contact*. The first is directed toward the haunches in upper level dressage riding, the second is directed toward balanced or military riding, and the third is directed toward the shoulders in hunt and race riding. The length of the reins, the position of the arms against the body, and, mainly, the formation of the fists, must be selected to correspond to these gradations.

For a *light contact*, the reins are the longest since there should be as little tension as possible; the rider's body is slightly behind the vertical and his hands are closer to his body because he does not need much room for his very light tightening of the reins. The fist is half open so that only the thumb and forefinger hold the ends of the reins; however, the little finger and the ring finger are not closed. This type of fist formation has a dual advantage. Because of its weakened position, it is unable to have any harsh effect, and by alternately closing and opening his two lower fingers, the rider can influence the horse in a fine, imperceptible manner, without having to move his wrist. Because of the contact it produces, we will call this fist formation the *"light hand,"* which often produces miraculous results with difficult horses that refuse to accept the curb bit because it greatly softens the effect of this bit.

For a *soft contact*, the reins are a bit shorter, the rein tension a bit greater, the rider's position vertical, and the position of his hands a hand's width away from his body so as to give him enough room for stronger hand movements. His fists form the *"soft hand,"* meaning they are closed in such a way that the last joint of the fingers is extended and a hollow fist is formed. The soft fist is also conducive to a weaker effect and forms, in a way, the middle between the light and the firm hand. Many riders accept the soft fist formation as the only correct and permissible way, and they are right if they restrict themselves to training military horses. If they go beyond that, however, or if they want to use it to ride the horse in its natural carriage, they will soon discover its inadequacy.

The *firm contact* requires the shortest reins, partly because the rider's upper body is leaning more forward and his hands must be at a greater distance from the body for the often required strong pulls. While in the two previously discussed positions, the rider's lower arm should have a light, natural contact with his body, for the firm contact the upper arm and elbow must seek a steady and firm support at the body in the faster gaits to be able to produce the necessary resistance against the forward urging horse. For that reason, the hands must be formed into firmly closed fists so that all of the fingers participate in keeping the reins at the required length. With this type of contact, index finger and thumb cannot do this alone. This then is the *"firm hand,"*[2] which every trainer must use from time to time as an aid or a means for correction when he is training a young horse. For the racehorse or hunter, where this type of contact is the rule, the bit must be selected accordingly if the bars are not to be injured and all sensitivity lost. The Englishman, who is very experienced and practical in this field, has expediently combined the curb and the snaffle into the pelham, and has in it an excellent hunting and steeplechasing bit. But it would be just as wrong to make a dressage horse in a pelham as it would be to ride a hunter in a curb with strong lever action.

When working a horse, the trainer must know how to use these different hand actions, often in rapid succession. He must be able to keep the hesitant horse moving with a light hand, use his firm hand to get the horse that leans on the bit or pushes forward too much to settle down, and, in between, use his soft hand to invite his horse to take on a quiet and uniform contact. The steady application of a firmly closed fist is the only punishment appropriate for the rein hand, regardless of the type of bit employed and whether one rides with one or both hands. Pulling and yanking on the reins is good for nothing other than injuring the tender mouth, making the horse head-shy and ultimately forcing it into such resistance that it will escape the rider's control completely (as by rearing and flipping over, running away, etc.). If, in exceptional cases, the usual bit is of no avail, one should use the cavesson, the lunge line, or the pillars.[3] Trainers who do not know how to work their horses sensibly with the aid of these means are better off to give up riding and take on a different profession than to sin against such a noble creature as the horse with their lack of skill or unsuitable temperament.

For that reason I also cannot exclude from this rule the so-called "*sawing*" which some experts use and consider permissible. These are quick, unexpected jerks on the bit to punish the horse for some bad habit, such as leaning on the bit or sticking out its tongue. They will never serve the intended purpose, but will frighten the horse off the bit and make it distrustful of the rider's hands. This treatment is likewise a misunderstood inheritance from the time when the cavesson took the place of the plain snaffle. Used with the former, such jerks can give us the same good results as they gave the old masters because then we act on the nose with forceful success, but without the adverse effect on the established contact.

Contact is correct, no matter to which degree the individual horse takes it, depending on its training, as long as the horse reacts or responds to the action of the hand. If, for example, both reins act in uniform restraint, the horse should shorten its movement. If this is prevented by simultaneous driving with the legs, the horse must come together, relinquish the bit somewhat, and change from the now too firm contact to a lighter one.[4]

If one rein is stronger than the other, the horse should bend its head and neck to correspond to the greater pressure; if, with the stronger use of one rein, the other rein provides support, the horse should turn toward the side of the greater pressure. As I mentioned before, all of these hand aids are nothing by themselves; they become successful only through correct coaction with the other aids, particularly the driving aids. The latter must maintain gait and contact, and only by uninterrupted and completely harmonious interaction of seat, hands, and legs can the horse unfold all of its power and agility under the rider.

Correct contact is always connected with a good mouth. The mouth is called *good* or *lively* if it appears not only freshly reddened by freely circulating blood but is also kept *moist* by the generous secretion of saliva which changes to foam as a result of chewing on the bit. In this state, the mouth will always be sensitive and active. The rider must therefore invite horses that tend to have a dry mouth to chew on the bit by way of repeated gentle reminders with his hands, the so-called *light* "arrests" (half-halts), again enhancing the secretion of saliva. Although good contact requires a good mouth, a lively mouth is not always connected with the correct contact since the latter is the result of correct work and guidance of the horse while the former may be innate. Horses which by nature have a very acute sensitivity and develop extensive saliva flow from merely the presence of the bit, a foreign object in their mouth, may nevertheless completely lack the correct contact.

The *dead mouth* is already externally evident from its dry appearance and bluish coloration, the latter being produced by an accumulation of blood in the veins. The rider's hand recognizes it immediately when the horse does not react to his aids and responds to his half-halts neither by chewing nor taking on a lighter contact, but leans on the hand with unchanging pressure. This fault may be innate and may have its origin in great insensitivity and general laziness, or it may have been developed by incorrect treatment. Young, green horses, that are tight in the throat-latch and whose center of gravity by nature is far forward or which, because of weak hindquarters, cannot be trained to come off the fore-hand, often have this fault for a long time until its causes are gradually eliminated by training. Riders who use up their horses in their natural carriage and are unable or unwilling to eliminate such faults fear the dead mouth greatly and appreciate a naturally good mouth that much more.

A rider's *good hand* is distinguished by steadiness and lightness. If these two characteristics could be developed separately, the former by secure support of the arms on the upper body, the latter by correct fist formation, we would find riders with good hands much more frequently than is in fact the case. But how can the hand obtain a quiet position by way of support for the arms from the body, if the body itself is continuously shaken by the movement of the horse? If this is the case, the rider must, to the contrary, freely balance his arms by keeping their joints relaxed so as to absorb any shocks in the arms themselves, and thus maintain the hands steady (similar to the waiter who balances a tray of filled glasses, not with his elbow flexed, but with a freely extended, relaxed arm).

The same applies to the lightness of the hand. Just as the rider's body cannot always properly follow the horse's movement, the hand cannot do it either. It will always have an inhibiting and interfering influence on the horse's way of going, which is the reason why a hard, clumsy seat on a horse always results in a hard hand, no matter how lightly the hands carry the reins.

The *light and steady hand* depends on the light and steady position of the upper body, and it in turn depends partly on the correct position and the resulting correct gaits of the horse. With a green horse, where the movements are still irregular and restricted and do not yet allow the rider to take on a light and steady posture with the resulting light and steady hands, it is the trainer's main skill to nevertheless use his soft and elastic seat to produce a light and steady hand. However, to achieve this, he must often depart from the regularly accepted body posture and hand position, and it is therefore a sign of great ignorance if the public judges his work only by the position of his body. How should he move the clumsy horse which still hangs on to its natural tendencies if he does not use his arms and legs freely? The expert rider (including all those who train their own horses, be it for love of horse and riding or as a profession) should be judged only by the results of his work; that is, by the presentation of a horse he trained himself and more yet by the performance of that horse than by his own position.

Now that we have discussed the nature of the rider's hand, we will move on to its activity and will discuss the aids it produces. The *straight* position of the hand, in which the thumb points upward and the little finger downward, the fingernails facing the body, is the rest position. If the horse is straight, if both reins are of equal length, and if the hand is placed above the pommel in this position, the reins act with equal strength and will therefore keep the horse on a straight line. From this position, the hand is rotated to the left and right, the little finger indicating the direction of movement. As a result of this rotation laterally to the right, the left rein only is shortened and thus causes the head and neck to bend to the left; when the little finger is turned to the left, the right rein is shortened and a bend to the right is produced. Since opposition from the outside rein is also required to turn the horse in addition to the bend, such bend must be facilitated and secured by the corresponding shortening of the inside rein. The hands must then be turned halfway to the side and halfway to the rear toward the right or left hip. When riding with a shortened inside rein, the outside rein will become effective and produce the correct effect and contact only if the horse has taken on a bend corresponding to the shortening of the rein; that is, it has pushed away from the inside rein, which it must be invited to do by the action of leg aids.

Since the main task of the outside rein is to maintain the required elevation of the forehand, it is very wrong to want to guide or turn only with the aid of the inside rein. It is just as wrong to want to turn the horse only with the outside rein, as this is so often the case when the reins are both of the same length and the hand is incorrectly moved to the side. Good-natured and patient horses will gradually understand even this incorrect aid and will obey it as well as possible in its incorrectness; insensitive and spirited horses, however, will turn to the left when asked for a right turn and turn to the right when asked for a left turn, thus greatly embarrassing their riders.

For a change of direction, the horse must most of all have the correct contact; that is, it needs the secure and good effect of both reins to guide and support it. Therefore, during turning and changing position, the rider must pay attention to the length of his reins, the movement of his hands, and the other interacting aids. Since I can discuss the latter in detail only in connection with individual movements, I will here note merely the following generalities: for bending, the inside leg supports the inside rein in that it bends the horse's spine and advances the inside hind leg considerably underneath the load; for elevation, the outside leg supports the outside rein in that it fixes the horse's outside hind leg or keeps it from falling out. Both legs maintain contact by driving the horse into the hand and positioning it between the reins.

The alternating slight yielding and taking up of the reins which is so necessary for maintaining a sensitive, lively mouth is produced in a fine way by repeated opening and closing and softly raising and lowering of the hands, and by a twist in the wrist so that the little finger alternately faces the rider's body or the horse's neck. While doing this, it is not necessary to shorten or lengthen the reins, but if it is required for a transition to another movement, this must be done with the index finger and thumb of the right hand alone so that the left hand does not participate and can continue to maintain contact.

The same error which, as I have already mentioned elsewhere, is so often made in teaching the student the correct seat, also occurs frequently during his instruction in guiding a horse; namely, prescribing the same forms and aids for the improperly trained horse as if the student had a perfectly schooled animal underneath him. The result is that he tries in vain and without success, learns to understand neither the reason for the aids nor his horse, and finally doubts the whole affair. If the horse just is not schooled well enough to respond to very subtle aids, such as a mere twist of the wrist, the student should be asked to use shorter reins and pull a little harder.

Finally, I must speak quite emphatically against *rounding* of the hand in the wrist, which some instructors insist on so strictly. It definitely does not fulfill the intended purpose; namely, to impart lightness or resiliency to the hands. This artificial position must, in the long run, be connected with effort and finally produces a cramped appearance, that is, something harsh, aside from the fact that it limits the range for stronger restraining aids. The wrist, like every other part of the rider, should remain in its natural, relaxed position so that it will not tire needlessly and remain able to unimpededly develop its full power whenever this is required.[5]

ENDNOTES:

[1] Although a good hand can never be an isolated favorable characteristic of a rider and can therefore never be acquired on its own, the appropriate position and shape of the hands is extremely important. Just as the violinist is able to properly guide his bow only if he holds it correctly, the tennis player grips his racket, the fencer his rapier or his sword with an appropriately shaped hand, the rider can never acquire a good hand if he shapes and carries it incorrectly. The best action from the hand is ensured if it is closed lightly into a hollow fist and is held almost vertically at such a height that it is in line with the bit and the elbow joint, with the back of the hand, without any artificial rounding of the wrist, forming a straight line with the outer surface of the underarm. The fingers should not be forcibly closed but turned

in to such an extent that their uppermost joint forms an approximately right angle with the back of the hand, while the last finger joint remains stretched out. Only in this way will the hand always be supported by the small of the back during all actions and will be able to restrict itself more or less to giving its aids only by a firmer closing of its fingers—as if squeezing out a small, wet sponge—and bracing the back. If needed, an increased weight aid serves as support for the back. From this hand position and shape, the various types of fist formation described on pages ? to ? result all by themselves. (Hans von Heydebreck)

[2] The "firm" contact as well as the "firm" hand can easily be misinterpreted and lead to hard, rigid hands and contact. Steinbrecht probably selected the term "firm" because, just as for a "light" and "soft" hand and contact, the hands should be closed only "lightly" and "softly," he wants the hands closed firmly for a "firm contact and hand." But never must the horse become firm in my hand! Therefore, the degree of rein tension identified as "firm" should better be called "full" or "strong" and the shape of the hand required then should be called a "fully closed" hand; even in that shape it must remain sensitive and elastic. (Hans von Heydebreck)

[3] For horses that lean on the hand, the pillars are also a rather dangerous thing. They should be used only for the training of dressage horses and then only after prior collecting work in hand. Should there be difficulties, this training aid can then often be used with benefit. Otherwise, I refer to the statements about in-hand and pillars work in the section on Piaffe and Passage. (Hans von Heydebreck)

[4] The type of aid discussed here describes the process that we call a halt. It is a full halt or a full arrest, since the horse then already obeys both simultaneously acting reins. A description of how the weight and back aids interact is absent, however. For details about this, see Footnote 1.

[5] Riding manuals provide very different, often completely exclusionary, rules for the manipulations of the rein hand. I have refrained from discussing this aspect in more detail than I did above because correctly executed turns are not based on complicated twists of the wrist but on the correct bend of the horse and the correct distribution of the rider's weight. Whoever correctly understands the effective range of the reins and legs and has succeeded on the basis of this understanding in getting his horse to push off from the reins in any desired bend as a result of leg pressure will have no difficulty later on in guiding his horse with one hand, the manipulations of which he will know automatically. However to attain this degree of training in a horse it is first necessary to carefully work it in a snaffle. Only after the described yielding has been safely established on the snaffle should the horse be introduced to the curb. Once this has happened, all of the training must be repeated in the same sequence as for the snaffle in that, as with the snaffle, it is first necessary to produce contact with the curb by riding forward on straight lines through the entire arena before an attempt is made to produce yielding to an individual rein by exercises on curved lines. In the beginning, however, truly effective and correct work in exercises on curved lines in

a curb bit is possible only with divided reins; that is, each hand carries the snaffle and the curb rein of its side. If then the horse has learned, in a manner analogous to the snaffle work, to yield to the pressure of the curb rein under all conditions in response to a leg or spur aid and to chew on this bit, it will do the same if both reins are combined in the left hand. Guiding the horse with one hand will then no longer be a problem. Since I assume that a horse is *worked* in a curb bit with divided reins, I can set up the same rules for use of the reins for the individual exercises, regardless of whether the horse wears a snaffle or a curb bit. Modifications of these rules for guiding the thoroughly schooled horse with one hand will then be self-evident for the thinking rider.* (Paul Plinzner)

* Although riding with divided curb reins is certainly recommended at the beginning when the young horse is to become used to the new bit and is asked to confidently accept the bit, as soon as this goal has been attained, riding with a grip of the snaffle, with the curb reins both being carried in the left hand, should be made the subject of the exercise as soon as possible. It should never be forgotten that the curb bit does not have a broken mouthpiece and that therefore correct rein action always necessitates a counteracting second rein. This can be done properly only if the reins are combined in one hand. (Hans von Heydebreck)

(c) The Supporting Aids

These aids are produced by changes in the rider's position to support the aids described above and to make them more forceful and better understood by the horse. They become automatic and are at their finest if the horse's sensitivity to these aids can gradually be honed to such a degree that these aids alone suffice to bring the horse to the full development of its power and skill. At such a state of perfection in training, there are no longer any discernible aids from the rider; with his quiet, naturally beautiful posture, the rider follows all his horse's movements in seemingly complete inactivity, as if he were a natural part of the horse. Such a rider will not give rise to the statement that he seems to be nailed or glued to his horse, since that would always suggest a forced union. Such a comparison is better for a stable groom who is able, with luck, to sit out a couple of bucks under the force of his leg pressure. Instead, the skillful rider has become a part of his horse, the dominant part.

One of the supporting aids is the *weight in the stirrups*. The stirrups serve a dual purpose: first, they support the weight of the legs so that they do not tire from hanging, and second, the stirrups provide a secure support for the rider's entire body, or for parts of his body when needed. The use of the stirrups to bear the weight of the legs is actually not a stirrup aid, but more a resting of the foot in the stirrup, which is usually called *"holding the stirrups."* In this case, no more weight should rest on the stirrups than the weight of legs and feet in their natural position. If the rider artificially applies more weight, the stirrup aid results which has become indispensable for all driving aids. It becomes a major fault if it is used to hold onto the stirrups in order to prevent their loss, or if it becomes a support for the seat. Riders who make such an error are still lacking in the fundamentals of their art, and they must first perfect their seat, and particularly their balance. Other riders consider it the peak of perfection if they no longer require the stirrups at all for security, and claim that they feel closer and less encumbered without them. As recommendable as such a degree of perfected, secure seat may be, it is nevertheless obvious that such riders do not know the great advantages afforded by the fine use of the stirrups.

Of course, the stirrup must not be an object necessary to the rider's security. At any time, the rider must be able to do without the stirrups and be ready to replace them by closing his legs. But to a balanced seat with a soft, natural hang of the legs, the support of the stirrup is a great help. Since a rider's sensitivity is perfect only with such a seat, he should not relinquish the aid of the stirrups in moments when his sensitivity must help him to practically guess his horse's intentions. For that reason, it is completely wrong for trainers to intentionally relinquish the stirrups when they encounter dangerous disobediences from their horses, for fear of being caught in the stirrups in the case of a fall, with or without the horse. They thus rob themselves of the ability to lightly and safely follow all arbitrary movements of the horse. They also deprive themselves of the opportunity to promptly and energetically take advantage of the favorable, but mostly short, moments when the horse is unable or less able to resist (for example, when two or even all four feet are off the ground).

In such fights with the brute force of the horse, the necessity of sometimes passively following its movements and sometimes resisting them forcefully requires not only great skill and a secure seat but also equestrian tact in correctly assessing the individual moments. In such cases, the stirrups are an important aid. They not only facilitate the application of forceful aids and punishment, they also save the rider's strength, which he would lose if he were to exert firm and continued pressure with his legs. This explains the fact that physically weak, yet skillful and courageous riders are able to have great power over an animal that is perhaps ten times their superior in physical strength.

When the stirrups are in the correct position, they are practically the pans of the scales for the correct distribution of the rider's weight; if the rider's upper body is in equilibrium, his legs will rest in the stirrups freely and with their full weight. This weight is entirely sufficient to fix the stirrup on the ball of the foot or, rather, to keep the foot in uninterrupted contact with the bar of the stirrup.

If, at the various gaits, the rider is lifted out of the saddle somewhat at regular intervals, his legs are shortened and lengthened in the same rhythm, with the ball of the foot, due to the mobility of the leg joints, particularly the ankle joint, remaining quietly at its resting point, while the heel moves elastically up and down in rhythm with the movement. If the rider holds the stirrup with a stiff ankle, that is, with the toe raised, the movement naturally propagates up to the tip of his toes. The foot will then dance up and down in the stirrup in the rhythm of the movement, with the heel remaining low and fixed. Such riders will never know the usefulness of the stirrups nor learn to hold them securely. They will always lose the stirrups when they need them most, since the stirrups themselves experience every impact through legs that are stiff down to the toes, and are thus flung away. The skill of holding the stirrups securely and using them correctly, therefore, lies in a soft and elastic ankle and in the natural position of the foot as a whole.

The weight in the stirrups as an aid is twofold: it can be used either with the heels raised or with them pushed down. In the former case, the stirrup serves as support for the foot, enabling a more secure use of heel and lower leg for the spur or calf aids, much as the arm requires a support when writing or painting. In the second case, the stirrups serve as strong support for the entire body if the rider has to use the full strength of his arms, like someone who wants to pull a heavy weight toward himself or up to himself. He will first take care that he has made his entire body capable of offering enough resistance by securely placing his feet. In this case, the legs are stretched considerably so that the ankles are bent through and the heels are oriented towards the ground.

While I have already discussed the stirrup aid with raised heel in connection with the spur aids, this stirrup aid with the heel down often serves to bring the horse from a contact that is too firm to a lighter contact, namely, when elevating the forehand by putting weight on the hind legs and flexing them. In advanced dressage, this stirrup aid, used in a more refined manner, serves as a support for application of knee pressure. It is also used to strongly tension the calves, thus augmenting their usefulness as aids. For that reason, this aid is indispensable to all exercises where it is important to keep the hindquarters in a certain artificial position, for example, in the movements on two tracks. In this case, the stirrup aid is often used by only one leg while the other leg acts in opposition and remains in the shortened, soft position. The greater weight will then have to rest on the stirrup of the extended leg.

For that reason, the stirrups are much more indispensable to the rider for prompt, secure, and fine application of all of his aids than for securing his seat, and the instructor should take care to teach his student the usefulness of the stirrups in this respect. He should first make the student independent of the stirrups by exercises without them, so that the student will not incorrectly consider the stirrups to be only a support for his seat. Then he should have him diligently practice driving with his legs in the stirrups so that he becomes quite familiar with them. The old masters made their students ride without stirrups often and for long periods of time. They did not need them as much because their saddles offered sufficient artificial support and the horses of that time were not as nimble or agile. Nevertheless, they recognized the importance of the stirrups as an aid. Although they presented their fully trained dressage horses without spurs as a demonstration of absolute obedience, they did not ride without stirrups. In those days it was quite permissible in all the arts to be a bit pedantic; this was believed to dignify the art, and everyone took much more time and pains to learn things. Today, however, man evaluates his art strictly according to its usefulness for practical application, and there is no time for pedantry. The student should therefore not be made to systematically ride without stirrups for a prescribed period of time; instead, he should be schooled right from the start to ride with, as well as without, stirrups. Beginners who find it difficult to maintain their balance may be permitted to ride only with stirrups during their first lessons. After that, it will be enough if, at the beginning of the daily lesson, they repeat the exercise without stirrups for a short time.

The *length of the stirrup* cannot be set to a fixed standard but must be a function of the natural conformation of the horse and also of the position in which the horse is being ridden. A broad-chested horse with a full barrel, which gives the rider a large area of contact for his legs, requires longer stirrups than the narrow horse on which there is not as much contact area for a long leg. Moreover, when riding the horse in its natural carriage at free gaits, it will be more appropriate to ride with short stirrups, not only because the rider will require more support from the stirrups in view of his own position and to overcome the excess weight of the horse on the forehand, but also because the extended gaits reduce the volume of the body. Conversely, when the horse carries itself on his haunches, its body will be expanded to the same degree as it is shortened in length, and thus provides a larger contact area for the rider's legs. The dressage rider will therefore always use longer stirrups, as this permits freer movement of his legs and also favors their natural hanging from the hips, which in turn greatly facilitates control of the hindquarters. The length of the stirrups for a balanced carriage lies between the two extremes. It could, in a way, be considered the normal length if, in the spirit of the present time, the purpose of the equestrian art is only the production of utility horses for which the position of horse and rider in a balanced carriage constitutes the standard. In this carriage, the length of the stirrups is correct, if the leg, hanging freely and relaxed along the horse, finds a natural support for its weight in the stirrup. The stirrup must therefore always be a bit shorter than the leg measured to the heel. If the rider must artificially stretch his leg or lower the ball of his foot to hold on, then the stirrup is too long, and the rider is forced to assume a crotch seat, more or less relinquishing the secure support of his seat bones.

Stirrups that are too short not only deprive the legs of their free mobility and natural position, but also put the upper body into a clumsy, hard orientation towards the back, in which the rider is unable to softly absorb the hard jolts coming from the horse. The above indicates that it is tactful riding to always adjust the length of the stirrups correctly according to the particular requirement. The skillful rider will adjust his stirrups himself, without outside assistance, and will be able to do this at any gait. For that reason it is necessary to place the buckle of the stirrup strap in such a position that this can be done easily and quickly. Setting the stirrups according to the length of the rider's arm can at best be an approximation which must be modified at the rider's discretion after he is mounted.

Generally, the foot should rest in the stirrup on the broadest area of the sole, that is, from the little toe to the ball of the big toe. However, for the fine spur and calf aids, and in the open seat, the stirrup must be held with the tip of the toes as if it were to be enclosed by the toes. In this way, the rider can reach the horse better with the spurs without having to relinquish the support of the stirrup. In the dressage seat, the stirrup is also held lightly with the tip of the toes and this gives greater softness and elasticity to the leg, particularly the ankle.[1]

Following the weight in the stirrups, we will now discuss the supporting aid of the *open seat*. According to the principle that any body gains in circumference the more it is shortened by compression, the horse, as mentioned before, must broaden its rib cage and flanks when moving in collection. So as not to interfere with such expansion but to enhance it as much as possible, the rider must intentionally open his thighs and knees when collecting the horse in movements that require considerable lowering of the hindquarters. That is, he must move his legs away from the horse,[2] so that no pressure from these limbs, albeit their natural weight, will interfere with the desired shortening and broadening. The main requirement for this aid is that the legs remain in a flat position, so that the hips always retain their proper position and the legs are ready to grip at a moment's notice, should that become necessary. Unfortunately, weak riders often enough demonstrate the wrong seat with open legs.

They turn their thighs outward and try to replace the lack of knee pressure by wrapping their lower legs around the horse. The correct open seat, however, is a fine aid which requires perfect balance since the rider has no support left other than his seat bones and stirrups. For that reason, this open seat has an extraordinary effect: the horse, not hampered by any hard contact with the rider, whose finely balanced body weight is reduced by about half, will feel almost as if in a state of freedom, and will therefore work with such lightness and enjoyment as if left to play in the paddock at will. Even at lesser degrees of collection and in freer gaits, this seat, used according to the horse's carriage, gives lightness and elasticity to the animal's movements, as if it were blessed with wings. The foot in the stirrup, with the heel raised, is an indispensable aid here. It must serve to support legs that are kept almost floating in order to facilitate balance and help the lower legs in their necessary lively activity of driving forward. Such work is tiring and hard as long as the horse is unable to flex its lowered hind legs with ease and endurance. The horse's movements at this stage of training, particularly at the trot, are often so bouncy that the rider is forced to relinquish some support from his seat bones in order to absorb more of the shocks with his crotch. In this yielding body position, it is most difficult for the rider to maintain the proper elevation of the forehand and the correct position of the horse's head and neck. He who knows how to accomplish this is richly rewarded in developing to the greatest perfection all the power and elasticity that nature has imparted to the hind legs. He will, in this manner, give his horse gaits that make it appear to be moving on springs. To feel and understand such a horse is a rider's greatest pleasure; he will never forget this feeling and ordinary gaits will seem dull and spent to him. Riders who carry themselves stiffly and with rigidly closed knees will never get to know this greatest of equestrian joys because both interfere with obtaining a degree of collection that is absolutely necessary for the development of such elasticity. The more the horse develops its skill in lowering its hindquarters to carry the weight, the less the rider will be forced to artificially maintain his open seat. It will gradually cease to be an effort. The horse's strides become steadily softer, and the rider will again be able to naturally come back onto his seat bones. The collected horse with its broadened flanks will fill the rider's open legs in such a way that they are held in the open position and take up a soft contact with the horse's body.

With the horse in this frame, knee pressure alone may also be an effective driving aid. This knee aid stands in close relationship to the open seat, and the horse can be made receptive to knee pressure only through the application of such a seat.

Although the weight in the stirrups and the open seat are most deserving of the term "supporting aids," the most important and indispensable support for the aids, whatever they may be, is the proper distribution of the weight of the upper body. Generally, support of the driving and restraining aids by distribution of weight is ruled by the principle that relocating the weight further back has a forward pushing effect, while leaning forward has an inhibiting effect on the horse's way of going, much like the equilibrist who, when he walks on a ball, drives the ball forward faster, the more he keeps his weight back, and causes it to move backward if he lets his weight act ahead of the ball. This principle is confirmed in practice: a hot horse is calmed by leaning the body forward, and the lazy or resistant horse is driven forward by the aids with the body directed forcefully backward. The hot horse would be caused to run away by a body that leans back; the lazy horse would respond to a crotch seat by being resistant on the spot or creeping backward. In the chapter on the seat, I discuss the principle that, if the horse carries itself on its shoulders, the rider can increase the horse's speed by leaning forward and following with his body. This could be considered contradictory to the above developed principle. For this reason, I would like to point out that the hunt rider achieves his purpose only if he brings his center of gravity in precise coincidence with that of his horse, and also gives the horse a secure support for the excess weight up front. He will accomplish this by taking firm contact against which the thrust of the hind legs can better become effective. The crotch seat of a trainer is completely different from a hunt seat. It has the purpose of displacing the center of gravity forward on horses having weak hindquarters or kidneys so as to take the weight off these parts without influencing the thrust of the hind legs and giving the horse the support of a firm contact. Since the crotch seat, in contrast to the hunt seat, is not a normal seat for a certain carriage of the horse, it should be used as an aid only if necessary, and the rider should change to one of the normal positions as soon as the crotch seat has served its purpose.

It is the same with the distribution of weight to the rear. If the position of the body goes back behind the horse's center of gravity, such a seat acts as an aid, providing support for the driving legs. It is an aid in itself as well. By putting more weight on the hind legs, it better fixes them and keeps them and the back flexed more. This seat must be at the rider's disposal for correction of all faults in the carriage of the horse evidenced by a lack of forward movement, such as creeping back, sticking in place, and others. For movements that are somewhat susceptible to such a fault, for example, the rein back, or collection in place, it must always be available to the rider to check on his horse. The effect of this aid is augmented if the hips are momentarily lowered and the back relaxed, because this increases the weight of the body. However, this position should not be retained longer than required by circumstances or the rider will interfere with the horse's forward movement due to his lack of balance. Conversely, in the former position, the crotch seat, the hips must be pushed forward and the back tensioned the more the body leans forward. In this seat, the rider more or less loses support from his seat bones, and this support must be replaced in part by greater tension in the upper body and in part by his weight in the stirrups.[3]

Lateral weight displacement has the same strong effect and is therefore a truly supporting aid. Used by a rider whose seat is in full harmony with the horse, it enhances bending, turns, and lateral movements; increased in intensity, it becomes a strong aid for preventing or eliminating the faults that occur in such movements. Even as punishment for disobedience, as when the horse refuses to bend, or intentionally pushes to the side, this aid gives the actual impetus to the actions of legs and hands.

As long as it is intended to remain in harmony with the carriage of the laterally bent horse, the rider's position is based on the placement of his hips. To the degree that the horse is bent, the rider's hip must move forward on the bent side, for the horse must advance the hind leg of this shortened side to retain uniform distribution of its weight on all four legs. The placement of excess weight on the bent side, in complete harmony with the horse, by pushing forward the hip on the bent side, is different from the complete displacement of weight toward *one* side, which is done to put more weight on the hind leg that does not carry enough weight, or to fix an escaping leg. By temporarily relinquishing his balanced seat, the rider puts the full weight of his upper body toward the escaping side and must then compensate by greater weight in the respective stirrup. A rider in a steady, finely adjusted, balanced seat makes the fully trained horse so receptive to the aids of weight displacement that it can be kept in the required movements almost exclusively by such weight displacement. In its desire to keep in harmony with the rider, the horse will inadvertently follow the direction which the rider's position indicates. Such horses are living masterpieces on which the student can learn fine feeling and the perfectly natural, graceful seat. On such a horse, the student will gain a genial understanding of equestrian discipline worthy of such a beautiful art and science.

The best proof for the effectiveness of weight distribution aids comes from the famous gyrations of the Arabs, Circassians, and other people known for their horse breeding and riding skills. Here we have skilled, but purely natural riders, and green horses with excellent natural talents that are especially suited for riding purposes. We see these wild riders work their horses in an admirable manner, throw them to the right or to the left with utmost speed, stop suddenly, or throw them around on the hindquarters. Although they are quite generous with the use of their sharp bits and pointed spurs to maintain control over their horses, which have not been systematically prepared for such sudden changes in direction, they give their aids to turn only with their upper bodies, as the untrained horses understand the action of the hands and legs only as an order to stop or move forward.

To avoid misunderstandings in this very important point, I will briefly repeat that the rider's normal position is one in which his center of gravity coincides with that of his horse. Deviations from that position are either the result of an incorrect seat or intentional aids. I also repeat that when working a horse, depending on the degree of its training, the trainer is obliged to maintain his body in a certain position, leaning forward, sitting upright, or leaning back. On a thoroughly trained horse, which always seeks equilibrium with its rider, he can, by displacing his weight, move the horse's center of gravity forward or backward at will. On such a horse, a lateral displacement of his body weight allows him to move weight onto each individual hind leg as desired. By weight aids in general, the rider can restrain or reinforce every movement as desired. It is understood, of course, that in all these weight aids, hands and legs must participate correspondingly, but the less such participation is required, the greater is the perfection of dressage training.

A stiff, cramped seat makes all these aids and their manifold gradations impossible, as they are the result of a relaxed position of the rider and flexibility of his entire body. For this reason, I must remind the reader again and again to give up old prejudices and to derive the rules for the rider's position only from natural principles. The unchanging, so-called prescribed seat to which many instructors stubbornly adhere is the reason that the art has such a bad reputation. It prevents the student from becoming independent on his horse since, with such a seat, he will lack the necessary feeling to be able to correctly evaluate his horse's carriage and movement. The rider who has been schooled in such a seat will present, after a long struggle, not a thoroughly schooled horse - that is, a horse whose natural talents have not only been channeled and made subservient by dressage training but have also been developed by suitable exercises - but a wooden machine which, although working mechanically, is devoid of all elasticity and freshness in its way of going. Such horses are certainly not likely to produce enthusiasm for the art because their dull, mechanical way of going fatigues the rider and wears the horse out before its time. For that reason, many riders feel safer and more comfortable on a horse with good conformation that moves in its natural carriage, than on a confused, so-called dressage horse that has been robbed of all its vitality.

Whoever does not want to degrade this beautiful art to a mere trade - an art that has been held in high esteem from early times and will continue to be appreciated as long as there is courage and chivalry in the human race - should first be diligent in exercising his own body and making all its parts agile and mobile, so that his stiff limbs will not act as shackles on better understanding and feeling.

In distributing the weight, the *head* must also be considered a part of the upper body. The human head has a considerable weight in relationship to the weight of the rest of the body. The position of the head will therefore not remain without influence on the effect of the total body weight. It should always be positioned so that it rests vertically on the upright neck vertebrae, so that when weight aids are given, the head will not act by itself, but only as a part of the upper body. The position of the head is mainly a function of the use of the *eyes*. A skilled rider has his eyes everywhere and therefore turns his head freely in all directions, regardless of his general position. Out of doors, he must survey the terrain ahead of him over which he rides his horse so that he can spot any obstacles in time to either avoid them or to sufficiently prepare his horse to take them. He must notice objects in his environment in time to prevent his horse from being frightened or injured. In the woods his eyes must even look upward so that he will not have unpleasant encounters with branches. The student, however, will have many a lesson made easier if he is told in which direction to look. For the seat exercises, his line of sight should go between his horse's ears, since he can better calculate his position if he always keeps the horse's center line in view. For exercises where the horse is in a bent position on straight lines, circles, or on two tracks, the student must always keep the inside eye of the horse in view so that he can better judge the lines he is to maintain. Since in these movements, the rider's inside hip is placed according to the horse's inside hind leg, the rider must follow the bend of the horse's forehand with his upper body and turn his head toward the inside so that his inside shoulder is prevented from following the direction of the inside hip. Turning the outside shoulder back too much would have the drawback of making it impossible to bring the horse's outside shoulder forward enough. When practicing the dressage seat, the student should be instructed to look up high so that he is forced to hold his head back a little in order for it to remain in agreement with the position of the rest of his body and make it impossible for him to see his horse's movements. If he wants to become a rider, he must learn to dependably judge these by feel because nothing is less graceful and reveals a greater lack of independence than when a rider relinquishes his position to look at his horse's legs.

A good, sure eye is a treasured gift from nature under all conditions of life; for the rider it is worth twice as much since he can avoid or overcome many a danger much more dependably if he has such a gift.

With this I come to the end of the first section of this book in which I have attempted to discuss the natural means available to the rider for controlling his horse. These consist of the *use* of his limbs and the weight of his body under the guidance of correct feeling and understanding, such correct use being the result in turn only of a natural, soft, and agile seat. I will now turn to the systematic working and gymnastic education of the young, green horse, which we call dressage training.

ENDNOTES:

[1] This way of holding the stirrups should probably be allowed only if the stirrups are longer, as required for the dressage seat, and only for a fully trained riding master. (Hans von Heydebreck)

[2] This instruction is highly dangerous for the less experienced and not yet fully trained rider. It will therefore be better to be satisfied that young riders, when instructed in advanced

dressage, are admonished only to carry their thighs and knees in a quite natural, soft contact with the saddle, without the use of any kind of force. (Hans von Heydebreck)

3 The hunt rider with his forward seat continuously furthers forward movement in that he keeps his center of gravity in coincidence with that of the horse; leaning back behind the horse's center of gravity is used only as a temporary support of the driving aids. (Paul Plinzner)

B. The Purpose Of Dressage

1. General Comments

The noble horse is not only the animal most suited for riding, it is also the creature with the most versatile talents in the entire animal kingdom. From time immemorial, the horse has been, and still is, the animal for which the young boy feels the greatest love and which the man holds in the highest esteem. Poets and songsters have always sung the praises of the horse, and not without reason: it has faithfully shared humanity's fate, has participated in all great events recounted in history with active and courageous spirit, has followed man to the remotest corners of the earth, and has shared with him all hardships and privations. In peacetime and prosperity, it is the most precious luxury item; on the hunt, it is a cheerful companion to man, carrying its rider over hill and dale, across hedges and ditches, dependably catching up with any prey, even the fleetest, with the speed of the wind; in combat, it is the faithful friend and servant of the warrior with whom it willingly shares danger and toil.

Is there any way that man can show sufficient gratitude for such excellent service? Is it not in his own interest to take the greatest care and conduct the most serious research about the breeding, raising, and training of this creature? And yet, in these three areas which should provide us with a reliable and plentiful supply of good and useful horses, we see the worst errors made as a result of the wrong attitude, petty adherence to narrow-minded aims, and prejudices of all kinds. All arts and sciences of our time have made such rapid advances from the study of nature that the successes attained often approach the miraculous. It is time to follow this example, to eliminate all old-fashioned prejudices, and to listen only to nature in order to learn the basic principles of producing a good horse. Nature works according to strict, immutable laws, which can be discovered only by observing nature's unadulterated creations.

Since it is not my task to speak about breeding and raising horses, I will continue in this vein only with regard to schooling a horse.

If the trainer wants to have a correct view of the mechanism of the horse's movements, of the activity of the individual limbs, and of the coaction of all the limbs during forward movement, he must diligently observe the young, green horse in the pasture. He will then be convinced that mother nature has endowed the foal with everything that he has seen as beautiful and artistic in thoroughly trained military and dressage horses, and this with such freshness and grace as it can only be achieved when art is at its greatest perfection. In its mischievous games, the young colt will display quite a number of the higher-level movements, from a passage to airs above the ground. The trainer should study these short and beautiful moments carefully to acquaint himself with the position and carriage of the individual parts of the horse that result in naturally free and elastic motion. He will then see the way in which he can dependably fulfill the aims of dressage; that is, not only to develop the natural forces and capabilities of the horse to perfection through gradual and appropriate exercises, but also to make the horse absolutely obedient.

Correct dressage training is, therefore, a natural gymnastic exercise for the horse, which hardens its strength and supples its limbs. Such exercise causes the strong parts of its body to work harder in favor of the weaker ones. The latter are strengthened by gradual exercise, and hidden forces, held back because of the horse's natural tendency towards laziness, are thus awakened. The end result is complete harmony in the cooperation of the individual limbs with these forces, enabling the horse to continuously and effortlessly perform, with only the slightest aids from its rider, such regular and beautiful movements as it would demonstrate on its own only fleetingly in moments of excitement. The more perfect the horse's conformation and the nobler its origin, the more natural this desirable harmony of movement will be. However, horses of which it is said that their sire has already "taught" them dressage are very rare and precious and are so much in demand (mainly for riders who love a horse in its natural carriage) that they will seldom come into the hands of a trainer. The latter is therefore forced to practice his art primarily on weak horses with unfavorable, even faulty, conformation. For these, dressage training will be elevated to physical therapy. Just as the art of physical therapy has found such great recognition in our time and plays an important part in medicine today, and just as one is now convinced that deformations of the human body or diseased conditions of the individual limbs cannot be healed or treated by iron machines but only by appropriate gymnastic exercises, the trainer, if he has a clear understanding of his art, can overcome many natural deficiencies and weaknesses in his horse. He is often able to perform true miracles in connection with faults and infirmities that were produced by misuse or misunderstanding on the part of earlier riders. By adjusting the horse's body, he is often able to thoroughly heal a horse after all veterinary intervention has been in vain.

I have had horses whose front legs were completely worn out, but whom nature had endowed with strong hindquarters, and I have given them such complete freedom in the shoulder and such reliable gaits by bending their haunches that they could compete with the best and most valuable of their species. Under former riders, their strong hindquarters had merely helped to push all of the weight toward the forehand with great force, with such overloading ruining the forelegs in a short time. By taking the load from the forehand, these horses gradually regained their natural elasticity and agility. The higher elevation of the neck also gave them increased action from the shoulders.

In spite of the most careful and expensive stable care, the Englishman, as the representative of riding in natural carriage, must work on his hunters at the end of each season with poultices, liniments, and unrestricted movement in the boxes to retain the use of the horses' forelegs. They are all excellent horses, the best for practical use bred in England, which is one reason their prices are so high. Dealers do not bring them to the continent; they sell them in England itself. Nevertheless, after but a few hunting seasons, most of them are sold for a few guineas when they are still at a strapping age, and arrive at riding schools with bruised knees, bowed tendons, or other infirmities to spend the rest of their days pulling stagecoaches, streetcars, or taxicabs. It often hurt me to see these beautiful, strong creatures with powerful and completely unused hindquarters end up this way because their weakened forelegs could no longer assure sufficient safety to the hunt rider. If the English would understand how to properly work and stress the hindquarters of their horses in the times between hunting seasons, they would have them year in and year out, not only as the most pleasant hacks, but also as much safer and more enduring hunters, and they would be able to use them to a ripe old age without poultices and liniments. It is unfortunate that a nation, in which love for the horse is so widespread and which undeniably ranks first in the breeding and raising of horses, has been so completely estranged from an art which in the past had reached such heights there. For no country has a greater master of this art and a warmer champion of the noble horse than England in her famous Duke of Newcastle.[1]

The opponents of training the horse so that it carries itself in balance argue against a subject which they either do not understand at all, or of which they have gained a completely incorrect view from false disciples of the art who downgrade it by their incompetence and do damage to the same degree that they intend to be useful. The correctly trained horse has the same relationship to the green horse as has the sculptured work of art to the raw material from which it is formed; the nobler the material and the greater the artist, the higher will be the value of the result. Whoever owns a noble, thoroughly active horse and understands how to use it correctly, will be able to appreciate its value. Unfortunately, it is hard to believe how much ignorance exists today, particularly in this beautiful art, because every untalented or frivolous person who cannot make a living in other fields tries his luck as a horse trainer. Without any scientific knowledge of his task, often without even the necessary physical capabilities, he begins to work the noblest creature of the animal kingdom mechanically, like a carpenter treats wood, according to a pattern. He does not rest until he has either completely broken it, or the animal has become his lord and master. Instead of furthering the natural movements of the young horse with his seat and aids, he interferes with them and inhibits them by his own stiff and incorrect posture, by unnaturally elevating the forehand and by the harshness and untimeliness of his aids. Thus he gradually suppresses all of his horse's abilities and, when he has made a cripple out of the horse, he blames this on its naturally poor conformation. These people, who see in the horse only a dumb, obstinate creature that can be made subservient merely by much pushing and beating, are to blame that many horse breeders and fanciers consider breaking a young horse the equivalent of ruining it, and that this art continues to lose in esteem. Of all the fine arts, the equestrian art should be the most attractive to a young man. With the abandon of youth he sees only the bright and pleasant sides of it, and in his vanity, his vigor, and his high spirits, he believes he is able to master it. It is, of course, a charming spectacle for everyone to see a skillful rider exercise his just as skillful, courageous horse according to the rules of the art. Only a few have an idea of how much time, patience, and effort is required to give a horse such a complete education. If the art were not so difficult, we would have plenty of good riders and excellently ridden horses, but, as it is, the art requires, in addition to everything else, character traits that are not combined in everyone: inexhaustible patience, firm perseverance under stress, courage paired with quiet alertness. If the seed is present, only a true, deep love for the horse can develop these character traits to the height that alone will lead to the goal.

In no art should the saying, "Practice and experience make the master," be taken more to heart than in the equestrian art. Nature shows such versatility in her creations that we will find no two completely identical examples among the millions of beings of the same species, not even among the leaves of one and the same tree. The trainer can therefore only learn from experience to finely and correctly weigh and skillfully use nature's basic rules of his art for the individual horse and its particularities. Young people cannot be reminded often enough to treat their horses calmly and patiently; they always tend, in awareness of their power, to use force against a resistant horse and to break with brute force what they should gradually make supple and flexible. Many an old trainer is honest enough to admit that he did not become a sensible and fine rider until he had lost most of his physical strength and that, since then, he obtains from his horse in a calm and reliable manner everything which in the past he had thought could be accomplished only after a hard struggle.

As mentioned before, schooling the horse involves natural gymnastics in which its entire musculature is exercised and the skeleton is brought into the positions demanded by the rider. The forces of organic beings are of the nature of a magnet; as the magnet gains in power by a gradual increase in the weight it must support, the power of the horse continues to increase through properly adjusted exercises.

Since dressage training primarily aims at developing and regulating the physical forces of the horse, it inevitably also involves its mental capabilities and their perfection. In the long, intimate association with its master, the horse becomes infinitely intelligent and alert. Because it has so much to learn and is continuously asked to observe the slightest hint from its rider, the horse exercises its mental powers together with its physical ones, so that it becomes more attached and friendlier toward its master to the same degree that it increases in skillfulness in its lessons. Once training has been completed, the horse performs its lessons with a type of happy and proud self-confidence.

Like the soldier, who needs years to change, through painful schooling of his body and mind, from a green recruit to a functioning part of a large machine, the horse requires long and careful exercising of the individual parts of its body and of its mental capabilities before it is able to promptly follow the fine aids given by its rider and move its body in all directions easily and gracefully. It is therefore the sign of a charlatan, or sheer ignorance, if people contrive artificially construed bits or other devices supposed to eliminate the long hours of work and to enable the green horse to immediately correctly follow all aids like a well-trained animal. Of course, a painful experience may momentarily elicit an artificial carriage and the corresponding movements from any horse, but soon the horse will find a way to escape such unreasonable force. Such attempts always end in resistance, often in the breakdown of the horse. If the horse had the nature of iron, which can be softened by heating until it turns red and can then be shaped as desired, it would probably be possible to bring it into a balanced carriage or onto its haunches in a single lesson. But as long as this is not the case, people will search in vain for a way to make dressage training unnecessary, much as they would search for the philosopher's stone. All positions that are unfamiliar to the green horse require great freedom and mobility of the joints and necessitate thorough working of the muscles attached to the bones to be moved. This can be accomplished only very gradually by carefully planned exercises which are often very difficult and painful for the horse. Man should only remember how sore his limbs became when he started to exercise, how painful the back of his neck after swimming, his wrist and arm muscles after fencing, his joints and leg muscles after riding and skating, and after other physical exercises. The young horse is no better off if it has to move in an unaccustomed position. The trainer must therefore be very patient with the poor animal and not consider it stubborn if it fights in some of the lessons to take on a position in which it had done much better the day before; it is the joint and muscle pain against which it rebels.

For that reason it is empty boasting or proof of great ignorance for someone to say that he is able to break any horse within a certain period of time and to want to prescribe to his followers not only a step-by-step sequence of exercises that will make this possible as well as their duration. Every practically minded rider will know how much difficulty each individual part of the horse can produce in schooling if that part is by nature of unfavorable conformation, for example, the head and neck. It often takes months of work before it is possible to use these parts to act correctly and naturally on the hindquarters.

The greatest example of such quackery is Mr. Baucher, who, with the audacity of his claims and the enormity of his promises, has brought the entire equestrian world into uproar and confusion. His method consists in gradually and cunningly robbing the horse of its natural power, which Mr. Baucher considers to be the enemy, and to thus make it subservient. He renders his horses so wilted and limp by unnatural bending and twisting in place, and so thoroughly robs their hindquarters of their natural forward action, that the poor creatures lose all support and are no longer good for any practical purpose. The follower of the natural-carriage school of thought makes his horses useless prematurely because he weakens its shoulders and forehand by overloading them, but he does not rob them of the thrust of the hind legs; to the contrary, he develops the hind legs by using them naturally. A skilled trainer can make such horses useful again for riding purposes by bending their hindquarters, or they can at least be used in harness. But a Baucher-trained horse is incapable of that, since it has been robbed of the main prerequisite for pulling and moving forward: its thrust. Mr. Baucher can justly boast that he is unique in the art in that he has discovered movements no master before him has described and shown. These are the infamous movements of stepping backwards, for which he throws his reins on the horse's neck and digs his spurs into its side with all his might, as well as cantering backwards, doing which Mr. Baucher spends ten minutes being flung into the air as a result of his horse kicking out in a regular tempo. His method should be called the backwards system. Having haunted the equestrian world long enough, it has finally, to the relief of all horsekind, been banned to where it really belongs: the circus. There it can be used to perform tricks that make the public laugh and applaud the same way they view the grimaces and contortions of a clown: with a mixture of cheerfulness and disgust. The products of true art will never be distasteful to the spectator, for they continue to develop his sense of beauty to greater perfection. Travesties of such art will, however, fill the person of refined taste with disgust.

I therefore warn against anything that points in any way to this backwards system, particularly against working in place and without a rider.[2] Lazy, physically weak, and particularly timid riders usually tend to use inanimate tools to make it easier for themselves to work a young horse whose unchannelled expression of power they fear. They turn to the *dumb jockey* or *overchecks*, usually in such a way that the resiliency of the hind legs is suppressed before it has ever been developed, and the young horse is forced to either try to escape the excessive action of the bit by going behind it or to deaden the pain by taking a firm contact. In skillful and understanding hands, such tools may, under certain circumstances, be very useful and recommendable. However, they are misused very easily because the poor horse is the only one to bear the brunt, and the trainer will seldom be able to keep the proper perspective if his own feelings do not participate directly. Even in the most skillful hands, inanimate tools can only produce a certain degree of preliminary training; they can never completely replace a live rider. Only the fine tact of a skillful rider is able to reliably detect the moments and degrees of action, thus producing the correct cooperation between hands, legs, and weight, and facilitating the work for the horse by using an agile seat that is appropriate for the particular horse. Under the skillful rider, every horse will always make the most reliable and fastest progress, from the beginning of dressage training to the end.

If I have pointed out in these general comments the difficulties involved in the natural training of the riding horse on a scientific basis, this was not done to frighten amateurs away from the more serious studies of the art, but rather to motivate them for such studies. With a correct view of the principles of this art, it is quite possible to find a way to the desired goal by independent endeavors. Our generation is neither lacking in chivalrous spirit nor in talent, nor in the means to return this beautiful art to its highest flourish. If only half as much were done for the old, proven methods of riding dressage as is done for racing and hunting, not only would the entire equestrian art be in splendid shape, the horse breeding industry would also be improved considerably. The first prerequisite for reawakening a general interest in the art of riding and a contribution in this respect is the main reason for writing this book is to ban from the art everything that is stiff, forced, and pedantic, and to overcome the prejudices that a man on a horse must carry himself in strange posture, and that the dressage horse has to walk around as if screwed into an instrument of torture. Instead, the equestrian art is for both a type of natural gymnastic exercise with which it is possible to attain and demonstrate the highest development of physical strength and skill.

ENDNOTES:

[1] The Duke of Newcastle was active primarily in France and the Netherlands. He established a riding academy in Antwerp where he trained dressage horses. Also, his book entitled **Neue Art Pferde zuzureiten** [New Ways of Breaking Horses] was published in French. (Hans von Heydebreck)

[2] Reasonable work on the lunge and collected work in hand, as described in the chapter about Piaffe and Passage, are, however, aids that a trainer can often use to great advantage. (Hans von Heydebreck)

2. Letting the Horse Find Its Balance

Now that we have agreed that the purpose of dressage is to enable the horse's muscular system, by means of systematically ordered gymnastic exercises, to give its skeleton the carriage required for service as a riding horse, we want to examine what such carriage involves and mainly what we understand by the so often used term, "a horse in balance."

Balance in connection with a moving horse is understood to mean correct, uniform distribution of the weight of horse and rider on its four legs.[1] As easy and obvious as this interpretation may seem, this normal body position is difficult to determine and maintain with certainty in every individual horse. With the infinite variety in the conformation of horses, the carriage that determines balance will also be infinitely varied. In a state of rest, the horse cannot be balanced; due to the significant excess weight of head and neck, the forelegs carry a much heavier load than the hind legs. In freedom, this weight distribution not only makes it easier for the horse to feed itself by grazing, but also gives it a definite forward orientation. A dead body in equilibrium has found its resting point and becomes immobile. If the equilibrium is interfered with, the body will tend with all of its mass to move toward the point where the excess weight lies. According to this principle, the rider, if he demands speed from his horse, will relinquish the balanced carriage and urge with his seat and his aids a carriage toward the shoulders. In the oppositely imbalanced carriage, a carriage toward the haunches, the weight is unable to escape to the rear because the angles of the hind leg joints have a forward effect. In freedom, the horse will therefore never move backward on his own, only when forced, while all movements forward, sideways, and upward in moments of excitement are performed with assurance, sometimes out of sheer joy. In this state, the horse balances itself in such a correct cadence that it almost never takes a wrong step, falls, or sprains one of its limbs due to improper weight distribution. It passes through all degrees of load-bearing on its hind legs, from a balanced carriage to carrying its full weight on the haunches. In its natural state, therefore, the horse is always able to follow its tendency toward the shoulders. This is not harmful, since the animal does not have to carry any foreign weight, moves at will, and has its hind legs available when needed, and without restraint, to support the forehand. Under saddle, however, the horse must additionally carry the rider's weight and must take on not only certain gaits, but perform them at a prescribed tempo and for any desired period of time, as demanded by its rider. It must then carry itself in balance in order to perform safely and without damage to its legs, according to the principle that a correctly balanced load is much easier to carry and to support than an imbalanced one.

By nature, the forelegs are intended primarily as supports for the body; due to their structure, they are capable of moving forward uniformly with the hind legs to support the forward-driven body weight at the proper time; but they do not possess any thrust or spring force to move the body weight forward independently. The bones of the forelegs, therefore, usually rest vertically on one another, and the few deviations from this direction serve only the purpose of absorbing heavy shocks and making them harmless.

The bones of the hindquarters, however, are arranged at angles to one another and, with their spring-action joints, are capable of pushing the body mass forward with greater force or, if the mass acts in a more perpendicular direction, of thrusting it upward. The hindquarters therefore serve the dual purpose of providing support and forward movement. For this reason, nature has equipped them not only with greater strength in the skeleton but also with very powerful muscles. The hindquarters are thus the main seat of all displays of power by the horse, the source from which spring all of the excellent characteristics of its way of going. This is where, as the old masters would jokingly claim, we find the horse's seven-league boots and the new uppers for its worn-out forelegs.

The trainer must devote his undivided attention to working the hind legs, particularly the hip and knee joints, if he wants to bring out of his horse everything that nature has put into it. He has accomplished this task, and has trained his horse to perfection, if he has brought the two forces that are based in the hindquarters, *thrust* and *carrying power* (the latter in connection with spring force), to their greatest development, and is able to weigh their effects and their ratio to one another precisely and at will. He is then able to displace his horse's center of gravity from the shoulders to the haunches and back to the shoulders, or he can maintain it in balance, depending on whether he permits the thrust or the carrying power to prevail; or he lets both appear in regular alternation (a perfection of training which is evident only in the true dressage horse). The race horse trainer develops only the thrust of the hind legs to the utmost perfection. Yet, he cannot do this without disadvantaging the forelegs

[53]

because the forelegs must then carry too heavy a load. The military rider, whose aim is a balanced horse, needs to develop the carrying power of the hind legs only to such a degree that they take over the excess weight from the shoulders. The dressage rider, however, develops both thrust and carrying power uniformly to the utmost perfection and thus imparts the highest physical agility to his horse.

To correctly determine the balanced movement of each individual horse is more a thing of feeling on the part of the rider than of evaluating the horse's exterior conformation, since the courage inherent in the horse and the impulsion developed in its way of going play just as much a part as its physical condition. Generally, it is assumed that it is possible to evaluate the weight distribution of a horse from its way of going: the more the hind legs overtrack the footprints of the forelegs at the walk and trot, the more weight is carried on the shoulders; if the hind legs step precisely into the tracks of the forelegs the horse moves in balance; and the more the tracks of the hind legs lag behind the tracks of the forelegs, the more weight is carried on the hindquarters. However, this rule can be used only for correctly and well-built horses. If a horse's conformation deviates from the normal, this rule is insufficient because we come up against such significant exceptions that, in practice, we often observe the opposite, and see horses that, although carrying a heavy load on their shoulders, do not step with their hind legs into the tracks of their forelegs, while others must be collected considerably to prevent them from overtracking.

What is important is not to assign exactly the same weight to each one of the four legs; this would require once and for all that they each have the same strength. Rather, the load should be distributed to the four legs in a ratio commensurate with their natural carrying capability, so that, corresponding to its greater strength, the stronger part carries a greater load and the weaker part is relieved to the same degree. As noted before, the hindquarters are stronger by nature than the forehand, not only simply because they have stronger bones, joints, and muscles, but also indirectly because their joints, like compression springs, are able to bend under a heavy load. The forelegs do not have this property and must therefore be carefully protected against any sudden, heavy stresses as they occur in poorly performed turns and halts. It is therefore the desire of all riders who espouse a balanced carriage whether they actually understand it or not to bring their horses onto their haunches and relieve them in front. How ignorantly this is generally done and how frequently

[54]

the work is completely contrary to the nature of the horse is evident from the many broken-down creatures that are victims of dressage training.

The understanding trainer, gifted with a well developed rider's intuition, will soon sense from his horse's behavior how much he must load the hindquarters to bring the horse into balance, which will then be expressed by a beautiful, natural elevation of head and neck, by free, elastic movements of the forelegs from the shoulders, and by strong, determined follow-up of the hindquarters. He will select the means of achieving this goal with consideration for his horse's conformation, temperament, and age. The more careful he is in this selection, the faster he will reach his goal. With the infinite variety in the conformation of horses and with the innumerable and minor deviations from the desired, normal shape of the individual parts of the horse's body and their interconnections, experience is the only and most dependable teacher in the selection and use of the proper exercises under a rider. Each trainer must pay for his mistakes in this respect and may be considered fortunate indeed if it does not cost him too dearly. Young people should never look down on old experienced masters, but take eager advantage of every opportunity to obtain advice from them, or to work young horses under their direction. Talent and personal skill cannot replace experience in this art, since what is involved is not working on a piece of inanimate material, but training a living, independent being. It is not as much of an accomplishment to make an excellent military or dressage horse from a well-built, young horse, as it is to make a weak horse with irregular conformation into a conditionally useful, acceptable horse. To take the latter and try to make a good dressage horse out of it is nonsense, however, and will always end poorly. What nature has denied the horse, the rider and all his skill cannot put into it. So many people forget this and, as a result, or due to lack of experience, they evaluate their horses improperly and make these bad mistakes.

It is often very difficult to distinguish between talented horses and truly poor ones. Young or poorly kept horses often appear weak and crippled at the start of training, but they gradually develop their hidden talents and strengths in such a way that they seem to be transformed. Of course, the art of quickly developing weak forces into strengths by means of exercise deserves the credit for this transformation, but it cannot impart anything that is not already there. No artist is able to develop a horse that is truly weak or impaired in its hindquarters and back into a skillful dressage or

[55]

military horse. The sensible rider will be satisfied to leave such a horse in its natural carriage, to set it straight in this carriage, regulate its gaits as much as possible, and to then use the horse for services which correspond to this carriage. Such horses are, of course, rather thankless jobs in the art, but the young rider must not hesitate to work with them as well in order to exercise his patience and broaden his experience.

The general complaint about poor quality horses is correct in that more poor animals are being bred than good ones. If we count among the good horses only those that are natural-born riding horses, they are very rare indeed. Nevertheless, this complaint is the same as the complaint about the "good old times." Everyone thinks the good old times were better because he did not experience their unpleasant sides or has forgotten them, while he is directly affected by the vagaries of the present. I myself am of the opinion, considering the hundreds of horses I have worked with, that we here in Prussia cannot complain about our horse breeders. In our Trakehner horse and in the East Prussian horse refined by it—although since the days of the meritorious Mr. von Burgsdorff, the extensive use of English Thoroughbreds has perhaps reduced somewhat the correctness of their conformation—we still have, next to the Arabian, the best utility riding horse in the world, as evidenced sufficiently by the dominant position of our mounted cavalry.[2] Although, of course, the perfect specimen among those can also be counted on the fingers of one hand, it is the purpose of the equestrian art to eliminate or render harmless any natural flaws or irregularities, since the perfect horse is, by nature, already in balance, at least without a rider. This gives us that much more reason to complain about the lack of understanding and skillful riders than about the lack of horses, since, with the aid of the former, we could produce many more excellent horses from those which, as a result of incorrect training and lack of balance, are ruined before their time. One should take the horses as they come and train them as they should be trained by exercising their muscles naturally and systematically to enable them to carry their skeleton in a suitable manner. Never forget that dressage training should be controlled gymnastics, not forced exercises, and that the horse's body should not be pressed all at once into the desired mold, but should gradually be enabled to take on this shape without force.

Flaws in the carriage of the skeleton can be remedied without damage to health only by planned, patient exercises. They are then eradicated thoroughly. In this way, a horse that appears to be useless for riding service is transformed into a useful animal. Riders who still lack in experience should not despair if they sometimes have to spend months in simple trot exercises with horses that have stiff necks, tense backs, or high hindquarters, before they are able to work on the parts that must produce the missing balance. They will then recognize the gradual development of balance not only in the advantageous external transformation of the horse, which I have already mentioned, but also mainly by feel, in that the horse, which is now in balance, puts its rider into the vertical position and holds him there. Its contact with the bit becomes softer and more regular, and, during turns and artificial positions, it is able to remain regular in its movements.[3] The balanced carriage is more secure the more it is possible to put greater weight onto the hindquarters without detriment and thus develop the horses' carrying power more perfectly. The more correctly this is done, the more the irregularities in conformation of the green horse will disappear. It is then possible to reshape a naturally ugly horse into a harmoniously beautiful animal and make it much more valuable.

The rider who truly loves horses and riding should therefore strive to develop in himself, through instruction and particularly through practice, a sure evaluation of the green horse, with his eyes and his intuition, so that in his old age he will not have to accuse himself of regrettably having ruined many a good prospect, and to thus have caused himself and others great loss, not to mention the sin which it is to needlessly cripple such a useful and noble creature as the horse. He should practice his patience and his skill with weak horses and impart to them a degree of agility and regularity of movement that enables them to carry their load on their shoulders. He should further practice patience, perseverance, and strength with poorly conformed but strong horses. He should learn to correctly estimate their true capabilities from their ability to withstand and their natural expressions of strength.

ENDNOTES:

[1] Contradictory interpretations of the term balance found in equestrian literature are explained by the fact that, on the one hand, laws established for an inanimate body are also applied to a moving, living body and, on the other hand, research involving the laws of balance to which the moving horse's body is subjected does not consider impulsion. It is also not recognized that it is only the supporting limbs, the legs in touch with the ground, which support the equilibrium during movement, but also the limbs that are swinging

forward, the moving legs, which contribute to the maintenance of balance and impulsion. Impulsion is generated by the hind legs which push off from elastic joints in a forward-upward direction. The more the hind legs fling the body upward during this movement, the more of the load they have previously absorbed, thus relieving the forelegs. To do this, the upper joints of the hind legs must bend while supporting the weight, thus lowering the hindquarters and putting the horse's spine, which by nature forms a line that descends from the rear to the front, into a more horizontal orientation. To be able to produce this orientation at any time is the main goal of training the utility horse by way of gymnastic exercises. (Hans von Heydebreck)

[2] Good utilitarian riding horses are now also being bred in many other areas of Germany, primarily in Hanover and Holstein. (Hans von Heydebreck)

[3] The uniform contact with both reins can be realized only by setting the horse straight. A horse that moves crooked will always lean harder on one rein and will put more weight on the forelegs of that side, thus rendering impossible the uniform distribution of weight to all four legs which is necessary for a balanced carriage. (Hans von Heydebreck)

C. Systematic Training
of the Horse

1. Work on the Lunge

The first task of a trainer should be to preserve the mind of the young horse, an animal that has previously grown up in freedom, and protect it against mistrust or fear. He should therefore take care that, in the stall, its groom treats it gently, friendly, and with great patience. Caresses, playful interaction, and spoiling the animal with sugar or bread in the stall are inappropriate for young horses. They cause the young horses to become playful which very easily may end up as dangerous habits, particularly in stallions, in that it teaches them to bite and strike out. Regular and calm treatment will keep the kind horse gentle and gradually calm down the timid, nervous, or distrustful horse. - At the beginning of work, this principle should be always adhered to and the young animal should be forced as little as possible. First it should be lunged and, for this purpose, it should be tacked up in a simple surcingle, a full-cheek snaffle bridle, and a generously padded cavesson. The lunge line is then snapped into the cavesson and the snaffle reins are attached[1] so that, if the horse carries its head and neck naturally and with slight contact, they have a gentle tension. Then the horse should move in both directions[2] in appropriate repetitions; at the beginning, it is not necessary to precisely maintain a certain pace or a perfect circle. Not yet used to bending its body, the horse will always tend to leave the circle in a straight line and will therefore soon escape, sometimes toward the inside, sometimes toward the outside. The coordinated work of lunge line and whip must quietly counteract this tendency until the horse has learned to reliably make contact with the lunge line and follow its direction. The young horse takes up this contact more quickly and willingly in a well padded cavesson than if the lunge line is snapped into the chin piece of the snaffle bridle because the cavesson acts on the hard and less sensitive nose bone while a lunge line fastened to the chin piece will interfere with contact with the bit during every pull required to maintain the circle; it will scare the horse away from the bit and, in addition, easily teach it all kinds of bad habits, such as letting its tongue escape above the bit, sticking its tongue out, moving the lower jaw, and other bad habits which will later make the rider's work more difficult for a long time. The young, courageous horse which, in the past, was able to follow any of its whims without interference, will initially need to run and buck on the lunge to get rid of its exuberance and will not maintain a certain gait. The understanding trainer will forgive all such irregularities; they result from a feeling of vitality - called barn freshness by horsemen - and will cease on their own with the appropriate work. If, by the way, the locality is suitable for such work in that it has even and loose footing, such bucks and sudden forceful movements will not do damage to the horse since it is still practically in a state of freedom and in such a state it knows by instinct to support and balance itself correctly. If, however, incorrect pulls on the lunge line or excessive restraining action from the side reins interfere with the natural freedom of its limbs, it is easily possible for the horse to fall, slip, or misstep and be injured. It is therefore quite wrong to start out the lunge work by pushing the young horse together in a lunging rig using four reins, two acting toward the top and the other two toward the bottom so that the horse is inhibited in its freedom of movement, including its forward movement, and can be forced to move forward only with the aid of a whip. This then is the cause of all those lamenesses and other accidents that are feared in connection with work on the lunge. Dressage training means educating the horse. Why not take as an example the immense progress made recently in education, with the aid of which the youngest children learn easily in half the time what in the past it was believed had to be taught them piecemeal with the threat of a stick, and teach the young horse easily and unobtrusively things that do not require any serious effort on its part. If this is not demanded until training has progressed, the rider is often forced to use more punishment and force than he would like since he loves his pupil, or should if he doesn't. Just as the experienced teacher is able to distinguish between the youthful pranks of his students that result from high spirits and frivolity and those that reveal viciousness and malice, the trainer must be able to distinguish in his horse the expressions of youthful high spirits from those demonstrating a bad character. He will therefore forgive some sillinesses and let them run their course, but meet explicit stubbornness seriously and strictly, and treat biting, vicious kicking with the fore or hind legs, and other bad habits by emphatically punishing them with the whip or by a snap with the lunge line.

Once its barn freshness has been checked, the horse can be asked to bend to the side as much as necessary to maintain the circle in that the inner side rein is shortened relative to the outer rein by such an amount that both are tensioned the same way if the horse moves on the intended circle with the correct bend. Generally, one should remember that it is easier for the young horse to stay on the circle the larger the circle is because then the circle comes closer to a straight line. However, the smaller the circle, the more it inhibits forward movement. According to this principle, a reduction in the size of the circle should be used as a means of slowing down a horse that is too fast, and increasing the size of the circle to make reluctant gaits more ground-covering and livelier. Since a small circle requires the entire body of the horse to be bent considerably, this should be used as a true lesson only after the horse has been gradually prepared for it by longer exercises; but it can be used at any time as a temporary measure against running away.

To prevent the green horse from intentionally deviating from the prescribed circle, some people use the counter position in which the head and neck are moved toward the outside with the corresponding rein. But, how is a young horse in such a difficult position to maintain a line which it is unable to maintain for lack of contact and bend in its simple, natural position?! This merely forces it to push toward the outside, and the lunge line must then hold it on the circle by force, putting the horse's entire body into an oblique position and therefore forcibly abolishing the horse's natural equilibrium. Regularity of the gaits and staying on the circle come all by themselves if contact with the lunge line and the bit is correct since this can be done only with the necessary development of thrust by decisive forward movement and the required position of head and neck. Yet, contact can be established only gradually by the correct interaction of lunge line and whip.

Lunge line and whip, if they are not to do more harm than good, must be used by experts who understand one another well and are able to support one another promptly[3]. The lunge line holder stands in the middle of the circle and constitutes its center in that he participates in the circular movements of the horse by turning in place and keeping his outer shoulder opposite the inner shoulder of the horse, always keeping an eye on the horse's forehand. He takes the place of the rider's hand, that is, he gives the restraining aids and will therefore become active mainly if the horse moves too fast and pushes toward the outside. The whip, however, replacing the rider's driving aids, must maintain the gait and thus produce contact. The whip carrier therefore follows the horse at such a distance that he is able to reach it at any time and observes mainly the activity of the hindquarters. The closer he keeps to the circle the better it is because in that way he puts himself directly behind the horse, giving his aids a forward driving effect as well. For that reason, it is of advantage to train a young, agile assistant with good lungs for this task; such a person is able to easily follow a lazy and laid-back horse in the faster gaits. He carries the whip upright and facing the horse in such a way that the horse is able to see the whip with its inside eye; if necessary, the whip acts on the hind legs. To counteract developing irregularities, lunge line and whip must, however, change their aids in many ways. If the horse pushes toward the inside, the whip carrier must drive it outward again in that he directs the whip toward the horse's inside shoulder, approaching the lunge line somewhat. If the horse pushes toward the outside, the whip carrier must be passive and merely watch that the horse does not slow down. If the horse rushes forward too much, the whip carrier must take his position closely behind the lunge line holder to show himself and the whip to the horse as little as possible. If the horse stops suddenly, which is generally followed very soon by a change of hand, he must quickly jump behind the horse and drive it decisively forward to prevent this mistake if at all possible. If he is unsuccessful, however, he must rush toward the horse and energetically try to direct it back the way it is supposed to go. For all of these occurrences, the lunge line holder must provide the appropriate support. If the horse pushes toward the inside, slows down, and particularly if it stops, he must leave his position in order to be able to give forward driving tugs with the line and must move ahead of the horse on a small circle. If the horses pushes toward the outside, he must resist this forcefully by repeatedly tensioning the line until the horse yields and continues on the correct circle, taking on the required lateral bend. If the horse rushes off, he must reduce thrust by gradually reducing the circle and prevent the horse from leaning on the line by alternatingly quietly taking up and yielding with the lunge line. No tightening of the lunge line must ever be sudden and directed toward the center of the circle but must always act more or less forward so that the horse's direction of movement will never be suddenly and forcefully interfered with. Failure to observe this rule not only easily brings about a change of hand but often leads to shoulder lameness or sprained joints in the fore and hind legs. Never must the young horse be punished by a hard hit on its nose or even in its mouth, since such hard and incorrect halts have a very disadvantageous effect on the hind legs and may cause the development of spavin, curbs, or other leg damage. Calmness and patience are always the most reliable, particularly with a young horse, since what is involved here is generally more barn freshness than stubbornness. Appropriate work is the best and most expedient means against this youthful exuberance since it develops strength, regulates the temperament, and keeps the horse free of distrust and in a good mood. When assigning the work, don't forget that endurance can be achieved only by gradually increasing the exercises; this continues to develop and strengthen the motion apparatus. Don't be deceived by the temperamental horse if at the beginning of its work on the lunge it shows much fire and eagerness; often such horses, carried away by their lively temperament, go beyond their natural strength and do themselves harm instead of gaining strength. In any case, avoid getting a young horse too hot right from the start since our horse tends to easily catch cold and consequently all kinds of infections. The reason for this is that our care is too artificial; we try to get the finest possible coat by using warm barns and blankets. This fine hair then is insufficient protection against our rough climate. In its free state, nature provides the horse with the appropriate clothing so that horses from northerly latitudes are able to withstand the bitterest cold and the roughest weather without any disadvantage. Young horses that have just recently been taken inside must be accustomed to their new surroundings by small amounts of light feed and careful work. Strangles, persistent coughs, and sometimes even more serious illnesses will otherwise interrupt training that has hardly begun and often are the reason for long delays which could have been avoided with more care.

Work on the lunge is very advisable as a preparation for under-saddle exercises and is indispensable in many cases. Work on the lunge makes the green horse more familiar with humans and accustoms it to working, paying attention, and being obedient. It gains in flexibility and agility to the extent that this is possible with its natural body carriage; a proper circle requires that the horse's body be bent accordingly. For very young or weak horses this work on the lunge should be continued until they are able to carry the rider's weight without damage since any development of their strength under sensible control will always be more useful than a lazy existence. But don't believe that it is possible to have a straightening influence on the horse and gradually bring it into balance, or even cause it to bend its hocks, in this playful way. Although it is possible, in order to make life easier for the trainer or the horse, to enforce an artificial elevation of the forehand and thus a forced shift of the weight onto the hindquarters by dead machinery, such as an overcheck or a dumb jockey, this will always be at the expense of the horse's natural strength. These inanimate tools have such a deleterious effect because, although they load the tension springs of the hindquarters, they do not relieve them and thus gradually destroy their elasticity, similar to a spring of steel or some other metal which loses its effectiveness if it is compressed for a longer period of time under uniform pressure. Only a rider who is sensitive and feels correctly is able to properly work the organic springs of the hind legs, make them flexible, and increase the development of their strength. He alone is able to correctly determine the degree and moment of compression and enhance relief by yielding. Only with such alternating bending and stretching are the joints able to develop their greatest power and easily and elastically move forward the weight they are asked to carry. As mentioned once before, organic forces, like the force of a magnet, can be increased to infinity by appropriate exercises but not by dead machines; only by the action of a thinking and feeling rider. Don't be deceived by seemingly free and elevated movements under the dumb jockey; they are not natural but cramped. With a forcibly cranked-up neck position, the flexors of the forearms are contracted excessively and act spasmodically on the bones they move. The hind legs, which are more inhibited than weighted by this enforced position of the forehand, creep along behind, and so we see a horse that is forced and tensioned in all its parts and moves forward with effort in an unnatural way. Just as any unnatural effort leaves behind that much more fatigue the more strength it has consumed, the poor animal will collapse in itself without self-carriage after such exercises and its muscle activity will gradually weaken. These inanimate tools also have a deleterious effect on the mouth in that, with their constant, uniform pressure, they either cause the horse to lean on them the wrong way, thus producing a dead mouth, or they force it to escape the bit completely and go behind it. The rider's good hands reward any pushing away from the bit by yielding and facilitate the correct contact by steady but light pressure from the reins, while the dead and hard overcheck produces faults that can later be corrected only with difficulty, if at all. He who desires to fulfill the true purpose of dressage training and to fully develop but not weaken his horse's natural gifts, should use inanimate tools to obtain an artificial position only through the intermediary of a rider so that their effect can always be measured correctly and at the right time by the rider's feel for the horse. In skilled hands, any bit will become harmless and also effective so that it is not necessary to fear its selection; nevertheless at the beginning the simplest will be the best since it interferes the least with the young horse.

Whoever extends the work on the lunge for a long period of time because he likes it or in consideration of his horse, will always gain sufficiently if he develops the lunge work through the thrust of the hind legs, thus causing head and neck to stretch toward the bit, and makes the head and neck muscles supple through appropriate lateral bending exercises. This ensures him a certain contact under saddle, which is the first prerequisite for later on being able to act on the hindquarters by means of the reins. But whoever wants to advance his horse as quickly as possible should get on it as soon as the horse is able and prepared, because nothing can replace the rider's aids. All training is based on the correct interaction of driving and restraining aids whose proper ratio can be regulated only by feeling. And this is accomplished only by direct physical contact with the horse and by the vibrations transmitted to the rider's body due to its motion.

The horse's preparation should be completed in the correct sequence in that as the next step a saddle is put on its back instead of the surcingle. This requires care, and the first time the horse should be saddled on the lunge line and in the arena so that it will have the necessary room to buck around as much as necessary if it wants to fight this new pressure by humping its back. The stirrups must be pulled up and fastened well so that they will not hit the horse and frighten it and the girths should initially be tightened only moderately, a little more after each repetition so that the young horse will not learn to blow itself up. If it has a poor saddle position by nature, don't attempt to overcome this with a foregirth or a crupper but wait patiently until the increasing equilibrium, and the reshaping of the horse's body connected with it, produce the good, safe saddle position all by itself. If the young horse then tolerates, without becoming suspicious, stirrups that hang down its sides and hit it, the rider may carefully mount and dismount a few times after each lesson while avoiding any annoying contact with the horse. The rider should carefully support himself on the stirrup and saddle and perform all his movements slowly while talking to the horse in a friendly voice. If the horse again displays neither fear nor distrust, the lunge line holder should lead it around the circle once or twice at the walk. In this way it will be accustomed to an initially completely passive rider until the latter gradually takes over the guidance with his hands and legs to the same extent as the supporting interaction of lunge line and whip decreases and finally stops altogether. How long the individual steps of this exercise should last depends entirely on the character and intelligence of the horse and must be left solely to the evaluation of the trainer. The old saying that "Haste makes waste" should always be considered because haste is ultimately paid for with a great loss of time. Also, any new exercise should be done at the end of the lunge work since the horse then not only has most likely lost its barn freshness and the sensitivity in its back but also considers the end of work as a reward for its obedience.

ENDNOTES:

[1] In order to be able to always precisely determine the degree of the effect of both reins created by the attachment, it is recommended to use special side reins. Most appropriate are reins which have one end snapped to the top of the surcingle or into eyes in the breast plate, the other end at the bottom of the surcingle; they are pulled only through the snaffle rings. The length of the side reins is such that the horse is on the bit with a slight contact, carrying its head and neck in a natural position. The length of the reins is of particular importance since it is very difficult to adapt them properly to each particular horse right from the start. The correct length of the side reins can only be selected once the horse has relaxed and, coming from its back, tends to stretch its neck toward the bit. In the beginning both reins are set at the same length, later it is advisable to make the inner rein a bit shorter. (Hans von Heydebreck)

[2] Since almost all horses by nature prefer reversing to the left rather than the right, work on the lunge should always begin on the left hand. (Hans von Heydebreck)

[3] To ensure prompt interaction of lunge line and whip, the lunge line holder should take over both tasks as soon as the horse is relatively secure in staying on the circle. (Hans von Heydebreck)

2. Starting the Young Horse

Developing Thrust in Its Natural Carriage

It is a very popular but quite incorrect notion that the young horse, whose sensitivities have not yet been developed and which knows neither rein nor leg aids, does not require a fine rider for its first exercises but could be taught the basics by the first available groom who has a good enough seat that he will not be tossed. As any father prefers to have his children taught their first elementary lessons by a scientifically educated man rather than by a schoolmaster of limited skills, each horse owner should give his horse to an educated expert trainer right from the start. This trainer will not only teach the young horse in a few days that for which the green groom would have taken months, he will also, with his skill in adapting himself to the horse's natural movements and in measuring his aids always correctly in accordance with circumstances, protect it against any unfavorable impressions on his mind and character, whereas the untrained rider, with his harshness and insensitivity, will not only make every movement infinitely more difficult for the horse but will also quite often plant the seed for all those resistances which later will be so difficult to overcome and which are therefore so feared. As long as the horse still goes on the lunge and it is more important to accustom it to the rider's weight and the contact with him produced in that way, it is probably in order to use a light-weight, flexible, although otherwise uneducated apprentice rider for that purpose. However, as soon as the horse is to be independently guided, it is necessary to have a rider with equestrian training and sensitivity. For that reason, only the trainer should mount the young horse from that moment on and guard it jealously against any outside interference.

Initially it is only important to develop thrust and thus the willingness of the horse to move forward in its quite natural carriage. Any green horse will become slower and more restrained under the rider than in hand because the freedom of its movements is more or less limited by having to carry the rider's weight and by the unfamiliar contact produced by it. This can be observed quite clearly when inspecting young horses at a dealer's; probably trained only in hand, they practically fly toward you with majestically carried head and neck, tail raised high, while under saddle they raise their backs, pinch in their tails, and carry their necks in a stiff, extended position, presenting a completely different picture. This artificial tensioning of the muscles, particularly the back muscles, prevents the free movement of the limbs but is nevertheless the consequence of an instinctively followed natural law. Anyone carrying a heavy load is unable to do this with his back hollow; he must bend his back in order not to endanger his health, because a curved support is better able to carry than a straight one. For the same reason, the horse will initially receive the unfamiliar load with a humped back until practice and familiarity will make the load cease to be one. Therefore, the rider should make his weight as light and comfortable as possible for the horse by bringing his seat into coincidence with the horse's center of gravity. Since this center of gravity is initially situated more or less far forward, the rider should position himself likewise with a forward slant, thus not only furthering the thrust of the hind legs but also ameliorating the shocks generated between rider and horse by putting his weight strongly into the stirrups and sitting in a light crotch seat. He should also help develop the way of going by moving on the straightest possible lines along the track against the wall of the arena since the latter simultaneously provides an artificial support and serves as a guide to the young, unstraightened horse similar to the lunge line. Passing through the corners must then be made easier by rounding them. The rider's driving aids should be given by his legs and the whip, and, if the horse is lively, sensitive, or distrustful, he should leave the spurs off entirely so that he can first make the horse familiar with his legs by using his calves and heels freely and without restraint. The horse's bridle should be an ordinary snaffle, with no other auxiliary equipment except for a noseband, and guidance should be limited to keeping the horse on the correct track through very faint rein aids and to obtaining steady, full contact. The rider should keep his reins relatively short, put both his hands low, one facing the other, in such a way that the reins touch the horse's neck. He should not try to find the desired contact with his hands but should wait in a quiet position for the moment until the horse takes the bit on its own as a result of the driving aids and the resulting stretching of his neck[1]. When riding through the corners, the inside hand should be moved inward ever so slightly, with the outside rein yielding somewhat while the inside stirrup carries more weight. The shorter reins are necessary to give the rider in his forward position the necessary room between hands and body for pulling the reins and to be able to put his hands low so as to act quickly and reliably on the still awkward horse. Full contact is necessary to serve as a certain support for the horse if the thrust from its hindquarters is a heavy load on its forehand. The selection of the gait should depend on the ability of the horse as determined by its conformation and temperament. Although the trot must always be practiced with priority, the canter should by no means be excluded since it is a quite natural gait which requires the greatest thrust and impulsion from the haunches, like a jump. It is therefore an exaggerated cautionary action to want to exclude this gait as an exercise as soon as the stimulation and development of the forward driving forces of the hindquarters are involved. We have also had it confirmed in practice that for slow horses extensive exercises at a fast canter enable them to produce a deliberate trot much more easily and faster than by unchanging, tiring trot exercises. Such horses are much more easily caused to seek contact with the bit by the greater thrust produced by the canter and thus find the correct position of head and neck. In the chapter about the "Canter" the use of this pace in the natural carriage of the horse will be discussed in greater detail. At this point I merely want to recommend not to interfere with the young, agile horse if it wants to canter until it has obtained the desired contact and carriage of its forehand, whereupon it can be returned to the trot by now letting the inside rein and leg become a bit stronger to bring the inside hind leg more underneath the load. It is not advisable, however, to force young horses to canter, at least not in the arena where they are required to perform regular turns. In the horse's natural carriage the canter is a rather free and lively gait which requires a certain flexibility to travel through four corners. Clumsy or very inflexible horses must first be prepared for these turns in quiet gaits before they are able to provide full contact with reliability in the canter or the extended trot. Impetuous horses that are driven forward by their temperament and in which thrust need not be artificially produced must, for the same reason, be kept at a more moderate tempo so that their natural position will not be lost in the turns and their contact does not become hard. Continuous straight lines in an open field do not require this consideration for turns and are therefore better suited for developing forward movement in lazy, slow, and naturally clumsy horses than the interrupted lines of an arena, although the walls delimiting the arena provide more support and the corners enhance flexibility.

The walk, because of its lack of impulsion and the special sequence of the footfalls of the four legs, is not suitable for the development of thrust and should therefore be used in this stage of training only for rest periods and as breathers for the horses after faster gaits. However, the horse can be occupied once in a while during the walk and also during halts by alternatingly bending its neck to either side.

The first task for the green horse is accomplished when it has learned from the discussed exercises to move under the rider in carrying the load on its shoulders with the same naturalness, and to perform its gaits with the same reliability as it was able to do in the past without the added weight, and when it accepts the rider's hands and legs to the extent that this is possible in its carriage on the shoulders. It has then learned the basics and can begin with its actual dressage training; like a child must first know his alphabet and numbers before he is able to learn to read and do arithmetic.

ENDNOTES:

[1] In this way the horse will gradually let his head hang down naturally, thus transferring the action of the bit to the bars and ensuring for the future a light contact and a willingly yielding poll. (Hans von Heydebreck)

3. The Artificial Carriage of the Horse

In order to obtain the desired *artificial carriage* and to confirm it, the horse must perform many exercises which work its individual parts and make them active and which also practice the correct cooperation of all parts. I call the horse's carriage, which requires it to be in balance or even to put a greater load on its hindquarters, an artificial carriage because it is an art to teach the horse to take on this carriage when desired by its rider and to maintain it for any length of time in graduations as prescribed by the aids. If the horse is able by nature to assume this carriage on its own, it is, strictly speaking, also a natural carriage.

With the multitude of differently conformed horses, science is able to teach the practicing rider only general principles according to which he must act. In particular, however, science also defines individual movements and exercises, how they must be performed to perfection, and the effect they have on the movement of the horse. It is the rider's task to make the correct selection from these movements and exercises according to the special talents of his horse. The conscientious observance of certain main principles and the gradually gained experience will then be or become his reliable advisors.

As the first main principle of the art I urge every rider to *"ride your horse forward and set it straight!"*

When I say riding forward I do not mean driving the horse forward in the fastest and most extended gaits, but rather for the rider to take care to maintain an active thrust of the hindquarters in all exercises such that, not only in the movements in place, but even when moving backwards, the forward motion, namely the desire to move the load forward, remains in effect. The horse must therefore be enabled, through practice, to restrain its thrust to the utmost by increasing the load, but thrust should never be completely suppressed by overdoing it!

Additionally, I consider a horse to be straight not if it carries its body entirely without bending, but if its forehand is adjusted in a forward direction to the lines to be traveled, so that the horse's forelegs precede the hind legs under all circumstances, even if its body is bent to the greatest extent possible, and in the movements on two tracks. The hind legs in turn follow the forelegs unconditionally in that they always step forward in the direction of movement and never to the side of that direction.

If these two golden rules are not observed due to ignorance or negligence, all of the faults that make a horse resistant, and often even ruin it, develop during training. The adherent of the natural carriage, who usually rides his horse in free gaits and on straight lines, rarely violates these rules. We find in his horses innate faults that are caused by temperament, excitable nerves, or faulty eyesight, but rarely do we find stubbornness or learned vices. The trainer, however, has a difficult task in this respect right from the start because he works his horse in a limited space and is continuously forced to ride turns, that is, to artificially adjust the forehand forward. He cannot accomplish this by guidance alone but must support the work of his hands with his legs in order to cause the hind legs to follow correctly. This following alone determines the way of going because the thrust of the hindquarters becomes more effective the straighter it acts against the body mass, according to the principle that a pushing or lifting force must always be directed toward the center of gravity of the load.

Each horse is built narrower in the chest than in the hips; if one imagines it moving between two parallel lines that are drawn from its hips parallel to its spine, the horse would be correctly set straight only if it were kept away from these lines by the same amount that it is narrower in the shoulders than in the hips. It is therefore wrong for the rider to keep his horse's outside hip and shoulder the same distance from the wall since this puts it obliquely inward by several centimeters. This carriage will in turn reduce the development of force of the inside hind leg to a corresponding degree.[1] If, however, the shoulders are moved inward too much, without the corresponding bend, this will cause the thrust of the outside hind leg to be lost to an even greater degree, the more this leg departs from the direction toward the center of gravity.

When moving on a curved line this includes all turns on one track the horse must be a part of this line. It must be bent in its body to the extent required by the curve. The degree of the required bend depends on the size of the circle on which the horse moves, the smaller the circle, the greater the bend. This bend must extend over the entire spinal column so as not to have an adverse effect on the horse's way of going. The spinal column forms the firm basis to which the remaining parts of the skeleton are attached either directly or indirectly. The skeleton in turn not only serves as a firm support for the muscles but also as a protection for the precious internal organs. In the center of the vertebrae, well protected as an extension of the brain, extends the spinal cord which provides the entire body with the nervous system, the organ of sensation and animation. The direction of this main stem therefore also primarily determines the activity of the individual limbs during movement. To work it correctly, namely make it flexible, is one of the main tasks of a trainer. By nature the horse is able to bend this part considerably; the strong bends and curvatures that it is able to perform voluntarily, which are stronger than any ridden movement would require, are sufficient proof. It is the object of the art of riding to control this flexibility in such a way that the horse takes on a bend of a certain degree when certain aids are given and retains this bend uniformly and obediently. This then gives the rider the means to turn his horse easily and reliably and, doing so, to put more weight on its inside hind leg, enabling him to work it successfully.

If the lateral bending of the spinal column is developed sufficiently, if the riding of curved lines has accustomed each individual hind leg to carrying a greater load, if the extensor muscles of the neck are able to yield, and if the resistance of the poll has been overcome, it is time to put the weight on both hind legs. In this case the neck acts like a lever that transfers the load to the hindquarters; the more the neck is moved upward, the more it presses and puts weight on the hind legs. However, this work must be based on the principle that the greater load should never be forced onto the hind legs but that instead the horse must accept this load on its own.

The rider should not try to put the load on the hindquarters primarily with his hands. Through forward driving aids, he must cause the hind legs to step more underneath the weight and thus take on the load themselves. The hands must then either rest passively, preventing the horse from rushing forward, or they must act with so-called through-going half-halts to move the load even more decisively backward in order to bend the forward moving hind legs. The elevation of the forehand then comes automatically, the more the hindquarters are lowered and bent.

This rule is often disregarded, particularly by riders who, because their body is too stiff, have dead legs and therefore always tend to overcome this drawback by increased activity of their hands. Since under such riders, the insufficiently stimulated hind legs do not step far enough underneath the load to be truly bent, the activity of their hands is unsuccessful; they merely interfere with their horse's movement and thus deprive themselves of the only means for attaining the desired goal. Thrust cannot be regulated if none exists, and the horse cannot learn to

[73]

move correctly if it does not move.

If the rider wants to move the weight from the forehand to the rear, he must have a support onto which he can move the weight so that, after being lifted artificially, it will not fall back onto its former point of support, namely the forelegs. The proper supports, however, can only be the stronger hind legs which by nature are not subjected to as much weight. It is therefore quite a useless and unnatural undertaking if many riders attempt to force their horses' heads and necks into an elevated position before they are able to bring the hind legs under correspondingly with their legs. They will be forced to carry the lifted weight themselves, that is, continuously support it with their hands. They will not transfer the weight to the hindquarters but only unnaturally bend their horses' backs.[2]

Putting the weight on the hindquarters, in other words, collecting the horse, must therefore begin from the back in that, by doubled activity and attentiveness on the part of his legs, the rider stimulates the hind legs to lively and deliberate forward movement. He must always keep the hind legs positioned in such a way that they act against the center of gravity of the body mass. This body mass is now held back by the rider's hands, that is, the forward movement gradually generated by the thrust is limited in such a way that the hind legs must bend under the weight that they are no longer able to master.

The hands, even if they are limited to passive holding, must not hold back unilaterally but must enhance the uniformity of the movement by timely yielding and must support the correct sequence of the hind legs by skilled guidance in that, by appropriate lateral bending, they prevent the hind legs from escaping. If the horse is crooked, they move the forehand toward the line of the hindquarters.

The rider's seat must also facilitate movement and straightening of the horse in these exercises. Since, by elevating the forehand and lowering the hindquarters, the rider attempts to obtain a horizontal orientation of the horse's spine, he must consider the vertical position of his own upper body to be the normal position. However, he must deviate from this normal position in all directions as soon as circumstances require it. He will lean forward to make it easier for reluctant horses to move forward, to soften hard shocks and bumps, and to protect soft or sensitive backs. In a way, he asks the horse to protect its kidneys by gently raising its back. He will lean back in order to be able to drive deliberately forward in the direction of the forces and also to hold back by putting his own weight emphatically on a tight back and inflexible hind legs together with the weight of the held-back forehand. Finally, he will lean to the side, and thus increase the weight toward the right or left, to prevent a hind leg from dropping out. In these exercises, the rider's skill replaces a large amount of force, and the skillful rider will be better able to protect his horse, the more his skill allows him not to have to resort to force.

Nevertheless, skill and sensitivity alone will be sufficient only in rare cases, namely only with horses which by nature are already almost balanced and have much flexibility and elasticity in the hindquarters as well as a good temperament and the proper sensitivity to the rider's leg. As I mentioned several times before, the number of such excellent horses is very small. All others, which have to overcome natural obstacles, be they the result of the conformation and position of their neck, shoulders, back, or hindquarters, will need to be taught respect of the spurs to take on and maintain a body position that is connected with effort for them due to their oppositely directed natural tendencies and is twice as difficult under the weight of a rider. In the state of freedom they have practiced this body position only during short moments of excitement.

The work of collection, namely putting the load on both hind legs and bending them, gives the rider an opportunity to firmly establish the horse's obedience to the spurs. He must use the spurs not only to get the hind legs to act uniformly but also to strictly supervise their tracks and must not let them stray the least bit from the intended line. If the hind legs are under the rider's control, that is, if he is able to precisely determine the degree of their load and activity, the entire horse is under control since every movement originates in the hind legs and their controlled position also requires the correct effect of the moving forces on the body mass.

This obedience of the horse, which is brought about initially by its respect of the spurs, must be gradually converted into trust and attachment to its master for the relationship between the two to be correct. This is accomplished if the rider limits and refines his actions the more the horse, through measured and gradually increased exercises, gains in ability and willingness to obey his aids. If, in overcoming resistance, the rider is always diligent to practice moderation and fairness, that is, he will not resort to unnecessarily hard punishments for impetuousness nor will he make demands which exceed the horse's capabilities, he will not lose the horse's trust even if he must perhaps be strict here and there. The noble horse is an intelligent and brave creature which defends itself against intentional tyranny, often by sacrificing its health and strength, but it is a true friend and servant to a just master for whom he sacrifices both if circumstances require it.

Under a rider who has a heart for the animal, the correctly trained horse will work with joy and happiness, while a horse that carries its rider with fear and hesitation accuses him of being unfair and cruel. Riders who espouse the principle that one must intentionally challenge a horse's resistance in order to break it, should be careful that they do not experience the fate of the sorcerer's apprentice who eavesdropped on his master to learn the magic words about the evil spirits which he then was able to call into action but, filled with fear and terror, could not banish. Horses whose temperament and character make them tend to be obstinate will soon reveal such obstinacy upon the first jab of a spur and can then be made to obey only by thorough action from the spurs. However, to make gentle and willing horses forcibly resistant by purposeless mistreatment, is a cruelty which only brutal human beings are capable of. A rider should attempt to make all strenuous exercises easier for the horse by keeping the sessions short, rewarding each demonstration of willingness and obedience, and overcoming the horse's fear or its excitement, caused by strong spur aids, through friendly treatment and simple exercises at the end of each session.

As I mentioned once before, the elevation of the forehand must not be forced, rather, with correct work of the leg aids, the horse will offer it on its own. It will initially look to the forehand for a way out, or for relief, when it is being driven forward from the rear but held back in front and thus pushed together.

The rider must regulate the elevation and be strict in observing that the position of the head relative to the neck as well as the position of the cervical vertebrae relative to one another is always correct. The uniform, soft contact with the reins must be a measure for him. Since he is working toward getting the horse balanced, this degree of rein contact is the normal contact.

Necks that are incorrectly built by nature are very difficult for the trainer. They often require years of exercise before they are shaped correctly and this new position becomes second nature to the horse. The more the incorrect position makes the correct bend of neck and poll difficult or impossible, the greater are the obstacles encountered with respect to a uniform distribution of the weight to all four legs.

The correct angle between head and neck not only produces the correct effect of the bit on the bars and thus contact, it also makes it possible for the impulsion generated by the hind legs to travel through the back and neck to the mouth, making the horse light on the bit and yielding in its poll. Only then is the path free between hindquarters and forehand, and now the hands are enabled to transmit their effect through the entire spinal column and to the haunches. In this way, forehand and hindquarters are connected with one another, the horse's body becomes a closed unit, hands and legs are able to interact correctly; the horse becomes "through." If individual vertebrae are not in the correct connection, that is, their contact surfaces are not in proper alignment, they will interrupt the transmission of the aids, similarly to the way a crack or break in a hard, resonant body interferes with its vibrations.

Due to their structure and close connection with the torso, the dorsal and lumbar vertebrae are more fixed while the cervical vertebrae and their connection with the head permit a greater freedom of movement which often degenerates into bends and positions that are wrong for the purpose of riding. To prevent them is the main task of the hands, while the main task of the legs is to cause the hind legs to spring off lively and to keep them directed toward the center of gravity of the body mass.

Just as the hands must support the work of the legs by skillful guidance, the legs and seat must always come to the aid of the hands. If there is insufficient contact with the reins, the neck is not elevated or the poll is not bent, both legs must overcome this fault by increased activity. If the neck has escaped to one side due to a false bend, the leg on the same side must remove the horse from the excessively tensioned rein. If the horse hangs on the reins to take them out of the rider's hands and to bring about freedom for its head and neck by force, the rider's upper body must take on a strong and steady position to provide a secure support for his arms. This support for the arms enables the hands to resist this pressure by repeated, quiet holding until the horse yields, that is, returns to the prescribed position and with it to the correct contact.

During this work, which amounts to balancing the horse in an artificial body carriage to which it is not accustomed, the rider can obtain results quickly and reliably only if his own body is completely balanced. This balance will enable him to temporarily compensate for any lack of balance in the horse by skilled distribution of his own weight. His quick and energetic aids, made possible by the freedom of his own limbs, will also keep the individual limbs of the horse in the position required to attain its overall carriage.

Do not believe that the steadiness of a stiff posture of your body could give the horse the balance it lacks. On the contrary, it makes it impossible for the rider to realize such balance since it gives the horse an opportunity to use the rider as a false support, thus losing even more of its own carriage. If the horse's balance is well founded, if it has become second nature, the horse will offer the rider a secure and comfortable seat and will even make it easier for weak riders to maintain their balance.

As a conclusion of these general observations about the course of dressage training I want to add the serious admonition, not to hurry any of the exercises and to let them all follow one another in such a way that the preceding exercise always constitutes a secure basis for the next one. Violations of this rule will always exert payment later on, not only by a triple loss of time but very frequently by resistances which, for a long time if not forever, interfere with the relationship between horse and rider and often jeopardize the success of the entire enterprise.

ENDNOTES:

[1] Horses will tend to take up this oblique direction due to a natural tendency, which in the rider's language is called a "natural crookedness," particularly on the right hand. Details about the consideration and elimination of this fault can be found in the chapter on Bending the Poll. [See page 93.] (Hans von Heydebreck)

[2] This important principle cannot be emphasized strongly enough. The reader is therefore requested to remember it whenever this book mentions the "elevation of the forehand." (Paul Plinzner)

4. Bending the Horse

If the ridden horse has the advantage, among many others, over the unridden horse that it is able to move easily and with regularity in a small space in the gaits nature gave it, this is because of the *flexibility* of its entire body that dressage training has given it. The more this flexibility has been developed, without detriment to the thrust of the hind legs, the more perfect in every respect will be the training of the horse. All riders who consider it necessary at all to work the horse, therefore diligently try to remove any resistance in the throatlatch, neck, back, and hind legs, and they can often be seen bending and working these parts for hours. All such exercises, however, bring only limited success and often are even a disadvantage if they are performed without moving the horse. The horse is a harmonious whole in which the individual parts mutually support one another. The horse is unable to move without the cooperation of the entire driving mechanism of the skeleton moved by the muscles. As a consequence, it can be only of very little value to work individual parts of the horse, for example the poll, at the halt, because it is very questionable whether this would be beneficial at all for the proper working of the entire machine when moving.

Motion is the element of the horse and all motion starts in the hindquarters. If therefore the flexibility of the hindquarters must be the ultimate purpose of all dressage training, this in no way means that lateral bending of poll, neck, and spine are unnecessary. Rather, the flexibility of these parts must first be obtained so that it can then be used as a means for the main purpose, namely to work the hindquarters. In order to avoid the resistance of the hindquarters as much as possible during this bending of the poll and spinal column, the horse must be made to move forward. In the free, deliberate gaits it alternatingly has one, two, or three feet in the air - in the phase of suspension even all four - and therefore its capability of resisting is lower the fewer support points it has. Also, for its own safety, the horse is forced to take on the correct body position in order to remain in balance even without these supports. I repeat therefore once more my main principle to always work the horse forward and I cannot recommend warmly enough to adhere to this basic tenet. Riders who act against this principle do not make their horses flexible but weak; with incorrect bends they ruin their horses' way of going and the proper contact but teach them ways to be obstinate.

Bending not only makes the tendons and ligaments more resilient and thus the joints more mobile, it also affects primarily the participating muscles, the flexor and extensor muscles, which are loosened up, and their alternating effectiveness is practiced and equalized. Care must therefore be taken during the bending work to determine whether in this particular horse the extensor or the flexor muscles predominate by nature in the development of force. If the extensor muscles are stronger, their effect must be moderated by many and continuous exercises until they become yielding. If the flexor muscles are dominant, their activity must be determined precisely by the correct counteraction of the extensor muscles. The appropriate selection of gait and tempo gives the rider the reliable means for establishing the correct relationship between counteracting muscles. Free gaits require greater activity of the extensor muscles while quiet movements and shorter tempi reduce their activity.

The soft horse that has weak muscles by nature should therefore only be bent in free or at least very deliberate gaits so that the resulting tensioning of the extensor muscles prevents it from following its natural tendency to become crooked. Conversely, the naturally tight horse which consequently carries itself stiffly will be fully manageable in a free gait only after it has become possible to moderate pace and tempo by lateral bending work and eliminate the tension in the muscles that is the reason for the stiffness. In principle, the naturally tight and stiff horse should be worked in greater bends only at the walk[1] and at a collected trot until it has become so yielding that its extensor muscles can also be controlled in a free gait. Since, however, tight horses usually exhibit a tendency to hold back, they will first have to be made to want to move and stretch by working them in the free gaits for which the reins must leave them sufficient freedom, before they can be bent successfully also at the walk and collected trot. Only in this way will it be possible to ensure the required liveliness of the paces, particularly at the trot and to obtain the proper contact. The naturally flexible and thus agile horse, the born riding horse, has inherited in its genes the correctly weighed effectiveness of its muscles. It needs only practice to use this gift in a certain way in response to certain aids.

Although it is not possible to work individual parts of the horse individually since its entire body is forced to cooperate in any movement, it is possible to act primarily on certain parts of its body, and I will now discuss the working of these parts in the sequence prescribed by natural dressage training.

(a) Bending the Neck

For the riding horse the *neck* is one of the most important body parts and its structure must be carefully observed in the evaluation of any horse with respect to its suitability for riding purposes and in the selection of the means for training it. The horse's neck, which the warrior of the past also used as a shield against bullets and blows, in the rider's hand is not only the lever with which he is able to load the hindquarters at will and determine the action of the forelegs, but also the steering means with which he indicates the direction in which the horse's body is to move. In the selection of a riding horse, a naturally well constructed neck therefore compensates for many flaws in the remainder of the body. The shape of the neck depends on the position of the cerebral vertebrae and is the more suitable for riding purposes the more favorably the upper vertebrae are connected with the occipital bone of the head by way of a regular and soft arc, the more the middle vertebrae, by their almost vertical position, facilitate elevation and the lower vertebrae have a uniform bend that is followed by the dorsal vertebrae.

Although the skeleton of the neck would justify the use of the popular term *"swan's neck"* for the ideal horse's neck, the external shape in which such a neck is presented is very different from the neck of a swan. A horse's muscle formation can be considered to be favorable only if the muscles are very evident at the top and very little at the bottom so that, if the neck is pushed together and the nose brought closer to the body, the top line of the neck describes a quarter circle, while the bottom line is concave or at most straight but not convex. Another reason that a swan's neck is not desirable in a horse is that a neck that is too long, thin, and excessively bent would be too mobile and thus make the necessary secure and comfortable contact, particularly with the curb bit, more difficult[2].

If the neck is of a good shape and set on deep, if the cerebral vertebrae do not ascend from the withers but extend forward more or less in the direction of the spine, this makes elevation more difficult. But, with the gradually obtained lowering of the hindquarters, it is nevertheless possible to develop a neck that is similar to the normal neck. A neck of such a shape is therefore not a great impediment and should definitely be still included among the good ones.

If a deep set neck is straight and stiff, that is, the cerebral vertebrae near the head do not have the required natural flexibility, this will pose great difficulties for the trainer. With effort and patience he will be able to obtain the elevation of the neck he needs to balance the horse and to set it on the haunches. But he will always have to skillfully guide the horse to compensate for the unfavorable position of the head relative to the neck. If, because of a lack of natural bend in the poll, a horse must always be put on the bit artificially, it may perhaps be very agile under a skilled rider and if its hindquarters are good, but it will always have the tendency of escaping this carriage. For the skilled and diligent rider such a conformation of the neck is no obstacle in preparing his horse for military service and, insofar as the remainder of its conformation enables it, even for upper level dressage, while it forces the weak rider to leave such horses in their natural carriage.

The *upside-down or ewe (deer) neck*, next to weak or truly faulty hindquarters, is the greatest obstacle to putting the horse in balance. Incorrect bending of the cerebral vertebrae, in that the middle vertebrae, instead of standing at most perpendicular on one another, are inclined rearward, causes such a neck to give the head an unfavorable attachment with which it is usually impossible to obtain the head position required for reliable action on the bit. It also does not transmit this bit action correctly in that the transmission is interrupted by the incorrect elevation which the neck tends to always assume because of its incorrect bend.

For a deer[3] this neck conformation is favorable because, by leaning its head backward, the deer is able to transfer the weight of its antlers to the rear when leaping and running. On a horse, however, it prevents the rider from putting the weight on the hindquarters as he is then unable to hold back the body weight or to use the neck as a lever, because the elevation required to do this eliminates the head position required for correct contact. Since such a head and neck can be set only by a low carriage, the horse can receive only a degree of training that corresponds to a carriage on the forehand. Some ewe necks, because of their length and favorable curvature of the upper vertebrae, permit an on-the-bit position of the head, and this then ensures sufficient contact to make such horses usable for military service. Otherwise, the understanding trainer will not waste his time and effort on such unsuitable material since he is smart enough not to fight against nature. He will leave such horses in their natural carriage and use them where he can. He may be able to demand great performances from them on endurance rides and in special efforts of all types since they often also have good traits in common with the deer. But such horses are not comfortable because, due to their lack of position and reliable contact, they always demand from the rider that he follow them, while a comfortable horse is able to adapt itself to its rider. This is the reason that such horses are also not suitable for hunting, no matter how suitable they appear to be because of their demonstrated speed and endurance. Green, lean horses, in which the fat of the crest has disappeared, so that the upper edge of the neck appears to be hollow at the withers, often appear to have a ewe neck without this really being the case, while, conversely, meaty necks having thick layers of fat on their crests often appear to have a favorable conformation which in truth does not exist. The quality of the neck essentially depends on the carriage of the cerebral vertebrae and their connection with head and torso. The rider will discover this with certainty only when working the horse.

Unsteady and shaky necks appear in any shape since this characteristic has its origin either in a disproportionate length, fineness, and flexibility or in weak muscles. Such necks make the development of thrust and the establishment of a reliable contact very difficult and yet can be overcome only by both of them. It is therefore usually necessary to perform long exercises at deliberate gaits before the rider is able to act reliably on the hindquarters by collecting the horse. To attain a well founded steadiness, such necks must be completely reshaped in the course of these exercises by strengthening and developing their muscles.

Correct work gives the neck a certain shape which the correctly ridden horse may already exhibit when moving without a rider, even in its stall. It is based not only on elevation and a beautiful bend but primarily on the width and thickness of the neck at the shoulders from where it tapers steadily toward the poll. This shape is always the result of correct and thorough training and is produced in that the fleshy parts of the neck, which move the forehand, develop more intensively from this activity while this same activity makes all other useless fatty portions disappear. Just as any body stands more firmly, the broader its base, the neck will also gain in steadiness the more its width increases toward the bottom. Horses that have such a neck by nature have one of the most important prerequisites of the born riding horse.

As already mentioned, the cerebral vertebrae are the most movable parts of the spinal column since the horse in its natural state requires this mobility and always practices it. When working the neck, it is therefore more the task of the understanding trainer to control its natural mobility and to thus make it steady than to work only on making it yielding and soft. If the green horse initially appears to be very stiff and inflexible under the rider, this is more a consequence of resistance with which the horse acts against the unfamiliar load than a lack of flexibility. We know that it has the latter from observing it in the barn and when it is at liberty. The rider needs a flexible neck to obtain elevation and to get the horse on the bit as well as for lateral bends. Lateral bends are required to prepare the horse for elevation and contact and thus constitute the initial exercises for working the neck, while later on lateral bends are very restricted by the resulting elevation and correct bend in the throatlatch.

These exercises should always be begun with head and neck in a low position, since in this position the extensor muscles of the neck are relaxed and thus are more yielding. Also they should be explained to the young horse, initially in quiet gaits and while holding it back to the point of making it stand still, by teaching the horse to bend its head and neck to the side on which the reins act more strongly. The more the horse gains in willingness and ability to do this, the more the outer rein, together with the better developed thrust from the hindquarters, must gradually limit the bend and perfect it. Corresponding to the increasing elevation of the forehand as a result of the progressive lowering of the hindquarters, lateral bending must be reduced together with the gradually more elevated position of the neck. Even in the fully trained horse, the lateral bend of the neck must always be determined according to the degree of elevation realized and must be less the greater is the elevation until, with the neck fully elevated, the required lateral position of the horse is obtained merely be its bending in its throatlatch.

The lateral bending of its neck enables the horse to turn, to properly travel on curved lines, and to perform the movements on two tracks. Since this lateral bending of the neck is always connected with a correct, corresponding bend of the spine and of the hind legs, it simultaneously acts as a moderating effect on the thrust and prevents too heavy a contact.

The elevation of the neck places the cerebral vertebrae into an upward position and thus brings the weight of the neck closer to the horse's natural center of gravity. If it is perfected and well founded, it can be considered the quintessential proof of completed dressage training. The rider then has available a lever with which he can dependably and precisely determine the degree of the load on the hindquarters. It additionally ensures for him an always uniform contact in its various graduations and also determines precisely the action of the forelegs. The higher the attachment points of the muscles connecting neck and shoulder are positioned when the neck is elevated, the more these muscles will be able to influence the lifting of the forearms. The so-called freedom of the shoulders in the horse's movements is therefore also a function of the correct elevation of the neck and can be obtained only in that way.

The elevation of the neck, however, can be considered to be well founded only if it is always aided by the reliable and corresponding support of the hindquarters and if it is connected with an on-the-bit position of the head. Only then is the correct effect of the rein action ensured. The more the natural construction of the neck permits the on-the-bit position, the easier it is to work the entire horse because the rider is then able to proceed to the elevation to the same degree as he is able to put the load on the hindquarters. Incorrect necks require long and tedious work in a low position to become able to bend the upper vertebrae in such a way that they permit the head to come on the bit when elevated. If the elevation cannot be obtained because of a structure that is too unfavorable, the horse will never be able to find a pleasant, uniform contact with the curb bit but can be guided reliably only with snaffle-like bits.

As necessary as a flexible and agile neck is for the fully trained horse, it must be connected with perfect steadiness. This is so because for every bend and position of the neck, the joining surfaces of its vertebrae must remain sufficiently in contact to thus be able to transmit the driving as well as the restraining aids. If, however, the neck is bent too much at individual points so that the area of contact between the vertebrae in question becomes too small, a false bend appears at which the rein action from the hands as well as the driving aids are broken; to use the customary term, the aids are stuck in the incorrect bend. This produces the most dangerous type of "being behind the bit" in the horse since now the rider is no longer able to correctly hold the weight and work the hindquarters against it or drive them underneath it.

The Baucher method is a complete system for ruining horses in this way, and all other riders as well who work the head too much, and particularly in place, will sooner or later fall prey to the error of making the head wobbly instead of flexible. Necks tending to be unsteady by nature must be treated with particular care in this respect and can usually be worked only in free or very deliberate gaits.

Generally the most serious mistakes are made when working the neck. Its stiffness in the green horse initially appears unpleasant to the rider so that it is easy to explain the mistake of many who attempt to overcome this fault by unilateral bending and positioning without thinking that the neck can obtain its correct and well founded position only gradually, together with the step-wise schooling of the hindquarters. The lateral bending of the neck goes hand in hand with the progressive flexibility of the inside hind leg, the elevation of the neck, and the on-the-bit position with the bending of the entire hindquarters due to carrying the load. Therefore, whoever does not eliminate the constraint of the forehand in the hind legs and is unable to control the extensor muscles of the hind legs while maintaining the thrust fully in force, will never obtain a perfect carriage of the neck but will leave his horse the means to change from one exaggeration to another, that is, to become disobedient by taking too little or too much contact. We often see horses which, in the arena, when shown in the shortened gaits, appear to have an excellent position of head and neck but, when asked to move freely on long lines in free gaits, completely fall apart because the then awakened but not fully controlled thrust becomes a reinforcement for the resistance of all of the extensor muscles. The Baucher system which, with all its glaring errors and misuses in the noble equestrian art, can always serve as a warning example, here again furnishes the conclusive proof: every "baucherized" horse, when asked to move in free gaits, will either resist by going in circles or run away if it has been left sufficient natural strength.

With a correctly worked horse, head and neck are the main weight that enables the rider to control the distribution of weight at all. He will use it not only to transfer weight to the hindquarters and bend them but also to enhance the speed of the movement in that the forward extended position of head and neck moves more of the excess weight toward the front. In every position, however, the neck must remain a reliable guiding chain for the rider's hands, that is, it must transmit the action of the bit to the thoracic vertebrae through the correct connection between the individual vertebrae.

That the correct elevation of the neck has a bending effect on back and croup is also evident from the fact that the tail of the green horse will be raised accordingly. The experienced rider therefore does not need a surgeon's knife to give his horse the most beautiful and perfect tail carriage corresponding to its conformation. He produces it by riding and often makes his horses more beautiful to the point that they can hardly be recognized. The natural reason for this phenomenon is simply that the lifting tail muscles, which are an extension of the back muscles, are forced into greater activity when the back is bent and thus are gradually strengthened.

Another sign of the correctly obtained elevation of the neck is the formation of fine parallel skin folds that extend down from the crest and across the neck at certain intervals from one another. They are produced by the curvature of the neck which is gradually obtained by the greater bend in the individual cerebral vertebra joints.

It is not an easy task to make the seven cerebral vertebra joints flexible in all directions to meet the various equestrian requirements and to nevertheless keep them closed enough that they are unable to escape in any way from the direction they have been given. This requires great skill in the interaction of hand, leg, and seat aids, with their intensity being determined only by fine feeling on the part of the rider. But it turns into pomposity if very wise masters of the art attempt to work at bending individual vertebrae one after the other in special exercises. As mentioned before, it is not even possible to bend the entire neck alone without the cooperation of head, back, and hind legs; how could it be possible to usefully work such a little part all by itself? An art which is valuable only by its practical utility must not try to become popular by false erudition.

The correct contact with the reins is and remains the only reliable measure for the results of working the neck. If in lateral bending, both reins are tightened uniformly the horse has correctly responded to the shortening of the inside rein by bending, and the tightening of both reins will be transmitted to the hind legs. If, further, with uniform action of both reins, the contact corresponds to the carriage of the neck, that is, it becomes lighter in the elevated position but fuller in the lower and more stretched position, this proves that the neck not only was worked correctly, straight and steadily, but also its elevation is well founded by the secure support of the hindquarters.

The *steadiness* of the neck, that is, the secure connection of the individual cerebral vertebrae with one another and their correct position relative to one another can be ensured only by unweakened and well developed thrust. The flexibility of the neck, however, can be ensured only by the carrying capacity of the hindquarters. Forehand and hindquarters can therefore be worked only alternatingly against one another or simultaneously with one another in that the forehand constitutes the main weight against which and underneath which the hindquarters must express themselves by pushing and carrying their weight.

According to this principle, the understanding rider should determine on his own how great the errors are which are generally made in training a young horse. Instead of initially asking it to carry its head and neck, according to its natural structure, in a position which develops the thrust of its hind legs so that in that way the entire spinal column constitutes a connecting chain between head and hind legs and is made steady and straight and, by this carriage, to obtain the interaction between the rider's hands and legs, most riders attempt right from the start to immediately displace the weight of the forehand upward and backward. However, without preparation, the hind legs are unable to take up this load; their activity is inhibited by it. The natural way of going is lost, and the rider must carry head and neck by the strength of his arms. He must also fight the counter-efforts which the horse in this forced carriage of its forehand will of necessity produce. Tired, the less energetic rider will then resort to bending in place in order to make the obstinate poll and the stiff neck soft and transmissive. He will then more or less fall victim to the Baucher system and obtain corresponding results. Or, he will want to make his work easier by overchecks, lunge lines, and whip and will then make his young horse dull and spent before it has served under him. The strong and forceful rider, however, will break the apparent stubbornness of his horse by force and will want to compel the hind legs into activity with spurs and whip. But horses are unable, without preparation, to constantly bend and freely move under the unaccustomed load. Instead they will try to avoid the load by becoming stiff and escaping it. The natural harmony of the body will be interfered with, and the horse will be able to move only through unnatural efforts which quickly have a deleterious effect on the organism and destroy its strength. Such riders work by continuously fighting their horses and, consequently, their horses go lame and break down. As a result of their own efforts, these riders will always end up having to get rid of poor, worthless creatures.

The intelligent trainer, however, will strictly observe in his work the natural conformation and position of head and neck and will not attempt to move their weight backward until he is able to sufficiently pull the hindquarters forward to enable them to reliably carry the load. He will therefore use the natural movement of his horse as the primary means for obtaining a secure contact with the reins in that he positions the entire spinal column and the poll in such a way that the thrust of the hind legs acts directly and unweakened against his hands. If this is the case, his hands will act just as directly against the hindquarters since he is now able to hold the weight of the forehand to then gradually put it on the hindquarters. This transfer of the weight will give him a reliable means to unequivocally control the raw thrust.

Before the rider is able to reliably hold his horse, the horse will attempt to avoid such action by escaping with its head and neck since these are by nature the most mobile. It will often put them into unusual positions in that, depending on the structure of its head and neck, it will either resist by pushing downward or by forcibly stretching its neck and raising its head. The rider is then often forced to laboriously obtain the normal position by constant exercises in the opposite direction. He can make this easier by using special tack aids, but these will be of use to him only if they are used with skill. All inanimate devices and auxiliary reins, even those which, when tied or snapped on, produce a uniform effect, are without exception more damaging than useful since they all ruin the horse's mouth. The action of the bit can be weighed correctly only by a living and sensitive rider hand. The old masters used such auxiliary reins together with a cavesson, and we can draw the same advantages from this extraordinary resource if we know how to use it on our noble horses of today.[4]

Generally, the trainer has more difficulties in getting the neck to go down than to elevate it because, with unfavorable neck conformation, he can get the poll to yield only with the neck lowered. This requires the head to be in the on-the-bit position which must be complete and secure if the horse is to be prepared correctly for the lever effect of the curb bit. Faults in this respect will always come to light as soon as the horse is to be guided by the curb reins alone. The reliability with which this is possible can be considered as a test for the work with the poll and as a measure of the degree of equestrian schooling to which the horse is capable. The more perfectly the poll is bent by nature or from correct work, the easier and more perfectly will the hindquarters be developed because the trainer is then able to hold the weight with more reliance and let the hindquarters work against it at will, using this work to strengthen them and make them flexible.[5] The fixing of the head from the correct bend in the poll is, so to speak, the foundation stone for all of the work with the neck and is the primary goal endeavored by the rider for all necks of unfavorable structure. The elevation of the neck will develop gradually to the same degree as the hindquarters which, by taking over the weight, continue to remove the load from the forehand, according to the earlier stated principle that the hind legs must themselves take over the weight in that they are pushed forward toward the center of gravity of the mass. The possibility of elevating the neck therefore initially depends on the bending of the poll, that is, on the rider being able to reliably maintain the correct, steady position of the head, and then also on the capability of the hindquarters to take over the load. The more the forehand is relieved by the hindquarters and the more the thrust of the latter is simultaneously reduced thereby, the easier it will be for the rider to keep head and neck in the correct elevation from which then in turn results the freer and more elevated action of the forelegs.

Going behind the bit, namely the horse escaping by putting its head behind the vertical, occurs primarily with very long, excessively curved, or wobbly necks. If this structure of the forehand is connected with strong, well conformed hindquarters, it is possible to thoroughly eradicate this fault, albeit not easily but gradually, in that the forehand is elevated by bending the haunches and the correctly developed thrust always takes care of the correct contact with the reins. Such horses are therefore able to be trained to the highest levels of dressage. However, during their training they require very light, fine hands and prompt leg aids from the rider and, during their later use, a suitably light bit in order to keep them from regressing to their old, natural fault. If, however, the hindquarters are unable to develop strongly bent haunches with sufficient thrust, then such a horse should not be unnecessarily tortured with shortened, highly collected gaits, but should be brought to the aids by developing thrust only in free, deliberate gaits. In this way, they have at least a certain utility.

The old masters were very much aware of this fault in their horses and were often forced to give up their work entirely. This is explained very simply by the fact that they rode almost exclusively stallions that had heavy, greatly bent necks and were able to continuously support the weight of the forehand only if their hindquarters were very strong. Moreover, in order to meet the requirements of the time and enable their

[90]

horses to move around in a small space, they practiced almost only shortened and collected gaits. And finally, they were forced to tack up these heavy horses in powerful curb bits which, with their strong lever action, allowed them to control the horses with ease. Thus, horses with overbent necks had it easy to completely cancel out the action of the reins by supporting their heads against their chests when the reins were pulled.

We do not suffer as much from this fault and will, as long as the primary breeding goal is speed, have to fight more against stiff and stretched necks than the reverse. Also, with our lighter bits and our fleeting gaits, we now have excellent means available to make this fault harmless. Even horses with weak backs and rear ends, which are able to withstand only a slight elevation, may nevertheless serve as comfortable travelling or field mounts since they not only are better able to see where they are going but are also able to find a secure contact with the curb bit in the extended gaits that such use brings about. Under any circumstances, it is easier and more effective to elevate and straighten a low neck that is behind the bit than to lower and bend an upside-down neck that is carried too high.[6]

This is the reason for present-day attempts at finding ways and means to eliminate, if not completely, at least reduce, such difficulties created by this type of neck. For this purpose, a multitude of devices and instruments have been invented - pulleys of such effect that one could lift the entire horse with them - and yet the equestrian art has not been advanced by them. They are passing phenomena which will be forgotten as quickly as they perhaps initially created a stir. The understanding trainer only smiles about them since he knows that the only way to achieve success is through patient, systematic work.

Mr. Baucher believed to have found the philosopher's stone particularly in this respect, and a large part of the equestrian world believed with him, since he was able to soften a neck in a very short time so that even horses with stiff and upside-down necks appeared to become through and could easily be put into the correct position when standing still. However, if we look a little closer at this miracle, we find that he simply is a master at getting horses behind the bit - that is to say, to escape the rein aids - in that he robs them of their thrust. Such a trained-in or forcibly obtained behind-the-bit carriage is very different from an innate behind-the-bit carriage of the neck due to faulty conformation. For the latter, the trainer is aided in counteracting such a conformation fault by the unweakened forces of the hindquarters and an unspoiled character, while with the former he would initially have to attempt to regain the natural state through suitable exercises, that is, to attempt to revive the suppressed or robbed thrust. This will be the more difficult the more the Baucher system has already exerted its influence. Like Cato, who closed each one of his speeches with the admonition that Carthage must be destroyed, I want to close each chapter by warning against the Baucher system.

ENDNOTES:

[1] To do this, however, dressage training must have progressed to the point that the walk can be used for working. (Hans von Heydebreck)

[2] If such light, excessively bent, thin necks are initially loosened up by forward riding and, in the further course of training, the rider always remembers to work from the back toward the front and, again and again, with sensitive hands and relatively long reins, permits the neck to stretch, such difficulties can gradually be overcome after all. (Hans von Heydebreck)

[3] Translator's note: the German word for ewe neck, "Hirschhals," literally translates as "deer neck;" hence the reference to the deer.

[4] As the reader knows, the old masters did not use the snaffle to work the green horses for the first time but a cavesson. The latter not only has the advantage that it leaves the mouth completely untouched but also the even greater advantage that it allows the unequivocal yielding of the poll to be established in a much more reliable way than with a snaffle. Since the major neck muscles extend beyond the poll and are attached at the upper jaw, a horse tacked up in a snaffle, while yielding to the pressure on the bars with its lower jaw, will nevertheless stiffen its neck muscles and remain completely unyielding in the poll. Although we attempt to overcome this problem by using the so-called dropped noseband, we can never do it in such an effective way as with a cavesson in which the holding hand acts directly on the upper jaw. My instructor, Louis Seeger, always attributed the unequalled successes of the old masters with respect to bending of the haunches to their work with the cavesson and has spent much time modifying or replacing the cavesson with a view toward our more noble and more sensitive horses of today. He was the first to use the bridle piece now known as the "dropped noseband" for which I want to officially give him recognition here. In the later course of dressage training, when the horse is already ridden in a curb bit, the old masters, particularly the Duke of Newcastle, used the cavesson for the attachment of auxiliary reins. For the strong bends they worked with, they fastened a rope to the inside of the cavesson toward the saddle so that the horse found an insurmountable resistance if it tried to free itself from the bend into which it was forced by the reins. Of course this work could be successful only with the cooperation of corresponding driving aids that took care at any time that the horse not only continued to move forward but also continued to push away from this fixed rope and became soft. (Paul Plinzner)

[5] The bending of the poll, namely its throughness, can be obtained only by the impulsion generated in the hindquarters and flowing through the entire body of the horse. Both, yielding of the poll and making the hindquarters flexible go hand in hand; correctly working hindquarters create the throughness of the poll, and this in turn permits and enhances the further development of the hindquarters. (Hans von Heydebreck)

[6] I can only conditionally agree with this view because all of the work on the neck always goes hand in hand with working the hindquarters. It will therefore primarily depend on the conformation of the hindquarters whether it will be possible to give the neck the position that ensures correct contact and thus a proper effect on the rein aids. However, necks that are too low and behind the bit always interfere with the establishment of balance and self-carriage, the most important requirements to be met by a riding horse. (Hans von Heydebreck)

(b) Bending the Poll

If I discussed the working of the neck before this chapter, although the forehand begins with the head, this was done because the neck must first have gained a certain steadiness before the rider is able to successfully act on the *poll*.[1] This joint connects the head with the first cerebral vertebra and its construction permits free movement in all directions as we can observe it on a horse in freedom. If these parts often appear very stiff and inflexible on a green horse under saddle, this is caused by the unaccustomed carriage that the rider requires for his purposes and in which the natural mobility of the joint can be developed only through gradual exercises.

The conformation of head and neck may greatly facilitate this work or may pose great impediments. Since in the preceding chapter I discussed how the natural position of the neck has a significant influence on the carriage of the head, in that an elevated, well curved neck naturally puts the head on the bit, while a straight, short, or upside-down neck makes it increasingly difficult or impossible to put the head in the on-the-bit position, I will now call your attention to the difficulties which the structure of the head itself may pose to dressage training.

Although a small, fine, and well chiseled head is not only much more beautiful, it is also far more advantageous because of its lower weight than a large, fleshy head. Nevertheless, even more important than the weight of the head is the manner of its connection with the neck and the structure of its throatlatch, namely the bones of the lower jaw. Even if the natural conformation of the neck is somewhat unfavorable and, in particular, the first vertebrae do not have the desired curvature, unless the rear edges of the lower jaw bones are too thick and fleshy and take up much room by being spread far apart, the correct position is easier for the horse, the smaller the angle formed by head and neck in their natural carriage. If, however, these advantages are more or less absent, it will become increasingly more difficult to put the poll in such a position that the rein aids are propagated easily and without attenuation through the entire spinal column and to the hindquarters. The poll is the first joint through which the rein action must pass later on and as long as this joint is not completely relaxed, the rider's action is limited to the horse's mouth alone.

The lateral flexion of the head may be made more difficult by a short, thick neck and by a thick, fleshy throatlatch, but such impediments can always be overcome by diligent and patient exercises to the extent that they will not adversely affect the influence on the hindquarters, that is, collection. Yet, they will always have a disadvantageous influence on the agility of the horse during turns.

The fleshy and soft portions of head and neck are in any case an obstacle for their artificial positions and bends, but an obstacle that can be overcome relatively easily if the position and connection of the skeletal basis is favorable. In young stallions we often find neck and poll covered with so much flesh and fat that it makes them appear to be quite misshapen and deformed. They will only gradually become pleasant in appearance and agile by means of sweat treatments.

The soft portions that sometimes make lateral flexion more difficult also include the parotid glands. They are the source of the secretion of saliva and extend in an elongate shape from the ear to the posterior edge of the upper jaws; the saliva channel opens into the interior of the oral cavity. This tender and sensitive part can easily be bruised and compressed by the lower jaw during lateral bending and the resulting pain often stimulates young horses into obstinate resistance and disobedience. It is therefore the duty of the understanding trainer, to perform the bending work carefully. Excessive demands will only lose him time since the resulting infections of these glands not only prevent the horse from eating but also result in a dead mouth.[2]

In the thoroughly worked horse, this gland seems to have completely disappeared and some people believe that it has been absorbed as a result of all the work. They attempt to further this absorption by special treatments and try to get the gland to disappear by stroking, kneading, and massaging it with their hands. Fortunately this is a great fallacy because the disappearance of the gland would also cause the secretion of saliva to cease so that horse and rider would be seriously disadvantaged: the horse with respect to its digestion, the rider with respect to contact.

At the beginning of training the gland is pushed outward to escape the pressure and is then clearly visible. However, when during the course of work the fat later disappears and the muscles become more ductile to provide more space for the gland, it will usually be retracted into the interior where during bending it can be accommodated underneath the edge of the jaw. Only then is the *work on the throatlatch* completed because only then does the activity of the parotid glands experience no interference and the influx of saliva will not be impeded during bending. This then is also the end of the horse's moodiness with which the rider might have to struggle under certain circumstances if one day it has a wonderful mouth and consequently takes on all positions willingly and obediently, while the next day it refuses to chew on the bit and resists the actions of the hands. Only then will the horse achieve not only perfect freedom but also regularity in all its movements, no matter how much the rider changes its direction and bend in many different ways. This is then the result of perfect work: the rein hand finds no resistance to its action, neither hardness nor false yielding. Instead, even the slightest pull on the reins is quickly and reliably transmitted all the way to the joints of the hindquarters. That such a result can be attained only by simultaneous working of the hindquarters is understood because, as mentioned repeatedly, the horse's skeleton can be adjusted in its entirety as a harmonious whole only if the thrust from the hindquarters gives the forehand the necessary steadiness while the weight of the forehand, transferred to the hindquarters, causes the latter to bend.

Nevertheless it is necessary to work the neck and poll diligently and in a special way in order to give these parts the flexibility and steadiness which the rider requires for his purposes, and these special exercises are called "breaking off."

The exercise involves bending the head, alternatingly to the right, to the left, and toward the neck when halted, with the neck and the remaining body of the horse always being straight and steady so that only the joint between head and neck takes on the required bend. As useful as this exercise is, if performed correctly, to make the poll perfectly soft and free, as damaging are the consequences of an incorrect execution. In the mobility of its seven cerebral vertebrae and its lower jaw, the horse has eight means available to avoid the correct flexion of its poll and, when standing still, where it also has the secure support of its four legs, it is quite skillful in using them.

A very fine feeling on the part of the rider is needed to judge whether his horse maintains the uniform distribution of its weight to its four legs during these exercises, that is, whether it remains straight, whether it might not lean unnoticeably on the outside legs, whether its neck inadvertently follows the bend, or whether it follows the bending rein only with its lower jaw instead of with the poll. If he feels this, the rider is able to prevent such avoidances only if the his horse's obedience to the spur is confirmed. That is why this exercise, in its purest sense, can be considered only as the *concluding exercise* of dressage training for higher levels since it enables the horse, whose neck is elevated as the result of the bending of its haunches, to maintain its head position easily and freely.

The old masters used much diligence and time for this exercise and the way they worked it appears ridiculous and barbarous today. However, if we consider the obstacles they had to overcome in training their heavy dressage stallions and the results they nevertheless knew to attain, we must confess that they were superior to us and will remain so until we no longer step into their footsteps. Then we will be able to excel over them because we will have available more perfect horse material. Just imagine a heavy Belgian or Danish coldblood stallion, as they are seen today as strong load carriers, being trained for higher level dressage. You will then no longer be surprised if the old masters needed four men to put the fat neck and the bull's poll of such an animal into position and to flex it. Their main tool for this purpose was the cavesson which, because it acts only on the nose bone, makes escape and displacement of the lower jaw impossible during breaking off and bending, thus giving these horse entirely proper positions.

Breaking off and bending of the poll always presupposes a high, steady position of the neck and a correct, uniform distribution of the body weight at the halt. It can therefore be practiced successfully only if the rider is able to reliably control the hindquarters with his spurs. This must not be confused with bending of neck, head, and spine in place which can be performed in all stages of dressage training.

In the beginning, these bends fill the recovery pauses which the young horse is given after each work section. They begin with simple, natural bending of the neck in that the horse is taught in this way to yield to the stronger action of one rein. A low position of head and neck facilitates these first exercises since it relaxes the neck muscles. The stiffer, thicker, and clumsier these parts are by nature, the greater this initial bend should be, and the horse should be left in this position for a while so that the muscles and ligaments can get accustomed to the greater expansion. Just like a human being, who has a stiff or painful neck, will not turn his head but his entire body to see to the side or rear, the clumsy, green horse will also always tend in these exercises to make things easier for itself by escaping with its hindquarters toward the opposite side. As long as the rider is unable to prevent this with his outside leg, he should use the wall as a substitute and always position his horse against the wall in such a way that its outside shoulder is half a step away from the wall and the outside hind leg takes the wall as its support. In this seemingly crooked position, the horse is effectively forced to keep itself straight since its forehand no longer finds support at the wall. Nevertheless, in the beginning it will not be possible to prevent the horse from putting its body weight more onto the outside legs and thus to lean toward the outside. The rider must therefore correct this fault by distributing his own weight toward the inside and by holding the inside hind leg against the outside hind leg by means of the whip or his inside leg. The success of this bending in place is primarily dependent on the correct body position, that is, on the same weight resting on the inside and outside legs, regardless of whether the forehand or the hindquarters carry more weight. Bending exercises of this type, in which rider and horse often lean toward the outside until they fall over, are not only useless but teach the horse the means to escape the bending of the inside hind leg and sew the seed for backing up, rearing, and disobediences of all kinds.

The straight position of the horse is therefore the primary prerequisite right from the start for all bending in place, while the adjustment of the balance or the carriage on the haunches can be furthered in this way only to the extent that the rider is able to hold the hindquarters with his legs, supported by the urging of the spurs. Once he is able to push the hind legs underneath the weight and to hold them there, he will be able to gradually request a higher elevation of the neck and thus perfect the bend until ultimately he will have a pure bend of poll and throatlatch.

However, as already mentioned elsewhere, it is much more difficult to obtain the correct body position in place since the horse, resting on all four legs, has it much easier to relieve one of the legs in an incorrect way than, for example, at the trot, where it must balance itself on alternating two legs and is thus forced to keep its body more in balance in any case. It is therefore wrong to state that dressage training is facilitated for horse and rider and flexibility in movement is furthered by much bending and working in place.

The gradually obtained flexion when moving is instead the preparation for exercises in place in that the correct bending in place is always an advanced task for the horse and can be used as a test for its obedience to the hands and legs. The rider should therefore bend his horse in place with his hands and legs and weight distribution according to the same rules he uses when moving, only with twice the attention and energy since he does not have the support of thrust and balance which he has in motion.

Riders who stand up their horse in a stretched-out position and then move its head and neck to the right and left, up and down, only with their arms, without caring how the remainder of the body turns and bends, who lean outward in order to gain more force when they pull on the reins and are satisfied if the horse ultimately takes on the positions on its own, will soon have to fight with wobbly necks, insufficient contact, and lifeless paces.

Mr. Baucher's system, the best scarecrow among all the errors and faults in our art, again provides the most convincing proof in this respect. He works his horses in place to get them as soft as a washrag and thus takes away all their desire to move forward. I warn my readers seriously against making long and tiring exercises of bending in place. The horse, perhaps enabled by its natural conformation, might soon escape from his control by bending incorrectly before the rider has a clue.

Such a *false bend* in the neck develops as soon as two of its cerebral vertebrae are no longer aligned correctly with one another but, by bending the joint too much, remain in contact with one another over too small a portion of their joining surfaces, thus producing a gap in the connecting chain between head and hindquarters. The interaction of hands and legs transmitted through the spinal column is interrupted in that not only the thrust from the hindquarters but also the rein actions from the hands get stuck in such a false bend and the horse now has found a means to avoid the rider's control. Such a fault extends through all gaits and exercises and may at times make an otherwise excellent horse uncomfortable and unreliable. Once such a fault has taken root, it can often be eliminated only with the greatest difficulty since it is much easier to bend an inflexible part than to make a part that is too soft steady and taught. The fault always develops because the antagonist muscles of the bent side do not counteract strongly enough. That is the reason why I mentioned right at the start that the straight carriage of the horse, that is, its weight resting uniformly on all four legs, is the main prerequisite for these exercises since this straight position of its body is still the best foundation for the correct counteraction of the antagonist muscles.

If such a single fault of this type is able to adversely affect the way of going and obedience of the horse, how destructive must the Baucher system be for both as it teaches only the art of bending the spinal column at every possible location.

The still inexperienced rider should therefore follow my advice and work his horse while moving forward. He can then be much more confident of achieving success since the movement itself is his best ally against all evasions and hidden tendencies of the horse. Moving initially requires the horse to keep its body straight for its own safety and thus to put the load more uniformly on the outside and inside legs; its thrust also produces a certain tension in its muscles and skeleton so that it is not so easy for the bent portions to yield too much by bending the wrong way. Finally, movement serves the rider as the only reliable measure to determine whether his work is correct in that it either gives him confirmation by its liveliness and its regular rhythm, or, if these characteristics are absent, it advises him not to continue with the work. Riders who bend and work their horses during deliberate forward riding will be unable to protect their own limbs and will shed many a drop of sweat to overcome the resistant forces of the horse, but they will soon experience the joy of seeing the way of going and carriage of their charges change to such advantage that the riders will seem to be in the possession of some special secrets that produce these miracles. Such special secrets are: a skillfully and timely used spur and sensitive hands which close temporarily and are supported in the rider's small of the back to repeatedly hold tight until the horse's resistance has been overcome and the desired position has been attained.

The hands thus constitute the barrier against which the legs and spurs cause the horse to push off. For riders who work playfully with long reins, stop their horse after every dozen strides, and let it back up if it tries to escape for a second from the demanded position, who let their legs rest so that the horse moves nice and quiet and comfortably, this rule is probably strange and hard to understand. They would consider full thrust and the greater contact with the reins resulting from it to be a sign of the horse running away and would believe themselves to be in danger. Yet, there is no other way of making wobbly necks steady and straightening bent and twisted necks.

In connection with this work, I again warn against any exaggeration because too firm a contact not only produces such pressure on the soft tissue that the free flow of blood to and from the head is restricted, but it also interferes with breathing in that a throatlatch that is too tight may adversely affect that natural activity of the large blood vessels of the neck, the larynx, and the trachea. Ignorant and tactless trainers should therefore not be surprised if their horses turn out to be uncoordinated, dizzy, or roarers. The first two faults are produced by an accumulation of blood in the head, causing the blood vessels to expand and exert pressure onto the brain to the extent that the horse is temporarily dazed. In noble horses this will gradually turn to vertigo, in more common ones to staggers.

Roaring, however, is produced and develops into a permanent vice if the mucous membrane of the larynx is inflamed by pressure and bruising and this inflammation results in oozing, often constricting the air passages to such an extent that breathing becomes noisy already without exertion. This noise becomes a whistle and roar as soon as the poor animal is urged in some way to breathe faster. During his bending work, the rider should observe with particular care all catarrhal states, such as strangles, quinsy, and other diseases of the breathing apparatus as they frequently occur, particularly in young horses, from catching cold. Better yet, he should discontinue any bending work so that the inflammation of these parts will not become worse due to irritation.

Since the introduction of English racehorses as breeding stock, this fault has become very widespread here. When put on the bit, these horses, with their long, stiff necks and narrow throatlatches, often are constricted so much that they begin to roar and are then used in their natural carriage in order not to make the roaring permanent. Because of the narrowness of its throat, the English horse has a great tendency to become a roarer so that an unproportionate number of horses imported from England, once they have gotten over the continental strangles which they usually get during their acclimatization period, become subject to this fault and almost the same number become roarers still during their training. The Arabian horse with its short, broad head, usually has a wide throatlatch and a round poll and rarely, if ever, tends to become a roarer.

The experienced and skilled trainer will avoid the drawbacks of such compressions, which he sometimes cannot quite prevent in spite of all his experience, and will prevent their dangerous consequences in that he rewards the slightest yielding of the horse by his own yielding, by changing hands or by a pause and will thus gradually overcome any natural resistance with the greatest of patience. He will also protect very sensitive parts as long as possible by the correct selection of his exercises until this

[101]

state has been overcome and the young horse is again working willingly. Blood circulation is inhibited only partially in all lateral bends since the outer side remains free. However, the unilateral pressure exerted on the larynx by lateral bends often has a rather annoying effect and must therefore be used as gently as possible to avoid any disadvantageous results.

The simultaneous pressure of both sides of the throatlatch during bending of the poll and neck to put the horse on the bit is the type of work for which I recommend that the young rider observe particular caution. Doing this, he will often suppress the influx of saliva and will have to confront a dry, dead mouth. In this period of its training, we often observe the horse moving for several minutes fighting for its breath, with a dry, insensitive mouth, staring ahead seemingly half unconscious. It pushes with its full thrust against the restraining reins so that the rider often needs to use all of his strength and energy to keep the horse on the correct line and not to yield to the forward urging weight. As soon as, however, the rider has caused the horse to yield by the tickle of his spurs and his endurance, all of these ugly phenomena disappear; the unseeing eyes start moving and become friendly again, the mouth becomes moist and lively, and breathing becomes freer as evidenced by lively snorting. This should be welcome music for the trainer during the entire training period since it is always a sign of yielding and comfort in the horse. Yielding also signals the recovered relaxation of the horse in that it bends the parts to be bent.

In his fight against the superior physical force of the horse, the rider should always take refuge in suitable auxiliary resources, such as a martingale, side reins, and preliminary work on the lunge in a cavesson. Never should he believe that he could save his arms and legs by replacing them with a dumb-jockey, an overcheck, or other inanimate objects. As long as he guides these tools in his own hands, he is able to precisely measure and calculate their effect and will be able to reliably avoid the above-indicated dangers of this work. This ability ceases as soon as his own feeling no longer supports him. And even if he does not make all horses uncoordinated, dizzy, or roarers, he will always rob them of their natural freshness and elasticity the more he uses these false auxiliary resources. Machines are extremely useful for working inanimate materials and save us an infinite amount of manpower today, but without exception they can act on living, organic beings only by ruining them.[3]

Horses that tend by nature to have a dry, dead mouth, can be cured of this fault only by working their poll and by teaching them to be absolutely obedient to the spurs. Some riders try to overcome it with external stimulants such as sugar or salt, or they use things on the bit for the tongue to play with, sharp bits, and similar things. But such means will always have only a temporary effect since they are unable to eliminate the actual cause of the problem which is either to be found in some constrictive pressure that makes the flow of saliva from the parotid glands more difficult or suppresses it, causing the nerves of the mouth to become insensitive, or it is caused by general laziness and insensitivity. If a constrictive pressure is the cause, its removal, in which the spurs play a major role, will also eliminate the fault. A lazy and insensitive horse can be awakened from its dreams only by spurs and whip. More lively activity of the entire body will then also increase the sensitivity of the nerves. Young horses which are fed relatively generously with little physical exercise, that is, are more fattened than suitably nourished, usually develop a sleepy, phlegmatic temperament, although by nature they might have a completely different type of mind. Such deadening of the temperament disappears together with the fat and lazy flesh through sweat and work, and the true spirit of the animal will be revealed. If, however, the spurs are not able to permanently overcome natural weakness and laziness, the horse is no riding horse; it belongs in front of a wagon where the driver always has his whip available.[4] The spurs are thus the proper means for making a dead, insensitive mouth lively and sensitive enough that the slightest action of the bit is sufficient to control the entire horse.

It is a generally known fact that green horses have more difficulties on one side than on the other and that most horses initially have these difficulties on the right hand.

To discover the actual reason for this phenomenon is more the task of a researcher in natural sciences than of the practical horse trainer. For the latter it is sufficient to know that most horses are naturally crooked to a certain extent in that they tend to assume a false bend to the right. This false bend is produced in that their right hind leg does not step straight underneath the load but to the right of it so that the left shoulder tends to fall away toward the left with the result that the horse leans on the left rein and refuses to accept the right rein. This often causes the rider to perform a hollow bend toward the left right from the start, which only worsens the problem.[5]

I want to mention this phenomenon also to warn against the mistake which it often brings about and which resides in the predominant working of one side while neglecting the other. It may be indicated to bend the stiff side more frequently by practicing the appropriate exercises a greater number of times, and the old masters generally observed this rule by beginning all exercises on the right hand, to then change to the left hand and ending after another change back to the right hand so that the bends to the right were always practiced twice as much.[6] Yet, it would be entirely wrong to work only one part for weeks and thus put the counteracting forces into an improper ratio. This will not only move the difficulty to the other side but will also convert the original side to the opposite, namely false flexibility.

As already mentioned, difficulties in the poll and neck are not seated in these parts but find their main support in the hind legs. The latter must thus simultaneously be made flexible as well, to serve as the inner hind leg, depending on the bend. If this is done too forcefully or without any change, so that the leg in question becomes the outside leg and is again urged to push forcefully, the reliable contact with the rein and with it the horse's obedience will be lost. This also explains the seemingly sudden change from stiffness to crookedness. If a horse is always worked only to the right because of its crookedness, with its left hind leg being asked less to carry than to push, it will be unable, because of the extended activity of its extensor muscles, to easily take on the required bend if this leg suddenly becomes the inside hind leg. All exercises to establish correct, uniform contact should therefore always be done with regular changes of hand in which case the more difficult side can be considered by doing the exercises twice as long or longer on that side; any counter-exercises always have a supplementing effect.

As already mentioned in passing, when work is done on the horse's forehand, and particularly its poll, the horse may develop great difficulties by escaping with its tongue and lower jaw. Only if these parts of the horse's mouth are in a quiet position, can the bit lie securely and uniformly on both bars and exert its unweakened effect. By taking back or shifting the lower jaw to the right or left, the horse appears to yield to the pull of the bending rein, but the action gets stuck in the stiffer parts and is thus canceled out. The old masters in their practical thoroughness prevented this fault by using a cavesson to keep the sensitive mouth of the young horse completely untouched and exerted their first influences on the nose bone. This firm, bony member is able to escape the pressure of the cavesson only by bending the poll and the neck vertebrae. Thus with the aid of this piece of equipment it was possible to prepare the horses thoroughly for the pure, unadulterated effect of the curb bit.

Our time with its prejudice against the cavesson tries to replace it by nosebands and mouth straps, which is, however, only partially successful because the influence on the horse's mouth is not avoided. Truly deep-rooted bad habits in the mouth, which prevent or interfere with proper contact, are almost exclusively the fault of the rider himself. Every young and very stiff horse, before it has obtained the means for freedom through the correct bend, will try to somehow escape the pressure of the bit. However, it is unable to do this continuously as long as the rider keeps the thrust of the hind legs active by moving briskly forward and here and there relinquishes the pressure by yielding at the proper time.

Hard hands as a result of a hard, stiff seat, very easily produce such faults, but more so, as mentioned earlier, work with inanimate tools. The surest way to eliminate these faults is a diligent leg and, if necessary, strong use of whip and spurs, connected with light, fine hands. The selection of bit is here not arbitrary but it plays only a minor role. The most obstinate manifestation of the bad habit of sticking out the tongue occurs when the horse puts its tongue over the bit. The curb bit can be constructed with a special mouthpiece to make sticking out the tongue more difficult and to gradually overcome this bad habit. Work in a snaffle often requires much time and effort to thoroughly cure the horse of this vice - yet, this is the only way that promises lasting success. It can be accomplished only in that whip and spur drive the horse against the hands, which maintain the connection with the mouth, until the tongue is in the correct position underneath the bit which the horse itself considers to be easier and more pleasant.

I believe I have now touched on everything that is important in bending work and will conclude the chapter by briefly summarizing its basic rules. First I remind you not to use the outside leg and the inside rein for bending, as this is done so often, but vice versa, primarily the inside leg and the outside rein.[7] These aids must produce the correct carriage of the entire body, that is, the uniform distribution of the weight to all four legs, in that the rider's inside leg keeps the weight on the inside hind leg by driving against the outside hind leg. The outside rein, with its inward action, always positions the shoulders so much toward the bent side that they precede the hindquarters in the correct alignment, thus keeping the weight on the inside foreleg. If the croup drops outward, this reduces or more or less cancels out the intended flexion, but leaves no lasting, disadvantageous influence, since it does not give the horse the means of escaping by bending incorrectly. This does happen, however, if the horse is made crooked by too much action with the outside leg and the inside rein, if the hindquarters are positioned relative to the forehand in such a way that both hind legs no longer act uniformly in the direction toward the shoulders. This rule regarding the alignment of forelegs and hindquarters and the other rule that the hind legs must, under all circumstances, expend their unweakened force *forward*, is actually the basis of all riding.

If this chapter has become rather long, the unexperienced reader should nevertheless not consider it boring. In a well ridden horse, the proper position of head and neck is always proof of the trainer having mastered his art. His skill and his talent in the art are to be considered greater, the greater were the obstacles which nature posed against such a perfect carriage as it can evolve only from correctly working the hindquarters and the entire body. It is a reliable proof for correct contact and thus also for the absolute obedience of the horse. If the difficulties are greater, physical skill and diligence are not enough to accomplish anything; the rider must carefully research his horse's characteristics and select the exercises accordingly, while searching for an ally in the horse's natural strength. He must be very patient and wait until progressive development of the young horse makes the desired position of individual body parts well established so that it becomes a natural position.

Following the above about working the forehand, I might as well also discuss now the so-called *freedom in the shoulders*. This highly praised characteristic of the horse, namely the regular, elevated, and light movement of its forelegs in the various gaits when raising, striding out with, and putting down the leg, is the result of a well established elevation of the neck. The cerebral vertebrae constitute the firm points of attachment for the lifting muscles of the forearms. The higher and more toward the rear these vertebrae are positioned, the more forceful and effectively the muscles are able to manage the weights assigned to them. Freedom in the shoulders is therefore not to be found in the shoulder blades or in the forelegs, but in the carriage of the neck and, consequently, always more or less in the hindquarters, since the forehand is able to find a reliable support only on the hindquarters. The degree of freedom of the shoulders to be attained is therefore also a function of the strength of the hindquarters, namely of the degree to which they can be loaded; the more weight is taken away from the forelegs and the more the activity of the lifting muscles is supported, the easier and more elevated will the movement of the forehand become. The saying, often used in everyday life, that "the green horse must first be ridden to be as light as a feather," leads to the conclusion that in some horses the shoulder blade is by nature grown so tightly to the body that this produces the constrained way of going of such horses. Therefore they must be forced to step over by putting them into lateral positions which are claimed to loosen these body parts. How wrong this view is, becomes evident from the victims of such work. Prematurely and excessively used lateral movements not only rob the horse of its natural mobility and carriage but also ruin its forelegs since this stepping over creates splints and swollen tendons. The excessive stress on the forehand, which finds no support in the hindquarters, causes the horse to become stiff in the shoulders and pasterns.

Every horse is by nature free in the shoulders, as we can observe when we see them in freedom when it surprises us by the freedom of its strides at the moment of excitement. If it moves constrained and stiff under the rider, this is only the result of its body being tense and the weight being carried on the forehand with the addition of the rider's weight which is unfamiliar and uncomfortable for the horse. Once it attains the natural, relaxed carriage and the weight is generally taken away from the forehand, the natural freedom of the shoulders will return. The foreleg is only a support for the body and does not by itself contribute to forward movement; it must be asked to do so by the hind leg. The rider can therefore strengthen and develop this body part only by taking as much of the load away from it as possible. He must protect it and further the freedom and ease of its movements in that he moves as much of the weight assigned to it by nature toward the back to the extent that the hindquarters are able to carry it.[8] To make the hind legs flexible and able to carry weight is the main purpose of dressage training, partially because it gives the rider an opportunity to correctly relieve the forelegs - which by nature are weaker and subjected to greater stress - at any time corresponding to circumstances and to protect them against all dangerous bruises. Only in this way is it possible to keep the horse sound, fresh, and surefooted as well as suitable for service under the rider up to a high age.

Skilled and insightful riders always have the reputation that they know how to give their horses freedom of the shoulders. Often they are believed to possess special, secret means with which they accomplish that. When a layman sees previously stiff, cumbersome movements turned into elastic gaits and the otherwise forwardly inclined body to take on a well positioned and harmonious shape at the completion of dressage training, the conversion of a green, naturally not so well conformed horse, or a horse that is very much on the forehand, often seems to him to be a miracle. He sees steep shoulders that apparently are set back further, hidden withers that have become visible. Often a completely natural saddle position develops in horses on which in the past the saddle could be held in the correct position neither by a foregirth, flank girth, or crupper. Nevertheless the rider owes all of these successes solely to the correct working of the hindquarters, and it is entirely wrong to believe that special exercises must be used to work the shoulders in particular.

Although Mr. Baucher and his followers also give their horses a certain freedom in the shoulders in that they teach them to lift their forelegs higher when hit with the whip and to hold them there, with the hindquarters following stiffly and spread out, such means may be suitable to train dogs and monkeys for the circus, they are not worthy of an expertly educated horse trainer since they are based on the absence of knowledge.

The conclusion of this chapter is therefore the repeated assurance that freedom of the shoulders can spring only from the hindquarters and that every horse that has a good back and strong hind legs can be worked with freedom in the shoulders, even though its forehand may be rather constrained by nature. In contrast, if the hindquarters are weak, all attempts at increasing the freedom of the shoulders are in vain, and a horse affected with this fault, if it is not to be ruined, must be used in its natural way of going.

ENDNOTES:

[1] On the other hand, in many cases the neck can attain its steadiness only after the poll has become flexible; both usually go hand in hand. (Hans von Heydebreck)

[2] To avoid all of these unpleasant consequences, the neck must initially be loosened in its natural position and then made to stretch toward the bit by forward riding in lively gaits before the carefully introduced bending of the poll can begin. In this way, head and neck are not unnaturally pulled together which is the sole cause of such bruises. (Hans von

Heydebreck)

3 The above thoughts about overcoming so-called throatlatch difficulties reveal two directly contradictory opinions and methods of working. One of them intends to overcome the horse's resistance with power and force, to "break" it, the other preaches patience and gentleness. I have attempted here to remove from earlier editions only obvious errors in terminology which contradicts Steinbrecht's basic views and could possibly lead the unexperienced rider onto the wrong track; for example, I have omitted the "sharp" spur and called the rein action caused by an "iron-firm hand" and a "hard" contact a "forcefully restraining" hand and "full" or "stronger" contact. However, at this opportunity I want to point out once more with emphasis that resistances resulting from physical flaws, whatever their origin, can be overcome only by removing tension from muscles and ligaments. Steinbrecht's bending work, which is the characteristic feature of his entire system based on systematic gymnastics and flows like a red thread through his entire **Gymnasium**, gives us the only truly effective means for this purpose. Although it is possible to enforce what looks like yielding with "sharp spurs" and an "iron-firm hand," this can never be lasting because it causes the loss of self-carriage. If you want to avoid such ugly phenomena as "labored breathing," "insensitive mouth," and a "lifeless eye" and their consequences, such as "staggers," "vertigo," and "roaring," you must follow Steinbrecht's other suggestions. He preaches gentleness, patience, and giving in to ensure that relaxation and self-carriage are maintained. (Hand von Heydebreck)

4 Frequently weakness and laziness in an overfed horse are based on digestive problems which produce painful tensions and thus reluctance to move. Suitable feeding or no food before work are most effective in eliminating or at least ameliorating such a state. (Hans von Heydebreck)

5 Based on the fact that the right hind leg, as mentioned above, tends to step toward the side to thus escape in part from accepting the weight so that the diagonal front leg, that is, the left fore, and the left shoulder are given more load to carry, setting the horse straight and thus obtaining uniform contact with both reins can initially never be obtained by action of the left rein. Instead, the rider will initially have to try to remain passive and soft with this rein, without losing contact with the mouth, and drive the horse with his right leg to step into the right rein. Once this is accomplished, the right rein will be able to effectively support the leg on the same side which must get the right hind leg to step underneath the weight. The left leg, acting as far forward as possible, will then take care mainly of maintaining forward movement and will have to urge the hind leg on the same side to step forward.
For a horse that moves crooked from the right hind to the left fore, these aids, supported as always by seat, weight, and lower back, should initially not only be used when riding on the right hand, but also on the left hand until the horse stretches the left side of its neck and uniformly accepts both reins, albeit while being positioned slightly to the right. Only in this way can it find its natural position and its natural balance and can now be made uniformly receptive for the aids and "through" on both sides. Yet, even the best trained horse will

never become completely straight; when mounted and not yet warmed up, it will try to meet new demands or external circumstances that cause it to resist by using its innate crookedness to escape the rider's actions in some way. Bending exercises on one or two tracks and the proper interaction of the aids will, however, straighten it very quickly and make it willing to be obedient. (Hans von Heydebreck)

6 When Steinbrecht speaks in the same sense of the difficult side and the stiff side, he refers to the right side since he always looks for the cause of front difficulties and resistances in the rear, that is, in the hind legs. The right hind leg, which avoids the load and thus the right rein, transfers the weight to the left shoulder by stepping to the side, puts more weight on the left shoulder and thus also on the left rein. It is therefore absolutely necessary to make a precise distinction between the stiff side and the difficult side. The difficult side is generally the right side, but the left side is then stiffer since its neck muscles contract and are tensioned because of the crookedness so that lateral flexion in the poll becomes more difficult.

In the Third Edition, Plinzner changed the original language and mentioned the left side to be the more difficult side instead of the right, because it was his experience that this side was usually the stiff side without becoming aware that there is a difference between the difficult side and the stiff side. (Hans von Heydebreck)

7 This rule, however, does not apply for a very green or crooked horse, nor for the finished horse. It applies primarily for that part of dressage training in which the shoulder-in work is the core of the bending work. First, the outside rein must predominate only if the horse accepts it, that is, stretches into it, without leaning on it. The horse must no longer push against the right leg and put more weight on the outside shoulder. In the advanced dressage horse, the bending must be perfected by traverse-like actions. (Hans von Heydebreck)

8 This principle must not lead to the conclusion that the hind legs should continuously carry the weight to the greatest possible degree and their joints should always be extensively bent. Rather, the hind legs should softly receive the weight assigned to them with loose joints and should push it away again with elastic resiliency. Flexion of the joints must be followed by stretching, not only in the military horse, but also in the dressage horse. (Hans von Heydebreck)

(c) Bending the Spine[1]

The spine as the main stem of the entire skeleton of the horse constitutes the connection between forehand and hindquarters and thus transmits the movement from the hind legs through neck and head to the mouth for which purpose it must have a certain resilient flexibility. In addition, a riding horse's spine must also carry the rider's weight and therefore requires a certain strength. To accomplish these different, important tasks the spine, as the main stem of the entire body of the horse, must also be exercised to take on the positions required for service under saddle. Like the other parts of the horse's body discussed in the preceding chapter, the spine, on the one hand, must be made flexible, which can be accomplished only by loosening the muscles that move its joints, and, on the other hand, it must be steeled by strengthening the muscles that must counteract the pressure of the rider's weight.

However, before the rider can think about any work on the spine, the horse must have overcome the tension in its back produced by the unaccustomed weight. This is the case when the horse resumes its natural carriage and its natural way of going under the rider. The tension may express itself in different ways: for example, the horse either hollows its back or it forcefully humps it, both preventing correct activity of the back. The first phenomenon will appear particularly in horses that have a very long back, while the opposite conformation usually results in the opposite, the humped back.

As already pointed out in the chapter about "Starting the Young Horse," the rider must initially avoid any active influence and patiently wait until this first tension has disappeared. Yielding of the back must be voluntary. It is primarily a question of trust.

We see that the conformation of the back has a decisive significance for its correct activity and must be considered with the utmost care during training. Generally the carrying ability of a back is less, the greater its length, similarly to a pipe that is placed horizontally onto two supports and weighted in the center. It gains or loses flexibility depending on whether the supports are moved further away from the load or brought closer to it. The horse whose back is too *long* will therefore be suitable neither for heavy weights nor for a collected body carriage since it is unable, as required for both, to bring the hindquarters close to the forehand. The distance between them is too great. Even in its natural body position, it will be unable to move with the endurance and decisiveness of the well coupled horse since the overall effectiveness of the muscles is a function of the structure of the skeleton. However, the long back with its greater flexibility will break all shocks received from the limbs or from the rider, and the way of going of such a horse is pleasant and comfortable for the rider.

The *short* back will exhibit precisely the opposite characteristics. A horse with a short back will not tire under a heavy weight and will usually move in a certain natural carriage since it is, in a way, collected already, but its back will be inflexible and hard and will transmit all shocks without amelioration, thus not only being uncomfortable for the rider but also adversely affecting the horse's legs. Such horses will therefore perform extremely well in an unconstrained carriage in strenuous service under saddle, but they are less suitable for higher level dressage since, with their overwhelming strength, they are able to put up too much resistance to any bending of their spine and their hindquarters so that the time required would usually be in no relationship to their value.

A *well built back*, in which strength and flexibility are well matched to one another, will therefore be appreciated greatly, particularly by hunt and steeplechase riders, since it ensures them performance capability and comfort at the same time. The experienced horse breeder will always strive to produce horses whose back is not too short, but with long withers and somewhat rounded loins. This shape of the back ensures greater carrying ability, reliably protects the kidneys if a heavy weight is carried on the back, and has therefore taken the place of the straight back and croup which used to be so popular and was considered to be favorable.

The horse's back must be flexible in both directions, that is vertically as well as horizontally. Its mobility in these two directions is only slight, more so the shorter the back and the closer the spinal processes of the vertebrae are to the ribs. The joints of the spine are moved by the dorsal muscles disposed above it and on its sides and by the abdominal muscles. Working of the back must initially be limited to loosening these muscles and thus making the spine flexible. This, however, can be accomplished only by lateral bending work since the rider is able to influence the horse effectively and reliably only in this direction. If the horse has thus been relaxed and loosened, the supple up and down movement of the back under the natural influence of the rider's weight will develop automatically and is expressed in elastic swinging of the spine.

The lateral flexion of the spine produced by lateral bending work is called, in the rider's language, rib cage flexion. This term is actually misleading since there is no bending of the rib cage, which is a fixed bone structure. Rather what we understand to be "rib cage flexion" is a lateral bending of the spine which somewhat pushes the ribs together on the bent side. Although it was necessary, when working the neck, to exercise bending of the vertebrae in all directions, the dorsal vertebrae require primarily correct and practiced lateral bending. The horse is able to raise and lower its back, curve it and bend it, and the rider is able to further or prevent both types of bending with his seat and the distribution of his weight, but he can make the back flexible only by loosening it with lateral bending work.

The correct and well founded *flexion of the rib cage* or lateral flexion of the spine is a main characteristic of a well ridden horse because it is the source for harmonious cooperation and interaction between forehand and hindquarters in dressage gaits, enabling the horse primarily to travel correctly on curved lines, perform short and sharp turns promptly and easily and produce pure and fluent gaits on two tracks. With the aid of this flexion, the rider is able, in all these difficult exercises, to keep weight on the inside hind leg, and the forehand in the proper alignment so that the action of both hind legs remains directed uniformly and unweakened against the forehand.

Flexion in the rib cage is therefore part of the soul of the equestrian art, and the rider must pay the same attention to it as to the flexion of the neck, if he does not want to feel the lack of it during every exercise, even every stride. As a part of the skeleton, the dorsal vertebrae must be bent laterally according to the same rules as the cerebral vertebrae, but working them is easier because they are more fixed by the rib cage and therefore have less of a tendency to bend incorrectly and in an exaggerated manner. To avoid unnecessary repetitions, I refer here to the preceding chapters, but emphasize again the basic rule: *the body must be set straight*, that is, the outside and inside legs must carry the same load through the correct action of the inside leg and the outside rein. I also warn against too frequent and premature exercises in place which, for bending the rib cage as well, can be considered only an advanced exercise to further increase and solidify obedience to the spurs.

In any case, work on the rib cage should begin only after the young horse has learned to accept, that is, notice, the spurs; it can be bent in the rib cage only by being asked to move away from the inside spur while being prevented from doing so by the outside leg, thus contracting the side threatened by the spur and bending as a result. Curved lines, that is, large and small circles, are the most suitable ways to begin these exercises since they already cause the horse to bend its spine. A correctly ridden circle requires a bend in which the spine follows the line of the circle, and this exercise is more difficult for the horse, the smaller a circle it is asked to describe. Sufficiently prepared by work on curved lines, shoulder-in will perfect rib cage flexion and thus enable the horse to perform all dressage movements to which nature has enabled it. I refer to the chapter about shoulder-in.

The natural structure of the body contributes significantly to the ease or difficulty of rib cage flexion. A long back facilitates it because it is unable to exert the same resistance as a short back. But, in the flexed state, it does not have the same expanding force and will therefore more easily tend to produce a false bend. A horse that is too short in the rib cage will be unable to assume the greater bends in a natural and distinct way, or only after long, tedious efforts since its ribs are very close together by nature in any case. Such horses are therefore not suitable for higher level dressage since all its movements require increased rib cage flexion. The golden mean is again infinitely more valuable and, since it is rarely found to perfection, will be greatly appreciated.

The rider recognizes the correct, well founded rib cage flexion immediately by his secure, comfortable seat with a slight, natural tendency toward the inside which the horse will produce automatically by relaxing its muscles when he turns it or rides it on two tracks.2 He also recognizes it in that his inside leg always finds a quiet, natural position while, with insufficient flexion, the leg is pushed away by the movement. This pleasant seat comes from the elastic working of the inside hind leg as it is always produced by the correct rib cage flexion and pushes the leg more underneath the weight. During all turns, this results in a corresponding lowering of the horse's inside hip and thus again in the tendency of the rider to hang inward, keeping both bodies in harmony and simultaneously obeying the laws of centrifugal forces on curved lines.

In lateral gaits, only the rib cage flexion enables the horse to have the thrust of the hindquarters act against the forehand without attenuation, since the hind legs of the bent horse are able to step underneath the load in these exercises, while, in the unbent horse, they must step to the side of the load to keep the lateral movement in force. Correct movements on two tracks are therefore inconceivable without rib cage flexion, and insufficiencies in this respect will always become evident by the croup drifting outward and the gait being uneven as well as by insufficient contact. These faults in particular make it very easy for the horse to be resistant since they limit the absolute control by the rider. One should therefore always take great care to avoid such faults since it will always take much time and effort to get horses that have learned to withhold their strength in this way, to fully use it again.

Once the horse's spine has been loosened and made flexible by lateral bending work and the rider is thus able to set the horse straight at any time, the unrestrained, resilient activity of the back will have been furthered considerably. The impulsion generated by the hind legs is now able to travel unimpededly through back and neck to the poll and mouth and cause the horse to yield its poll and chew on the bit. This brings forehand and hindquarters in connection with one another. With lively leg aids, the rider is now able to cause the hind legs to forcefully push off, and the thus increased impulsion is able to flow through back and neck to the front while half-halts and a displacement of the rider's weight to the back cause part of the impulsion to travel through the entire body of the horse back to the hindquarters so that not only the resilient activity of the back but also the flexibility of the hind legs are increased. In this way the horse, by lowering its hindquarters, automatically elevates its forehand and puts its head and neck in a higher position.

The cerebral vertebrae together with the dorsal vertebrae constitute a two-armed lever which has the forelegs as its fulcrum; the raising of one of the lever arms has a lowering effect on the other and vice versa.[3] For that reason the horse will instinctively strike out when it bucks, will hold its head and neck low when pulling heavy loads and will raise head and neck for rearing and pushing a load backward. The lever effect of the neck gives the rider an effective means to control the parts behind the neck, namely to lower the hindquarters and to determine the degree of their thrust to thus make the back sufficiently flexible by putting weight on it and to take away enough of its hardness to make its movement comfortable for the rider.[4]

Left to itself, the horse will always be able to correctly follow the lowering of one lever arm with the raising of the other. The rider, however, must be careful in the use of the leverage of the neck since its misuse will quickly have a damaging effect on the hindquarters. If he brings about elevation of the neck by force before the hind legs are able to carry the load and bend accordingly, the entire weight drops onto the lumbar vertebrae which then are lowered too much and interrupt the thrust. The horse will then move as if it were sore in the back which, after a time, will actually be the case. For that reason, foals whose feed trough is attached too high and young horses that are strapped in with their head too high in front of a carriage or for lunging, will become sway-backed.

The understanding rider will therefore always adapt the elevation of the forehand to the conformation and natural strength of the back and hind legs. He will protect the long, soft, and weak back by putting head and neck in a somewhat lower position and by sitting lighter to thus develop a raising of the back which will gradually strengthen it. But he will attempt to make horses that have a hard, tight back carry their head and neck higher and make the back yielding by bending work and by more frequently using a deep seat and an upright posture.

It takes a very fine feeling and much experience to always reliably determine the true condition of the back, since the outward appearance alone does not constitute a reliable measure. We find horses with a low back and long loins that are no worse performers than horses with good conformation because their energy or other special characteristics of their haunches compensate for these flaws if the rider understands to protect the weak parts and lets the stronger parts work harder. We also find backs that are very strong and even appear stiff because of the horse's bumpy way of going as long as saddle and rider stimulate unnatural tension in them. But when this stimulation disappears, they appear weak and soft and quickly tire under the rider's weight. The only correct measure for the condition of the back is the endurance with which it is able to carry and move greater weights.

If the strength of a back is accompanied by the necessary flexibility to sufficiently absorb the shocks created by the exertion of force of the hindquarters, so that they are less noticeable for the rider and the forehand, this alone gives the back its actual value, at least for a riding horse. Only the correct elasticity is able to impart to the kidney area the connection between forehand and hindquarters and between both of them and the rider in a pleasant manner.

For these reasons it is particularly important for the rider to determine the true condition of the back and to select the carriage of the forehand, his own seat, and the tempo of the gaits correctly. He should make a stiff back yielding by longer periods in free gaits which urge the dorsal muscles into increased activity and relieve their tension so that the spine is stretched as a result of the greater distance between the forelegs and the hind legs, which form its base of support.[5] He should follow this with periods in a shortened, collected tempo in which his own strong, backward leaning position puts more weight on the hindquarters. These exercises should be alternated until the desired flexibility is attained. The elevation of the forehand will then gradually come on its own. By the way, among the free gaits the canter is particularly suitable, the walk and trot are better for collected exercises.

In contrast, the trainer will attempt to make a *soft* back stronger and enable it to carry more weight in that he lets the thrust work against the lower carried forehand in lively but not too free gaits, with his own weight being placed as far forward as possible by using a light crotch seat. This deep and on-the-bit position of head and neck is the more necessary for weak horses the more they tend, because of an unfavorable conformation of these parts, to carry too much weight in an incorrect elevation, as this is usually the case with upside-down necks. The support the horse finds for its forehand by a secure contact with the rider's hand, has a stress relieving effect on the weak back.[6]

The *stiff back* which appears to a greater or lesser extent in almost all green horses is the consequence of increased tension in the muscles that move the back due to stimulation from the unaccustomed load and contact by saddle and rider. It is therefore unreasonable to act forcibly against such a natural phenomenon; it will disappear on its own after the horse has gradually become accustomed to the added weight. Nevertheless it is often the reason that young horses are ruined early on. Not only do they learn the means for getting rid of their riders, but also the shocks from these violent bucks in which the entire body is frantically stiffened may inflict damage to their skeleton for the rest of their life and thus these horses lose greatly in value. Forceful punishment worsens the situation while quiet and patience overcome it reliably albeit sometimes very slowly.

Forcing the head and neck to elevate and punishment with spurs and whip while the seat is stiff and clamping, will not prevent the unbroken horse from bucking, the horse will instead be invited to buck because its fear and discomfort are increased even more by such action. If, however, the rider leaves the horse in its natural carriage, protects the sensitive back by using a light crotch seat, touches it as little as possible with his legs and asks the horse to move forward with a light hand, the horse will remain unaffected and soon, after sufficient exercise, lose its artificial tension. If the horse is very sensitive, the irritation of the saddle can be reduced, in addition to the light crotch seat, also by a soft pad and a girth that is tightened only slightly. The more a strong back is connected with such sensitivity, the longer it will take to remove the unnatural tension. We find horses that will never quite lose this irritation or ticklishness and, up to an advanced age, will move with a raised back when the saddle is first put on.[7] Strenuous and long rides seem to overcome the sensitivity but, once the horse is rested and saddled again, it will reappear.

Just like a ticklish person is unable to control the irritability of his nerves, a sensitive horse is unable, in spite of being accustomed and obedient, to suppress such irritability. I have myself known horses that had been in service for a long time and were well trained which, if the girth was immediately tightened firmly, would fall over backwards when first asked to move forward and thus cause great danger to themselves and the rider. Such horses require much patience and caution and no effort should be spared to saddle them a long time before they are mounted, with the girth being gradually tightened a bit more in several incremental intervals; force is completely inappropriate here.

A stiff back is often the reason that unexperienced riders evaluate a horse incorrectly and therefore do not work them correctly. They often believe that a soft and weak back which pushes them hard out of the saddle, as long as it is humped by the tensed muscles, is a strong back and therefore they put too much weight on it. Or, they believe their horse is perhaps not weak but irregular and not built suitably for riding if it has tense paces because of a very strong and short back and appears to be bumpy and unsure. Yet, with increasing flexibility of the back, such horses would move freely and with elasticity. The correct evaluation of the horse is possible only if the thrust of the hindquarters is no longer prevented from acting on the forehand by the false curvature of the back, and the frantic tension of the dorsal and abdominal muscles is no longer an invitation to the other muscles of the body to do the same. For this reason it is necessary to move the young horse in simple gaits until its back is no longer stiff. Only then should the actual bending and collecting exercises begin. Whoever does not follow this rule, will always provoke resistance.

And if he himself need not worry about such resistance, he should avoid it for the protection of the horse since a tensioned body suffers much greater shock during violent movements than a soft and flexible body.

If the rider has recognized the true condition of the back he knows which degree of load it is able to carry without damage. Then he need not be misled in his work if this body part appears to be hurting and is sensitive during individual training sessions. As long as the hind legs do not flex sufficiently when the hindquarters are loaded, the weight will primarily fall into the kidney area. This will often act adversely on the kidneys disposed underneath and the horse will exhibit its discomfort after the riding session by frequent stretching and a great tendency to urinate. Even the most careful rider is unable to completely avoid this in some horses when he wants to thoroughly work their haunches because he must often urge them with his weight to bend the strong but rigid joints of the hind legs. As soon as this is accomplished, the back will be free again because then the hind legs take on more of the load more perfectly the closer they are to the center of gravity of the weight, that is, the more they have been pushed forward.

It is not easy to correctly load a back that has an unfavorable conformation and to set it in such a way that it constitutes the most perfect connection between forehand and hindquarters. Any excess load will weaken the thrust of the hind legs, while an insufficient load will be a detriment for the control of the hindquarters since a loin area that is curved up too much counteracts the elevation of the forehand. A soft back can be made acceptable in part by strong hind legs. A rigid back, if it is connected with strong hindquarters, will become flexible together with the hindquarters. In connection with weak haunches, however, the rigid back will be unconquerable since it will ruin the haunches before it yields.

When a horse is selected for riding purposes, its back should always be given the most careful consideration if time and effort, which often are expended entirely in vain, are of the essence. Don't believe that a heavy weight, that is, a heavy rider, or sand bags in front of a saddle that has been pushed far back, could make a high, hard back flexible. This would only weaken the back, and with it all of the hindquarters, and make it lame but not elastic. The only correct means for this purpose is the natural lever action of the forehand. The finer the rider is able to manage this lever action by properly positioning the forehand, the more precisely he will be able to determine the force exerted by the back.

For that reason, Mr. Baucher, the great artist, has no power over this part of the horse's body. He bends and kinks the back during the lateral bending of the spine in that he turns his horses by moving the hindquarters about the fixed forehand and thereby destroys the reliable connection between the two, and thus also any exertion of force of the hind legs from the rear to the front, but he is unable to make a stiff back resilient and to lower a raised back. His horses instead curve and raise their backs that much more the more he attempts to collect them in his way. They therefore are similar to a billy goat on the peak of a rock with its four feet placed close together. It is natural for them to take on this position because, on the one hand, he pushes the forelegs back by pulling head and neck behind the vertical and, on the other hand, he forces the hind legs, which carry no load and are therefore not bent, forward in the direction of the forehand. His horse can then bring its four legs together only by curving its back. The movements of such a distorted animal that has been robbed of its thrust act more backward than forward, and the poor rider is completely helpless and perplexed on such a high, tensioned, and distorted back. With a young horse that tends to buck he knows that the movement, be it ever so rough, is directed forward and the unweakened thrust of the hind legs will also affect him in this direction, while with the baucherized horse he will never know where he will end up.

ENDNOTES:

[1] This heading covers a combination of the two chapters About Bending the Rib Cage and About Bending the Back which were discussed separately in the earlier editions. This was done because in both cases the only thing involved is making the horse's spine flexible which is possible only by lateral bending work, that is, by bending the rib cage. (Hans von Heydebreck)

[2] This natural tendency toward the inside must not prevent the rider from following the direction of movement of the lateral movement. (Hans von Heydebreck)

[3] Steinbrecht took over the theory of the two-armed lever from his mentor Seeger. The latter, however, compares the entire skeleton with two-armed levers by proving that the lumbar vertebrae as well form such a lever with the pelvis. Seeger claims that, since the front arm of this lever is in immediate connection with the rear arm of the front lever, any change in the direction of the arms of one lever must also be transferred to the other lever. (Hans von Heydebreck)

4 But the back must never be pressed down for this reason, its loosening and yielding must be produced by lateral bending work. (Hans von Heydebreck)

5 The pace must here be kept fluid and natural by light guidance to let the strides come out freely. Any forced action leads to tension in the strides which just makes things worse. (Hans von Heydebreck)

6 The correct activity of the back produces a swinging movement and becomes evident to the rider by a swinging back and resilient chewing on the bit. A swinging back must therefore be one of the trainer's main goals during the entire course of training. For the large majority of today's horses, it can be attained only with a relatively low position of head and neck.* If the hind legs are weighted and bend due to elevation of the forehand, this must de done with particular care because there is a great danger that the swinging back and thus the impulsion in the movement will be suppressed. (Paul Plinzner)
*Since the position to be attained here is subject to many erroneous opinions, it should be pointed out again that the most favorable position of head and neck to attain the correct activity of the back is always the position in which the horse finds its natural self-carriage and its natural way of going. Generally, this will be the case when the horse, with a naturally extended neck, carries its head in such a way that the bit is at the same height as its spine.

7 Experience has taught us that such difficulties in the back are caused more often than you think not by sensitivity of the back itself but because the horse has some problems in its digestive tract which cause it to convulsively tense its back. This is quite understandable since the abdominal muscles constitute the flexor muscles for the back and, understandably, painful digestive processes cause them to convulsively contract. (Hans von Heydebreck)

(d) Bending the Hind Legs

As I mentioned earlier, the *hind legs* are the actual engine producing the forward movement. The horse's speed, agility, and endurance depend primarily on their power and strength. Their individual components are arranged relative to one another and are connected with one another by way of joints in such a way that they act in the manner of a compression spring on the weight to be carried and moved. The more correctly the relationship between the length of the individual bones and their angulation follows the laws of mechanics[1], the stronger the structure of the joints is by nature, and the more developed the muscles of the hind legs, the more energetic will be their overall effect during forward movement. A normal configuration of these parts increases the value of the horse immensely because, with an otherwise just acceptable conformation, it gives it naturally what otherwise the trainer would have to produce with so much effort, namely regular, elastic, and enduring paces. With the aid of good, strong hind legs, the trainer is also able to completely compensate, or at least ameliorate, obvious flaws in the remaining physical structure and shortcomings in the forehand or the back. To make such hind legs flexible is more a pleasure than work since they are flexible by nature so that it is merely necessary to make the horse understand the rider's will.

However, the obstacles that confront the trainer in a horse with an insufficient structure of these limbs may be great. These obstacles originate either from incorrect angulation, an insufficient relationship between the individual parts to one another, or weakness. If weakness is a consequence of general softness in the articulation of the entire organism, all human efforts cannot prevail because it is impossible to produce a diamond from a plain piece of stone. If it is only a consequence of youth, poor nourishment, or inactivity, gradual, well measured exercise can do an infinite amount of good. If the structure of the bones and joints of the hind legs is obviously too weak in relationship to the remainder of the body, such a horse should become a driving horse where it need not carry any loads and can put more weight on its forehand without problems.

But don't confuse fine bones with weak bones. When you evaluate a horse, look at the total conformation of the horse. The harmony of the whole is the deciding factor and a horse that is fine all over, under the proper weight, may develop an infinite strength with its seemingly tender limbs. The thickness, that is the circumference of the bones, is in no way a measure of their strength but of their interior structure, just like the circumference of a muscle does not determine its strength which is a function of its tightness. Just think of some animals in the woods, like the deer, with its dry, fine legs and look how it performs. This will eliminate the prejudice that only thick limbs can be strong. Generally, however, the rule may apply that strong, short limbs are better suitable for carrying heavy weights but that there then is a corresponding loss in speed and elasticity. The stocky farm lad will easily carry away a sack of wheat that would pin the light-footed tailor's apprentice to the ground; the former will make the dance floor rumble with his stomping and will soon become breathless if the music speeds up, while the latter will never tire.

Regarding the angulation or overall conformation of the hind leg, the horse cannot be judged according to a standard pattern. Temperament, elasticity, and a certain toughness often appear to be able to replace a lack of strength, while, if these traits are missing, a seemingly good bone structure produces perhaps only average results. If I have repeatedly said that the exterior shape of a horse does not provide a reliable measure for its inherent strength, that the rider can find this strength only through feeling, this applies particularly for the hind legs and the entire hindquarters. We find that horse enthusiasts who are more steeped in theory than practice and select their horses with a yardstick and according to mathematical formulas never select a good high-performance horse but almost always a poor one.

Generally, however, it is a fact that a straight hind leg in particular, with its too obtuse angles, is not able to sustain greater flexion in its joints with the same facility and endurance as a horse that was shortened and bent by nature through more acute angles. In contrast, during the phase when both stretch the bent joints again, hind legs with angles that are too small are unable to develop the elasticity and spring in their movements as this is possible for the horse with large angles. With the same natural strength, the straight leg will always be able to develop more thrust while the bent leg is able to carry more weight. Great deviations from the normal angulation must be moderated by oppositely directed exercises. The straight hind leg must be gradually accustomed to bending by shortened, collected gaits, while the horse with excessive angulation must be asked to develop thrust in free paces. The first task is always very difficult and requires much time, patience, and skill. It is worthwhile and advisable only if the hindquarters are naturally strong and the forehand is constructed to favor the lever effect of the neck. Otherwise it is not worth the effort and the horse should be destined for another purpose since it is impossible to make a straight and stiff hind leg flexible and elastic unless the entire spinal column reliably and easily transmits the rider's aids, and the joints of the legs are strong enough to sustain the efforts of the first exercises without disadvantage.

The other exaggeration in the structure of the hind legs in the horse, unless it is connected with weakness, will enable the horse very much for service under saddle since it will be very willing to perform in collected gaits. The rider must merely take care that the hindquarters, which are so willing to take up the load, are not overloaded and thrust is not suppressed[2].

If, after these general remarks, we approach the question of bending the hind legs, we should first understand that of all the joints in the hindquarters the two uppermost joints, that is, the hip and stifle joints, are by far the strongest due to their strength of bone as well as the numerous and powerful muscle groups that surround them. These muscles form the so-called trousers of the horse which, with their tendinous extensions, also move the lower portions of the leg, while the two mentioned joints are the actual haunches. The main forces for supporting and moving the entire body lie in the haunches, and it is the most important task of the understanding rider to develop these forces and make them subordinate.

There are many riders who are able to speak about bending the haunches and they also believe that they are working the haunches of their horses without ever having felt correctly bent haunches. Yes, there are enough of them who think the hocks are the haunches, and they have hardly an idea that there are even stronger and more important joints above the hocks. All of these riders do not progress in their work beyond bending the leg from the hocks downward and therefore obtain only very mediocre results in training their horses. Hundreds of horses with good haunches are used up before their time because their valuable strengths remained untapped, while they should have been used to relieve the forelegs and to protect the lower joints of the hind legs under load. To bend strong haunches is of course not an easy task because, according to their natural power, they are able to resist the required flexion. Don't believe that this resistance can be overcome by physical force. While a rider is able to bend the back of a horse by rough, forceful means, and can also break up the hock and fetlock joints, he is unable to bend the haunch joints. This is the prerogative of the scientifically educated and experienced trainer who knows that he can create a reliable lever by working the spinal column in stages and whose fine feeling enables him to use this lever always according to the horse's strength. Making the haunches flexible is therefore always the limit for the artisan rider beyond which he cannot go without breaking down his horse or making it the boss.

The follower of the natural carriage knows well, if he is a prudent rider, how to evaluate the power of the haunches and appreciates their natural flexibility immeasurably because it gives him easy and elastic jumps. But he is unable to control them, that is, to let them push or carry at will. They will therefore contribute the more to the rapid ruin of the overstressed forelegs the more their strength or rigidity predominates and the more they are able to resist any bending attempted by adding weight.

The old masters knew how to thoroughly work the haunches and have become a lasting example for us for years to come. Their extraordinary accomplishments, which at present are considered to be almost miracles, were the result of only this work. If we are serious in maintaining the equestrian art as a fine art and not let it be degraded to philistinism and puppetry, there is only one way: we must try to follow the old masters. The borderline between military riding and upper level dressage, if such a line is to be drawn, is defined in that military riding has as its goal to put the horse in balance, that is, to put equal weight on the forehand and the hindquarters, while in upper level dressage the movements become the more perfect the more the center of gravity of the weight can be moved backwards without interfering with the freedom of the hindquarters.

If we speak of a well built horse, the so-called born riding horse, we understand this to be a horse that is balanced by nature, whose natural conformation enables it to effortlessly put its skeleton in a position in which its four legs carry equal weight. It will be easy to train such a horse because the work is limited essentially to teaching and accustoming. If, however, there are discordant relationships between forehand and hind-quarters or between individual parts of them, the art must take an arbitrating approach and produce as well as strengthen the horse's in-balance state by a system of gymnastic exercises.

Overloaded or steep shoulders, a heavy forehand, weak forelegs, high, uphill hindquarters, for example, often require more intensive bending in the haunches, and the rider must subject these horses to difficult dressage work to merely produce simple utility gaits. Each horse, even the completely green horse, has a natural flexibility in its haunch joints because every time it raises and puts down a hind leg, all of the joints of that leg must bend so as to shorten it. How and to what degree this occurs determines the beauty and perfection of the gait. The closer the hind leg remains to the horse's center of gravity when it takes up the load and moves it forward by stretching the joints[3], the more beautiful is its way of going. Such a green horse is called a good mover. The less the way of going exhibits this characteristic, the more unsatisfactory it is in every respect, be it lingering and dull or falling apart and dragging, and must be improved by the art. This will be impossible only if back or hindquarters are simply too weak to carry their assigned load. In such horses there is no setting them in balance or even onto the haunches; the horse must be used in its natural carriage. A faulty way of going can be improved in a truly effective manner only by thoroughly working the haunches, as is done in dressage, and this is absolutely necessary when training horses with irregular conformation as long as they are strong enough.

Among the lower joints of the hind leg, the *hock* is the most important. It is called the jumping joint because its main purpose is to produce the jump-like movements. For this purpose it is specially equipped by nature in that its spring-like force and resistibility are significantly augmented by the ingenious assembly of seven different, small joint bones which form a movable but closed unit. The hock is also equipped with very strong extensor muscles that are attached to the point of the hock by the achilles tendon and whose effect is significantly augmented by the projecting structure of this bone. The hock is therefore the main source of activity for thrust and carrying force, depending on whether its strength is made evident, which depends on whether the hind leg acts more against the weight or underneath it. This joint is therefore of great significance for every practicing rider. Not only the dressage rider but also the hunt rider will very carefully examine this very important part of the horse's body. As wisely as nature has constructed this joint for its intended activity, it suffers most under the rider if used incorrectly, and no joint is subjected to so many faulty formations, such as spavins, curbs, bog spavins, thoroughpins, and capped hocks, as the hock. This is easily explained in that whenever the hind leg is bent to a great extent and has to work, the hock does most of the work unless the upper, stronger joints are made to participate correctly. Riders who favor the natural carriage and let their horses gallop and jump too much will not only ruin the forelegs by overloading them but also the hocks if their angulation is unfavorable. The followers of the artificial carriage will also damage primarily the hocks if they make the mistake in their work of prematurely or excessively loading the hindquarters. Forced elevation of the forehand, hard halts, and primarily gaits with the horse in a crooked position in which the horse steps, instead of underneath the weight, to the side of it, are certain to damage the hocks.

At the present state of the equestrian art it is not surprising that the mentioned faults in the hock appear as genetic traits already in whole families of our horses and that horses intended as hunters and for other strenuous service are routinely fired as a precautionary measure against spavin and curb. This English custom, which came to us from across the channel with the English horses and the English way of riding, was really not needed here and was unknown to us as long as the good old German school was being taught and honored. There is no doubt that the English are the top breeders of all animal species and can certainly be recognized as teachers, but as riders they have no other merit than being known not to be afraid to challenge the raw power of the horse with masculine courage and to quickly use up the material they have bred with so much effort and expense. If the English were riders who operate with as much perfection according to correct, scientific principles as they are good horse breeders, they would definitely have the most perfect riding horses for any practical use.

In view of the importance of the hock during the sequence of movements of the hind legs, the trainer must attempt not only to keep it sound but also, if possible, to increase its strength through appropriate exercises. For this purpose there is no other way of making the hock itself and also the joints of the haunches flexible because only this will prevent all strains and overextensions of the ligaments and joint capsules as well as bruises on the periosteum in and at the joints. The well trained horse, that is, the horse that is flexible in its haunches, is then protected forever against such diseases in its hind legs. The spring-like flexibility of its joints will render any hard stress or bruise harmless. Bending of the haunches also requires bending of the hocks and the lower joints since the horse will initially bend in these weaker and more yielding parts before it gives up resisting with the stronger joints. The lower joints must therefore be bent with the more caution, the less the haunches facilitate this work through natural flexibility but instead push downward with reluctance. The stronger and stiffer the hindquarters are by nature, the more carefully and patiently they must be worked. The success will then be the better, the greater is the elasticity of these parts after they have been worked.

When training the practical utility horse, it is nowadays often necessary to make the lower joints flexible since at present it is generally sufficient to have the horse carry itself in balance. For horses, in which barely favorable relationships in conformation permit this carriage even without much bending in the haunches, it will be possible to meet requirements by merely working the lower joints. If, due to lack of time or for reasons of cost, the trainer must be satisfied with such a task, he should at least lay a good foundation for the flexibility of hock and fetlock joint which, by softly yielding, can make harmless those moments in which the resistance of the ground and the pressure of the load act equally strongly on them. He will accomplish this goal reliably and without damage for his horse if he is able to correctly evaluate the natural strength imparted to these parts and begins accordingly with easy and short exercises.

If, however, it is intended to more or less thoroughly bend the hindquarters, then the first bending exercises must always be performed primarily while moving forward because, when moving, the load always changes from one hind leg to the other and the thrust developed thereby simultaneously serves as a measure for the rider to what extent he can produce a bend by means of weight. If he suppresses forward movement, if the joints are unable to freely stretch after being bent but must struggle on, compressed under the load, this is too much stress for initial exercises and must be reduced until the rider again notices the fresh emergence of thrust.

Moreover, the hind legs must first be made flexible individually until they have been prepared for simultaneous bending by alternating exercises. The rider will then have to overcome mainly the resistance of one hind leg, that is, only half the resistance, and the horse will be able to rest the leg that has been previously stressed more when changing from one hand to the other. This now involves lateral bending of the horse which is the only way to intensively work each hind leg individually as the inside hind leg. The more perfectly the entire spinal column is able to assume the necessary carriage and lateral flexion, the finer and more reliably will the rider be able to act on the individual hind leg.[4]

Work on the spine and the hind legs is so intimately related that it cannot be performed separately at all. The spine finds one of its main supports in the hind legs; the resistance which the horse poses against lateral flexion of its body is thus usually to be found in the hind legs. If the horse bends correctly in the spine on a circle it bends the inside hind leg. An increased bend in the individual hind leg is conceivable only on a curved track and with the horse bent accordingly. Bending the spine is therefore the only means for primarily working the individual hind leg. It must unconditionally precede the uniform bending of both legs. This work on the inside hind leg by letting the horse carry itself in a bent position begins on one track on a circle and on other bent lines. From this then develops the shoulder-in with its various gradations which must be so well established that the remaining exercises on two tracks evolve correctly from it. These exercises initially begin with little elevation and will gradually be perfected by increasing the elevation. They must be practiced in all natural gaits which must initially be selected with care according to the talents of the horse. They should begin at a free tempo; gradually more collection should be demanded.

Once the horse has happily passed through these stages, it is exercised to simultaneously bend both hind legs. This is done by more action of the outside rein which reduces the bending of the spine and neck, but increases the elevation of the forehand and puts weight onto the outside hind leg. This work is perfected and solidified by halts, particularly also in the lateral movements, by holding in place after the transition to the halt and by stepping back, thus preparing the horse for the upper level movements.

The *fetlock, coronet, and hoof joints* are automatically worked as well in all exercises for bending the hind legs since they actively participate in their movement. Due to the shortness of the lower bones, the activity of these joints is less a participation in the development of thrust and spring than a reduction of the shocks produced by contact with the ground. Horses with soft pasterns, that is, whose fetlock joints bend through considerably, therefore have a very soft, comfortable way of going. If this configuration is connected with weakness, then it is, however, a severe fault; we often find it in the most noble and hardiest horses whose elasticity in the hindquarters can then even be increased considerably.

A soft pastern is not necessarily a fault, it may even be of great

[129]

advantage for some riding purposes. However, the rider must carefully consider this lower portion of the leg with respect to its structure and the strength inherent in it; the more so since it is not only weaker but also more affected by contact with the ground. As long as the flexibility of the upper joints does not impart any elasticity to the way of going and the lower joints are not protected by yielding of the upper joint when the load is greater, the lower joints will suffer from a harsh contact between the legs and the ground, the more so the harder the ground and the greater the load on the hindquarters. That is the reason why horses that are used a lot on paved roads in their natural carriage quickly become dull and weak in their pasterns which, however, can be remedied again by quiet work on soft ground. We also note that young horses whose riders work them in difficult exercises and movements for which they are insufficiently prepared very quickly suffer damage and, in addition to the mentioned flaws in the hocks, they also acquire windpuffs, ringbone, or joint lamenesses from twists or sprains.

At this opportunity it should be noted that it is the duty of a sensible trainer and of every true horse lover to always seek out the most favorable riding area. No effort and work should be spared to find level, soft, and springy footing for one's horses. One should be willing even to pay a fine if instead of moving on the hard, dry road, a good path in the fields is available. A rider who from carelessness or his own laziness unnecessarily tires his horse or even damages it on poor footing if better footing is available is no true horse lover and does not deserve to ride a noble, well trained horse. Every race rider knows the importance of the footing for performance and endurance of the horse. He much appreciates a uniformly firm but elastic racetrack while he is very much afraid of a hard and dry track as he knows precisely that his horse may damage its tendons, become lame in its joints, or even break a bone on such a hard track.

If it is possible for the rider, on good footing, to let his horse work barefoot, this gives him double advantages. Nature has not only equipped the hoof with great toughness but also with elasticity so that it sufficiently protects the internal, soft parts and is able to soften the contact with the ground. Consequently an unshod horse not only moves more comfortably for the rider, its own limbs are also not stressed as much as those of the shod horse and the natural growth patterns of its hooves are not interfered with by unknowing farriers. The paved roads in our civilized countries often do not permit the riding of unshod horses in practical life, but wherever it is possible it should be taken advantage of!

To briefly summarize the main thoughts of this important chapter, I again compare the hind leg and its joints, particularly the three upper joints, with a compression spring. As such a spring, if used reasonably, generally retains its force although it will become softer and more pleasant in its effect through such use, the same applies to the hind leg with the difference that organic forces equal to the magnetic forces are multiplied by exercise. Reasonable work will not only make the hind legs softer and more elastic, they will generally also become stronger, while the dead spring at most can retain its capability that is inherent in it due to the elasticity of its components.

Just like a compression spring is suppressed in its action by too heavy a load in that its desire to resume the state of rest, that is, the extended position, is inhibited, and like this tendency or, in other words, its elasticity, is gradually weakened and finally completely canceled out by too frequent or too long an action of a load that is more than it can handle, the joints of the hind leg are weakened by overloads or their strength is completely taken away, that is, they become lame. Finally, like the compression spring reacts to a force it can handle with the same degree of force and, for example, quickly returns a jolt, the hind legs, without preparation, will not accept a load but will defend themselves against actions produced by sudden, hard jerks by letting their joints spring against them.

The hind legs can be made flexible only by stressing them, there is no other way for the rider. To bend them more, he must load them more, and the weight required for this purpose can only come from the forehand. By temporarily directing the weights of the forehand toward the rear, that is, closer to the center of gravity of the horse, he is able to act in a downward pressing lever-like manner on the dorsal and lumbar vertebrae and transfer this action to the hind legs if he brings them sufficiently forward.[5]

Mr. Baucher, as usual, can serve as a warning example for us, particularly for working the hind legs. Instead of developing and controlling their natural power, primarily their forward driving action, he interferes with it in any way he can because he considers it his natural adversary. For that reason, he immediately tacks up the young, green horse, that has not yet established contact with the simplest snaffle bit, in a full bridle. With this unpositioned animal, which is unable to even move on a straight line, he practices bends and turns in place which only the completely trained horse is able to perform correctly. He does not rest until he has suppressed the thrust of the hind legs by bringing the horse completely behind the bit and twisting its spine. He suppresses and destroys the thrust not by overloading, as this is done by careless riders, but prevents its action by removing everything against which it could be directed.

Once he has weakened the horse in this way so that its behind-the-bit position no longer bothers him, then he begins to bend the hindquarters, in his opinion, with his backward lessons in all gaits and with his spur attacks in place, namely the senseless application of the spurs. Since, however, due to the lack of contact, he has no lever action and also is unable to put weight on the hindquarters, they remain high while the forehand is lowered. In this position, as already mentioned, the horse is able to hump its back and push its four feet together like a billy goat, but its joints remain unflexed and ultimately lose their natural flexibility from the unnatural and frantic efforts to which they are forced by the endless, senseless jabs with the spurs. In that way he robs his horses of all natural abilities and forces them into movements that are contrary to nature, about which he then boasts as newly discovered training successes.

This type of training is indeed new because Mr. Baucher cannot be denied the reputation that no one before him has discredited the noble art in the way he does by working against all its natural principles and systematically teaching such action. The results of his work are therefore a series of vices and resistances which the proper trainer seriously avoids, each individually, and if he is unable to do this, fights them seriously and strongly, while Mr. Baucher teaches them to the horse, establishes them as firmly as possible, and then calls them upper level dressage. Any rider who has already developed a feeling for the correct way of going and the proper contact, needs only five minutes after mounting a baucherized horse to thoroughly convince himself of the correctness of these statements. The entire behavior of these poor creatures, their swishing tails and grinding teeth, their squeals and grunts in response to the spurs reveal that they can have been caused to perform such unnatural movements only by cruel force and coercion.

With this I close this chapter and with it the section of this book in which I wanted to draw a picture of how to evaluate and work the individual body parts of the horse so as not to interfere with their overall harmony in their activity together. I now move to the special exercises and lessons with which the goal of dressage training is attained in stages. I will maintain the sequence determined by the gradual increase in the tasks placed before the horse, but must leave it to the practical rider to develop a specific lesson plan for each individual horse depending on its aptitude and to perhaps change this lesson plan again from time to time according to circumstances. Precise rules and dead letters allow the rider to make a horse into a machine, but he cannot train it that way. This he can do only if he lets his own feeling and his own judgement be the guide.

ENDNOTES:

[1] The mechanically most favorable angulation exists if the pelvis forms a right angle with the thigh bone and the thigh bone with the tibia, with a vertical cannon bone forming an angle of 135° with the tibia. (Hans von Heydebreck)

[2] Generally, extensively angulated hind legs, which are usually connected with pushed-out hocks, are less suitable for higher-level dressage and have more difficulty carrying the weight correctly than straight hind legs. In contrast, horses having excessively angled hind legs but otherwise a favorable conformation usually perform well as jumpers. (Hans von Heydebreck)

[3] Decisive for a good way of going is whether the hind leg that has just been put down receives and supports the load in an elastically resilient manner while bent in order to then move it elastically forward at the proper time by forcefully stretching its joints after striding out. (Hans von Heydebreck)

[4] Working the individual hind legs is also enhanced by a bent carriage when moving on straight lines since the inside hind leg can be brought forward underneath the weight in such a way that it learns to reliably balance the weight and is required to step forward passing closely by the other hind leg. This work, however, intends and produces only the loosening and control of the individual hind leg, not its greater load carrying ability and bending. This can be accomplished only on curved tracks or if the rider, riding on a straight line, holds one hind leg temporarily with a half-halt and loads it. If this can be accomplished on both sides, the rider has obtained the means for holding the hind legs together on a close track and to ask them to carry the weight. (Hans von Heydebreck)

[5] The work described here presupposes that the horse has successfully completed the earlier described steps of training, that is, all of its limbs have been loosened and made flexible by bending work and the rider is thus able to bring the hind legs forward underneath the weight

where they must, so to speak, take on the load themselves. The hands here always play only a temporary role in that they either hold the weight for a brief moment or displace it toward the rear by through-going half-halts. (Hans von Heydebreck)

5. Bending the Horse on One Track

Every *line* traveled by the horse is a function of its own body carriage. The unbent horse follows a straight, continuous line, the bent horse a circular line corresponding to its bend. As long as they both set their feet down straight in front of them and do not change the direction of their body, they will not leave these lines because the laws of mechanics bind them. Therefore, like the unbent horse, the bent horse is actually not performing a turn, although it may appear that way; both simply follow the natural inclination of their bodies. It is impossible for the unbent horse to describe a circle, it can be guided around the arena only on straight lines that are oriented at an angle to one another. The bent horse can also be guided in a straight direction if it is caused to move its legs sideways instead of directly in front of one another. In nature, the horse must maintain the line that corresponds to the direction of its body and can leave it only by changing this direction.

The forehand determines the direction of movement, but the drive for the movement comes from the hindquarters; the more accurately the hindquarters are attuned to the forehand, the more perfect will be movement and carriage of the horse. Any deviation in the forehand or in the hindquarters from the common direction must adversely affect both of them. A change in the previously maintained direction may emanate either from the forehand or from the hindquarters or may be effected simultaneously by both.

For example, when turning right, the forehand deviates to the right of the previous line, the hindquarters to the left. Depending on the displacement of the center of gravity of the horse, it will tend to take his support, when changing direction or turning, more on its forelegs or on its hind legs, with the part carrying more weight always being less mobile and therefore participating less in the turn.

Depending on the position of the center of gravity during turning, we must distinguish between *turns on the forehand, turns on the haunches,* and *balanced turns.*

In the turn on the forehand, the center of gravity lies in front, the forelegs constitute the support about which the hindquarters, which carry less of a load and are more mobile, turn like on an axis to the extent necessary to attain the intended direction of movement. In a balanced turn, the center of gravity lies in the center and the forehand is sufficiently supported by the hindquarters to make it easier to take on a new direction without interfering with the pace. The line through the center of gravity then forms the rotation axis and the hindquarters must always maintain the equilibrium by correctly and precisely following the tracks of the forehand. In the turn on the haunches the center of gravity lies further back, the hindquarters carry more weight and are bent more, constituting the axis about which the thus relieved forehand is easily able to turn.

The first type of turning can be called the natural way, not because the horse uses it in its state of freedom but because it is the only means available to the adherents of the natural carriage.

Left to itself the horse will often, because it tends to be lazy, turn more on the forehand than on the hindquarters, which is perfectly alright if it moves quietly and does not carry the extra load of the rider's weight. But observe young horses in their paddocks, when they are chased around or play with one another in a limited space, where they are forced to turn often and quickly. See how skilled they are in using their hindquarters for support and turning the forehand as swiftly as an arrow about the hindquarters, how they are able to quickly change the direction of their movement at full speed by breaking out to the right or left on curved lines and instinctively taking on the necessary flexion and collection of their body because their natural feeling teaches them that this will protect them against injury.

Things are quite different with the green horse or, more precisely, the horse carrying itself on its shoulders, when turning under saddle. The added extra weight on its shoulders as well as the rider's guidance impede its natural movement and inclinations. Because of a lack of flexibility and collection, it will always tend to use the heavier forehand as the support for its turns. That is the reason why such a horse is so clumsy and awkward when it is asked to move in a limited space. Comparing it with a trained horse, this is quite obvious in a riding arena. Because of its carriage and flexibility, the trained horse is easily able to change from a straight line to a curved line, to ride through the corners precisely and securely, always in the same tempo of its gait and, after a few brief half-halts, to quickly throw around its forehand, for which it does not require much space. The untrained horse, however, will be unable to change its straight-on direction without interrupting its pace and seeking support in the rider's hands. The rider is then forced to pull the forehand into the desired direction while with a trained horse he just takes up the forehand and is then able to move it laterally with ease. For that reason, the adherents of the natural carriage shy away from riding in an arena if the bridle paths cannot be used and prefer to give up the pleasure of riding altogether rather than struggling in vain with their untalented horses in such a small space. For the same reason, the naturally talented race and steeplechase horse will often win over a faster but less nimble opponent because its agility saves it much room going around corners and when collecting in front of the obstacle.

In contrast to the turns on the forehand of the horse ridden in its natural carriage, all dressage turns - whatever they may be called - fall into one of *two* classes, namely those in which the hindquarters correctly follow the forehand, either on one or two tracks, and those in which the held-steady hindquarters form the axis about which the forehand turns until it has attained the desired direction of movement. Flexibility and self-carriage are the source of the horse's agility. Good turns, which develop its agility, are obtained only by making the horse flexible, putting it into balance, and thus giving it self-carriage. This involves not merely the lateral flexion of the entire spinal column but more so the flexibility of the hind legs. Only the latter enables the horse to perform quick and reliable turns under the rider, since the forehand is able to turn and change direction easily without danger for the health of its limbs only from the always secure support of the hindquarters. In some respects, this lateral flexibility of the spinal column is only a means to an end. If we did not require it for other reasons, for example, as the major means for making the hindquarters flexible, we could spend much less time working on it.[1]

The proof for the importance of flexible hindquarters are the few excellent horses that nature has blessed with strong but flexible hindquarters. They will be skillful under saddle right from the start when moving and performing turns because they do not exhibit the main base for all stiffness, the stiffness of the hind legs.

Exercises involving changes of direction must always be adjusted to how much the horse is able to follow with its hindquarters, that is, to support. If it is very willing to move forward, that is, has a naturally well developed thrust, you can soon begin to moderate this willingness to go forward on a larger circle in that you request the corresponding lateral flexion and greater bending of the inside hind leg. If there is no tendency to rush forward, contact and forward drive must first be securely established on straight lines. Changes of direction interfere more with the way

[137]

of going the more the thrust of the hindquarters is impeded by their oblique orientation relative to the forehand. The regular change of direction requires the rider to always ensure that the hind legs constantly and sufficiently support the forehand and move it forward. For that reason the rider will use his feeling to prepare his horse corresponding to the size of the turn in that he produces the necessary collection by preceding the turn with half-halts and by increasing the horse's lateral position for the bend corresponding to the intended turn, thus preventing any inaccuracies in carriage and way of going. The unskilled rider will be unable to maintain correct lines or avoid interruptions in the way of going, even on the best trained horse, because he is unable to correctly adjust flexion and collection.

Just as the unskilled rider will practically inhibit the way of going of his horse by incorrect turns, the skilled rider will merely moderate and regulate the pace by using turns correctly. For impetuous horses and those that want to rush off too much, he will not only develop flexibility by frequent turning but also be able to reduce their thrust by putting more weight on one of the two hind legs to the extent this is required by the size of the turn. Under certain circumstances, he will be able to restrict the excess thrust of his horse by forcing it into a crooked position if he feels that there is no other way to master the brute force. He will then be able to quickly stop the run-away horse if he is able to interrupt the straight orientation of the hindquarters relative to the forehand, or he will be able to gradually moderate the runaway pace if he manages to force the horse onto a circle. Without the corresponding bend, the horse is unable to maintain such a circle and will therefore assume a crooked carriage in that its hindquarters fall out, thus breaking its thrust. Extraordinary circumstances require extraordinary measures; even the well trained dressage rider will sometimes be forced to perform such turns although they are contrary to the rules.

By saving the discussion of turns on the hindquarters for later chapters, we will now discuss the turns in which the hindquarters precisely follow the forehand *on one track*. If the bent carriage of the horse's body they require is maintained, such turns then result in *riding on curved lines*. This riding on curved lines or turns on one track is based primarily on the flexibility of the spinal column and will be more successful the more this flexibility is developed, similarly to a fish bone being easily guided through a bent tube because it is able to assume the shape of the tube, while a stiff rod would break or get stuck in the tube.

The unbent, green horse will quickly develop its natural way of going on uninterrupted straight lines and will thus establish secure contact with the rider's hands. If the horse is to turn to the right or left from this direction, its forehand can be laboriously directed to do so by forcible action of the reins, but the hindquarters will be unable to follow correctly. Instead, they will either fall out or remain on the old line so that the horse becomes crooked. As long as this is the case, pace and contact are interfered with or even interrupted. We therefore see the unskilled horse slow down or become faster and change gait when it is first asked to turn until, with great effort, it has regained contact and thus the secure carriage on the new line.

Before we discuss how the trainer gradually obtains from the horse the uniform longitudinal flexion required for travel on curved lines, we want to initially imagine - in order to draw up our lesson plan, so to speak - how the young horse in the arena is forced right from the start to go through four turns each time around. This is not easy for any green, not yet flexible horse and requires much patience and calmness on the part of the rider. The accomplishment of this task is possible for the horse only in that the rider asks it to round off each corner according to the horse's natural ability, that is, to leave the wall at a certain distance before the corner and to return to it on a curved line at the same distance behind the corner. By thus riding four partial circles each time around, the rider is able to redevelop thrust on the straight line after each turn and to regulate the contact if both were interfered with during the turn due to the unaccustomed and still insufficient flexion. Every rounded corner, to be ridden correctly, should constitute part of a circle which, depending on the degree of flexion, will be larger or smaller.

Once the horse has become secure enough in riding through the corners, the task can be increased by using only half the arena from time to time. In this way the rider does not ride the long lines but instead has available four uniformly short lines, assuming the arena is twice as long as it is wide. He also gains a free line on which the horse must be without the accustomed support of the wall. The support given the horse by the wall is a great help to the rider since it enables him to use more inside rein and leg and thus obtain lateral flexion. The free line will force him to also use the outside rein and leg to keep the horse from falling out, thus enabling him to firmly establish the horse's obedience to these aids.[2]

Only after the horse is able to correctly travel through half the arena, can the rider begin to form the first large circle in that he uniformly rounds the four corners of the square until the periphery of the circle just touches the center of each side.[3] This hold at the wall, which continues to give the horse a little support, will make the new task easier for it at the beginning. Once it has assumed the bend corresponding to the circle and travels precisely on this circular track, the circle can gradually be made smaller, but only in stages, so that the greater flexion to be assumed by the horse does not increase too suddenly. In young horses whose skeleton is still sensitive and soft this increase must stay within certain limits so that their elasticity is not weakened by too much and continued flexion.

If the circle has reached a diameter of about three horse's lengths, the smaller circles should be ridden in the form of a volte which has the advantage that it can be alternated with a straight line by riding such a volte from the regular track of the whole arena as often and as large as desired. This change in lines, and consequently in the rider's guidance, will simultaneously make the horse more attentive so that the transition to the volte can be considered a step up in the exercise even if it is no tighter than the preceding circles. It is of advantage to use the corners for the first voltes because the horse will then find more support on the wall from two sides. This support from the wall is only imaginary since the horse is not actually able to lean its body against the sloped wall - at least not without endangering the rider as proven sufficiently by unresponsive horses that push against the wall. The wall, however, provides immense support during work because it is not only a reliable guideline for rider and horse but also because the horse worries that it might bump into the wall when it falls outward.[4]

We see how important the activity of the eye is for the reliability of the movement when we consider that a human being with his eyes covered is unable to maintain a straight direction even for a few steps, and it also becomes very difficult on a surface that gives no target point for the eye. The riding arena with its solid delimitation therefore provides great advantages in making the horse flexible and agile by having to turn often although it makes it more difficult for the rider to develop the gaits correctly in green horses, particularly those that are very stiff, and to develop reliable contact; therefore the rider needs more skill and consideration.

After these first exercises in riding small circles facilitated by the walls, such small circles must gradually be further perfected with progressing collection and throughness by practicing them in any size and at any desired point of the arena.

Regarding the manner of obtaining the required flexibility of the spinal column in stages and, in connection with it, the flexibility of the inside hind leg, the basis on which this is possible at all is the securely established *contact*. As long as the young, green horse has not found contact with the reins, the rider is unable to reliably determine either lines on the track or the tempo of the gait and is therefore more or less at the horse's mercy, particularly since there is a great discrepancy between the physical strengths of the two. Knowing, however, that this first prerequisite for reliable guidance, the contact, can be obtained only through thrust from the hind legs, that is, through forward movement, the understanding rider will avoid everything that would counteract this. Like a wise field marshal who tries to evade the superior enemy as long as possible until the necessary reinforcements have arrived, the rider will primarily maintain forward movement, regardless of whether the horse changes gaits arbitrarily or deviates from the intended lines. Although he will counteract these irregularities and attempt to stop them, he will not do this by active behavior but by passive behavior in that he gradually returns the horse to the correct track by giving it only slight hints with his hands and through skillful distribution of his weight. In this way the horse remains calm, learns not to squander its strength through resistance and gains confidence and contact. The lighter the seat and hand actions and the finer the rider's feeling, the greater will be his success because it enables him to always remain in harmony with his horse and to maintain the coincidence of the centers of gravity of both bodies so perfectly that they seem to become one. For these reasons it is a very serious error to leave the first rides on young horses to unskilled and rude riders.

In the arena, as already mentioned, the corners constitute the first difficulties in keeping the movement regular. The unbent horse, following the straight direction, will go too deep into the corners and then be unable to turn out of them because it lacks the flexibility this requires. The rider must therefore artificially round the corners in that, with his reins and the skilled application of his weight, he indicates the direction to be taken by the horse. In this case I assume that the reins are carried short enough that they securely enclose the neck and the still inexperienced horse without any self-carriage can always feel them.

[141]

The action of both reins required for a turn toward the right or left will usually make the horse slow down so that it becomes necessary to increase the driving leg aids already before and perhaps also during the turn, possibly reinforcing them with the whip if the horse initially does not pay sufficient attention to the leg aids in order for the thrust that is so very necessary to be available. The reins must restrain as little as possible. Instead, both hands should produce a short, hinting pressure toward the inside, with the inside rein acting more sideways as if it wanted to bend head and neck. Simultaneously, the outside rein, acting slightly toward the inside and somewhat in opposition, prevents too much yielding to the bending rein and rushing into the turn. It also guides the outside shoulder toward the inside.[5]

If the rider skillfully reinforces these aids with his seat by not only putting more weight on the inside stirrup but also by gently turning his upper body and moving his outside shoulder forward correspondingly, the horse will obey this triple signal and perform its turn with hardly any flexion but flowingly and without slowing down. Perhaps it will initially lean more on the hands because it tries to replace the support that it temporarily loses when its hindquarters do not follow properly, or it will perhaps begin to rush or change gaits in response to the greater driving of the aids. Both need not be considered especially as long as the major conditions, sufficient thrust and contact, remain in effect.[6]

The young horse quickly tires from lively and irregular movement and will then return to a quiet pace on its own. Initially only the trot should be used, in a moderate but active tempo, without in any way attempting to artificially position the horse. The pace should be natural, diligent, and in no way collected. To rest the horse, the trot should frequently alternate with the walk and a canter should not be excluded in principle if young, lively, and agile horses voluntarily take it up. It should then not be furthered by the seat and the aids but it should also not be forcibly suppressed by slowing the horse down. The rider should wait for the trot to be resumed with his body in a quiet position. The canter should be continued until the horse voluntarily drops back into a trot.

Unfortunately, the above described natural procedure will often not be followed; instead, an incorrect, active elevation as well as an excessively bent neck will be the deviation. In both cases thrust is limited before it has been properly developed and the horse will be robbed of its natural carriage. It is therefore not surprising if, with such treatment, the horse sometimes pushes against the wall and sometimes toward the inside, or it ultimately completely stops moving unless movement is forcibly maintained by rude punishment. But this will ruin the spirited young animal, perhaps not forever but certainly for a long time, because its first impressions, just like those of humans, are always the most lasting.

I repeat again that the securely established contact, that is, the correct tension in the reins for the gait, can be obtained fastest and easiest only with the horse in its natural carriage. This carriage does not necessarily mean the carriage that each individual horse happens to take on at the moment and attempts to maintain, but generally the carriage on the shoulders which the horse usually tends to assume more or less because of its natural structure and tendency to be lazy. If it has such a tendency, it should be left in it. If, however, its conformation mandates that it carry its head and neck too high, one should attempt to produce a lower position through seat aids and guidance.

If a secure contact is firmly established and the horse moves forward with determination in response to the whip and leg, the rider should initially utilize this to teach the horse to move correctly and straight along the wall. Every green horse is guided on the track along the wall in such a way that its outside foreleg remains as close to the wall as its outside hind leg. But this puts it into a crooked position because its shoulders are narrower than its hips. To overcome this fault, the outside shoulder must be kept somewhat farther away from the wall than the outside hip so that the inside hind leg no longer steps to the side of the load but straight underneath it. The aids for this work are the same as for rounding the corners, only to a lesser degree but lasting longer and are repeated more frequently. The outside rein must act inward with slight pressure primarily on the outside shoulder, with the inside rein being taken up half backward, half inward. While both legs maintain the pace, the inside leg must simultaneously prevent the hindquarters from escaping inward and must be in contact with the horse's body for immediate action. The predominant effect in this work is thus produced by the outside rein and the inside leg.[7]

Whoever bends his horse contrary to this rule with the inside rein and drives it inward with the outside leg before he has set it straight correctly, will only increase the crooked position in which the inside hind leg steps to the side of the load and will reinforce it. He must not be surprised if he is unable to strengthen and perfect the walk and trot of his horses but instead robs them of more and more of their natural freedom in the shoulders in relation to the work they perform.

If we now increase the removal of the outside shoulder from the wall to the extent that the inside shoulder is positioned just in front of the inside hip, this requires the first degree of rib cage flexion to prevent the outside hind leg from falling out. This position of the horse is the basis for all flexion exercises *on one as well as on two tracks* and is the first stage of the "flexed straight position" of the horse. Let us give this position the name *"shoulder-fore"* once and for all. To assume this position, the rider's outside leg must produce the flexion in the rib cage and must act in the proper opposition to his inside leg and thus at the same time hold the outside hind leg.

To discuss in more detail the important work of bending: As soon as the exercise of *moving the shoulder away from the wall* has taught the horse to obey the outside rein, and the rider is able to keep it straight with the aid of the outside rein, he can begin to let the inside rein have a bending effect. This is accomplished by simply taking up the inside hand repeatedly until the desired lateral flexion of head and neck has been obtained. However, this flexion is correct and useful only if the horse takes it on voluntarily and is not held in it by constant, forcible action of the bending rein. That is the reason why the rider must prevent the horse from leaning on the inside rein or resisting it by alternatingly taking up and yielding with this rein and by frequent opposition of the outside rein, and he must gradually accustom the horse to carrying itself in this position. This the rider accomplishes quickly and securely only by timely, alternating yielding with which he temporarily takes away from the horse the discovered or searched for support, but not by forced pulling which would result only in a dead mouth but not in yielding.

Positioning and bending by holding the reins steady belongs to a later stage of training, namely when the aim is to bend the hindquarters by putting weight on them and to firmly establish obedience to hands and spurs. Nevertheless, even in these first bending exercises, the hands require the active cooperation of the legs, firstly in order to keep the pace fresh and the remaining body straight, and secondly, to bend the entire spine corresponding to the resulting bend in the neck. This then again causes the inside hind leg to step forward underneath the load.

While both legs, supported by the whip, must take care that the pace does not suffer from the activity of the hands, the special action of the inside leg must also produce rib cage flexion. This is accomplished by timely, short, and lively contacts with the spurs, the so-called spur jabs, which initially introduce the young, unconstrained horse to this auxiliary tool the rider has available. If this is done while the horse is moving in a rather lively and fresh gait, the horse needs its four legs as support for its body and cannot use them as a weapon against the rider. At the same time, its attention is deflected from the unfamiliar spur aid by the work of the hands and it will soon become familiar with it and obey it. The need to use the spurs depends on the horse's obedience to the bending rein. As soon as this rein encounters hardness and resistance, the inside leg or the spur must support it because both are inseparable companions in this work. Their finely tuned interaction alone assures success.[8]

The correct moment for using the leg or spur aid is when the horse raises the inside hind leg[9] because it can then not stiffen itself through the leg and the main pillar for resistance against flexion of the entire spinal column is not available. To seize this moment correctly is not as difficult as it may appear because the horse indicates it to the rider in a natural seat by its way of going. The rider's body is caused to swing in every gait in a corresponding rhythm and his limbs participate in the cadenced movement of the gait unless they are prevented from doing so by artificial tensing of the muscles. The hands are moved regularly up and down as the forelegs are picked up and put down and the belly walls cause the rider's lower legs to swing in the manner of a pendulum when the hind legs leave the ground, thus in a way indicating the cadence of the gait.

If you wish to have this demonstrated more clearly, observe the farmer boy riding his draft horse into the watering pond and, on the way home, making it trot or canter; you will then be able to study the natural aids and the mobility of his arms and legs. The pedantic riding instructor takes so much pain and effort to completely suppress these natural movements in his students and make their bodies stiff and motionless.

The principle of teaching the rider to sit as stiff and stretched out as possible in order to give him steadiness and strength in the saddle is the reason that we have so many riders without feeling and equestrian tact. The skilled rider becomes one with his horse since he is sensitive enough to be able to calculate its movements in advance and to properly prepare it for every movement of its limbs through his never absent aids. The unnaturally tense rider, however, always remains a strange, uncomfortable load for his horse, which prevents it from moving with freedom and impulsion. Whoever has gained a feeling for the movement of his horse will instinctively use the hand and leg aids at the proper time. If you don't have this feeling, you will never acquire it but always remain in doubt and uncertainty. It cannot be taught because the moments of leg movement are much too short for the instructor to point them out at the right time and then for the student to give the aid with sufficient promptness.

It is therefore understandable that many riding schools and riding instructors train riders that carry themselves in a dainty position, but they are unable to teach them to regulate carriage and gait of their horses. It is necessary to give a student the necessary steadiness and posture to prevent him from sitting on the horse like a farmer, but one should not take away the agility of his limbs with which he can instinctively feel the rhythm of the gait and thus the proper moment for giving an aid.

It leads to nothing and always goes at the expense of good riding if one worries too much about hitting the right moment for the hand and leg aids since these must result merely from the natural swinging of the relaxed body. Nevertheless, self-observation teaches that hand and leg on the same side must always work together and in a way accompany the movement of the horse's shoulder on the same side. Taking up the rein and the leg aid are in opposition to the forward moving hind leg, the leg aid to enhance its forward movement and the rein aid to move the weight of the forehand backward to load the hind leg.[10]

The degree of the aids and the time and manner of their use depend on the rider's intentions, whether he wants to bend, elevate, or activate. The unexperienced rider will soon find a reliable yardstick for using the aids in their results as long as he knows to apply them in time and in harmony with the movement of the horse.

The unbent horse will initially tend to turn inward when it receives a bending aid because this is the natural effect of the inside rein and leg. Only if the rider prevents it from doing so by the corresponding opposite action of the outside aids, will the horse understand that the only way it can overcome the unpleasant effect of these aids is by bending its body. By yielding to the rein and leg aids, it gradually gains in flexibility. This the rider now utilizes in practice in that he works his horse on curved lines, beginning with the correct rounding of the corners, then changing to a large circle, and perfecting these exercises with smaller circles.[11]

Through lateral flexion of the spinal column, the forehand is directed inward and the inside hind leg is pushed further forward so that both inside legs approach one another, similar to a flexible body being bent by approaching its two end points to each other. The extensor muscles of the bent side are thus relaxed to the same degree as those on the outside are tensed, and the inside legs carry a greater load due to the inward inclination of the center of gravity, the more the outside legs are relieved.[12] Only in this way is the horse able to maintain a regular pace on a circle on which its inside legs perform a smaller circle than its outside legs. It restricts the activity of the inside legs by putting more weight on them and reduces their elasticity to the extent required by the difference in size between the two circles.

Just like the correctly straightened horse is bound to a straight line, the correctly bent horse is bound to a circular line whose diameter is just as reliably determined by the degree of its arc as the circular movement of a carriage can be determined by the angle position of its pole. A rider can ride a perfect circle with his eyes closed, if he is able to maintain the corresponding bend in his horse by feeling. The bend can only be correct if each individual vertebra of the entire spinal column participates so that the spinal column precisely covers the part of the circle that corresponds to its length. It also requires, however, because it is natural, that the legs move in synchronism and with regularity, so that the gait can be used as a reliable yardstick for evaluating the bend. If the inside legs step forward too much compared to the outside legs, the bend is insufficient, if they do not step forward enough, it is either excessive or wrong in some of its parts.

The horse is asked to bend by the inside aids, with the rein bending the throatlatch and the neck, while the leg bends the spine. The degree of this bend, however, is determined by the opposition of the outside rein and leg. The correct opposition is therefore the more important part of the bending work and disregarding this principle is the reason why so often success is not forthcoming in spite of all the bending.

The *outside rein* must not only keep the intended flexion of the forehand from being exceeded, it must also maintain it correctly by taking care of the necessary elevation and not permitting the shoulders to escape toward the outside. In addition to a certain, through-going opposition to the inside rein, the outside rein must sometimes elevate by giving collecting pulls and sometimes, by pressing toward the inside, it must protect the outside shoulder against excessive loads. It will generally best accomplish its tasks, if the hand takes on a position at the point where the neck comes out of the withers, from where it can reliably control the bent horse. If, however, it is necessary to provide more effective elevation, the outside rein will have to be carried somewhat higher than the bending, inside rein.

The *inside rein* must not only produce the bend by its stronger action but must also maintain it, with it being desirable for the horse to gradually maintain the bend voluntarily, that is, remain in the attained position even if the rein tension is reduced to normal contact. This is accomplished by alternatingly taking up the reins and yielding so that the horse is unable to find a constant, firm support on the bit but learns to carry itself independently. The bend is removed not only by yielding the inside rein but also by the simultaneous greater action of the outside rein so that contact is not interrupted at any time when the position is changed.

Just as the forehand can be bent only by the correct interaction and coaction of both reins, the spine and inside hind leg can be bent only through the work of both legs. The rider's *outside leg* here has the important task of preventing the hindquarters from falling out, that is from escaping toward the outside. The position of the outside leg is therefore placed further back so that it is closer to the outside hind leg and is able to prevent it more effectively from escaping. In addition, it must give the required driving aids together with the inside leg so that the pace always remains regular and fresh.

The rider's *inside leg* has a triple task: accepting the bend; preventing the hindquarters from escaping toward the inside; and giving the predominant aids for maintaining the pace, which requires much activity and skill and is not compatible with an unchanging, stiff leg position. Its position is more forward, just behind the girth where it is best able to bend the spine. However, it must often temporarily leave this position and act more toward the rear to prevent the inside hind leg from escaping or, together with the outside leg, drive energetically forward.

Just like the inside rein initially requests bending by repeated, stronger pulls and then gradually returns to the usual contact, the inside leg must also initially produce rib cage flexion by repeated lively spur aids, but must then know how to gradually reduce them so that ultimately a gentle, calm pressure is sufficient to keep the horse's spine bent. The rider accomplishes this by weakening his active aids the more the horse has learned to pay attention to and obey the spur. He will therefore change from spur jabs and pricks to a threatening leg position, from it to firm pressure with a tensed calf, until this, too, can gradually be softened to the extent that a gently increased contact of the naturally positioned inside leg is sufficient to cause the horse to yield, be it in the form of flexing its rib cage or moving its hindquarters sideways, depending on the opposite demands made by the outside leg.

The rider must support the work of hands and legs with his seat in that he artificially puts his body into the direction automatically indicated by the correctly bent horse. I refer to the seat in which the inside hip is forward and the outside leg is put further back while the inside leg is put further forward and, when riding curved lines, the inside seat bone carries more weight. This type of seat not only facilitates the assumption of the correct position of the legs but is also an instruction for the horse to move its center of gravity further to the inside to come into coincidence with the rider's center of gravity. As I already mentioned, the correctly bent horse, when traveling on a circle, must put more weight on its inside legs by moving its center of gravity toward the inside. The inside hip is then lowered due to the greater flexion of the hind leg and this lowering gives the rider a natural tendency to lean toward the inside to bring his center of gravity into coincidence with that of the horse so that both bodies become one and are able to move easily and securely on curved lines just like under the straight positioned rider on straight lines.

The artificial carriage of the rider's hips must, however, not be transferred to his shoulders because an advanced inside shoulder puts the outside shoulder back which then gives the rein pulls a direction from the inside toward the outside and the rider hangs behind the movement on the outside. This, however, would counteract the relief of the outside foreleg in that it would drive the forehand toward the outside and put the horse into a crooked position with an incorrect bend. The rein pulls must instead act, at least predominantly, from the outside toward the inside in the direction toward the inside hind leg so that the shoulders always remain forward and the bend becomes correct.

If we observe a correctly sitting rider on a correctly bent horse riding a circle, we see the inner sides of both lowered so that the inside stirrup comes closer to the ground. The greater weight on the inside stirrup is therefore the main purpose of this type of seat and that is the reason that it must be limited to adjusting the hips, while the shoulders must generally be adjusted according to the horse's shoulders if their position is to be an aid for the guiding aids of the hands. Just like the hips determine the position of the legs, the shoulders determine the position of the arms and have a significant influence on their activity. If therefore the rider rides on curved lines where the outside shoulder of the horse describes the larger circle, he must put this shoulder forward and his own shoulder must be put forward correspondingly so that the outside rein is able to give light and comfortable rein aids to relieve and turn. His inside hip and shoulder must then act in the opposite direction, a task that only a few riders are able to accomplish because most of them find it easier and more natural to keep both shoulders in the same position. This type of seat of the rider, to which I will refer in all later lessons on curved lines, and which, for the sake of simplicity, we will call the "bent seat," is correct and well established by the horse's carriage if the rider need no longer maintain it by artificial means such as closing his legs and pushing hip and shoulder forward, but can passively follow the movement; in other words, if there is full accord with the horse.

Although for the sake of clarity, the individual aids for bending have been discussed separately, success will always depend on the correct coaction of all and their prompt mutual support. The rider's feeling is here the only reliable adviser and, until this feeling has been developed sufficiently, the horse's way of going must be the characteristic for the correctness of the work. Generally, inside rein and leg support each other when developing and maintaining the bend, outside rein and leg support each other for elevation, both reins together support each other for producing uniform contact, and both legs together for maintaining the pace and thus contact. The outside rein and the inside leg guide the bent horse toward the outside; the outside leg and the inside rein guide it toward the inside, with forehand and hindquarters being pushed outward or inward simultaneously, while the opposite aids must perform the necessary opposition action.

If the young horse no longer takes on a false bend so easily when moving forward, it will be able to put up more resistance against the bend itself. In particular, it will try to keep its main pillar, the inside hind leg, free to be able, with its support, to stiffen those parts of its body that are by nature most difficult for it to bend. The rider should therefore pay primary attention to the inside hind leg and ask it, through lively action of his inside leg and spur, not only to step forward but simultaneously also to *step toward the outside hind leg*. Only in this way can it be pushed correctly underneath the weight and become flexible.

This rule, as simple as it seems, is the basic rule for all dressage training up to its highest perfection. It constitutes the correct beginning for the highly touted *"shoulder-in,"* or rather it is the basis on which the shoulder-in is established. Without this basis, neither pace nor flexibility of the horse can be perfected, and with it, any obstacle in its way can be overcome. The importance of this rule is so great that all flaws in the gaits and all resistances of the horse, without exception, can be traced back to non-observance of this rule.

Some horses are very skilled in pretending to yield to the bending aids and, in spite of partial bending of the spinal column, leaving the inside hind leg without weight by letting it step inward and to the side. Riders with the correct feeling notice this right away because of the faulty contact and the irregular or dull way of going, primarily, however, because of the fact that the inside hip is not lowered, thus forcing the rider to artificially move his own center of gravity toward the inside, while this should be the natural consequence of the correct bending of the hind leg.[13] Strong forward and sideways driving aids from the inside leg and spur, supported by the whip, in lively paces on corresponding circles are the only suitable means for overcoming such resistance and establishing obedience to the legs.

If a hind leg escapes by letting the croup fall to the outside, this is less misleading since even the unskilled rider must notice such deviations from the position of the horse and can counteract them by stronger opposing action from the outside rein and leg.

During bending as well as turning, the inside leg must generally develop the greater activity. If bending occurs along the wall, the wall, for the most part, takes the place of the outside leg and the latter need act in opposition only at those moments when the horse, while moving through a corner, misses the wall. On the circle, where the croup is free, the outside must travel the longer path and it is therefore incorrect to place the outside leg firmly against the horse's body since it makes the free, forceful movement of the outside hind leg more difficult. If the horse is very stiff in the throatlatch or in other parts of the spinal column, the tendency of the croup to fall out is often very great and if obedience to the spur is not yet firmly established, the rider must sometimes not only hold the outside hind leg with his weight but must also bring the forehand to the outside through the predominant action of the outside rein to thus produce the straight position of the horse to such an extent that no interruption of the pace occurs which would constitute the onset of a reversal or other obstinacies. The horse's forward movement is the surest and most effective means for overcoming its natural resistance if it is expressed in irregular and even incorrect gaits until the rider is able to regulate them.

Because they tire the horse more quickly, irregularities of gait are often the means for making the horse more willing to yield because it will then have to voluntarily use the parts which it has obstinately protected until now in order to support the fatigued parts and must make them available to the rider. Fatigue from forward movement is therefore not only a permitted means but even a major means for the expert trainer to obtain obedience from the horse as long as he is still unable to obtain it through the spurs. It is a natural and simple way since it does not hurt the organism, rather it increases and steels its strength. But it is unnatural and cruel to obtain obedience by suppression of the horse's natural strength as Mr. Baucher teaches us; this is the obedience of a poor, mutilated slave.

The rider should never forget during the above-described work that obedience to leg and rein is synonymous with flexibility of the horse because one is the condition for the other and both can be obtained only uniformly and in stages. Although obedience stems from following hands and spurs, it is foolish to believe that forceful use of these aids would shorten the work. Rather, their misuse will lead to obstinacies which will either ruin the horse or cause the rider to completely lose control. Proof for this is furnished only too often by rude riders who through brute physical force bring about positions and exercises for which they have not sufficiently prepared the horse. Willing and weak horses are then completely ruined in a short period of time, noble and strong horses become obstinate and vicious.

The sensible trainer will divide the bending work into three time sections and will not deviate from this division. The *first section* is the lateral bending of the spinal column discussed in this chapter and the special work with the individual hind legs as the inside hind leg on one track, with riding on curved tracks making the inside hind leg flexible and able to carry more weight. The *second section* is the same, but more difficult, exercise on two tracks, and the *third* involves the bending of both hind legs by means of even greater weight.

Before I conclude this chapter about the first phase of training, I want to call attention once more to the fact that this phase requires only a slight lateral flexion of the horse's body as needed for rounded corners, circles, and voltes, which make its natural movement only a little bit more difficult, but that the horse must have learned from these exercises to correctly put its outside shoulder forward and to step with its inside hind leg toward the outside hind leg in order to be sufficiently prepared for the first lesson of the second phase, namely the shoulder-in. This movement alone proves the correctness of the bend and must serve the trainer as a yardstick for its evaluation. Both conditions are always met simultaneously since one depends on the other and they can both be considered the actual goal of this work.

The rider should make the work easy for the young horse by often changing from one hand to the other for which, as long as he is working on *straight lines*, he uses straight lines. When he changes to curved lines, he changes hands through *curved lines*. When changing position, the horse must always remain positioned between both reins in that the rider gradually yields with the bending rein to the same degree as he takes up the other rein that requests the new bend. He must then just as carefully change the position of his hands, the direction of his body, and with it the weight in the stirrups. Hard, sudden, or insufficient changes of the aids will always be detrimental for contact and with it for the way of going of the horse. To maintain both, the rider should, after the first few exercises on the circle, always change to a straight line before he concludes the movement with a halt. Not only is he able to relinquish the greater bend on the straight line and drive the horse again deliberately into his hands, at the halt on the straight line he is also able to put weight on both hind legs through his rein aids more reliably than would be possible on a curved line and with a greatly bent horse. For the same reasons, the rider should initially not change directly from one position to the other, but should instead give up the old position, secure himself a good contact by developing thrust, which is much easier in the straight direction, and only then take up the new position. The straight position of the horse and straight lines must therefore always be used to regulate and freshen up the way of going of the young horse if it has become insufficient in some way during the first exercises on large and small circles.

The rider should determine the gait and its tempo according to the individual horse. The trot must always be the major gait but the canter may be very useful under certain circumstances and, for many reasons, the walk is also necessary. Generally the principle applies that great thrust increases the horse's resistance during bending; impetuous horses as well as those with much natural stiffness must be worked in quiet gaits and tempos while lazy horses that tend to take on false bends should be worked in fresher gaits and at free tempos.

To briefly summarize this chapter, the proper turn for the horse is based on its capability of precisely taking on the bend and body position required by the line it is to travel, be this line more or less curved, and for the rider it is based on the ability to impart this position to the horse in a well calculated and timely manner.

ENDNOTES

[1] After all, lateral bending work is the only means for acquiring suppleness, that is, the relaxation of all joints and muscles, and thus setting the horse straight, giving it an impulsive way of going, a swinging back, balance, and self-carriage. (Hans von Heydebreck)

[2] These aids will be that the rider, once he has initiated the turn in the manner indicated on Page ?? [Pages 5-6 of the translation of this chapter], places the whip against the outside shoulder, supporting the aid by slight tapping, thus preventing the horse from falling out. As soon as it has gone on the new free line, he drives it energetically forward with both legs and the whip. This procedure is recommended particularly on the right hand, since right turns are harder for the horse because of its natural crookedness. (Hans von Heydebreck)

[3] Riding through half the arena is very difficult for rider and horse and may produce very grievous problems, while riding a circle hardly ever produces significant difficulties in horses, particularly if they have already been lunged. (Hans von Heydebreck)

[4] Even if the first voltes are ridden in the corners, these tight circles already require a certain amount of collection which the horse cannot possibly have attained in this stage of its training as it has not yet learned to obey half-halts. It is therefore suggested that such tighter turns are initially begun only by reversing in the corner. In any case, the horse should be acquainted with the full volte only at the walk. (Hans von Heydebreck)

[5] The procedure described here cannot yet be used for the first rides through the corners; it is for later. Most importantly, the outside rein must not yet attempt to guide the shoulder on its side toward the inside but must yield to the same degree as the inside rein holds back; both hands must turn inward together with the shoulders. The action of the hands must only be in the form of rein signals that are repeated in the rhythm of the gait, with the inside hand acting more away from the neck laterally toward the inside. The outside hand leads softly and, with equally light outwardly directed rein signals, limits itself to preventing the horse from rushing into the turn. (Hans von Heydebreck)

[6] However, contact must not become hard, the horse must not lean on the reins. This can be avoided if the instructions in the previous endnote are observed and in addition the rider's legs do not drive at the moment when the reins are active but only during the yielding phase. (Hans von Heydebreck)

[7] The statement made here that any green horse is crooked on the right hand as well as on the left hand, that its outside shoulder moves too close to the wall and its inside hind leg moves on the track, cannot be maintained as a general principle. It is true that every green horse is crooked under saddle, initially not only in the riding arena, but also out in the open. At first, it is always crooked in the same direction, usually from the right hind to the left fore, regardless on which hand it moves. Setting the horse straight must therefore be accomplished on each hand. For details about this crookedness see Page 102. (Hans von Heydebreck)

[8] In this phase of dressage training, the interaction of hands and legs must, however, not take place in such a way that both become active simultaneously; this must happen only in a later phase of the training. Initially they must act one after the other: first the hand, when the hind leg is in the air, and then the leg, when the hind leg touches the ground and no resistance is felt in the hand on the same side. (Paul Plinzner)

[9] The process takes place in a somewhat different way since a hind leg cannot become stiff when it is raised but only as long as it is on the ground. If thus the inside hind leg becomes stiff, the spur must release if from the ground, whereupon the rider's leg can ask it to step forward underneath the weight. (Hans von Heydebreck)

[10] As discussed in Endnote 8, the hand must initially act before the leg. In the next phase of training, which relates to bending and putting weight on the hindquarters, the rider's leg must act first, namely when the hind leg is in the air, to urge it to step far forward; the hand acts later, when the hind leg is on the ground, to put weight on it. (Hans von Heydebreck)

[11] The reader should note that the rib cage flexion required for riding on curved lines on one track should be confirmed in the horse by working in the shoulder-fore position along the wall. Whoever wants to skip this preparation and obtain the first flexibility in the horse by riding curved lines, will have to expect great difficulties since the absence of the wall on such lines gives the horse too much opportunity to let its outside hind leg fall out. In practice it will be better to ride curved lines more to test and solidify the attained flexibility, and to do the actual bending work along the wall. (Paul Plinzner)

[12] As discussed and proven in detail before, the center of gravity inclines inward only on a curved track, and this is not due to lateral flexion but only because of the laws of centrifugal forces. (Hans von Heydebreck)

[13] The correctly bent horse may perhaps be able, by relaxing the muscles of its body on the hollow inside, to somewhat lower the rider's inside hip, thus also placing his inside seat bone a little bit lower than the outside seat bone. The horse's own hip, however, can be lowered only on a curved track. Here, again, we see the opinion, frequently proven to be erroneous, that the inside hind leg also carries a greater load on a straight line as long as the horse is flexed laterally. (Hans von Heydebreck)

6. Lessons on Two Tracks

The lessons on *two tracks* include all the exercises in which the horse is forced by its carriage to travel two different, identical lines with its forehand and hindquarters in contrast to the lessons on one track in which the hind legs follow on the same line as the forelegs. The greater the distance between these two identical lines, the more oblique is the direction of the hindquarters relative to the forehand and the more the horse is required, in order to move forward, to step with its inside legs over the outside legs or vice versa.

However, the greater this oblique direction, the more the thrust of the hind legs is adversely affected. Therefore, these lessons require a very accurate feeling on the part of the rider in order not to be misused and have an adverse or deleterious effect on the horse's way of going. We see this confirmed in practice since most young horses are ruined by premature and incorrect lateral movements which initially rob them of their way of going and then make them stubborn through driving aids.

A lateral position of the horse can become a correct movement on two tracks only under two conditions: firstly, the shoulders must always remain forward with the correct flexion, that is, the forehand must precede the hindquarters in the direction of the lateral movement to the extent that it simultaneously receives the necessary forward drive from the movement of the hindquarters; secondly, the hind legs must be brought close to the forelegs through increased collection and thus both parallel lines are brought closer to each other. Only through the greater support which the hindquarters provide for the forehand can the drawbacks of an oblique direction between the two be compensated. Therefore, the degree of the lateral position must always depend on how much the horse can be collected, namely how much its hindquarters can be pushed forward to carry weight. Lateral movements without flexion and collection are always the wrong exercises; they can be compared with the croup falling out or in, as mentioned in the preceding chapter, and produce the same drawbacks. They cause swollen knees and tendons in the horse, splints and injuries from overreaching, and rob it of its movement because its striding leg is unable to correctly step forward over the resting leg.

In any case, it is erroneous to believe that stepping over would make the horse's limbs more agile. Correct lateral movements make the horse agile because they require greater flexibility of the spinal column and the hindquarters, with the lateral movement being a natural consequence but more a side-effect. Generally useful effects of this movement for the joints and muscles of the limbs are a matter of course but it is impossible to regulate and perfect the way of going with them alone. Nevertheless many riders are tempted by this prejudice to practice lateral movements much too early and at too great an angle so that they damage their horses instead of furthering their dressage training. These lessons must instead be begun with the same patience and care and must be perfected and completed by step-wise increases like the preceding exercises on one track, since they are only a continuation of them and serve to solidify the horse's obedience to the hands and legs. They accomplish this to a high degree and thus are very important for every experienced trainer.

If it was difficult already on one track to guide the four legs correctly on their two lines through bends and turns, it requires even more activity on the part of the rider and greater attention and obedience to hands and legs from the horse to keep forehand and hindquarters not only on their separate lines in lateral movements but also aligned with each other in such a way that the thrust of the hindquarters, although moderated accordingly, remains sufficiently active. The thrust is reduced already when riding curved lines on one track since the inside hind leg which supports more weight carries more than pushes, while the outside hind leg still retains its full thrust. In the lessons on two tracks, however, the thrust of the outside hind leg is limited by the oblique direction. The thrust must initially be developed securely, but must then be moderated to facilitate the first degrees of weight carrying also for the outside hind leg. Beginning with the lateral position, the collection of the horse, that is, both hind legs carrying weight, must also begin. This is accomplished for the inside hind leg by flexion and for the outside hind leg by elevating rein aids from the outside rein. Both purposes of this work, flexion and collection, supplement each other and must be adjusted correctly relative to each other. Brought into harmony with each other, they then regulate the ratio of thrust to carrying force of the hindquarters, with the degree of lateral deviation being the best way to accomplish this. Whenever the excess thrust counteracts the loading of the hindquarters, the pace must be moderated by temporarily increasing the angle of the lateral position, while, in the reverse, the angle of the lateral position must immediately be decreased as soon as the pace becomes dull or irregular, indicating that thrust has been suppressed too much.

Collection and flexion enable the horse to correctly move on two tracks. Collection requires an elevation of the forehand which gives the pace regularity and expression; flexion permits effortless, natural stepping over. If now flexion and collection are facilitated by the lateral position, the degree of the lateral position must, however, be carefully adjusted to the degree of the resulting flexion and collection unless the drawbacks of crookedness come into the foreground.

The practical utility of lateral movements is so great that the entire training of the horse can be judged according to the degree of their development. When they are perfected, the dressage training of the military horse can be considered completed. They require complete obedience to hands and legs and a sufficient degree of flexion and collection for the balanced carriage. In this way, the military horse in rank and file is enabled to move easily and accurately in all directions and, trained in this way, it will also enable the rider to always swarm around the front of his opponent to discover his weakest side while skillfully protecting his own.[1]

In addition to good conformation of the horse, the perfect development of the lateral paces also requires perfect riding on the part of the rider. In our times, we see them only rarely in perfection, and these movements are usually considered upper level dressage movements. However, in the opinion of many of today's riders, upper level dressage movements are useless tricks that make the horse unfit for practical use. The old masters, however, saw in them the end of lower level training and the beginning of the upper levels. Their school trot and school canter was the regulated trot and canter in the correct position on two tracks and was always the basis for higher training of their dressage horses. These lessons are of course diametrically opposed to the crooked positions and non-positioned movements that are today considered to be movements on two tracks and are one of the main reasons that, with the poor success of such dressage training, the reputation of our art continues to drop more and more.

May this general observation suffice to make the separate discussion of the individual lessons of this type more understandable and emphasize their importance.

(a) Shoulder-In

For the further development of the horse's flexibility, the shoulder-in has the same importance as "shoulder-fore" and "setting straight" have for its initial development in bends and turns on one track. As we know, "setting straight" is not the unflexed carriage of the horse but the correct position of the hindquarters relative to the forehand and vice versa. *Shoulder-in* is actually a greater shoulder-fore and therefore constitutes the actual core of dressage training in this phase of schooling. Travers and renvers, precise riding through corners, turns of the forehand around the hindquarters, are inconceivable without shoulder-in, namely without the correct flexion and shoulder position required by the true shoulder-in. All mentioned movements can only evolve as the result of a well established shoulder-in.

It is to the great credit of the old French master and writer [de la] Guérinière, and has made him famous, that he recognized the great importance of this school, has perfected and left it for posterity in his work under its present name with a clear, convincing description. However, its actual inventor or discoverer should be considered to be the very famous, unexcelled Duke of Newcastle who achieved his extraordinary successes easily and naturally with the particular characteristic of this movement, namely the forward directed shoulders and the correct weight on the inside hind leg.[2] His contemporaries were able to achieve the same only in part and then always with a great waste of time and effort. The ingenious work left by this great master is proof that he is correctly called the reformer of the beautiful art, which was highly esteemed at the time, and gradually overcame prejudices developed through eccentricity and arrogance that had become the general rule.

The name of this movement already indicates the horse's position in this exercise: its shoulders or forehand should be positioned toward the inside, that is, on the inner line, and the croup on the outer line, thus forcing the horse, depending on the degree of its lateral position, to move its inside legs forward and over the outside legs. This stepping forward and across can be done easily and naturally only if the inside legs are advanced through correct flexion, but the outside legs are prevented from falling out by the appropriate opposition from the outside aids, that is, they are prevented from stepping too far to the side. This movement is developed in that the horse, once it has taken on the correct flexion, turns its forehand to the inside to such an extent that its forelegs travel on the intended inner line on which they will remain just as the hindquarters must remain on the original line. The inside rein, supported by the outside rein, initially produces a turn of the forehand, with both of the rider's legs keeping the hindquarters on the outer line. Once the lateral position has been attained, the lateral movement begins, with the outside rein guiding and the rider's inside leg acting stronger, together with the inside rein, not only to maintain flexion but also to cause the horse to yield, while the rider's outside leg, together with his inside leg, guides the hindquarters and supports the outside rein during collection. Since in this movement the bending inside leg simultaneously drives sideways, it is obvious that the horse, by yielding from this doubly strong aid, will try to escape the flexion by falling out with its hindquarters. The rider must therefore produce the correct opposition to his inside leg by well adjusted use of outside rein and leg to keep the pace regular and not let it degenerate into falling sideways.

In the shoulder-in the rider must therefore often work more with the outside rein and leg and even put his weight more on the outside so as to always remain in control and be able to determine the degree of sideways travel of the horse's outside legs, because the correct and unforced stepping over of the inside legs primarily depends on this. This control of the outer side is produced by collection as well as by greater weight on the outside hind leg, thus limiting its freedom of movement correspondingly. It is therefore a general rule that, when practicing this movement and as long as the outside hind leg is still unflexed, the outside aids must predominate so that this excess weight will generally increase its flexibility. The more this is done, the more the rider will be able to let the inside and outside aids act uniformly until, in the correct and firmly established shoulder-in, he actually no longer requires any visible aids at all but relies only on the gentle effect of the outside rein toward the side to guide the forehand, and the soft hang of the rider's weight toward the inside to drive the hindquarters sideways.

Horses that do not yield sufficiently to the rider's inside leg are flexed insufficiently or incorrectly, usually too much in the neck and not enough in the poll and spine. They must first learn to listen to the spurs. The counter-shoulder-in position is better suited for such correction with strong spur aids than the shoulder-in. With respect to flexion and foot placement and consequently also with respect to the aids, *counter-shoul-*

der-in and *shoulder-in* are exactly the same movements and differ only in that the counter-shoulder-in is ridden opposite to the flexion so that the forehand comes against the wall, that is, steps on the outer line, while the hindquarters are set into the arena and travel on the inner line. In the counter-shoulder-in to the right the horse is bent to the right and moves, forehand against the wall, hindquarters into the arena, by stepping with its inside, that is, its right, legs over the outside, that is, the left, legs, around the track to the left; conversely in the shoulder-in to the left. In this lesson the wall is a support for the rider if the horse presses against his legs, a support that is absent in the simple shoulder-in since the sideways driving leg is on the inside of the track.[3]

I am taking the liberty of discussing the work in counter positions and their gradations in greater detail *in a separate chapter*, since they are too important to be taken care of just in passing.

Just as bending the young horse on one track can be accomplished only by gradual exercises on curved lines and in turns, the shoulder-in must also be developed in stages. In the beginning, the forehand should only be moved about 30 to 40 cm to the inside so that the horse first learns to step with its inside leg not toward but *in front of* the outside leg. This first degree of the exercise is quite correctly called the "trot position" because in this carriage it becomes very difficult for the young horse to break into the canter and it is therefore the safest and most natural means to prevent it from selecting the canter or to return it from the canter to the trot.

Starting from this basis, the lateral position should be increased together with the flexion and with it the demand for the inside legs to step over the outside legs. Never forget, however, that this stepping over is not the purpose of the exercise but is only a yardstick for the correctness of the position. As long as flexion and collection are lacking, the angle of the lateral position must be smaller so that the forehand always remains in a forward orientation. With increasing flexion and collection, the line of the hindquarters approaches that of the forehand in that the hind legs are pushed underneath it. But never, neither in the shoulder-in nor in any other movements on two tracks, should the distance between the two lines be more than 80 cm.

It is therefore a great error if riders, at the beginning of shoulder-in work, force their horses sideways with the inside spur because they believe the yielding to the spur and crossing over are the purpose of the exercise. Such inappropriatenesses bring the uncollected horse even more on its shoulders because the oblique direction of the horse's body takes the support of the hindquarters away from the shoulders more than on a straight line. This can also be seen immediately in the stiff, forced movements of the forelegs which then carry too much weight to be able to be raised and move without constraint. Whoever fails to appreciate the purpose and idea of the shoulder-in will, in his desire to make his horse free in the shoulders through this exercise, make the shoulders stiff instead and the horse lame. The correct shoulder-in as a basic pillar of dressage training does, however, free the shoulders and with them all of the horse's limbs, not by the lateral movement, but through flexion and collection which it requires.

If shoulder-in is considered exclusively as the means for freeing the shoulders in the walk and trot, this is easily explained by the fact that its greater degrees, when the horse's legs truly cross over, do not permit a canter which must be limited to the trot position, that is, a position of stepping forward. Nevertheless the freedom of the shoulders in all gaits is always only the result of elevation, and this in turn is the result of the hindquarters carrying the correct weight. Proper collection thus produces freedom of the shoulders or weight relief for the forehand, regardless of whether this occurs with the horse in a straight, bent, or lateral direction. However, in the young, green horse collection is obtained more easily and naturally if its thrust is initially moderated by bending the inside hind leg on curved lines and later by positioning the hindquarters in a lateral direction relative to the forehand, because too much exertion of thrust is counterproductive to the flexion of the hind legs produced by the weight. Since collection is the essential element of the shoulder-in movement, walk[4] and trot, which are more easily maintained in their appropriate tempo, are the only suitable gaits for this movement until the canter has been sufficiently prepared, that is, until the horse has developed sufficient carriage to canter in an elevated and flexed manner. Then the canter in the shoulder-in position furnishes proof for the correct development of this gait because in it the flexed horse must canter straight. It is therefore the basic lesson to perfect and solidify the jump-like movements of the horse, which we will discuss in greater detail in the respective chapters.

Depending on the horse's talents, particularly with respect to its willingness to go forward, this lesson should be practiced alternatingly at the walk and trot, with the tempo, although lively, being kept shortened.

The forward and sideways movement of the outside feet must be limited sufficiently to enable the inside legs to easily cross over. Free, extended gaits on two tracks are nonsense because they do not permit the necessary flexion to execute them. Instead of free and extended, the movement in the correct shoulder-in will be elevated corresponding to the degree of collection and thus primarily makes possible the easy and pleasant crossing over.

In the shoulder-in work the outside rein is of great importance because it has the dual task of guidance and collection. By acting toward the *inside* it initially guides, together with the inside rein, the shoulders to the inner line and then prevents them from deviating toward the outside, that is, it prevents the forehand from falling out and the outside front leg from stepping too far out and to the side. By acting toward the outside, the outside rein guides the forehand sideways on the intended line and, when weighted with elevating half-halts, it puts weight onto and flexes the outside hind leg. During turns and collection, the outside rein is supported by the rider's outside leg which must prevent the croup from falling out. For guiding, however, the outside rein is supported by the rider's inside leg which must drive the hindquarters sideways in harmony with the forehand which is guided by the outside rein. It is therefore the main task of outside rein and inside leg to maintain forward movement and the correct lateral position, with the other aids acting in opposition, correspondingly and simultaneously. The latter are used stronger or predominantly only if deviations from the correct position occur. Horses which, due to lacking rib cage flexion, tend to fall out with the croup must be worked with a predominant inside rein and outside leg, with the counter-aids having more of a supporting effect,[6] while those horses that tend to escape the correct shoulder position by incorrect flexion in the neck must be corrected with the inside leg and the outside rein and must be driven forcefully into the hands by the coaction of the outside spur.

As long as a horse tends to free itself from the shoulder-in position, which still bothers it and to which it is not yet accustomed - and this will be the case to the degree in which it must overcome physical difficulties - the rider must develop great attention and activity to prevent this with skill and prompt aids and to prevent misunderstandings. His main attention should here, too, be directed toward maintaining regular paces. It is much easier to recover the momentarily lost or given-up position during forward movement than to re-establish an interrupted gait.[7] This gait must be maintained in any way possible, for example, if the croup drops out[8] and if he cannot prevent this with his outside leg supported by the outside rein, the rider quickly leads the forehand toward the outside to the line of the hindquarters. If the forehand is stuck, flexion must be reduced and the hindquarters brought toward the inside to the line of the forehand so that the timely approach to the straight direction always maintains the effect of thrust toward the forehand.

In the lessons on two tracks as in the exercises on one track, the pure tempo of the gait is the yardstick for the correct flexion and contact. In lateral movements this is combined yet with natural, unconstrained crossing over. Any contact of the crossing legs with the supporting leg is proof that flexion or collection of the horse do not correspond to the lateral position it has taken up.

It is therefore a sign of great ignorance if riders force their horses to cross over too much before they are able to collect them sufficiently. If such riders do not have the feeling to recognize the incorrectness of these movements, they would have to simply use their ears to notice the banging together of bones and hooves during the crossover. Instead of removing errors of this type by reducing the lateral direction and increasing collection, they are often augmented because the rider believes that he has to excite the crossing legs by driving more to the side. How should these horses cover enough ground if the legs that are to be crossed over are not sufficiently shortened by added weight?! A pure gait and pure crossing over must always be the guiding thread in this work. They must determine how much the rider must move the forehand forward and how much to restrict the sideways movement of the legs to be stepped over.

In the shoulder-in, where the horse's inside legs step over the outside legs, the rider's inside leg bends the rib cage and simultaneously drives the horse sideways, the correctness of the bend and of the pace depends on the control of the outside hind leg. If this leg escapes toward the outside, not only the bend is canceled but the hindquarters also move ahead of the forehand and there is insufficient forward movement. This is called "the croup falls out," a fault to which horses have a particular tendency in this movement as long as it is difficult for them to take on greater lateral flexion. If the outside hind leg does not drop out but moves only sideways and not sufficiently forward, the forehand not only does not have sufficient support, making elevation of head and neck impossible, contact and with it freshness and purity of the pace are lost as well.

[165]

Such horses creep unnoticeably behind the hand and then slink backwards from their correct lines and out of the correct position.

The first-mentioned serious fault more or less inhibits and interrupts the pace and, because of its unnatural character, soon invites the horse to resist and become disobedient. Only very rude and insensitive riders will force the horse to do it. The second fault, however, easily fools better but still inexperienced riders due to the seeming complaisance of the horse in flexion and lateral movement. These riders are unable, however, to keep the horse either in suitable elevation or precisely on the line. Both faults are prevented or overcome by the correct opposition of the rider's outside leg supported by the outside rein. If the croup falls out the outside hind leg forcibly frees itself and must be pulled back again. This can only be done by the spur if the respect for the spur is already greater than the aversion to the requested flexion. Otherwise the outside rein must moderate the flexion until the spur is able to control the hind leg. More weight on the hind leg transferred from the forehand by means of half-halts from the outside rein and the rider's weight in a seat in which the outside hip is set back will secure success that much faster.

If the second fault occurs, that is, if the outside hind leg does not step forward sufficiently, the outside spur must drive it forward against the forehand, with the outside rein sufficiently holding the weights generated by the exertion of force by this hind leg so that its activity becomes not only a pushing action but also a carrying and supporting action.

In the shoulder-in the rider maintains the correct lateral movement by half-halts in that he uses them to regulate contact, pace, and collection. These half-halts consist in the rider driving the horse forward from time to time in the direction of the lateral deviation as if he wanted to ride it into the arena on one track. He either lets it step forward somewhat, if it is necessary to reinforce contact and counter the horse's tendency to suck back, to then immediately guide it sideways again into the shoulder-in position. Or the rider keeps it on its lines by temporarily holding back with his hands precisely to the same extent as he drives forward with his legs. This produces a purely collecting effect since the forward driven hind legs must now bend under the weight.

Only one means exists to firmly establish the shoulder-in and to avoid with certainty the many errors that it may easily cause, namely to practice it patiently and consistently by slowly advancing to its different degrees. These step-wise gradations of an artificial carriage should serve only as a means to further develop obedience to hands and legs and thus fulfill the true purpose of dressage training. Since flexion and collection must increase uniformly with increasing lateral position as practical results of obedience to the reins and legs, it would amount to skipping a step in the step-wise education of the young horse if, after a laboriously obtained position on one track, in which the nucleus is that the hindquarters follow correctly on the line of the forehand, one were suddenly to change to a body position in which forehand and hindquarters travel on two widely separated lines. Instead, this distance between the two lines must be obtained centimeter by centimeter, and the rider must not tire if it takes him months to thoroughly climb this stepladder.

For that reason, the rider should begin his lesson by directing the horse's outside shoulder to the line of the inside hind leg so that initially the inside shoulder leaves the direction for a single track by the width of the chest. This position should be securely confirmed at the walk and trot on both hands, on straight as well as curved lines. For the next step up, he puts the outside shoulder perhaps five to ten centimeters inward and does not go any further until he fully and securely masters this position as well. In this way, with increasing flexibility, he very systematically increases the angular position of his horse on two tracks. With this increase the movement must become more elevated and its tempo more precise and distinct, with the activity of the hindquarters remaining correct, that is, their thrust remaining unweakened and directed sufficiently toward the forehand. The shortening of the pace as a necessary consequence of increased flexion and collection must not result in a loss of its freshness. This freshness must be evidenced by lively raising and a longer suspension of the bent leg as proof that the body is in secure balance on the supporting legs. It is not the shortening of the pace that is the yardstick for the correctness of the movement but the expressiveness of it, since this is always in the same relationship with collection. An inexpressive, tired way of going is, as always, particularly in this movement, a sign that the hindquarters do not carry sufficient weight or are not sufficiently active under the weight.

For collecting the horse in the shoulder-in, the rider must especially drive the free outside hind leg correctly underneath the load since the inside hind leg is sufficiently secured by the lateral bend and the increased action of his inside leg. In the travers and renvers - may this anticipatory comment be permitted - the inside hind leg must be watched well so that it cannot escape the load by trailing behind or stepping to the side. Therefore, in the shoulder-in, the outside rein and leg must predominate while in the travers and renvers the outside rein and the inside leg predominate during the collecting half-halts.[9]

Just as the rider must proceed with care when increasing the lateral position and must often spend a long time with great patience in the first stages, that is, in the trot position, he should also select the lines with care so that the task is not made unnecessarily difficult for the young horse. As for the bends on one track, the rider should initially use the walls of the arena not only as a guideline but also as a support for his outside leg to prevent the hindquarters from falling out. He should round the corners and thus accustom his horse to the first exercises on curved lines. Once it is able to travel through the corners in a good position, namely while maintaining its correct carriage, only half the arena should be used and, by gradually uniformly rounding the corners, this should develop into the first large circle.

In the shoulder-in, the circle as well as every turn on a curved line require the corresponding behavior of the forehand since the latter must travel on a smaller circle in synchronism with the hindquarters which move on a larger circle. On one track, the correct appropriate lateral flexion and the weight on the inside legs resulted in the regular stepping of the inside and outside legs. In the shoulder-in, however, the forward movement of the forehand, while maintaining this bend, must also be artificially shortened to the extent that the hindquarters are able to follow similarly on a larger arc. This requires a very secure and fine feeling for the right pace on the part of the rider as well as great activity of hands and legs so that not only the horse's four feet travel on four different lines but also in a regular pace. Of these four lines, the inside foreleg describes the smallest circle, the outside foreleg the next larger, the inside hind leg the third largest, and the outside hind leg the outside circle, that is, the largest circle.[10]

It is not too difficult to hold back the forehand by rein action. The main difficulty is to let the outside hind foot step sufficiently far forward and yet keep sufficient weight on it. This must be accomplished by the rider's outside leg which, by prompt opposition, determines the degree of sideways stepping and by driving produces the strides forward and underneath. As long as the outside hind leg cannot yet be held sufficiently steady by putting weight on it, the rider's outside leg, if the horse willingly moves away from his inside leg, must be dually active on lines on which there is no support from the wall, so as to fulfill its dual task. It will be able to do this more easily the less the circular lines of the individual feet are spaced from each other, the less the horse is thus directed toward two tracks because this reduces the required flexion and thus the tendency to fall out.

The movement in the shoulder-in position initially poses three difficulties for the horse: firstly, the horse moves in the direction opposite to the bend; secondly, the greater the flexion, the position of head and neck consequently makes seeing the track more difficult; and finally, the legs that are stressed more by the flexion are the ones that must cross over.[10]

The main difficulty for the rider, however, in the execution of the movement is that the hindquarters are assigned the outermost line. The intensive flexion of the forehand produced by the inside rein requires great obedience to the outside rein which must guide and relieve it. The intensive flexion of the spine requires perfect obedience to the spur which must overcome or suppress the horse's tendency to escape this flexion by letting the hindquarters fall out. The fact that the hindquarters travel a longer path on curved lines, that is, through all turns, requires them to be pushed under greatly toward the forehand in order to shorten this path by approaching the forehand. Regardless of these difficulties, the shoulder-in must constitute the first and basic lesson not alone for the movements on two tracks but generally for correct lower and upper level dressage, because it alone makes it possible to obtain rib cage flexion and flexion of the hind legs most securely and perfectly in stages. If, in addition, work on the circle has already accustomed the individual hind leg as the inside leg to carry the most weight and thus flex the most, it will be more willing, as the outside leg, to carry the weight if it is asked to do so in the travers and renvers or when both hind legs are asked to carry equal portions of a greater weight.

The essence of this lesson is the correct *rib cage flexion*. It requires absolute obedience to the inside and outside spur since the horse must move away from the inside spur and observe the outside spur. The rider should therefore direct his main attention to the rib cage flexion and use it to determine the degree of flexion of the forehand so that the entire spinal column is flexed uniformly. Only then is it possible to obtain quick, direct, and unweakened action of the rein aids on which obedience is based. Riders who deviate from this and do not make the rib cage flexion the nucleus of the exercise, but attempt to obtain the shoulder-in position by putting head and neck to the inside, will put their horses onto the shoulders and behind the aids because they make the required collection impossible and make the neck unsteady due to the false bend.

Horses which by conformation, namely due to long, thin necks, tend to take on false bends must be worked with twice the care in the shoulder-in since they love to escape the rib cage flexion by bending their necks too much. They yield too much to the inside rein and do not correctly move away from the rider's inside leg, thus keeping the inside hind leg unflexed and the weights, which it should be carrying, are pushed to the outside supports whose free movement is thus interfered with. The horse then tries to replace the balance, which of necessity it lost, by using the rider's hand as an artificial support and leans on the outside rein. To get it away again from the outside rein, the forehand must not only be relieved by strong half-halts from this rein but must also be moved toward the inside by energetic turns whereupon the inside leg and spur drive the inside hind leg underneath the load and thus re-establish balance. Such horses must first have their neck position well confirmed before they are taken more extensively on two tracks. They should be worked diligently in the trot position which permits a lively tempo and strong opposition from the outside rein. Both produce secure contact, which is the only means to make the neck steady.

The *trot position*, that is, the degree of shoulder-in in which the inside feet actually do not cross over but step forward only, is not only the most suitable form of this exercise for the military horse but the alpha and omega of dressage training of a horse for military purposes. It is a reliable means for the rider to reduce thrust appropriately at any time and to be able to obtain uniform weight distribution on the inside and outside legs, that is, set the horse straight while it is flexed. With it the rider is able to make his horse secure even in free gaits and to move around in a restricted space. It also enables the rider to prevent or overcome any rushing and irregularities of pace resulting from the escape of the inside hind leg.

By firmly establishing the trot position in all gaits, particularly at the canter in which this is possible only with secure control over the outside hind leg which in turn can be obtained only by the correct weight distribution on both, the lateral flexion of the spinal column and the gymnastic development of the inside hind leg can be realized to a degree which can be considered to be sufficient for the military horse. The trainer who envisages only the training of a horse to serve military purposes should therefore not bother himself and his horse with excessive lateral positions but instead consider the trot position of the shoulder-in and later the canter position of the travers and renvers as the nucleus of his work. To perfect both, that is, to make the horse very familiar with them, he will at times also practice the lateral movements at greater angles. But he should do this only for short periods and at a quiet tempo and always return to a smaller angle position in order to always keep the thrust sufficiently active and thus maintain contact unweakened.[12] He will thus protect his horses against physical and mental damage, will attain his goal securely and quickly and save himself and the horse effort and unnecessary use of energy.

Just as the trot position is essential for the establishment and secure development of balance, the complete shoulder-in is essential for the carriage on the haunches, that is, for upper level dressage. It really belongs more to the latter where the primary object is to securely prepare the turns on the hindquarters and can be obtained only by stepwise increases and only with horses that are naturally able to do it. The true shoulder-in displays the highest possible rib cage flexion and flexibility of the inside hind leg without adversely affecting the proper forward movement. The horse, through its uniform, semi-circular flexion, has the entire front of its forehand oriented toward the inside and its hindquarters are pushed under to such an extent that the tracks approach each other to a distance of 40 to 50 cm. The perfection of the shoulder-in will thus always be dependent on the ability of the hindquarters to carry weight.

The old masters put great emphasis, and rightly so, on this movement and began their presentations always with a dressage trot in the shoulder-in. They not always rode through the corners on two tracks but often used the corners to obtain renewed collection in that they brought their horses onto one track one to two horse's lengths before the corner and pushed the horses through the corners with the full flexion of the shoulder-in, causing initially the outside shoulder and then the outside hip to traverse the outermost angle of the corner. The inside rein and leg guided the forehand and hindquarters into the corner, the outside rein and leg guided them out and resumed the shoulder-in position after the corner.[13]

Shoulder-in enabled their horses to perform all difficult turns promptly and accurately since it urges the inside hind leg to step, without support, directly underneath the weight and, by taking over this weight, to sufficiently relieve the outside hind leg so that its thrust maintains the pace through the turn. If the shoulder-in is thus truly considered the basis for all turns, turns in the shoulder-in are actually quite difficult because the hindquarters must travel the longer path and nevertheless support the forehand. Small circles and voltes should therefore be ridden in the shoulder-in position only after entirely sufficient preparation in order to keep the horse from going onto the shoulders and behind the bit.

The rider recognizes the correct shoulder-in, in whatever lateral position it is ridden, through his seat and the contact with rein and legs. Every true dressage movement, that is, every proper carriage of the horse, indicates to the rider what body position to assume from which the aids required to maintain the movement evolve almost naturally and through which these aids are best furthered and facilitated. This also applies for the shoulder-in and all other movements on two tracks. As for bends on one track, the rider will hang slightly inward depending on the degree of flexion because the relaxation of the muscles of the inside, the bent side, causes his inside hip to be lowered somewhat. Doing this, and also due to the flexion in the rib cage, the rider's inside leg comes into closer contact with the horse. This natural contact is already sufficient for the well trained horse to cause it to yield to the rider's inside leg, and the rider then requires no artificial reinforcement of the leg aid to keep such a horse in the shoulder-in position. Once the horse has correctly bent its spine and assumed the lateral position, it is sufficient, in addition to the above-described increased contact of the rider's inside leg, for this leg to gently drop against the horse in the rhythm of the movement.

The rider's outside leg which, due to the set-back outside hip, is carried further back will not find the quiet and natural contact with the curved outside ribs as does the inside leg on the hollow side, and must therefore be kept in contact with this side artificially the more its opposition becomes necessary. The inside rein must take on the bend of neck and jowls corresponding to the rib cage flexion and must be shorter than the outside rein by the same amount as the inner side is shortened by the bend. Only in this way will the inside hand have enough room to perform the required rein aids without constraint, without having to take the shoulder back too much. A certain taking back of the rider's inside shoulder, however, results from the bend of the forehand just as naturally as this bend takes the rider's outside shoulder forward to the extent that the rider's shoulders

[172]

are in the same direction as those of the horse. Only in this carriage of the shoulders will the outside hand be able to perform correctly its triple task, namely: to determine the degree of flexion; to maintain the necessary collection; and to guide the forehand. In the same way, the position of the rider's hip parallel to the horse's hips will bring the rider's legs into the correct position. From this position of the rider, which the correct shoulder-in gives him naturally, the predominant action of his inside leg and outside rein result quite automatically. One can therefore almost say that the rider is able to keep a horse that is correctly flexed in all its parts in the correct shoulder-in with these aids alone while merely having the counter-aids in readiness.

As long as the shoulder-in does not come quite easily to the rider from the described type of guidance, seat and leg position, as they result naturally from the correct contact, flexion of the spinal column and hindquarters, these basics of the movement still harbor inadequacies. Although these inadequacies often become apparent at a quite defined location, it would be foolish to want to overcome them by locally limited exercises. Rather, their origin must always be searched for in the whole and must be overcome by joint activity of hands, seat, and legs. Exercises à la Baucher, in which the hindquarters are forced to yield and turn about the fixed forehand by the sole action of the inside rein and spur, can never serve to prepare or improve the shoulder-in but will only teach the horse to evade the correct performance of the movement through false bends which will bring it behind the bit and thus out of the rider's control in a short time.

The actual essence of the shoulder-in is not the yielding to the inside rein and leg but a lateral movement based on increased lateral flexion of the horse's entire body and regulated by the correct weight distribution to the four legs. Only this correct weight distribution, that is, balance, enables the horse to naturally and freely step forward and over in such an artificial position. This is usually called the *good position of the horse* and is expressed in the correct contact resulting from it. Inadequacies in contact are therefore always a demand for the rider to more correctly adjust the thrust of the hindquarters by moderating or increasing it and to distribute the weight more uniformly.

Riders who have enjoyed the advantage of developing their equestrian feeling on correctly worked horses and under the guidance of a diligent instructor, will have no doubt about its correctness when they check the

[173]

shoulder-in position. All others, however, should take good care that they do not mistake false bends of the neck and skillful falling out of the croup for well established obedience to the inside rein and leg. Such less well trained riders should feel the errors of their shoulder-in work, if not by their contact and seat, at least in that their horse will always have a tendency to leave the prescribed track line to the side and rear and to become irregular. And they should hardly miss that in such a faulty lateral movement they have difficulty sitting correctly because they must try to maintain the direction of their body that would correspond to the shoulder-in artificially and with effort. In a proper dressage shoulder-in, the rider's inside hip is pushed forward and lowered and he thus leans gently to the inside which is beneficial for the sideways movement of the hindquarters, while its incorrect performance, if the horse yields to the side without rib cage flexion, causes the rider's outside hip to urge forward and thus brings him into a direction in which he is not only unable to prevent the falling out, that is, the sideways rearward yielding of the hindquarters, but which even furthers it.

If I now close this important chapter, it is done with the serious admonition to every rider to unflaggingly study the correct shoulder-in and to consider it as the main pillar of all dressage through which he obtains and develops from the horse everything that nature has given it and which also enables him to thoroughly eliminate errors in carriage and movement that have crept in from incorrect work. Riders who fully recognize the wonderful power of this exercise will not trouble themselves with making their horses flexible and obedient by constant changes into the most varied positions because they know that all other movements they need for attaining their intended goal evolve from the correct shoulder-in, be it the well established balanced carriage, be it the carriage on the haunches.

ENDNOTES

[1] In modern warfare, the tasks of the mounted troops reside neither in the attack of closed cavalry ranks nor in individual combat with drawn weapons. Therefore, the military horse of today no longer needs such a high degree of collection. Consequently, lateral movements are used more than ever only to the extent required for each individual horse to overcome physical shortcomings, to bring them into balance and develop self-carriage. (Hans von Heydebreck)

[2] Newcastle rode this movement only on a curved line and called it "head into the volte." Therefore he was justified to speak about the increased weight on the inside hind leg. (Hans von Heydebreck)

[3] A particular advantage of work in the counter-shoulder-in is that in all turns the horse must always turn about the hindquarters. (Hans von Heydebreck)

[4] If here and at other locations relating to work in flexed movements, the walk is recommended in addition to the trot, this is understood to mean a collected but still lively walk which would perhaps better be called a school walk. As long as this school walk cannot yet be ridden, the walk is suitable preferably for teaching the horse the respective movement but for the actual work the only suitable gait is the trot. (Paul Plinzner)

5 To do this, collection must already be advanced to the extent that the horse moving in a restrained trot tempo on one track is able to carry itself in the correct flexion. (Hans von Heydebreck)

[6] In particular, the rider's inside leg will then have to take care of forward movement. (Hans von Heydebreck)

[7] As important as it may be to maintain flowing forward movement also in a lateral movement, one must not lose track of the fact that horses which have difficulty maintaining themselves in balance and therefore tend to rush can recover the lost position only through repeated half-halts. (Hans von Heydebreck)

[8] In this stage of development of dressage training it will be more correct to give up the lateral position, to regulate the pace on the single track, and then re-establish the lateral movement with less angular position than before. (Hans von Heydebreck)

[9] The collecting half-halts are short pulls on the rein that are finely adapted to the cadence of the gait which must, however, be given in alternation with the likewise cadenced, light leg or spur aids, not simultaneously. If thrust is to be reduced, the hand will act first and then the leg, while the leg aid must precede the aid from the hand if the hind legs are not sufficiently active. (Hans von Heydebreck)

[10] In the shoulder-in of a lesser degree of angular position, that is, in the trot position, the four feet do not step on four but only on three different lines in that the outside fore and the inside hind both travel the same line. (Hans von Heydebreck)

[11] As already pointed out several times, the inside legs carry a greater load from the lateral bend only when riding on curved lines. (Hans von Heydebreck)

[12] The practicing of greater degrees of the lateral position, even if they remain within the

limits stated here, always requires secure equestrian tact if they are not to be damaging. It would therefore be better if inexperienced riders and instructors of military dressage units did not concern themselves with greater lateral position angles than required by the trot and canter positions. (Paul Plinzner)

[13] The above procedure, however, is not recommended for the first shoulder-in exercises. At the beginning the shoulder-in should be ridden only on larger circles. It would then be of advantage to round the corners if it is intended to maintain the shoulder-in position. Or one remains in the shoulder-in only until the horse's forehand has almost reached the opposite wall to then guide it through the corner on one track while maintaining the lateral flexion, whereupon the shoulder-in is newly developed out of the corner. (Hans von Heydebreck)

(b) Travers

A correct travers, this should be the premise, can evolve only from the shoulder-in; it must thus include a correct shoulder-in. Everything said so far in general about the lessons on two tracks and particularly about the shoulder-in applies for the travers as well except for the deviations that result from the differences between the two movements. To further illuminate these differences is the main task of this chapter.

Shoulder-in and travers, these two lessons which are so closely related in their characteristics, are different from each other in the picture they offer to the eye: in the travers the hindquarters are initially directed onto the inner line, then the outside feet step forward and over the inside feet, and finally the horse yields to the rider's outside leg and steps forward and sideways in the direction of the bent side.

For all turns on curved lines, the direction of the hindquarters on the inner line requires that the hindquarters are held back relative to the forehand so that both are able to travel their paths of different length simultaneously in the same rhythm of the movement. This holding back of the hindquarters is effected by the rider's legs, particularly his inside leg, while in the shoulder-in the reins, particularly the outside rein, serve the same purpose for the forehand. The forehand must be aided in its movement on the longer path, in part by diligent guidance with both reins, in part by relieving it at the expense of the hindquarters. The more the forehand is relieved, the more agile it becomes and the more ground-covering it will be able to stride if necessary. In this lesson as well, the degree of collection therefore determines the perfection of its performance since collection not only elevates the action, as in the shoulder-in, and thus makes crossing over easier, it also holds back the hindquarters and makes the forehand more turnable. In this lateral movement, as in the shoulder-in, the shorter steps of the hind feet on their tighter line require greater weight on the hindquarters so that these lessons must be considered more difficult tasks.

Although it is actually easier for the horse's outside legs to step over the inside legs because the legs of the unflexed side are freer and the lateral movement is enhanced in the direction of the bend, the yielding of the croup into the bend results in other difficulties. It not only increases rib cage flexion and with it stress on the inside hind leg, it also drives the outside hind leg more underneath the weight if the lesson is ridden correctly. Because the bending rein and the rider's sideways driving leg work in opposition to one another, the yielding of the croup in this lesson is much more difficult and cannot be forced in the young horse as in the shoulder-in. Instead, it must evolve from the shoulder-in and can be considered, so to speak, its result because the correct and fluent flexion resulting from the shoulder-in is the only thing that can overcome the obstacle placed against yielding to the rider's outside leg.

During training the travers may therefore serve the rider as a test for the shoulder-in. The more willing the horse gradually appears to be in the travers the more secure it has become in the shoulder-in. It is, however, a serious error if riders force their young horses into unprepared travers positions or alternate them regularly with the first shoulder-in exercises, because the incorrect travers positions have an even more adverse effect than those of the shoulder-in. In the shoulder-in the outside hind leg always remains free and is kept moving forward only by its thrust as long as it is directed in some way toward the weight, but in the travers the inside hind leg escapes the load by escaping toward the inside and thus overloads the outside leg in such a way that its thrust is interrupted. Irregular, restrained paces and lack of contact are the direct consequences and this to a much greater degree than if the croup falls out in the shoulder-in. They easily give rise to the most stubborn resistances because they are always produced by the escape of the inside hind leg.

As in the shoulder-in where the rider's inside leg has to take care of rib cage flexion and guidance of the hindquarters, in the travers the inside rein must simultaneously produce flexion of the forehand and its guidance. The rider's outside leg leads the hindquarters, that is, produces its lateral position, with the rider's inside leg acting in opposition to provide not only rib cage flexion but also to watch the inside hind leg in order to hold it strictly on its assigned line. Inside rein and outside leg must therefore provide guidance and forward movement in the lateral position; the aids of opposition produce flexion and collection. As long as the latter two have not yet been sufficiently attained and confirmed, the rider must practice his travers more with the outside rein and his inside leg, that is, with the predominant aids of the shoulder-in, similarly to the shoulder-in where he initially required more of his outside leg to fix the outside hind leg. Only when he no longer needs to artificially maintain the flexion in the travers can he consider the travers to be perfect. He will then present the movement seemingly with the inside rein and the outside leg, that is, he will be able to obtain it easily and naturally with the predominant effect of these aids and uniform opposition of the others.

The correct travers is one of the most beautiful movements and most advantageously emphasizes the shape and skill of the horse because initially the shorter line of the hindquarters requires them to carry more weight, giving the forehand more freedom and a pleasant appearance, and also because the forward movement occurs in the direction of the bend, making the bend more natural, with the horse moving its own center of gravity to the inside and being able to see its way. The naturally greater collection and the fact that the outside legs step over the inside legs also permit greater flexion of the forehand since this causes the inside shoulder to be set back further which makes it easier for the outside foreleg to cross over.

Just as the shoulder-in has a furthering and solidifying effect on the young horse's trot, because the horse's inside legs must step forward and across in order to move forward - which is possible to perfection only in gaits with diagonal footfalls and only within limits in the canter so that its lower levels, which belong to the beginning exercises, are also called the *trot position* - the travers is furthering and preparatory for the canter because it requires the inner side to be set forward and both inside legs to reach forward almost simultaneously. The first level of the travers can therefore be considered the *canter position* and it can be used to make it easier for young horses to learn the transition to the canter since in this position it is easiest for them to naturally find the correct footfalls of the canter.

However, the canter position should be employed with care for this purpose and not be misused through premature or unnecessary attempts since otherwise it would result in the drawbacks of an incorrect travers and would teach the young horse to escape with its inside hind leg. In the trot, errors in the travers become clearly evident through irregularities in the cadence and in the crossover steps as well as by a retreat from the correct lines; in the canter, however, the faults are so hidden that only a very sensitive rider can discover them because the canter is naturally related to the travers position.

One should therefore follow the example of the old masters who evaluated the perfection of their movements according to the purity of the gaits in non-related positions and therefore used the trot as a test for the travers and the canter as a test for the shoulder-in. They would not assume travers positions at the canter until these positions were perfectly established in a pure and collected trot tempo and until they had developed the canter in the most perfect trot position so that they had complete control over the inside hind leg. Then they often used the canter in the travers position in order to further develop their horses' hindquarters, particularly their carrying force, and displayed the results of this work later as canter in place and canter pirouettes, which will be discussed in detail in the chapter about the canter.

If the shoulder-in performed to perfection, that is, at a great angle, requires true crossovers of the inside over the outside legs, which should be considered part of upper level dressage because it requires a degree of flexion and collection that exceeds the customary requirements for the training of military horses, this will be even more so the case with the perfect travers since this lateral movement requires even more weight on the hindquarters which move on the shorter line in that the inside hind leg must maintain the flexion of the shoulder-in and the outside hind leg must be directed more underneath the weight. The rider should therefore take particular care to adjust the degree of the lateral position according to the degree to which he is able to collect his horse.

The travers position is obtained in that the rider uses his outside leg to direct the hindquarters of his horse to the inside after it has previously been well flexed in the shoulder-in, while the forehand is held on its line. Both of the rider's legs and the reins then keep forehand and hindquarters in their assigned direction relative to each other by way of mutually adjusted activity, with the rider's legs simultaneously taking care that the pace is lively. The inside rein and leg support each other in maintaining flexion, the outside rein and leg in maintaining the lateral position. This occurs in such a way that the horse is balanced in a manner of speaking by the skillful interaction of inside and outside aids. Since the main effect of the inside rein and outside leg is of course that they hold the horse in its position, they must be supported through strong cooperation of the aids of opposition, that is, the inside leg and the outside rein, when half-halts are employed to overcome a lack of collection and carriage of the horse.

The rider's inside leg and the outside rein are therefore the collecting aids in the travers. Riders who ride the travers by hanging toward the outside and stretching their inside leg away, will harvest even sadder results than those who enforce the shoulder-in with their inside leg alone.

Yet, this is the customary error of all those who demand the lateral positions of both movements without sufficient preparation. Due to lack of flexibility, the horse will be unable to yield easily and willingly and must instead be forced to yield through violent, unilateral use of rein and spur. Perhaps it will yield to the individual spur out of fear but this will not lastingly influence its carriage; it may even teach the horse to escape the rider's control by false yielding.

The understanding rider will therefore prepare his young horse quietly and patiently for the first levels of the shoulder-in by riding curved lines on one track, then developing the movement in stages and not change to the travers until he is able to obtain the first levels of this movement with some certainty. The shoulder-in is entirely sufficient to overcome all obstacles facing the travers because these obstacles are primarily always a lack of sufficient flexibility which the horse gains in an unconstrained manner by performing the shoulder-in.

The correct travers requires greater flexion of the forehand than the shoulder-in, in part so that the center of gravity falls more in the direction of the forward movement and the forehand keeps well forward on its further travel and also to make it as easy as possible for the outside foreleg to cross over. By keeping the steps of the hindquarters shorter on the smaller circles and the freer movement of the forehand on the larger circles, all turns in the travers already approach the collected turn on the haunches and can therefore be considered a preparation for it.

In the correct travers the horse gives its rider the same slight hang toward inside as in the shoulder-in because of the same, greater load on the inside hind leg. But the rider's inside hip is oriented more forward to the same degree as the horse's inside hip is oriented more forward. The rider must now be careful not to commit the usual error of letting his shoulders follow the direction of his hips but instead position his shoulders to coincide with those of the horse.

In the previous lesson I warned against this error. In the travers this warning is even more urgent since in this movement the horse's outside shoulder must be especially forward oriented and must be kept relieved of weight if the lateral movement is to remain a correct forward movement. This can be accomplished only by the active and timely cooperation of the outside rein. The rider should therefore pay less attention to his own inside shoulder and position his outside shoulder in such a way that he is able to let the outside rein act successfully to sometimes turn, sometimes collect.

The rider's hang toward the inside brings his inside leg into closer contact with the horse. If in the shoulder-in this leg acts on the croup to drive it sideways, it must create the opposite effect in the travers which brings the advantage that this always keeps the horse's inside hind leg under control so that it is unable to deviate from its line even by a hair's width. In the shoulder-in, body position and flexion depend on the control of the outside hind leg, in the traverse they depend on the control of the inside hind leg. In the travers in which the forward movement takes place in the same direction as the inclination of the load, the slight increase in body weight on the inside connected with the slight hang of the rider toward that side has a furthering effect on the pace as long as the line of the rider's center of gravity coincides with that of the horse. Once this harmony between the two bodies is disturbed, the rider acts as a foreign body that impedes movement. Likewise, a coinciding but excessive inclination of the common load toward one side, although it increases forward movement in that direction, will interfere with overall balance. A lack of carriage and impure tempo of the gait are signs that this is happening.

In the shoulder-in where the hang of the rider and the inclination of the common load act counter to forward movement, it is necessary not only to have a more decisive guiding activity from the outside rein but also a reduced degree of this inclination to counteract the consequences of this natural fact that interfere with the way of going. For this reason, it will be sufficient to have the forehand in the correct position to keep the well trained horse on its line when performing the travers. The inside rein then needs to act less as a guiding aid than a bending aid, while in the shoulder-in the correct position of the forehand can be obtained only by decisive guidance from the outside rein.

ENDNOTES

[1] The term "redopp" doesn't really have an English equivalent. Zdzislaw Baranowski, in his **International Horseman's Dictionary**, translates it as "canter on two tracks" or, in French, "galop de deux pistes." However, according to all the other statements by Steinbrecht, I am certan that a high degree of collection must be present to call a two-track canter a "redop." (Translator)

[2] It is more advantageous and more appropriate for proper dressage training to initially

obtain the travers position from the shoulder-in position, namely while changing hands through the arena. Even later it is not advisable to develop the travers by putting the hindquarters to the inside; it should be developed from a corner or from a volte because every turn of the hindquarters about the forehand, even if performed while moving, always puts more weight on the forehand and thus adversely affects collection. (Hans von Heydebreck)

3 In the travers the inside leg does carry more weight but not due to lateral flexion, simply because the direction of movement is toward this side. As demonstrated, this is not the case, however, in the shoulder-in. (Hans von Heydebreck)

4 As already demonstrated several times, in the shoulder-in as well the weight of rider and horse must be inclined somewhat in the direction of movement. (Hans von Heydebreck)

(c) Counter-Movements

Each one of the previously discussed movements and positions on curved lines has its *counter-movement*. This is generally understood to mean those movements on curved lines in which the horse must turn in a direction opposite to its bend, that is, if it is bent to the right it turns to the left and if it is bent to the left it turns to the right. Counter-movements are therefore conceivable only as long as the rider works his horse on a circle or in a square; no counter-movements can be developed on straight lines because their difference from the simple movement becomes evident only in the turn. Counter-movements should not be considered something unique and existing individually but rather a continuation of the corresponding simple exercises with a change in the direction of the tracks. They therefore serve to strengthen and improve the simple movement and to securely prepare for the next one. Selected and used correctly, they are of extraordinary effectiveness and often bring the desired results more quickly than dwelling long and unilaterally on the simple movements.

The counter-movements require exactly the same aids from the rider as the simple ones, only under consideration of the changed direction of the tracks. I cannot emphasize enough and state with enough determination that the change of hands must be the only difference between the counter-movements and the corresponding simple movements; position, flexion, and pace of the horse must be the same in both. If the rider always adheres to this principle, he will not only soon understand the counter-movements correctly, he will also be able to correctly distinguish between and arrange all of the different movements. The horse's flexion always decides on which hand it is traveling; if it is positioned and flexed to the right, its right side is the inner side even if that side faces the wall and the horse moves to the left around the arena. In that case we have a counter-movement to the right, and the rider must arrange his seat and guidance precisely in the same way as if he were riding his horse in the same position on the right hand. If thus the horse's inner, flexed side faces the center of the arena, that is, it turns in the direction of·its own bend, this is a simple movement, whatever name it might carry; if, conversely, its inner, flexed side faces the exterior of the arena and it is thus forced to turn in a direction opposite to its bend, this becomes a counter-movement. Turning is then more difficult because the weight is unable to follow the natural inclination of the center of gravity but must move in the opposite direction. For that reason the rider must take care that his horse is in a good position and must prevent, in particular, with timely and increased action of the outside rein, the outside foreleg from carrying too much weight. Of course, these aids, if they are to be successful, must be supported by other, corresponding aids, such as the hang of the rider toward the inside, that is, toward the horse's bent side and, under certain circumstances, the active cooperation of the rider's legs so that the inside hind leg cannot escape. With the correct flexion and increased collection of the horse thus secured, the rider must additionally see that the outside, freer legs travel the inside, shorter lines of the track in all counter-turns. Accordingly they must be held back if the pace is to remain pure and in the correct tempo. The greater effect of the outside rein should therefore not only be collecting and weighting for the hindquarters, it should also be restraining and thus inhibiting for the outside legs. However, in order not to adversely affect the liveliness of the pace, the horse's inside legs should be given relatively more freedom to stride out by way of a well adjusted reduction of flexion so that the harmony of the pace is enhanced. If the counter-movement always requires greater collection from the horse and a shortened pace, one evolving from the other, this sufficiently explains that the movement is a step up from the corresponding simple movement and therefore contributes significantly to perfection and strengthening. Insufficiently and incorrectly performed, however, the counter-movements will for the same reason tend to bring the horse onto its shoulders and into disarray that much quicker. Due to the greater difficulty of the counter-movements, the unskilled rider will soon reveal his insufficient riding skills which the horse will quickly learn to use to its advantage.

After these general comments about the characteristics of the counter-movements, I want to make a general statement about their development and use: they should always evolve from the corresponding simple movements, but only as their continuation under changed and more difficult circumstances. They must therefore follow one another in the same order and each individual movement must be developed with the same care as the simple movements, through stepwise increases of the demands. Only after the horse has obtained a certain security in the simple movement can the rider begin to think about a transition to the corresponding counter-movement and must then initially select the lines in such a way that any short and difficult turns are avoided as much as possible. To make it easier for the horse to understand what is wanted, the movements should initially be developed in such a way that, beginning with the simple movement, and strictly maintaining the position required by that movement, the horse is ridden on a change of hand through the arena or on a large half-circle to begin the counter-movement, with the corners being well rounded and the movement being ridden only for a short time. In the beginning the counter-movement is best ended by a change to the opposite simple position on one track, that is, for example, from the counter-trot position to the right to the simple position to the left in which the horse can then be stopped or halted. If the young horse still appears awkward or restrained in the counter-movement, it should not be forced into it. This should be considered as a sign that the horse has not been prepared sufficiently and the rider should patiently return to the simple movement or practice at the walk if it does not quite work at the trot or canter. Fights in counter-movements are twice as dangerous for the horse's limbs because they interfere very much with the natural movements. With increasing skill on the part of the horse the rider can change more frequently and quickly between simple movement and counter-movement on a continuous line. He must then not forget that at the moment of the change in position he must always change from one hand to the other and consequently must change his own seat.

Counter-work starts with the *counter-position on one track* or the simple counter-bend as the first stage of these movements. Just as the main task in the corresponding simple movement was to teach the horse to move straight while flexed, that is, to let the hindquarters follow correctly the lines of the forehand and, doing that, letting the inside hind leg step toward the outside hind leg, the rider must also take care of this in the counter-bend where he uses the same, already mentioned aids. Since, however, now the horse's inside legs are directed toward the outer line, and the horse's bent side faces the wall, the outside rein becomes the guiding rein through the turn as it must direct the forehand to turn in the direction opposite to its bend. The outside rein, with its stronger, restraining action, must also limit the forward movement of the outside hind leg to the extent that the inside hind leg is able to follow sufficiently. The rider's outside leg must strongly support the outside rein during this procedure so that its sometimes guiding, sometimes collecting aids are always successful. Herein lies the reason why the counter-position is much faster in making the young horse more obedient and attentive to the outside rein and leg. The rider is able to discern this by the horse's better carriage in the simple position. For that reason, skilled riders will be successful more quickly with horses which try to resist flexing by falling out with the croup or pushing against the rider's inside leg and spur if they use the counter-bend as a means for obtaining the simple bend. Since, as we have seen, the outside hind leg can be worked more successfully in the counter-position because it has the inside line, the inside spur can more reliably bend the rib cage and the inside hind leg, which, moreover, is being held in by the wall. A head position toward the exterior of the arena provides greater protection if stubborn horses press toward the wall. But, the rider must have the skill of not letting the pace slow down by skillfully guiding the forehand since this is always the beginning of resistance.

To practice the counter-position, only walk and trot are suitable in the beginning and the latter only in a collected or medium tempo. The counter-canter, to be of any value, already requires the horse to carry itself well in the canter. It is therefore unreasonable for many riders to attempt to school their horses in the counter-canter before they have sufficiently prepared them by turns on a single track in this gait. It demonstrates a complete lack of riding tact and understanding to change their horses into counter-positions when just riding around without particularly considering such counter-positions as such. As mentioned once before, counter-positions always require increased collection and more shortening of the pace and, for turns, special preparation of the horse by relieving its outside shoulder. Very short and sharp turns in the counter-position require great collection, that is, complete bending of the haunches, and are therefore tasks to be performed only by the dressage horse. The military rider should be satisfied with moderately rounded corners, circles, and larger voltes.

The next higher level of counter-flexion we give to the horse through the *counter-trot position* or the *half-counter-shoulder-in*. I have already declared that the corresponding simple movement is the main pillar of military dressage training; this movement is it to a greater degree. Performed and used correctly it is the most effective means in this phase of dressage training not only to strengthen the young horse in the preceding exercises, but also to prepare it well for subsequent lessons. I can therefore not recommend them enough since I have always had reliable and shining successes with them, and I make this recommendation that much more urgently because generally I have very rarely seen them practiced correctly. Their decisive characteristic is, of course, the relaxed forward striding of the inside legs in front of the outside legs while simultaneously maintaining the straight direction in the bend, that is, with uniform weight on the horse's inside and outside legs.

The rider accomplishes this through his soft hang toward the inside and relieving the horse's outside legs by means of his outside leg and rein. With these aids he can carefully watch his horse since it otherwise has full freedom in the counter-movement to fall out with its outside legs, which step on the inner lines, and to let them move ahead of the inside legs. The collecting aids, as already mentioned, permit the rider to work the outside hind leg even more in the counter-bend than in the simple bend. For unskilled riders the release of the outer side, which is always connected with a false bend and an impure pace that are the result of it, is more difficult to detect in the counter-movement because the falling out of the horse's outside legs on the shorter lines might be only very slight but will interfere with the body's balance. The sensitive rider recognizes this error already in its initial development from the harder foot fall of the horse's outside legs due to their carrying more or less weight even if this does not yet interfere with the uniform cadence of the pace. However, the horse's outward urging body mass will not only exert greater pressure against the rider's outside leg and rein, it will soon also attempt to support itself by stepping farther and faster with its outside legs, so that the pace then becomes uneven, rolling, and falling. The horse's inside legs, which are then relieved but restricted in their freedom of movement and are not pushed sufficiently underneath the center of gravity of the body mass, are no longer able to participate in the carrying due to their dull, forced movement and only augment the irregularity of the pace.

The counter-movements of the shoulder-in, in their stepwise sequence, are related to the individual levels of the travers in that the hindquarters are directed onto the inside track line in both. They therefore constitute the most natural preliminary exercise and transition movement for the travers exercises since they already require the same greater weight on the hindquarters as does the travers and they additionally give the advantage to the rider that the horse's flexion facilitates its lateral carriage, while in the travers the opposite is the case. That is the reason why they are so effective in firmly establishing the horse's obedience to the rider's inside leg and spur so that the horse will also yield sufficiently to these aids when they later become the outside aids.

In this phase of dressage training, the rider will often alternate these two movements in such a way, for example, that he changes from the counter-trot position to the right to the half-travers to the left. For such a change he should only gradually change the bend to the right by yielding with the bending rein; then, as soon as the horse is straight, he should push his horse more forcefully against the hand by using both his legs; and then he should change just as carefully to the bend and the travers position to the left. He must then change, in synchronism with the changing bend of his horse, not only his seat but also his weight distribution and also the position of his legs in that, when yielding with the inside rein, he also relinquishes his hang to the inside. Thus the horse gradually becomes straight, with both the rider's seat bones being weighted evenly whereupon, with the bend to the left, he changes to greater weight on the left side. Consequently the rider's legs must also change their position together with the changed direction of his hips so that his right leg, which so far has been positioned more forward - so as to give not only a bending aid but also a sideways driving aid slightly behind the girth - now takes on a rearward oriented position. It becomes the outside leg which limits flexion while the rider's left leg becomes the inside, bending leg and consequently pushes itself more forward, just behind the girth. It should be particularly emphasized in this connection that the nucleus of the entire transition is that, in spite of their changing activity, both hind legs of the horse remain loaded uniformly and work with elastic resiliency. The horse will be very willing to let its previously inside right hind leg, which is now free, act as the outside hind leg, but it will be less willing to put the previously outside leg forward enough to load it correctly. Without this condition, however, the entire bend cannot be correct and the change will of necessity become wrong or insufficient. Therefore the rider's legs should not timidly remain in the lateral position of the counter-shoulder-in; instead the previously outside leg must act more strongly so that this lateral position is gradually relinquished and the horse, when it reaches the straight position, is on one track, perhaps not completely but almost. The rider then utilizes this moment not only to make the pace more lively again but also to prepare himself and his horse for the new position. Developing this new position, it is then easier for the rider to bend the horse's left hind leg by correctly acting and

[189]

counter-acting with his legs, than if, in the lateral position, he must suddenly change his pushing action to a supporting action.

As I already noted elsewhere, this rule applies for all changes from one bend to the other, particularly, however, if these changes are connected with lateral positions, that is, with travel on two tracks. Whoever does not observe this rule will bring his horse into disarray and lose the pace or the correct tempo, or at least impulsion. The old masters with their fine equestrian tact never failed to obey this rule, no matter how quickly the movements of their securely schooled horses seemed to appear. We, with our generally more superficial work, are much more inclined to do so!

Correctly performed, changes from the simple to the corresponding counter-movement bring great advantages. They save the rider many turns that often interfere with the pace in that he is able to continue the good tempo of his young horse, which he perhaps has won only after great effort, without interference on a large track and with support from the wall. The horse will not only remain more attentive to hands and legs if their aids change more frequently, but it will also find its work easier if its position and bend and the activity of its legs are changed from time to time since this also changes the tension and relaxation of the body parts involved. The rider should therefore diligently use the counter-movements but always corresponding to his horse's capabilities. He should begin with simple flexion on one track and the opposite counter-flexion, let the simple trot position be followed by the counter-trot position on the other hand, whereupon he rides the perfect shoulder-in alternating with the counter-shoulder-in and only at the end the travers positions with the renvers or the counter-travers.

The counter-shoulder-in exercises are also an excellent means for the skilled rider to quickly and promptly stop naughtinesses and resistances of young horses. My remarks in this respect regarding the simple counter-bend apply even more here. Impatient or already distrustful horses that tend to obstinately refuse to obey can be prevented from sudden reversals, running away, and sticking to the wall by making the outside hind leg the inside hind leg at the moment when the horse wants to use its thrust to forcibly free itself, thus removing all support from their resistance.

In spite of all the advantages that this, my favorite, movement provides, one should not forget that the best and most effective aid may become ruinous in unskilled hands. It should therefore be used neither without preparation nor at an inopportune time, in other words, only if one knows how to use it correctly. This movement should initially be practiced only at the walk and trot, always at a moderate tempo which gradually must become more lively but at the same time more collected so that collection increases in stages. Only on this basis is it possible to obtain slowly and patiently the correct counter-shoulder-in at the canter, if this position permits the canter at all.

Although the counter-canter will also be discussed in detail in the chapter about the canter, it can only contribute to the understanding of the movements discussed so far if I emphasize repeatedly that the canter in the trot position constitutes such a high development of this gait because it requires perfect control of the outside hind leg and the closest possible approach of the inside hind leg to the outside hind leg. In this way, both hind legs act directly and unattenuated against the weight, which gives the rider an infinitely secure and pleasant feeling because the horse is unable to deviate from its assigned direction by even the breadth of a hair. The counter-canter of this movement requires from the rider, in addition to securely balancing the horse between his hands and legs, a finer and more skillful guidance since turns are extraordinarily more difficult in the counter-position. Whoever is able to confidently present a well-schooled horse in this movement can be called a fine and skillful rider, but whoever is able to school his horse correctly up to this level of training is justified in claiming to be a master of the lower levels of dressage. I need therefore not note that this counter-canter is diametrically different from the type of counter-canter that we see daily in insufficient or incorrect renvers positions performed by laymen and false disciples of the noble equestrian art.

The further development of the counter-trot position to the perfect counter-shoulder-in, like the shoulder-in itself, is actually already part of upper level dressage because this movement requires such a high degree of flexion from the horse and loading of the hindquarters that it cannot be demanded of every horse. But if the military rider wants to provide a basis for the shoulder-in position that is truly entirely sufficient for his purposes he must practice it beyond the trot position simply and in the counter-movement. This he can accomplish only by step-wise increases in his demands with respect to flexion, collection and lateral position. The more obedience to hands and legs is confirmed, the more the horse will be perfected and developed in these three requirements.

Since I have already discussed the means for achieving this in the chapter about the shoulder-in, I want to note here only that in the counter-lessons the movement of the hindquarters must be shortened in the turns the more the degree of sideways displacement directs them onto a tighter, that is, shorter line. This shortening of the forward movement of the hind legs, however, must not reduce their lively, elastically springing activity but must increase it so that they will be able to support the forehand that much more strongly when it describes the larger arc. If the rider's rein aids are to be not only restraining but also correctly collecting, he must support the aids from his hands with lively driving leg aids.

The more perfectly the counter-shoulder-in has been developed, the more secure is the basis for the subsequent travers and renvers. The time spent for this is never lost but is made up more than adequately in these movements. I want to repeat again here that only the shoulder-in with its gradations and variations can produce the other movements securely and correctly. Before the horse's inside hind leg is under control and is able to unreservedly step underneath the load, one cannot speak of pure carriages and paces. However, the rider attains the flexibility of the inside hind leg required for this purpose faster and more securely if he lets the horse step against, in front of, and across the outside hind leg than vice versa, because he more easily feels it if the outside hind leg falls out, and is able to prevent it, than the escape of the inside hind leg.

It is understood that the counter-shoulder-in, like the simple shoulder-in, can be practiced in its higher levels only at the walk and trot and, because of the required collection, also only in a rather restrained tempo. The canter by nature does not permit the actual crossing over of the inside leg over the outside leg and is therefore a physical impossibility in this movement. The highest perfection of the shoulder-in position in the canter is attained if the horse's inside leg steps in front of the outside leg, that is, in the trot position.

The discussion of the counter-positions of the travers, also called the *renvers positions*, shall be initiated with the *counter-canter position* or the *half-renvers*. There are many riders who believe the only counter-position is the renvers, that is, the position of the horse in which its outside legs must step toward or across its inside legs. In their ignorance, they skip the preceding, so very important movements and encounter the renvers exercise unprepared. It will usually be those riders that proceed in this erroneous manner who suffer from the cardinal error against which I have warned so seriously during the discussion of the simple flexion on one track, namely those riders who do not understand how to completely eradicate the crooked carriage which the young horse tends to assume by nature in the first exercises in the arena in its desire to keep its shoulders and hips at the same distance from the wall and which becomes reinforced more and more by excessive use of the inside rein and the rider's outside leg. Riders who have this fault will always tend to do incorrect travers and renvers movements, incorrect because they do not include the correct stepping under of the horse's inside hind leg. On this crooked basis they will never be able to construct a firm structure and, although it seems that their horses are obedient to hands and legs, they will always lack the proper balance and the necessary collection, making their pace restrained, dull, and uncertain.

All levels of the true renvers, based on a correct shoulder-in, are exercises that are beautiful as well as effective for the horse. The renvers is described perfectly by the term counter-travers and is related to the shoulder-in since in both the hindquarters are directed onto the outer track. They are opposites in that the bend in the renvers is taken in the direction in which the horse moves so that it counteracts the sideways movement of the croup. Just like the travers, this movement gives the rider great power to watch the horse's inside hind leg by way of the degree of the bend - insofar as the bend is correct. Since the renvers requires the same high degree of collection as the travers, and the highly loaded hindquarters must step in larger strides than the forehand which is directed onto the inner line, it requires lively and strong work from the horse's hind legs. The rider must therefore use his aids to ask the horse for such work, unless the horse is able to do this due to its natural abilities, particularly in the turns in which the hindquarters must move in a larger arc around a more fixed forehand.

This can be done by the stronger action of the outside rein, which restrains the forehand, and simultaneously by slightly yielding with the inside rein so that an unnoticeable reduction of flexion gives the inside hind leg more freedom, and also by the corresponding lively urging of the hindquarters with the outside spur to make them cover more ground. These further steps or strides must emanate from the outside hind leg, however, and not be caused by the escape of the inside hind leg since the horse would then fall onto the forehand. Therefore the rider must hang slightly inward and provide forceful counteraction with his inside leg to keep the horse's inside hind leg correctly bent under its load. He must never forget that, particularly in the movements on two tracks, the correct collection always depends on the continuing flexibility of the hind legs which can be brought about only by well adjusted, alternating action of the inside and outside rein and leg aids in that the rider directs the horse's inside leg against the outside leg or vice versa.

Just as the canter position of the travers is sufficient for military purposes, so is the counter-canter position of the renvers. However, practiced in the appropriate tempo of walk and trot, it also requires higher levels of the renvers to strengthen it to the point that the lower level paces are secure and pure. The rules for working the various gradations of the renvers are precisely the same as for the travers. In particular, before the start of the canter work, the rider must attempt to establish a secure foundation for the trot in this movement. He should always remember that the trot position as well as the canter position obtained their names from their relationship with the respective gait, and the true test of the confirmation of these basic paces can therefore lie only in the reverse use of both movements. I cannot repeat often enough that, just like the canter gains in perfection the more it approaches the trot position, the trot is also improved the more securely it is developed in the travers and renvers positions. The best proof for the canter not having been practiced too prematurely, too excessively, or incorrectly is always the fact that it has not robbed the trot in these movements of any of its freshness and purity.

When practicing the counter-movements of the shoulder-in on the large track of the arena, the wall constitutes the guideline for the forehand so that rider and horse can comfortably utilize it as such. In the renvers, however, just as in the shoulder-in, the rider's feeling must always keep the forehand a suitable, uniform distance from the wall in order to keep the lateral position of the hindquarters unperturbed. Riders whose feeling is not yet that well developed that they no longer need their eyes to maintain the proper lines will often be seen attempting unsuccessfully to drive the horse's croup sideways in the renvers position although they did not give it the necessary room for yielding by correctly moving the shoulders away from the wall. In particular, they will miss doing this when riding through the corners because they do not restrain the forehand sufficiently and soon enough, and therefore come too close with it to the new side of the arena. In the renvers the rider should direct his primary attention to guiding the forehand so that it is always kept at the same distance from the wall, and using his legs to direct the hindquarters correspondingly toward the shoulders. Just as he adjusts the restraint or rearward escape of the horse in the counter-shoulder-in by decisive forward driving toward the wall, in the renvers he must drive the horse forward into the arena in the direction of his sideways position. With horses that are too willing to yield to the rider's outside leg and do not sufficiently listen to the inside leg, the rider must find support for his inside leg by bringing the inside shoulder as close to the wall as possible so that the hindquarters do not have any room to escape. In such cases, renvers exercises can be used very well to improve the travers and, as an exception, may precede it. The superiority of an understanding and experienced trainer is based primarily on the art of correctly selecting the respective exercises for the natural characteristics and aptitudes of his young horse without anxiously and pedantically binding himself to a certain sequence if exceptions are in order.

The perfect development of the renvers or the counter-travers, just like the correct simple travers, is not a task for lower level dressage training. The balanced carriage, that is, the collection of the horse to this degree is not sufficient. The more, however, the trainer is able to approach this goal - perhaps because his horse has favorable aptitudes or he has sufficient time to work thoroughly - the greater will be the advantageous effect of this movement, the more his horse will gain in exterior beauty and suppleness as well as in elevation and purity of its paces.

The old masters loved and treasured this movement very much and often used it to demonstrate the power and suppleness of their horses, particularly in the canter, the canter in place, and in the courbettes. In times where man still fought man on horseback, this movement had great practical significance because it best enabled the rider to skillfully circle his foe eye to eye. It constitutes the keystone of the movements on two tracks and justifiably so since, with the correct weight distribution of the travers, it is more difficult to keep the hindquarters on the outer line than on the inner line.

Before I close this section of such important movements I want to point out the rule which is applicable for checking the correctness of all counter-movements, that the horse must be easier to turn from them toward the inner, bent side than toward the outside. For example, from the renvers right the horse should be more willing to perform a volte or half-volte to the right than to the left. If this is the case, it is proof that the center of gravity, due to the correct bend, is inclined sufficiently toward the inside legs so that movement in this direction is facilitated. If, conversely, the center of gravity is inclined toward the outside legs, the load on them is too heavy and they are unable to suddenly travel on the longer outside lines; instead, they tend more toward the shorter lines, that is, toward turning to the left in the counter position. Turns in this direction then appear to be easier but are always incorrect. Too much weight on the outside legs can only be the result of incorrect flexion and from this in turn results the insufficient support of the inside hind leg. Such turns will therefore always be performed on the shoulders. It is understood that this proof of the counter-movements can be obtained only on a circle since the full arena does not provide sufficient room toward the outside.

All movements on two tracks, so I admonish my young, eager readers, need diligent practice more than anything else. Performed correctly, they will always have the same, quick and good success, performed incorrectly, however, they will just as quickly rob the horse of its thrust, that is, its way of going. To avoid this, I remind you of the main rule, to place less value on a large lateral angle than on the correct flexion and collection. If the rider, when moving in lateral movements, must anxiously watch that his horse does not bump its nose or heels against the wall, these are no movements on two tracks but only unnatural distortions of these movements brought about by pulling and pushing the horse to the side. In a proper dressage shoulder-in, the outside hip, and in the renvers the inside hip, constitutes the outer limit of the track. In both lateral movements, the heels are protected sufficiently against any contact with the wall in that the hind legs step under very far. In the travers the outside shoulder constitutes this line, and head and neck must be bent to the side to precede the shoulder in the direction of the movement. I refer here to the pictures of the masters of that time appearing in old riding books that were handed down to us. Although these pictures were often technically quite imperfect and often full of errors with respect to the depiction of the horse, we always find the haunches bent and the lateral flexion of the entire body so distinctly expressed that we are justified to conclude that the living originals must have been perfect. If the strong, living image had not impressed itself deeply on every observer, how would these inferior and often clumsy horse painters of that time have been able to capture the expression and depict it!?

ENDNOTES

[1] The center of gravity must always be inclined into the turn, even in the counter position. On a straight line, it is by nature inclined toward the curved side, thus to the outside in the counter-shoulder-in and in the renvers. For that reason, the rider riding the renvers on a straight line, where the direction of movement is in the direction of the hollow side, must put more weight on his inside seat bone so as to remain in harmony with the movement. In a turn, the increased inclination of the center of gravity toward the outside due to the laws of centrifugal forces is added to the natural inclination toward the outside so that the rider must sit more to the inside to maintain the equilibrium. (Hans von Heydebreck)

[2] In the counter-shoulder-in to the right the rider must sit straight because if he were to sit to the right his center of gravity would deviate from the direction of movement which goes to the left. In the travers, however, he must sit to the left because the direction of movement goes to the left. (Hans von Heydebreck)

[3] Although one hind leg does not push more than the other, the important thing here is after all to maintain collection and balance during the change-over, for which both hind legs must carry the same weight and must work with elastic resiliency. (Hans von Heyde-breck)

[4] According to today's views for military utility riding, this is no longer correct. Today's military riders have relinquished all travers movements and the only lateral movement they use is the shoulder-in. To obtain a balanced carriage, which is the goal of the perfected military school, however, travers and renvers exercises in a moderate lateral position are absolutely necessary. (Hans von Heydebreck)

[5] Particularly the thoughts developed in the last paragraph and the conclusions drawn from them indicate clearly how untenable the repeatedly stated principle in this book is that simply because of the lateral bend the inside hind leg carries more weight that the outside hind leg.

The concluding sentence must contribute particularly to this realization in which it is pointed out that the proof for the correct work in the counter-movements can be obtained only on a circle. Imagine the following scenario: The horse moves in the counter-shoulder-in or in the renvers to the right on a line bent to the left on which, following the laws of centrifugal forces, it must incline its body to the left and thus put more weight on its outside legs. But the rider is asked to displace his weight to the right so that "the center of gravity is inclined towards the inside legs." This is an impossible requirement! If the rider meets it, he must inevitably turn his horse to the right, that is, from a line bent to the left to a line bent to the right. For that reason he must change this weight distribution only if he wants to leave the left-bent line to the right, similarly as when riding serpentines without changing the lateral bend. To be able to remain in the counter-bend on the left-bend line, the rider must keep his center of gravity in coincidence with the center of gravity of the horse which is inclined toward the left, that is, he must place his weight to the left as well.

If, however, the rider travels on a straight line in a counter-movement, his weight must enter into the direction of movement, that is, in the counter-shoulder-in right he must sit toward the left, in the renvers right toward the right. Assuming he is in an open field where there are no outside delimitations, the horse, if the lateral movement is ridden correctly, will be more willing to perform a volte to the right from the renvers right than a volte to the left because the rider already sits to the right; to be able to perform a volte to the right from a counter-shoulder-in right, the rider must change his seat to the right; that is, he must move his weight, which up to now was hanging toward the left.

The difficulty of the counter-movements lies in the turns, particularly in the renvers, since the rider, in order to perform a turn to the left from the renvers right, must displace his weight from the right more to the left to be able to follow the movement and remain in harmony with his horse. In order to prevent the hindquarters from falling out, he must also temporarily put weight again on the horse's right hind leg. In addition, the inside and outside hand and leg aids must alternate to support the horse in maintaining its balance during the turn. (Hans von Heydebreck)

7. The Canter

The attentive reader and the fairly well schooled rider, when following the general guidelines established in the preceding chapters, will also be able to train his horse in the canter, but he should again adhere to the main principle: "Ride Your Horse Forward And Set It Straight!" and should not forget that, in the canter as well, collection - by means of which we want to perfect this gait - "must begin from behind in that the rider causes the hind legs to move forward in a lively and decisive manner by doubly active and watchful leg aids and always keeps them positioned in such a way that they act against the center of gravity of the body mass." In addition, the chapters about "Starting the Young Horse," "Bending the Horse on One Track," and "Movements on Two Tracks" contain almost all of the important teachings for the initial development and for the perfection of the canter. If nevertheless a supplemental chapter is devoted to this gait, as it was in the earlier editions, this is done because, at the canter, the activity of the limbs differs significantly from that in the walk and trot, and this circumstance must be considered in the development and perfection of the canter to prevent disadvantageous consequences from resulting.

As already mentioned in the chapter on "Starting the Young Horse," the canter is a natural jump-like gait. It is composed of a series of immediately consecutive strides, with the hooves of one side reaching farther forward than those of the other side. In the freely suspended phase of each stride, the forward and downward directed weight of the horse's body, which acts in the manner of a jumping pole, is initially caught by the outside hind leg and is then transferred to the inside hind leg and the outside foreleg, which track up simultaneously, to finally be transferred back in the ascending direction to again enter the freely suspended phase.

To initially explain what it is that we desire to attain when working the horse at the canter: it is nothing other than to enable the horse, by way of gradually increasing gymnastic exercises, to move with ease in this gait as well in a carriage which is easy on its limbs but ensures the rider of absolute mastery in its use in addition to the best possible comfort. This goal, the self-carriage, can be realized at the canter, just like at the trot, only by getting the horse to relax and setting it straight through bending work, thus creating the basis on which self-carriage is founded, namely the rider in balance with the horse.

However, before we turn to answering the question of how we attain this goal, we must understand when we may begin the canter work and how we initiate it.

In the chapter "Starting the Young Horse," it has already been pointed out that the canter can be of use already in the first phase of the horse's training where the preferred goal is the development of thrust into the hands. This gait, in particular, has the advantage that it best develops this force. On the other hand, a warning was also given not to force young horses to change to the canter, particularly in the arena where they must continuously perform turns. From the advice given there not to interfere with the young, talented horse if it selects the canter itself we can also draw the conclusion that the greater or lesser willingness with which the horse takes up the canter is always the most reliable yardstick for when we can use the canter without doing damage. Conformation and temperament of the horse will be the primary determining factors.

Mentioning the dangers to the soundness of their limbs inherent in premature or faulty use of the canter in young horses, the reasons that force us to restrain ourselves during the first canter should be discussed in greater detail. Although it is doubtlessly correct that the horse's natural canter has the advantage of developing the greatest thrust, this fact and the footfalls inherent to this gait, in which the two diagonal pairs of legs do not, as in the trot, alternate in supporting the load, also result in increased wear of the limbs. The body weight is thrown to the forehand with much impulsion, until the inside hind leg participates sufficiently in carrying the load. The forelegs are thus used increasingly as support and are stressed slightly. This becomes particularly apparent in all turns in the arena, that is, when riding through the four corners. At that time, particularly the outside foreleg is stressed considerably due to being forced to support the entire weight of horse and rider and push it to the side until the simultaneously stepping inside hind leg supports it sufficiently. Consequently, we must first exclude the canter during the first training phase for horses that do not carry themselves sufficiently in natural balance, that is, all clumsy, inflexible horses, and use it only after we have given them, through trot work, the necessary self-carriage and thus the ability to carry the load primarily on the hind legs. Second, we must avoid tight turns in the first canter exercises and therefore use either continuous straight lines or a large circle whose track is curved only slightly. If a large riding ring is not available and one is forced to canter for the first time in an indoor arena, the entire arena should be used with the corners being rounded in an arc-like fashion.

If these facts and recommendations are considered the canter may also be very useful in the early stages of training since it is the fastest way to cause the young horse to willingly yield its back muscles, takes away its barn freshness, and best prevents it from being foolish. All of these goals are also attained with much less effort on the part of the rider than in continuous trot work. Early canter work with young horses may therefore considerably facilitate and accelerate their training.

After these preliminary remarks we want to generally comment on the canter question with respect to two rather roughly opposite opinions we can initialy admit that the teaching of earlier times, according to which the young horse was allowed to canter only after it had found its perfect balance in the walk and the trot, can now be considered to be old-fashioned. On the other hand, we must qualify the statement that early canter exercises are extremely useful in the first phase of training to be accurate only conditionally. For systematic dressage training the trot offers such great advantages that it will probably always remain its main gait. It not only brings about a degree of activity for the entire body of the horse as is necessary for gymnastic work directed toward developing and strengthening all muscles and joints, but it is also not very stressful for the horse since it stresses all four legs uniformly.

Nevertheless, it cannot be denied that an impulsive canter is the main prerequisite for a good riding horse, not only for a soldier or the hunt or race rider but also for those who ride only for pleasure. The canter is preferred if the rider's comfort must be considered, for example for older people or persons of ill health. And it is justified on the promenade where one wishes to present the most advantageous picture and wishes to hold unconstrained conversations. The selection of a riding horse will therefore most certainly be based on a special test of its natural canter, particularly since innate deficiencies in this gait, just as in the walk, cannot be completely eradicated even by the most careful dressage training, while the trot can be improved considerably through appropriate work, if the horse has a good canter and displays a regular and ground covering walk with a pure sequence of footfalls. Count Lehndorf is still correct today, writing in his book about horse breeding, that here in Germany, when we evaluate horses, we pay much too much attention to the trot, a mistake not made by the practical Englishman.

If we now turn to the natural development of the canter, we should note initially that the horse, in freedom, almost always changes into the canter from the trot although it is very well equipped by nature to start cantering from the walk or even from the halt. The transition generally takes place in that the trotting horse moves one foreleg forward more quickly and farther out than the diagonally opposite hind leg in order to support the weight that is being moved forward. This hind leg is thus prevented from stepping forward and transfers the load that much faster to the other two diagonal legs of which the inside hind leg by nature steps that much more forward the more the outside hind leg remains behind. In this way there first results an impure trot, a three-beat movement, from which the horse then falls into the canter. This observation indicates that, if we want to canter a young horse during its first training phases, before we have collected the trot, we only have available the development of the canter that the horse uses naturally. Our aids will therefore reside in restraining the outside shoulder with the outside rein, thus holding back the outside foreleg to give more freedom to the inside shoulder and its foreleg, while our inside leg urges the inside hind leg to step further forward. In addition we relieve the inner side by putting more of our weight on the outside seat bone.

In this connection it should be pointed out right away that the trained horse that starts cantering from the collected trot performs a different transition. Here, after the inside diagonal has been put down, the outside hind leg is caused to step off early by the rider's leg on the same side. Then the inside foreleg first pushes the horse's body into the freely suspended phase and the previously put down outside hind leg reaches the ground first, earlier than the two simultaneously tracking legs of the other diagonal.

In the first development of the canter it is only important to practice a quiet canter depart with the young horse. For this purpose, the rider must not push the horse into the canter with sudden, hard, or even rough aids; instead he must use lightly touching leg aids which are skillfully supported by his voice (clicking) and whip, to repeatedly ask the horse to reach out with its inside legs. Horses that tend to rush away at the trot when they receive the driving aids must always be taken back into a restrained trot tempo before the above-described driving aids are given again.

Likewise, horses that are unable to carry themselves sufficiently in the canter because of insufficient natural self-carriage and therefore soon drop back to the trot must not be pushed back into the canter immediately with stronger aids, but instead must be returned to a quiet, regular trot by means of finely tuned aids before another attempt can be made to make them canter.

In any case, all forcible actions must absolutely be avoided during these first canter exercises. If a horse still appears very awkward, usually because of an unfavorable conformation and, because of it, a lack of flexibility and natural self-carriage, further canter exercises should be discontinued and the horse first confirmed in obtaining carriage and pace at the trot.

Horses that frequently strike out on the wrong lead should also not be forced in any way since this phenomenon is usually based on natural crookedness which cannot be overcome so quickly in this phase of the horse's training. Only cross-cantering must not be permitted. In that case the horse should gradually be returned to a moderate trot tempo and then asked again to canter.

To strengthen the horse in the canter, the canter exercises should initially be very short and should only gradually be extended for longer periods of time after the horse's fitness state increases and the better the horse is able to carry itself naturally without rushing.

If, in especially difficult cases, it appears that the canter would be very advantageous in the first phase of dressage training, while the trainer feels that its use would be objectionable not only for the horse's legs but also for the rider's own safety due to an unfavorable conformation and the resulting awkwardness of the horse, it is advisable to canter such a horse initially on the *lunge line* for a while. This will appear to be of practical use particularly for those horses which, due to their neck being attached in an unfavorable manner and a difficult poll, are unable to find their natural head and neck position, without which cantering is completely useless. Only with a correct head and neck position can the full thrust and push into the hands be obtained.

Warming up the canter on the lunge line is done in the same way as recommended at the beginning of this book for working young horses on the lunge line. The horse is tacked up in a simple snaffle without overcheck, in side reins that correspond to the lateral bend on the intended large circle. After being started at the trot, the horse is then quietly asked to canter. The tempo must be selected so that the pace is maintained by its own impulsion. In this way, all irregularities, false canter, and cross-canter will disappear on their own, particularly since the horse is required to remain on a circle. Its tendency to push its nose out will gradually disappear on its own during this work because the horse will soon let its head and poll drop as a result of the impulsion of the gait. All irregular movements and the greater weight on the shoulders are much less damaging to the legs in this type of work than if the weight of the rider were added. Due to the fact that the circular movement secured by the lunge line is much more favorable for the canter than a straight line, because on the circle the inside hind leg is asked to stride farther forward in any case, and because the somewhat restricted thrust as a result of the bent direction soon dampens any all too stormy forward movement, the horse will also understand much more quickly what it is supposed to do, and much useless effort is avoided.

In any case this work can be used to great advantage in all those cases in which it is required because of the lack of innate balance or because there is not enough time. It saves rider and horse much effort and annoyance. It is, however, more proper for dressage training if in such cases the canter is excluded until the naturally missing balance has been established well enough through systematic work at the trot. This is always the best assurance that the legs are protected. I recommend the early canter only if there is not enough time in difficult cases and the canter must be utilized as soon as possible, or if the canter appears to be particularly desirable because of great temperament difficulties, a noticeably laid-back character, or excessive impetuosity, although physical discrepancies make its use doubtful.

If now this work on the lunge line has developed to the point that the horse is able to easily carry itself in a quiet but impulsive natural canter on both hands, with a moderate attitude and without significant aids, which will generally be the case after one to two weeks, the rider should mount after some preparatory lunge work, but let his assistant hold the still attached lunge line. Usually a very advantageous change will be noticed already at the trot. The horse will take a more secure contact in improved self-carriage. Since the horse has already learned to some extent to quietly strike out at a canter from the trot without a rider, it will obey the canter aids better and, held on the circle by the lunge line, will continue to canter quietly under the rider as long as the rider knows how to put himself in harmony with the horse by way of the correct weight distribution and quiet guidance. Once this has been practiced for a few days with the aid of the lunge line, the line can be detached for a while and attached again until it can finally be kept off altogether. If this goal has been attained, it will be better to ride through the entire arena again since straight lines are more favorable than a circle for the development of thrust which must always remain our main purpose. On the other hand, the circle can be used again whenever it is felt that the thrust should be moderated for a while.

The described procedure allows us to use the canter as a training aid at the beginning of work also for less well conformed horses without raising too many fears with respect to the safety of our person and of the horse's legs. However, if you have the time and want to proceed on the safest possible ground, you should, as already mentioned, avoid the canter until the horse is able to uniformly distribute the load to its four legs at the trot.

Assuming that this is the way the rider proceeds, there is, of course, no general rule for when the time has come to begin with the canter. Following the principle of not cantering until the horse offers the canter itself may in some cases extend the training itself beyond the time available even under the most favorable circumstances. Yet, one should not be satisfied with one's trot preparations until the horse is at least able to perform a canter depart without considerable difficulty. Too slow is always less of an error in the training of a horse than too fast; but one should not go too far with such slowness. Decisive for the evaluation of the stage of training the horse has entered should always be the degree of independence with which the horse is able to go on the bit. In the term "on the bit" the "on" cannot be taken too literally, since when the horse goes on the bit and no longer above the bit, it carries itself and is in a certain natural balance.

If our horse has completed the lessons discussed in earlier chapters and is able to move on the bit at the trot with transitions from the shortened to the medium and the extended trot and back again on one track, we are safe to try the canter and need not worry if initially the horse exhibits some awkwardness. The principle of not asking for anything new until the horse is able to do it on the basis of the preparation it has received is probably theoretically correct but must be qualified somewhat in practice. A certain familiarization period cannot be avoided for every new task and only after the timidity toward the new requirement has been overcome can this principle be applied with justification. If thus a horse with unfavorable talents has been prepared to the point that it is able to perform the above-mentioned trot test, we can be certain to expect that, after a short period of familiarization, it will be able to start the canter without difficulty and maintain a quiet but impulsive natural canter. More than such a natural canter cannot yet be expected nor demanded. Although we have prepared our horse to the point that it is able to move on the bit at the trot, that is, in balance, this has not in any way been confirmed to the point that the horse can also do it at the canter. Careful work in trot exercises only enabled us to achieve what many a favorably constructed horse does naturally.

If we start to canter at this point, we can only expect the natural canter, namely a canter that is performed with more weight on the forehand; that is, not on the bit but above the bit. It would also be completely wrong to assume any type of collection at the canter even if the horse should offer this already against our expectations. Such premature shortening could easily result in irregular strides and the above-described dragging canter. It can therefore not be repeated often enough that, initially, shortening is not the aim but quietness, relaxation, and regularity of the canter.

These characteristics cannot be obtained through long periods of canter but only through repeated quiet canter departs. The horse must not display any restlessness and the required aids must become increasingly finer and lighter. On this basis the rider will then be able to further the canter to such a degree that the horse learns to carry itself in a quiet, natural tempo for longer periods of time. By often yielding with the reins, moving the hands up and down the crest of the neck and patting the horse, the rider must continue to convince himself that he has firmly established the necessary natural self-carriage.

The more the rider is now able to gradually collect the working trot, the more elevated, regular, and therefore more carrying the natural canter developed from it will become. The easier and calmer the horse starts the canter, the better is the first canter stride and the subsequent period of canter. The working canter then develops all on its own from the natural canter.

It must at this point be emphatically stated that, at this stage of training, the rider must never attempt to obtain collection in the canter by more rein action. All attempts in this direction will only result in the horse leaning on the hands, becoming crooked, and losing its natural sequence of strides. The canter, particularly its collection, requires a much more complicated and careful development than the other gaits. Mistakes made here are very difficult to eradicate later, sometimes not at all.

At this opportunity reference should also be made quite generally to the significant difference between the first collecting work at the canter and that at the trot and walk. In the latter gaits the rider obtains the first collection by temporarily changing from a freer to a more restrained tempo, that is by using half-halts. In the canter, however, this collection must be obtained initially only by frequent transitions obtained with fine, light aids, first from a working trot, then from the walk, with the transition to the original gait also being executed with the same light, carefully measured aids.

After the collection at this gait has been improved, another transition is made to the canter, again by adhering to the above points regarding the aids, and this procedure is repeated several times. When the horse begins to understand the aids, which must gradually become finer and gentler, the intervals between half-halts and canter departs can become shorter. In this way the horse will ultimately learn to perform these transitions in response to hardly visible, almost signal-like aids. The better the half-halt, the better is the preparation for the renewed canter depart, the quieter the first canter stride and also the next following strides, particularly if the rider makes the work easier by letting the stride come out and going with the horse's movement and, if the horse does a good job, he does not skimp with his praise.

With such a systematic way of proceeding, which must be carefully adapted to the particularity of the horse and its present state of training, self-carriage and, with it, the horse's throughness will gradually improve so that increased collection can now be attempted directly through special exercises, particularly the riding of tight turns, making the circle smaller and larger, counter-canter, and exercises on two tracks as well as the use of half and full halts.

In all these exercises we must always remember that under all circumstances impulsion must characterize the canter, be it a free canter or a collected canter. In the free tempo, this characteristic is generally more or less secured by the speed of movement, but in the collected tempo we often miss it. If we paint the ideal picture of a canter that has been shortened correctly by way of collection, the spectator must gain the impression that the horse is imbued with the liveliest eagerness to go forward although it does not gain any more ground than is possible for someone riding along at the walk. Such a canter is natural only by the spring-like activity of the three major joints of the hindquarters: the hip joint, the stifle, and the hock. This spring force must be developed to perfection, and the degree of its effect must be determined unconditionally by the rider's hands. The slightest pressure of the bit on the bars must be sufficient to compress the springs which must then retain enough force to be able to immediately elastically open when the pressure is reduced and there is the concomitant relief. It would be foolish to expect such a canter from every horse. Only the noble horse that is willing to go forward, whom nature has given a well conformed forehand, a back of medium length, and, most importantly, strong, flexible, and well-angled hindquarters, will be able to perform it to this perfection. The rider must always have its image before his eyes during work so that he will not be led astray while collecting the canter. If his horse has not been endowed by nature with the physical prerequisites necessary to accomplish this, it is the rider's task to develop them at least in approximation by carefully selected and systematically performed gymnastic exercises. If the horse has no willingness to go forward, there is only one way to develop it: with energetically and promptly used spurs which can do wonders in lazy but noble and courageous horses. If the horse is lacking in blood and courage, if its basic fiber is weak, one should not hold on to dreams because in that case the spurs will bring success only temporarily. Nature calls peremptorily here: cobbler, stick to your last!

The described, ideal collected canter in which each stride gives birth to the next is then also the parent of a free canter in which the rider has the uniquely exquisite feeling that he owns the world. Yielding with his hands and moving his upper body from leaning back to sitting upright and leaning forward relieves the haunches which now will let their thrust work with that much more joy and energy. Nevertheless, they are willing, at any moment, when the reins are taken up and the upper body moves back, to take over the load again as desired. It is such an invaluable, precious feeling for the rider to be able to control the motion mechanism with just his hand, or better yet, only with the ring finger of his hand; the hind legs require no reminders from his legs or spurs because the spirit sets their forces in motion. The weights are distributed as precisely around the rider's seat as they are around the fulcrum of a scale for weighing gold, so that a slight raising or giving with the hand, supported by indiscernible changes in direction of the upper body, is sufficient to put them in motion as desired. This feeling is so wonderful that fate allows mortals to experience it only rarely, just as moments of serene rapture are so very rare in life. Only a horse with exceptional mental and physical talents is able to grant such happiness and this only after sensible and careful training.

Although the art is unable to bring every horse to the point that it comes at least close to the ideal, it does so with some. Often attaining this goal takes a long time which nowadays the trainer is rarely allowed to spend. The expectations in this regard have shifted in such a way that the demands placed on the poor professional are often almost ridiculous. It is not unusual that someone buys from a dealer a completely green or even ruined, unresponsive beast with an upside-down neck and broad, tight jowls and then, as if nothing else were possible, demands from the unfortunate trainer that this abnormal creature be completely trained in a few weeks. With views regarding the training of horses as they evolve from the mentioned example, it is not surprising if many riders believe the above description of the ideal canter to be a great exaggeration because they have never even come close to enjoying such a feeling. The eradication of physical difficulties in training is naturally a very time-con-suming job and cannot be speeded up. Everyone who has ever done some sort of physical exercises should know this. So-called temperament faults, however, if that is what they really are and not only appear to be, can be overcome, if at all, only after years of work. Frequently these faults only appear to be temperament related and are seated in some sort of physical difficulty.

To emphasize even more the picture of the ideal, collected canter and the free canter developed from it, I would like to refer to the two faulty degenerations of the collected canter, namely the shortened running gallop and the clumsy, dragging canter.

The *shortened running gallop* - the reader please forgive this arbitrary designation - is characterized by showing no jump-like strides; the horse does not jump but runs. It simply moves its legs in the sequence of the canter, usually even in a four-beat, under a back that remains rigid and lifeless. If the observer sees a horse cantering this way - and this might make the picture clearer - coming towards him, he is unable to distinguish whether the horse is trotting or cantering because the elevation of the forehand is absent which results when the hindquarters jump correctly underneath the horse. For the rider this canter is characterized by a certain uncomfortably rotating feeling underneath his seat bones which cannot find the quiet seat in the saddle that results from the good canter.

This faulty canter usually is a result of the natural canter being shortened by incorrect elevation from the hands and without a poll that is through. Although this does produce a shortening of the pace, because the secure contact on the bit is interrupted and thus the thrust loses the point against which it must act. But since the back is then bent through, its flexor muscles are simultaneously relaxed too much so that it is impossible for the horse to let its hindquarters work energetically. Horses worked in this way leave their hindquarters far behind the center of gravity with the result that the forehand must of course remain low.

This canter results if collection is desired too early. Usually the use of an incorrect elevation is involved which interrupts the thrust. Obviously such a faulty, shortened canter can be corrected only by first returning the horse to the natural canter in which it lets the thrust act correctly in a natural carriage and finds the correct sequence of strides again. Such horses will always want to take up the faulty running gallop whenever they are asked to collect; they must then immediately be put into a free tempo, and the spurs must ask their hindquarters to become more active. This driving spur, possibly supported by the whip, must also never be absent later, whenever there is an attempt at collection, until it is possible to obtain a few strides in which the hind legs jump under energetically. However, initially, collection should always be limited to only a few strides. These must be performed with the hindquarters pushed under, and then a transition to a freer tempo must follow.

The correction of this faulty canter must follow the rule that no stride can be allowed in which the hindquarters are not working energetically. At this opportunity the warning must be repeated that the rider should not have the ambition, as it is seen too often from laymen and beginners in the equestrian art, to ride the shortest possible canter. The characteristic of the canter must always be its impulsion; shortening at the expense of impulsion is always wrong. One should never forget that the collected canter does not exist to show off; it has a practical purpose, actually a dual purpose. We use the *collected* canter to improve the *free* canter and also to have a means available to exercise our horse in a small space. Both purposes are accomplished only if the horse always has its hind legs underneath itself in lively activity. A short canter with the hindquarters hanging out behind can neither improve the free canter nor can we throw the horse around quickly in it.

The *clumsy, dragging short canter* is characterized already by its name. This degenerate version has something that easily misleads the unexperienced person and tempts him to even favor it instead of suppressing it as it develops. A large number of horses, particularly those which have a lazy temperament and strong hindquarters, offer a shortened canter very early because it favors their way of going and is not difficult physically for them. Such a shortened canter, however, does not have the major characteristics of this type of canter, namely liveliness and impulsion. Nevertheless, it often impresses the non-expert in spite of its flaws which are primarily that the strides follow one another too slowly and each time the horse lands after the freely suspended phase, the forehand is lifted too high, which people often believe is quite pretty. But whoever has felt or at least seen a truly collected canter can see this type of work only as a distortion.

Such a dragging, short canter is useless for the horse's training because the hindquarters in no way work in the manner desired for collection; there is no spring-like compression and springing apart of all three joints of the hindquarters. These joints which are the most powerful joints of the hindquarters, that is, the hip joint and the stifle, whose resilient activity are the major characteristics of a good collected canter, become stiff in this degenerate version and the horse catches its clumsy strides only with its hocks. It is then obvious that such a collected canter must also remain useless for the development of this pace since it neither improves the free canter nor the agile riding around in a small space nor does it ensure the correct activity of the hindquarters.

A uniform and correct contact with the rein will never be accomplished in this dragging canter. Instead the horse will throw its weight more or less into the rider's hands with every one of its awkward strides so that the rider feels a greater weight in his hands in the final phase of each stride. Here again the horse must be asked to correct itself to a lively, free canter from which collection can then be attempted with lively aids from spurs and whip and repeated, cadenced picking up and letting out the stride from the hands, but only for short periods. Spur and whip must ask the horse to spring off lively with its hind legs, while the hands attempt with light half-halts to return part of the impulsion generated by the hind legs back to the hindquarters, and thus make them flexible.

Never must the hand act forcibly in any way or even want to collect because premature reaction from the hands defeats the purpose of these first canter exercises, and, when working young horses, one must reject in principle any idea of collection, particularly at the canter, for longer periods of time, rarely less than four to six weeks. Only after the thrust has been developed fully and correctly, will it be able to securely withstand the later rearward displacement of the load. If thrust is not fully developed, the shortening aids find no support. Premature collection either produces horses without impulsion or disobedient horses. The drive forward is the basis of all dressage training and cannot be established securely enough.

Mostly, however, the apparent necessity of strong hand aids will cause us to wonder whether the use of the canter in this first stage of dressage training was appropriate at all for the horse in question. The reason for this necessity can be found only in either a great lack of skill or lack of natural carriage, caused by physical deficiencies or general physical weakness, or ultimately in a violent temperament. In the first two cases, the use of the natural canter, as mentioned earlier, should not be considered because it would then be connected with too much danger for the forelegs. For a violent temperament we do not need the canter to develop thrust because this characteristic already drives the horse suffi-ciently into the hands in the trot as well. However, in that case, the canter might be useful for such horses because it produces the necessary calming down more quickly than the trot. If a back of considerable strength goes along with the violent temperament, early cantering is definitely advisable because it would take too much time to moderate the temperament at the trot and to get the back to relax, both absolute necessities for being able to begin working at all.

If we now assume that our different horses - the one with favorable conformation which we were able to canter at the beginning of work and the one with less favorable conformation which has already been sub-jected to preparation on the lunge or the more conscientious preparation in trot exercises - are at a stage where we can assume that their thrust has been sufficiently developed and has made our hand a reliable lever, it is now our task to use this lever at the canter as well in order to move the weight gradually more and more backwards until it is distributed uni-formly to all four legs and the horse canters in balance.

If it becomes evident from the above that the rider's task with respect to the canter is no different than for the development of the other gaits, it is obvious that the means to be employed will also in no way be different from those that serve primarily to distribute the weight uniformly to the four legs. Since such discussion would generally be only a repetition of earlier statements, we can be brief here, without affecting our thoroughness.

A uniform weight distribution onto the four legs can be realized only in that the skeleton, that is, the mechanical basis of the machine that is the horse, is given a position which moves the center of gravity, that nature has placed more onto the forehand, further to the rear. This is possible only by lowering the croup through bending the hind legs and having the hind legs step farther forward, and also by elevating head and neck, or better stated, the forehand. Both must go hand in hand and to the extent that the elevation is a result of the lowering of the hindquarters. Any pull on the reins to pull head and neck upward and backward must, because of the yielding poll, act through the spinal column on the hindquarters to put weight on them and thus flex them as long as the rider's legs, supported by spurs and whip, have previously caused them to step underneath the body to such an extent that the through-going rein aids, the half-halts, are truly able to have a loading and thus flexing effect on the hind legs.

If the thus identified goal were to be approached directly, one would doubtlessly encounter significant difficulties and decisive resistance in that the horse would stiffen its hind legs or push against the bit, or both, to make our efforts to naught. We therefore attempt to get the hind legs to step forward and to flex under the load by asking the horse to take on a carriage in which we first ask at least one hind leg to step forward underneath the load and are thus able to make it flexible. Only after each individual hind leg has been made flexible by careful work in these exercises, can we expect that the horse will now be willing to flex both legs under these weight imparting rein aids.

To be able to employ this theory also to perfect the canter, we will first attempt to set our horse straight after it has been prepared one way or the other to let the thrust of its hindquarters produce a secure contact with the hand in a quiet but impulsive natural canter with relaxed poll. To accomplish this we must move the forehand away from the wall with both reins, primarily, however, with the outside rein, to the extent that the inside shoulder is directed in front of the inside hind leg. Doing this, we cause the spinal column to take on a slight bend about our inside leg as it results from the aids given from a bent seat. By thus asking the inside hind leg to no longer step sideways but underneath the load, we prepare the horse to perform turns and to canter correctly on a circle.

Such a circle we will now use with preference for the canter work. If the horse is bent correctly, corresponding to the line of the circle, the circle makes the inside hind leg more flexible as it steps more forward at the canter in any case than the outside hind leg.

The more the work on the circle makes the inside hind leg flexible and willing to change from pushing to carrying, the more the tempo of the canter will be moderated without any further action by the rider, only as a result of quiet, resilient holding of the load with the hands, and contact will become lighter. Because the horse is now a little higher in front of us and a little lower behind us, our seat will become more reclining and thus more comfortable. Yet these advantages will come about only if the horse is cantering on the circle truly in a straight carriage with the correct flexion so that neither the inside hind leg nor the outside hind leg ever acts sideways. Instead both always act directly forward and against the load. The rider must watch this with the utmost care and with all means he has available, that is, with rein, leg, and weight aids, by alternating between positioning the hindquarters correctly against the forehand and positioning the forehand in front of the hindquarters.

Experience shows that most green horses are, in a matter of speaking, right-travers horses and therefore have a tendency to set the right hind leg sideways instead of underneath the load. The trainer can generally eliminate this particularity only by initially riding more shoulder-in-like on the right hand and more travers-like on the left hand, particularly on a circle where there is no limiting and supporting wall. However, this one difficulty usually produces a second, namely that almost always the bend to the left becomes more correct and purer than the bend to the right. This is explained quite naturally by the fact that on the left hand, as emphasized above, it was possible or rather necessary to work with travers-like aids and the travers-like carriage produces pure flexion much more easily than the shoulder-in-like carriage. The trainer must be familiar with this phenomenon, which has already been mentioned in preceding chapters, in order to act correctly when it occurs. This occurrence should not cause him to immediately leave the path he has been traveling. He should instead consider that a bent cane can become straight only by bending it to the opposite side. He should therefore calmly continue to favor a bend to the left with travers-like aids and only after he has been feeling for a longer period of time that the tension on the right side that had been absent by nature has been developed sufficiently, should he change to produce the purity of the bend to the right also through travers-like aids.

As in the development of the trot, the straight, flexed carriage is also the secure basis for success for the development of the canter, since it is the only means for making the hind legs pliable and willing to carry in an unconstrained way. Flexion without straightness, in which both hind legs do not truly step straight ahead underneath the load, can naturally not fulfill this, its major purpose. To be able to work successfully, the trainer must have a quite infallible feeling for this, and this feeling he can acquire only if he sits in a soft seat that conforms to the horse's movements. However, the travers-like aids in the shoulder-in and the shoulder-in-like aids in the travers, the smooth transitions from travers-like aids to shoulder-in-like aids and vice versa, are the only way to establish a reliable foundation for the straight and flexed carriage of the horse in preparation for true collection.

If we keep this in view as a guideline when developing the canter, then the canter will no doubt also become gradually more collected, softer, more comfortable, and more pleasant to the eye without the rider having to resort to forced and strenuous attempts at shortening which always have an adverse effect on the purity and freshness of the pace. If exercises on curved lines are used, one should always remember that these exercises can serve their purpose only if the full development of thrust into the hands has previously been realized; only then do the springs of the hindquarters gain the strength to remain effective even under load.

In this phase of training in which we attempt to collect the canter by bending, one should not forget to interrupt the work from time to time by a free forward gallop on a straight line in order to revive the thrust and ensure the correct contact by letting the horse stretch into the hands. Otherwise the springs will inevitably lose their resiliency after some time. The rider will notice this very clearly when his horse, depending on the conformation of its neck and poll, either creeps behind the bit or goes above the bit. If the trainer notices this phenomenon, which is always based on an incorrect procedure, it is absolutely necessary to completely cease any collecting work for the time being and to ride forward with energy until the thrust has been revived to the extent that the horse goes correctly on the aids and pushes away from the hands. The correct contact, based on this going toward the hands and pushing away from the bit, must under all circumstances be the prerequisite for any collection. A horse which goes above or behind the bit, may it perform a figure eight in the shortest possible canter and in the smallest possible space without changing leads or three strides to the left, three strides to the right, has not become one iota better for practical use by learning these tricks. Performed without the correct contact, the most beautiful canter exercises do not provide the slightest assurance that the horse will not go completely out of control on a fast ride.

The canter is a gait which very easily leads the unexperienced rider to incorrect shortening attempts. Not only is it a very widespread prejudice that a shortened canter is the touchstone of dressage training, the majority of horses also soon learn to escape correct work by incorrectly shortening their gaits. It can therefore not be repeated often enough to all aspiring trainers: "Not *shortness* but *impulsion* characterizes a good collected canter." However, impulsion is inseparable from correct contact. Therefore, the rider who canters more forward will do more for true collection than the rider who puts his horse to sleep in an incorrectly shortened canter.

"Riding forward" has today become such a generally known term that it appears to be superfluous to discuss it any further. Nevertheless, I cannot banish the fear that perhaps some people still misunderstand me since "riding forward" in the sense of a stable manager is by no means synonymous with "riding fast." A horse that goes forward in our sense must have secure contact "on the bit." That a horse that is "behind the bit" is not "on the bit" will be clear to anyone just as generally the term "above the bit" is also not easily misunderstood. Yet only too frequently one encounters confusion between the two terms "leaning on the bit" and "on the bit". When admonishing someone, "Your horse is not on the bit," one might receive the reply, "I wouldn't know; I can hardly hold it." The pressure on the hands is considered to be a sign of the horse being "on the bit" while the opposite is true: the horse that is "on the bit", even if it puts weight into the rider's hands because of the action of thrust, will not make this weight an uncomfortable load because the horse has previously gained confidence in the rider's hands. The resistance developed by the horse "leaning on the bit" produces an uncomfortable, dying feeling in arms and hands which must never be produced by even the fullest "contact." A firm contact, which may be necessary under certain circumstances, must never become hard or rigid; it must remain soft. The light contact must then develop from it very gradually. Any horse that is "on the bit" must be through and must have yielded its poll.

The yielding of the poll must never be attempted and achieved directly, that is by actively putting the horse on the bit with the hands, but by impulsion generated by the hind legs. In order to enable this impulsion to travel unimpededly toward the front into the mouth and cause the horse to push away from the bit, the path to the bit must be clear which is possible only by taking away the tension from all body parts there between. This is accomplished with bending work in conjunction with riding forward, as clearly developed in the preceding chapters. A transmissive poll must be expressed in that the horse is always willing, when asked by its rider, not only to move its head closer to its neck by yielding in the poll but also to immediately move it away from the neck again by pushing its nose forward. The neck must be made freely mobile in both directions, forward as well as backward, and also to the sides, if it is to be considered "through."

The position of head and neck taken on by the horse after it yields in the poll will differ from horse to horse depending on its conformation and also on its degree of training; no absolute standard can be established. Even on the thoroughly trained horse the position of head and neck must always be adapted to the degree of collection and must never prevent it from maintaining its balance, that is, its self-carriage. The freer the pace, the freer must be the carriage of the entire horse, and the longer must be the frame it fills out. A head carriage with the "nose vertical" which is often identified as the ideal head position, even if a horse with favorable conformation is able to take it on without adverse effects in the highest degree of collection, must never be maintained after a transition to freer paces; as soon as the thrust increases, the nose must spring slightly forward and the neck must be stretched more.

The horse that carries itself in balance, in self-carriage, in which thrust and carrying force are developed to such a degree that the rider is able to determine the effect of both forces at will, will itself correctly select its head and neck position according to the tempo of the gait and will usually exhibit a head position in which the nose is slightly ahead of the vertical. Since, however, it can have developed its self-carriage only after all its muscles and joints had been loosened, it is also through in the poll and will be willing, when requested by the rider, to move its head temporarily into a more vertical position. If, however, the nose is already in a vertical position, it must go behind the vertical with every shortening pull on the reins; in such a position, neither self-carriage nor throughness are completely ensured. If the horse's conformation is unfavorable and does not permit sufficient bending of the haunches and, as a result, no elevation of the forehand, the horse will always tend to put its nose behind the vertical. As discussed in the chapter on bending the neck, it will never find a pleasant and uniform contact with the curb bit and consequently can be guided securely only with snaffle-like bits.

When correcting horses that go above the bit and hollow their backs, it will usually be unavoidable that their nose initially goes behind the vertical. It will then always be the rider's task to get such horses to stretch again by riding them forward and to reject any idea of collection until the horse has accepted the bit, again going forward, and carries itself in light contact with the reins.

It is probably obvious that a few words should be said at this opportunity about auxiliary reins that help put the horse on the bit since such reins are often used for correction. Generally the use of all auxiliary reins, without exception, is dangerous because they too easily mislead the rider. Any auxiliary rein for putting the horse on the bit, whatever name it might have, actually works well only if it doesn't work at all. What Seidler says about the use of auxiliary reins for putting the horse on the bit is the best that can be said about this subject and I would like to refer to it here. According to Seidler, the auxiliary reins for putting the horse on the bit are intended to provide an upper limit beyond which the horse must not go. Their effect must therefore always be limited only to those moments in which the horse tries to go beyond this limit. In that case the forward driving aids must take care that these moments become as short as possible; that is, that the push away from the auxiliary reins happens as quickly as possible. A continuously tight auxiliary rein for putting the horse on the bit is the most disadvantageous thing imaginable because by leaning on it, the horse continuously tensions the lower neck muscles which it should relax. Therefore the continuous use of such auxiliary reins is a sure way to produce an ewe neck. A horse ridden with such auxiliary reins continuously misleads the unexperienced rider by performing all its exercises in a tensioned state instead of in a relaxed state and the horse finally becomes so accustomed to this support that, when it is taken away, the horse loses its carriage and becomes unsteerable. A horse worked in this way will never carry itself, which in the end is the ultimate goal of all dressage training.

Since the temptation of using the auxiliary reins in this incorrect way is very obvious for the inexperienced rider because the horse, supported by it, is able to perform some exercises which it would still be unable to do without this auxiliary means and for which it is not yet mature enough, it is advisable not to use such auxiliary reins for putting the horse on the bit at all, or at least ride without them from time to time to determine whether the rider's work is correct.

To return to the canter after this short digression, I hope that the above statements made it clear what is meant by "riding forward" in the stable manager's sense and that the correct contact "on the bit" - that is, with a yielding poll and without the support of auxiliary reins - must always be a prerequisite for any attempt at collection. As soon as the contact is no longer quite perfect and the horse begins to canter above or behind the bit, it is time to correct the contact by riding forward. If a horse is able to canter on a circle on both hands, in the correct bend, on the bit, it has unmistakably reached such a degree of preparatory collection by bending the respective inside hind leg that we can dare, without danger for impulsion and relaxation of the pace, to gradually shorten the tempo to enable us to ride counter-turns and movements on two tracks as a means for perfecting the canter.

This stage of the development of the canter very easily tempts a less experienced rider to neglect purity and impulsion of the pace in favor of shortening it. It must therefore be repeated once more that the pace must always be the most reliable yardstick for the correctness of our work. As long as the pace is regular and impulsive, in spite of being shortened, we are on the right way; as soon as it loses these characteristics, there is no doubt that we have gone beyond the degree of shortening that is appropriate for the present state of dressage training of the horse. As for all other gaits, this principle always applies for the canter. As soon as irregular, hesitant strides occur from time to time, as soon as the pace becomes dragging or running, we are on the wrong track and must think of changing it quickly in order to prevent these errors from taking root and becoming entrenched.

In an orderly course of dressage training, such incorrect phenomena should of course not appear at all; but even the experienced trainer will be unable to completely avoid them all the time. The beginner must therefore not be surprised about such unexpected setbacks. The art of riding is an infinitely difficult art, and no one has fully become its master before age has whitened his brow. There is an unbelievable multitude of means with which the horse sometimes almost imperceptibly resists his trainer and slowly and gradually escapes the full compliance for performing the tasks requested of it. Only the incessant and most attentive study of the characteristics of the horse and the utmost precision of his feeling give the trainer, after long years of hard work, the unmistakable judgement that enables him to predict unevennesses in the path of dressage training and to avoid them. Even with the greatest of care and the most serious diligence, no one should dream that it would be possible to reach the goal smoothly and without obstacles. With every horse you take in training, if it appears to be the most evidently suitable riding horse, be prepared for disappointments, embarrassments, and fights; then you might possibly not lose your good humor; and that is really the most important in all of our work.

Also note: your horse will make progress only if you and it are friends. Even if you fight against his bad tendencies, its natural obstinacy, your dealings with the horse must always be enveloped in an aura of benevolent friendliness. A bad mood, sullenness, impatience, lack of self-control make any true progress impossible in dressage training. Whoever really wants to become a master of the equestrian art must have the ability, in addition to many other good traits, to take pleasure in overcoming difficulties per se, and such difficulties must not put him in a bad mood but, to the contrary, make him happy.

To return to collecting the canter, this, as any collection of a gait, can naturally be achieved by holding back. The restraining aids, however, so as not to simply dissolve the canter, must counteract just as naturally the driving aids that maintain the impulsive pace. To get the restraining aids and the driving aids to coact correctly, that is, to make the restraining aids go all the way to the hind legs and the driving aids to the mouth, it is necessary above all to always keep the horse straight and to prevent it from stepping sideways or from one hind leg falling out. This is the most easily available way for the horse to escape bending its hindquarters. To advantageously counteract this tendency of the horse it will be good to use the whole arena in this stage of canter development since the solid wall is an inestimable aid for controlling the hind legs. To truly take full advantage of the wall, we will ask the horse to take on the shoulder-fore position or the bent-straight position, namely - to clarify this term once more - a carriage in which the inside shoulder is in front of the inside hind leg, but the spine is laterally bent to the appropriate degree so that the outside hind leg is forced, without being able to fall out, to act underneath the middle of the load.

In the canter more so than in the trot, the outside hind leg must be controlled. Its activity determines impulsion and roundness of the strides. These characteristics, which identify the correctly collected canter, can most quickly be re-established, if they begin to diminish in some way, by putting the horse into a slight travers position. The easy continuation of the bent-straight position is the only way to establish the effective coop-eration of driving and restraining aids and thus obtain true collection.

During all of the trot work, this bent-straight position was the basis and the starting point for all exercises with which we intended to establish balance. If it was not possible in that gait to keep the horse in this position by firmly gripping it with hands and legs like a vise, this is even more true for the canter since it offers the horse far more ways to escape the vise by stiffening its back and hind legs, by hopping, or changing leads. Only the correct distribution of the weight in a soft, flexed seat with occasional slight leg or spur aids and maintaining the bent-straight position, is able to re-establish that unconstrained state in the horse that is the only way to obtain a light, softly springing, and regular canter.

In addition to the bent-straight position, the success of the collecting work is determined by the correct ratio of the driving aids to the restraining aids. It is of course impossible to give binding rules for this since this ratio is different for every horse, depending on its temperament and willingness to go forward. To find the ratio of the aids that matches the particularity of the horse is a matter of equestrian tact, and while the experienced, finely educated trainer will certainly hit upon it easily, the beginner should not be vexed if he has to do some experimenting. If it sometimes appears to be miraculous how riders of poor physical strength magically produce much greater performances from their horses than those with the limbs of a Hercules, this miracle is simply explained by the fact that they are the ones who have this equestrian tact that provides them with certainty the appropriate ratio of the aids. This is usually called the "correct cooperation of hands and legs." Such equestrian tact can only be acquired in a soft, flexible dressage seat in which every nerve, so to speak, extends its feelers, and can only be developed to the utmost by long, incessant practice. To acquire such a seat as a permanent, inalienable possession and to maintain it as such should therefore be the diligent, serious striving of any trainer-to-be because then his feeling will also gradually develop to such a fine degree that he will be able to adjust his aids correctly relative to one another. That is all that can be said about the relationship of driving and restraining aids. The end result must be that the canter is shortened by restraining aids but that it is enlivened and kept impulsive by the driving aids.

Aside from the fact that the strength of the aids must always be carefully adapted to the nature of each individual horse, the selection of the correct moment at which they are applied is also of the greatest importance. Both types of aids, the driving aids as well as the restraining aids, must be applied in such a way that they enhance the flexibility of the hind legs. The driving aids cause them to spring off lively and step forward, while the restraining aids put weight on them and thus bend them. As emphasized earlier, the weight of the forehand must never be thrown to the hindquarters without warning. Only a hind leg that is sufficiently driven underneath the body by the rider's legs and spurs is able to accept the load and bend under it; if it has not stepped forward far enough, it will stiffen against it.

This indicates that the driving aids and the restraining aids must not act at precisely the same moment but the ones must always precede the others by a bit. The driving aids must generally be applied when the hind leg pushes off, the restraining aids shortly before it touches the ground.

To apply this general principle to the canter, it is first necessary to understand that of the three beats of the canter stride, the second beat is the one during which the main emphasis lies; a certain calm exists on the inside hind leg and on the outside foreleg, while naturally the other two beats, at which the load is supported only by one leg at a time, are transition beats only. This is the reason why the canter on the forehand is particularly hard on the outside foreleg. The perfection of the canter depends mainly on the fact that the inside hind leg tracks correctly undern ath the load at every stride and willingly bends under the load to then strongly push it off. A not yet fully worked horse will almost always try, if the canter is shortened, to escape having to bend the inside hind leg under the load by setting it out to the side, in which case the then only insufficiently supported load is burdened primarily onto the outside foreleg.

This will particularly be the case in the canter on the right lead since the earlier mentioned tendency of almost all green horses to set the right hind leg to the side in all gaits becomes particularly evident here. This is then also the main reason for the frequent lameness and crippling of the left foreleg.

The above shows quite clearly that the shoulder-fore position offers the most advantages for the collection of the canter since it, if the horse willingly submits to it, forces the inside hind leg to step correctly underneath the load. Of course this advantage also occurs if the horse relaxes completely in the carriage and flexion it is given, which leads me to return once more to the fact that any force is completely useless here.

Moreover, one should understand that the regular use of the shoulder-fore position on both hands is appropriate only if nature or training has already set the horse completely straight. Since this, however, is hardly ever the case from nature and, in the stage of training that we are presently concerned with, cannot yet have been accomplished, the wrong natural bend to the right will become evident. I want to remind you of what I have already discussed in connection with work on the circle at the canter, namely that on the left hand a more travers-like carriage will usually be necessary to fix the *then outside right hind leg and thus keep the bent-straight position pure. It is the only one that permits the correct interaction of the aids. But also if, in order to effectively work the inside hind leg, one selects the shoulder-fore position on the left hand as well, one should not forget to maintain the travers-like position in it, that is, to use his hands, legs, and weight distribution to prevent the outside hind leg from falling out.

If we thus attempt to collect the canter by selecting the carriage of the horse in such a way that it offers advantages for working the inside hind leg, we will have to take care just as much that our active aids are directed toward this main purpose. Since any working of a hind leg must begin by using the rider's leg on the same side, supported by spur and whip, to cause this hind leg to step off at the right time and in a lively fashion and to move further forward due to the stimulus exerted onto the stomach muscles, we come to the conclusion that the rider's inside leg must predominate during this work, while the rider's outside leg has the task of reaching a bit further back to watch the outside hind leg and counteract its tendency to escape the bent direction by falling out. The horse itself indicates to the softly and supply sitting rider the moment at which the

[223]

rider's inside leg must act in that its rib cage widens to a certain degree when the hind legs jump under and this becomes clearly noticeable to the softly contacting rider legs. In particular, the further forward reaching inside hind leg will produce its effect on the inside and thus in a way automatically produce this aid from the inside rider leg with every canter stride. The sensitive rider can therefore not help himself but enhance the forward movement of the inside hind leg by softly tapping his inside leg or spur against the horse's body during every stride.

It is the task of the reins to correctly utilize this stepping forward of the inside hind leg underneath the load in order to load it and flex it by means of through-going half-halts which transfer the weight of the forehand to the hindquarters. As we already explained during the discussion of the shoulder-in, the outside rein will here have the primary active role while the inside rein serves the purpose, together with the rider's outside leg, of keeping the bend around the inside leg clean. Here again the horse itself indicates to the rider the moments at which he can elevate the forehand and set it back and thus successfully put the weight on the hindquarters through the use of rearward-inward directed half-halts. These are naturally the moments at which the horse lifts itself up in front while its outside hind leg performs the transition from one stride to the next and takes up the load after the brief moment of suspension. Applied at this moment, the rein aid will express its influence on the immediately successive inside hind leg at the moment it is put down and will bend it by increasing the weight that it has fetched itself.

The sensitive rider will just as naturally see the necessity immediately thereafter to open the compressed springs by removing the weight, that is, by yielding with his hands. This again leads us to the realization that the essence of all good riding is to be found in the soft, pliable dressage seat in which the rider feels the horse's movements and gives the appropriate aids at the proper time as a result of this feeling.

However, the above-discussed aids will become fully effective only if the rider supports them with the correct weight distribution. In this respect, the rider can only be referred to the already repeatedly emphasized principle of distributing his weight in such a way that the gravity lines of rider and horse coincide at any time so that both bodies may truly be considered as one. Since the shortened canter can only be called a collected canter if the majority of the load is carried by the haunches, the rider will keep his upper body slightly leaning back and thus, in the manner required by the increased flexion of the inside hind leg, move his inside hip forward and put more weight on the inside stirrup. Doing this, he must take care, however, that he follows the horse's forward movement well in this position so that his weight at no time inhibits it. This can be accomplished, in particular, by a somewhat forward positioned outside shoulder.

Although in a correct collected canter the horse will indicate this weight distribution to the rider automatically, it is in no way an established fact that he must remain in this position as if bound by a spell. The work with the horse will often give him cause to change his position in order to fix problems that have developed. In particular, he will change from a leaning-back position of his upper body to a leaning-forward position in order to relieve the haunches if he feels that the horse puts too much weight on its hind legs and remains flexed, thus no longer being able to push off the load. This occurs easily in naturally soft and flexible horses. If during this load-relieving forward inclination of his upper body, the inside spur gives its slightly touching aids in the rhythm of the strides, this is one of the most emphatic means to enhance the strong push of the hind legs away from the ground, the so-called trill. Also, if the horse does not sufficiently bend its hind legs under the load, but stiffens up against it - this happens usually if the weight is not transferred to the hindquarters in stages but too suddenly - the rider must not make the so frequently seen error of trying to force the hind legs to flex by further increasing the load. This would only result in the hindquarters continuing the resistance with their strong upper joints and bending only in the fetlock joints or at most also in the hocks which would have a highly deleterious effect on these weaker parts.

The understanding trainer will instead properly recognize the reasons for this action and will try in this case as well to relieve the hindquarters by leaning his upper body forward and increasing the tempo, to then later return the load to the hindquarters gradually in a soft and unconstrained manner.

The lateral distribution of the rider's weight must also depend only on the circumstances. If, therefore, the correct collected canter brings about more weight on the inside stirrup or, which means the same, more pressure on the inside seat bone, the rider will change this weight distribution if necessary and, under certain circumstances, even put more weight on the outside stirrup and seat bone to emphatically support his outside leg in controlling the outside hind leg.

If we have thus compiled the main principles according to which we will proceed in collecting the canter, any not quite inexperienced rider will know that this work creates numerous problems that must be solved according to his own equestrian tact. To avoid serious embarrassments, one should again remember the basic rule: "Ride your horse forward and set it straight!" This applies to any work, yes anytime one sits astride a horse, be it cross-country in front of an obstacle, be it in the arena during highly collected dressage movements. Whoever knows to maintain the forward drive during collecting work and to always correctly adjust forehand and hindquarters relative to one another, will never be seriously at a loss for action. If the beginner nevertheless is in this predicament, he must certainly have violated the above principle. But he should not be discouraged since no man is born a master of his craft. He should merely be careful that he not blame the horse for the resulting difficulties and stubbornly insist on continuing the work. Instead he should quietly stop the collecting work and return to riding his horse through the whole arena in an impulsive canter or better yet truly forward outside to get him on the bit. Then from this basis he will be able to renew his efforts to collect the horse but with greater caution.

In this stage of dressage training, which involves the collection of the canter, *pace* and *contact* always remain visible and noticeable characteristics that indicate whether our work is correct. As long as the canter strides follow one another regularly, are round and fluid, and we are able to move the weight from the forehand to the hindquarters with a yielding poll by way of light half-halts that are adapted to the rhythm of the movement, we are on the right track; if this no longer is the case, we have made a mistake which must be corrected almost exclusively by immediately returning again to a freer tempo.

With respect to the position of head and neck, I want to emphasize once more that the elevation of the forehand, although it accompanies the collected canter, nevertheless is produced much more by bending the haunches than by rein aids directed toward the rear, and even if the horse has a good back and strong hindquarters, such elevation must absolutely be connected with throughness. To use the so-called "high elevation" to overcome a tight back, that is, to raise the head and neck so that the nose is almost in a horizontal position, is a risky undertaking against which I advise under all circumstances because it thoroughly interferes with the sequence of movements.

Now that we have furthered our horse with patience and consideration to the point that it is able to carry itself on its own on straight and curved lines without requiring any other aids than those that come on their own from the rider's soft, flexible balanced seat and we easily feel the inside hind leg underneath us during every stride, the time has come to move on to further perfect the pace and to prepare the horse for practical use by changing to the counter-canter.

The counter-canter is an extremely effective training aid particularly because we have the wall on the inside so that there always is a barrier against the horse's tendency to prevent the inside hind leg from flexing by stepping to the side. If we were able in the regular canter, where the outside hind leg is controlled with the support of the wall, to direct our aids more toward controlling and bending the inside hind leg, the counter-canter enables us to direct our attention more toward working the outside hind leg. Its increased activity naturally also enhances the activity of the inside hind leg.

In the regular canter we had to limit ourselves usually to just watching the outside hind leg since it was rather difficult, for the purpose of giving active aids, to keep the inside hind leg stepping underneath the load without force and thus making it so flexible that it receives the load and pushes it off again with relaxed joints, which is the primary prerequisite for a good collected canter. In the counter-canter, however, in which the wall ensures us control of the inside hind leg, there is no obstacle to actively working the outside hind leg, so that impulsion and rounding of the strides, as already indicated in connection with the regular canter, gain considerably. The counter-canter therefore makes it possible for us to give lively aids of both types as we were allowed to use them in the regular canter, without having to fear that the horse would escape them, either by stepping out with the inside hind leg or by changing leads.

If we have waited to put our horse in the bent-straight position until the counter-canter, in the counter-shoulder-in position, with cadenced half-halts of the outside rein directed toward the inside hind leg and if we drive the outside hind leg energetically forward with the outside spur we are able in a way to canter with every stride onto the wall that holds the inside hind leg. It is not difficult to see that this gives us a highly impressive means to push the horse together in itself in the canter.

This would be possible to an exponentially increased degree in the corners, on a circle, and in all other turns, if here the absence of the supporting wall would not force us to pay increased attention to controlling the inside hind leg. Since, however, the horse, in order to remain in the counter-canter during a turn, is unable to manage without an emphatic support of the load by the inside hind leg, it is not so difficult to hold it in these counter-turns, and no interference is necessary with the energetic forward driving of the outside hind leg and the repeated half-halts from the outside rein to relieve the forehand which are here necessary to a particular degree.

If thus the counter-canter gives us great power over the horse, it also harbors the danger of misuse for the unexperienced rider and it should therefore again be pointed out that the correctness of the work must always be checked through pace and contact. Here, as in all exercises which require very energetic activity from the horse, one should not forget to carefully adapt the length of the sessions to the capability of the horse and at any time better make them too short than too long. Nothing is more inducive to taking away the joy and desire of the horse than endless sessions of very hard work.

At this opportunity, a few words should be devoted to the length of the work at all since this is of unbelievable importance for its result. If one sees many riders whose horses are able to perform all kinds of movements but have a dead mouth and a weak way of going, giving a sad and weary impression, the reason is only that the poor animals have broken hearts as a result of unreasonable overwork, and any true friend of the noble horse will give more recognition to those riders whose horses know only the natural paces but exhibit strength and eagerness as well as a friendly, lively expression. Knowledge of theory, diligence, and skill alone are not enough in the training of horses if true love for this beautiful and lovable creature and an intimate understanding of its nature are not connected with it. I therefore beg of any young colleague in my field to always carefully observe his horse when it is working to see that it does not lose its fire and power so that he does not end up with a dead machine which is no fun to ride for anyone.

To briefly discuss the technique of the counter-canter work, it will be necessary here, as in all new exercises, to precede the actual work with a certain introductory procedure and this movement will be taught to the horse most easily by simply making the first attempt at counter-canter so that it directly follows the regular canter without a change of lead. After the collected canter has been developed to the above-described perfection, it will not be difficult for the horse to perform closer turns in it as well. The hindquarters must then carry the greater portion of the load. The inside hind leg is driven well underneath the center of gravity by the active inside spur but is restrained sufficiently by the rider's leg on the same side. Once we have asked our horse-in-training to depart at the regular canter, we will use the corner after a long side of the arena to change to the other hand by performing a reversal and will attempt to continue the canter unchanged through one or two corners which we round nicely. We use the outside rein and leg and more pressure on the outside seat bone to hold the outside hind leg. If this is possible we will stop the horse and praise it. If it is not possible we go quietly back to the other hand and repeat the exercise until the horse understands us. If our horse is sufficiently prepared in the collected canter, it is physically able to perform the counter-canter and it can then only be a question of understanding. If it turns out, however, quite clearly that the new requirement faces physical difficulties, this is definite proof that the collected canter had not been confirmed sufficiently. In that case it would be completely wrong to force the counter-canter. Instead, one must continue patiently to practice the collected canter on the correct lead until the horse has become more independent in it.

When our horse has performed the described first counter-canter on both hands, this is sufficient for the first lesson. Gradually we then increase our demands and, the more familiar the horse becomes with the counter-canter, the more we use it as a means to perfect the gait. With increasing certainty, we initially cease using our body weight to restrain the outside hind leg and take on the natural weight distribution again in which, as in every exercise on curved lines, the lowering of the horse's inside hip brings with it increased pressure on the inside stirrup and increased weight on the inside seat bone. If this reestablishes the correct weight ratio on the inside hind leg, we can accomplish it even more emphatically by gradually directing the half-halts from the outside rein, that initially were directed toward the outside hind leg, more toward the inside hind leg to thus put weight on it and flex it. If the rider's outside leg is the sole means for controlling the outside hind leg and simultaneously there is a slight rhythmical touch with the outside spur to enhance the lively push-off and forward striding of this hind leg, we have reached that stage of training in which the counter-canter is so outstandingly useful since it, like no other

[229]

exercise, develops the lively forward jumping of the hindquarters, their so-called trill which is the basis for all further canter movements, the redopp, and turns on the hindquarters at the canter.

Gradually we then increase our demands and change from the whole arena to the circle from which we then change to tighter turns and lines with greater curvatures. It must be pointed out in this connection that all turns at the counter-canter are useful only if we are able to maintain in them the bent seat with the correct weight distribution toward the inside and the half-halts from the outside rein which put weight on the inside hind leg.

The stage of perfection to which we elevate the canter by way of the correct counter-canter work, entitles us to set our eye now toward the ultimate goal, namely canter turns about the hindquarters. These turns which, becoming tighter and tighter, reach their peak in the *pirouette* are the beautiful result of systematic and diligent canter work. A well con-structed and noble horse that has reached this level of training will give his rider the sublime feeling of being the master of his destiny, be it in the arena for giving an eye-catching performance, be it on the drill-ground, be it on the serious battle field. Only about the hindquarters and only at the canter are we able to turn our horse securely in the smallest space, with agility and decorum.

These short canter turns about the hindquarters can only be performed on the inside hind leg which, the tighter the turns become, must carry the load more on its own, while the other three legs, particularly the outside hind leg, only perform the role of supporting the load for short instances and returning it again and again to the inside hind leg. It is therefore obvious that only the perfected flexibility of the inside hind leg, connected with an elasticity which is able to push off the weight of horse and rider elastically at any time, enable the horse to perform such turns. Although the counter-canter has established the foundation for this development of the hind leg, it is nevertheless not possible to change directly from the counter-canter to the turns on the hindquarters. Instead, we can achieve the required flexibility and resiliency of the inside hind leg in an unforced manner only by way of lateral movements at the canter.

If so far we have asked the horse usually to take on the bent-straight shoulder-fore position at the regular canter as well as at the counter-can-ter, we now increase this position gradually to the half-shoulder-in position. This position is certainly opposite to the way in which the untrained horse likes to canter, and it is therefore able to maintain it in a regular and forceful collected canter only with considerable effort of flexibility and strength on the part of the inside hind leg. Although correctly performed work in the preceding lessons, particularly at the counter-canter, may have enabled the strong and talented horse to take on this position, it is nevertheless certainly appropriate to proceed only centimeter by centimeter when increasing the lateral position.

With respect to seat and aids in this lesson, reference is made to the chapter on the shoulder-in and it need only be particularly emphasized at this occasion that the shoulder-in position is useful only if the flexion is pure, and this in turn is dependent primarily on the correct control of the outside hind leg. The idea that an increase in the lateral position is useless if it is at the expense of flexion must be emphasized even more at this point since the difficulty of a *shoulder-in canter* very easily causes the horse to escape in an incorrect bend. It should therefore be sufficient, particularly for horses that have an unfavorable conformation and are not very strong, to take on a lesser lateral position. Such horses should not go beyond the half-shoulder-in position. For the understanding trainer it needs no mention that for such a difficult lesson the length of the session must be short. It is advisable to push the horse straight forward with both legs from the shoulder-in canter and to change to a circle on one track or, if the horse approaches a corner in the shoulder-in canter, to push straight forward as if one wanted to change to the travers and to continue cantering on one track out of the corner.

If one believes to have sufficiently furthered the flexibility and suppleness of the entire horse through the shoulder-in canter and particularly the spring-like activity of the inside hind leg, one may dare to make the first attempt at a more distinct travers-canter out of the corner in a transition from the shoulder-in position. The travers position is enhanced considerably by the canter movement and is therefore generally gladly accepted by the horse, particularly on the right hand. The not expertly educated rider is usually surprised that the *travers-canter* is called a higher-level movement and believes to be performing such a movement if he pushes his horse's croup inside at the canter. The expert, however, is well aware of the difficulties of the correct travers-canter and dares to assume the specific travers position only after his horse has been carefully prepared for it in the above-described stages of canter work. The difficulties of the travers-canter are based particularly on the fact that the cantering horse by nature tends to push its croup inside, as anyone will understand who has followed our discussions to this point. The lateral position taken on by the untrained horse does not exhibit any rib cage flexion and the inside hind leg is set down to the side of the outside hind leg because it is lacking in flexibility. The essence of the true travers-canter, however, is a perfectly pure lateral bend of the entire spinal column, with its degree being in full harmony with that of the lateral position and, connected with it, the inside hind leg is put forward in the direction toward the center of gravity, closely past the outside hind leg.

The system developed in this book continues to adhere to the principle that all movements of true, classical dressage have direct or indirect practical utility and it emphatically contradicts the unfortunately so wide-spread erroneous opinion that the only purpose of dressage is to present the horse in artificial positions and movements. The travers-canter in particular is one of the dressage movements which has a direct practical purpose since it is perfectly suited to prepare and enable the horse for turns on the hindquarters.

The travers-canter is of course able to fulfill this purpose only if it embodies the above-mentioned characteristics. A turn about the hind-quarters is possible only if the inside hind leg is under the weight mass at the moment of the turn. A good travers at the canter, in which the inside hind leg jumps underneath the body in the direction toward the center of gravity, is conceivable only with a uniform, albeit slight, lateral flexion since the unbent horse would always tend to canter straight ahead instead of sideways. The above statements will hopefully have contributed to everyone's understanding that the correct travers-canter can be developed only from a correct shoulder-in canter, just as in the other gaits the proper dressage travers can be established only on careful preparation of the shoulder-in. For this reason it has also been recommended to develop the transition to the travers-canter in the described manner from the shoulder-in-canter because this is the best way to obtain the necessary correct longitudinal flexion and to carry it over into the travers-canter. Moreover, I must here again refer to the chapter about the travers and particularly to the fact that a flowing, regular pace is conceivable only if the inside hind leg works correctly after being asked by the rider's leg and spur on the same side to step diligently forward, and both reins, especially the inside rein, continue to move the forehand to the side, particularly in the turns.

From the travers-canter we will guide our horse to the counter-travers-canter or the renvers-canter and there find the means to give the gait its ultimate perfection. We then have the wall behind us and are permitted to use stronger half-halts which continue to increase the flexion of the hindquarters produced by the weight and make the canter stride ever more elevated. If we have already warned, in connection with the counter-canter, that the rider should not misuse the power that this movement gives him, this is even more true here.

If the horse's capabilities to perform are exceeded, resistance will suddenly and unexpectedly arise and the entire structure, set up with so much care and consideration, will collapse like a house of cards unless the rider can fall back on very mature experience. Most of all, the rider should again call to mind the two major principles: "Ride your horse forward and set it straight!" or stated differently, "Always take care that the forehand is leading the hindquarters." As soon as this rule is neglected and the horse is permitted, by letting it drag its forehand, to put the inside hind leg to the side, it would be very magnanimous of the horse if it did not take this opportunity to remove itself from the rider's authority. Almost every horse will not give up such an opportunity and will be even more willing to take advantage of it the more the rider asks it for a performance that goes beyond its capabilities and the more its temperament puts it either into an annoyed or irritated state. To avoid repetitions, reference is made here to the chapter on the renvers which also applies for the renvers-canter.

The more harmoniously a horse is constructed, the stronger its hind-quarters, the more lively and willing its temperament, the more elevated will be its stride in the travers- and renvers-canter until finally the outer diagonal, "the inside hind leg and the outside foreleg," will track separately, that is the three-beat becomes a four-beat, and the travers- and renvers-canter have become a redopp and counter-redopp, respectively. This upper level dressage movement is often misunderstood and a certain dragging canter of some horses is thought to be a redopp. The redopp differs considerably from such a faulty, dragging canter, which I have mentioned occasionally in this chapter, and against which the under-standing trainer will take decisive counter-measures, by the energetic trill-like jumping under of the hindquarters; the forehand is set down softly, as if the forelegs were trying not to touch the ground. A redopp is a dressage movement that only very gifted horses are able to perform. In them it develops from the travers- and renvers-canter, practically without any special assistance from the rider. Forcing less talented horses to perform this canter movement would be foolish because the result would always be only poor and would adversely affect the overall training.

At the conclusion of our canter work we crown it with turns on the hindquarters. In the travers work we already had the opportunity to prepare such turns in the corners and, with increasing proficiency in the travers- and renvers-canter, we will have occasionally interrupted our track along the whole arena by a turn or a transition to a circle. To now develop the turns on the hindquarters to their utmost perfection, we go on a circle in the travers-canter or the redopp and gradually reduce the size of the circle. This exercise is very suitable to further enhance the elevation of the forehand when the hindquarters land and to ask the latter to fully take over the load since this movement by nature also permits us to use strong half-halts. The rider's legs must of course always produce the corresponding counter-aid to these half-halts. The inside spur in particular must ask the inside hind leg at the proper time to willingly take up the load it is supposed to carry when the outside hind leg willingly follows the sideways driving aids.

As long as the horse still tends to fall out with the outside hind leg, the rider's outside leg must predominate, frequently supported by the outside rein and even by increased weight on the outside seat bone, as the control of the outside hind leg is the basic condition for the correct performance of this movement. With this predominant use of his outside leg, the rider must, however, be particularly careful that the forehand always properly precedes the hindquarters since only in this way can the correct lateral flexion and the flow of the movement be maintained.

The more perfect the travers-canter was, the more it became a redopp, the more we will be able to reduce the circle, until finally we come to the pirouette in which the inside hind leg works on the pivot point around which the forehand turns in redopp strides. The number of strides the horse needs for a pirouette depends on its strength, agility, and liveliness. The fewer strides, the more beautiful is the pirouette. There are a few, extraordinarily gifted horses which, with increasing practice, become able to perform the pirouette in one sweep or stride, while the number of those who get around in two strides is somewhat larger, although this movement is also not the forte of every horse.

At this opportunity it should be stated once and for all that the training of horses, although it is a systematic whole from the first beginnings to its highest perfection in which one lesson logically develops out of another, one must nevertheless not believe that every horse can be trained over time to perform the highest-level dressage movements. Nature has placed very defined limits here which bring very severe consequences if exceeded. The experienced trainer very soon discovers these limits in each horse. The unexperienced rider, however, must be urgently advised that he better be too modest in his expectations and requirements than setting them too high which unfortunately most riders have a tendency to do. Systematic and logical training of the horse brings the result that a horse, when trained quietly and expertly, will occasionally indicate itself that it is ready for the next movement. The principle can therefore be established that demands can be increased as long as one feels that he horse exhibits a certain willingness.

To return now to the *pirouette*, everyone will understand that it can be performed in but approximate perfection only by a horse whose strength and courage are sufficient to increase the travers-canter to the redopp since of course the pirouette requires a decisive elevation of the forehand on hindquarters that jump underneath it. With less talented horses one will have to be satisfied to reduce the size of the circle only to the extent that the inside hind leg describes the smallest possible circle. In this connection it should also be pointed out that the smaller the circle becomes, the horse will have more of a tendency to escape by its hindquarters falling out and that therefore the rider's outside leg, rein, and seat bone must control the outside hind leg that much more while his inside leg and seat bone maintain forward movement.

After we now have developed the reduction of the circle to a certain degree of reliability, we can occasionally interrupt the straight line at various locations in the arena, depending on the performance capability of the horse, by a travers-canter or redopp voltes, by quarter, half, and whole pirouettes or by corresponding turns about the hindquarters and would thus have arrived at the perfection of our canter work if we did not also have to develop the changes of lead in the canter.

The so-called flying changes of lead are also not every horse's strength since they require a certain agility and liveliness to be performed properly and without deleterious results. If one were to force a fat, phlegmatic horse to do flying changes, it would break its bones and still not bring about a good change. Here again the horse will indicate to the attentive rider

[235]

precisely how far it is able to go. Every talented horse, the stronger, more flexible, and sensitive it has become from its gymnastic work, will offer the flying change that much more easily if the rider skillfully changes seat and guidance when changing from one lead to the other. The flying change of lead should not be made a special exercise too early and one should especially not begin with it until the horse performs the simple change with increasing skill and gradually more securely and promptly.

Before we turn to the manner of its performance and the required aids, we want to explain again in connection with this exercise how the horse naturally uses its limbs. In the state of freedom we can also often observe the horse performing flying changes at the canter.

The sequence of footfalls at the canter makes it evident that a change of lead in this gait can occur only during the period of suspension in which the horse, after its inside foreleg has pushed the body off the ground, pulls all four of its legs underneath its body for a very short moment. To be able to catch the body now not with the previously outside hind leg but with the other hind leg, the latter must be given more weight and directed underneath the body mass while the former is relieved and is asked, while still in the air, to pull up more and swing forward so that it will land later than the first.

If we bring to mind the natural aids that this requires, the rider will primarily take his weight off the previously outside legs and cause them to swing forward while still in the air. But he will have to load the previously inside legs so that they track ahead of the outside legs. In connection with collecting the canter, it has already been pointed out what important task is performed by the outside hind leg. In the flying change its activity is also decisive for the fluent performance of this movement in which the footfalls are different from before. The outside hind leg is the pillar that supports the body and must enable the other limbs to securely change their sequence of footfalls. For this purpose they must receive the weight and the new inside hind leg must be enabled to remain in the air and swing forward, which it must simultaneously be asked to do by an aid from the rider's leg at the girth. Before the change, the rider will therefore already ask the new outside hind leg to jump forward well underneath the load and will have to take care that it is flexed. This is possible only by setting the horse straight and collecting it. Moving the rider's weight backward and half-halts in the direction toward the previously inside hind leg which has been pulled forward by the rider's leg on the same side will ensure both.

After this preparation, the change of aids takes place, the hand begins with the change of position and the rider's legs likewise change their position immediately thereafter. To do this, the previously outside leg of the rider initially slides toward the girth and the other leg almost simultaneously slides behind the girth. The former has the task of making the new left side hollow and asking the hind leg on the same side to swing forward lively. The previously inside leg of the rider must direct the hindquarters onto the line. At the moment of the change, the rider must sit up more, hollow his back, and push his inside hip and inside seat bone forward without moving his leg on the same side further forward than to the girth. He must, with his seat, seem to want to throw the horse forward-upward in a straight direction, with his new inside leg acting a little stronger and with the new inner side being allowed to lead. The rider's weight is then directed more toward the new outside seat bone.

As in all other exercises, the flying change must first be taught to the horse. To do this the necessary aids which, when performed to perfection, almost flow into one another, must be separated from one another, the rein aids coming first, then the leg aids, with the seat aids bringing the change to completion. The procedure should be similar when teaching the young rider to perform the change of lead. Particular care must be taken right from the start that the horse remains precisely on the line but the young rider does not look down or throw himself over to the side.

Before one can begin with the practice of changing leads, the straight canter depart on both leads, from the trot as well as from the walk, and the simple change of lead at the canter must be perfectly secure on a straight, open track and must be performed as a result of light, invisible aids. Before beginning the first exercises of flying changes, one should be convinced that these prerequisites are met. Likewise, the horse must be easily collected at the canter on a straight, open track and must remain completely straight and through.

There are several methods for practicing flying changes of lead and many riders, particularly those who are not trained in dressage, use the moment to change the horse from one position on a curved line indicated by its position to another, inversely curved line. Others perform the first changes of lead from the counter-canter by cantering along the wall and completely changing their aids when they reach a corner, using primarily the new inside rein and outside leg. However, to teach the horse to change in a straight forward direction under all circumstances, it is advantageous to practice the changes also on a straight track.

Best suited for this purpose is the diagonal through the whole arena. As soon as one steps on this line, one must take care that the horse is set completely straight and canters quietly. If this is the case, one should begin, as soon as one is approximately in the center of the arena, to increasingly collect the horse. Particular care should be taken to keep the horse straight, through, and cantering relaxed but diligently. If this is the case, one begins with changing its position and should arrange it so that this is completed shortly before the new track line is entered. As mentioned earlier, the aids for the change must be given separately from one another, in such a way that the rein aids come first, the leg aids follow, and the seat aids complete the change when the change point is reached.

If the horse becomes restless already during the preparatory collection and pushes sideways, the change must not yet be performed because all these phenomena indicate clearly that the horse is not yet ready for this new lesson.

Moreover, one must at first not repeat the change of lead too frequently and not always at the same location in the arena, but must interject pauses or in between ride the same tracks without changes. Also one must always be convinced that the horse continues to perform the simple change securely and quietly.

As in all other movements, the prompt and correct performance is dependent here, aside from the already frequently emphasized suitable preparation, primarily on the detection of the correct moments for giving the aids. This is a matter of equestrian tact and experience which can be acquired only by much practice. Whoever understands that a good flying change can only be performed from the period of suspension and that the individual tempi of the canter movement follow one another extremely quickly and almost flow into one another, will also be aware that the aids must begin already before the period of suspension. The preparatory collecting half-halt will have to be given at the movement when the previously outside hind leg sets down (the change of position, however, must follow immediately thereafter, when the legs of the outside diagonal step down). Such quick and prompt interaction of the aids can be accomplished only with increasing practice by the thus perfected feeling.

The further training must continue on the basis achieved by the above described exercises for a single flying change if one wishes to turn to the development of repeated successive flying changes, particularly after a set number of strides. One must not begin any earlier than when the horse is able to perform a change to the right or left lead easily and regularly at any location in the arena. In the beginning one should be satisfied to produce a single change to either lead after a certain, larger number of canter strides, that is, eight or ten, and one's demands should only very gradually be raised with respect to the repetition of the frequency of the changes and with respect to the reduction of the number of canter strides in between. As soon as the horse displays excitement, one should return to the simpler exercises. But if the horse performs the requested changes well - one must always intend to perform a certain number and must not exceed that number - it should be praised and a pause should be interjected or the day's work should be terminated completely. Slow and systematic progress on the correct basis is the most reliable way to arrive at one's goal. If one remains faithful to these principles, as should be a matter of course for the true expert, and the physical talents of the horse permit it, one will finally arrive at a point where the flying changes can be performed every stride. However, such changes can be considered proper dressage movements only if they are performed precisely on a straight forward line without any noticeable aids from the rider, particularly without any non-equestrian and unsightly throwing of the upper body from side to side as is unfortunately seen very frequently today.

In order to avoid repetition, the so often emphasized principle that pace and contact must always be the touchstone for the correctness of our work has no longer been referred to in connection with the last exercises at the canter. However, at the end of this important chapter, the urgent admonition must once more be repeated, even at the risk of becoming boring, that one should immediately change to a freer, more lively canter in order to refresh the thrust as soon as any kind of insufficiencies in pace and contact become evident.

If correctly riding forward is the soul of all equestrian art, this is particularly applicable for the distinctly impulsive gait of the canter.

ENDNOTES

[1] The strong holding of the weights in the rider's hand, as recommended for this purpose in earlier editions, must lead to renewed tension. The hands must hold tight only if this is possible without the exertion of force, or if the lively spring action of the hind legs need no

longer be asked for through spurs and whip. (Hans von Heydebreck)

2 However, with his straightening bending work the rider must not make the mistake of letting the neck flap toward the left against the shoulder; instead he should attempt to obtain the bend to the left primarily with his inside leg and spur and not with the left rein. (Hans von Heydebreck)

3 To work travers-like in the shoulder-in means to give the horse the correct longitudinal bend with the rider's outside leg behind the girt, and asking the horse's outside hind leg to step forward and underneath in the direction of the lateral position. To work shoulder-in-like in the travers means for the rider to use his inside leg to ask the horse's inside hind leg to step forward against the gravity line and to thus prevent it from escaping toward the inside. (Hans von Heydebreck)

4 In the earlier editions the urgent requirement was made at this point that every horse that is supposed to be "on the bit" "must move with a bent neck and its *nose vertical*," and it was added that "there is no neck and no poll that could free the rider from the requirement of putting the *nose vertical* or at least *almost vertical.*" This position was represented as a sign that the horse had given up any resistance in the poll. Such a schematic requirement obviously contradicts Steinbrecht's principles as laid out in the preceding paragraphs and cannot even be found in the chapter dealing with the bending of neck and poll. For the above detailed reasons, it cannot be maintained and has therefore been omitted. (Hans von Heydebreck)

5 Seidler generally recommends double side reins which have a similar effect as the side reins described in connection with work on the lunge, except that the rider has the upper ends in his hands. With shaky heads these auxiliary reins serve their purpose since they prevent the neck from escaping to the side. (Hans von Heydebreck)

6 Primarily it will be the horse's crookedness, even after it appears to have been overcome, that creates difficulties in every new exercise. It never leaves us until the end and appears to a greater or lesser degree even in a perfectly trained dressage horse; it must be eradicated again and again through bending work on one and two tracks. (Hans von Heydebreck)

7 To obtain a clear picture of the moment at which the aids for collecting the canter must act, one must observe the movement of the horse's body during a canter stride. One will then note that both forehand and hindquarters are raised and lowered alternatively. At the moment at which the inside foreleg solely supports the body weight and pushes it off, the forehand is lower than the hindquarters, while conversely the hindquarters are lowered and the forehand is raised as soon as the horse, after the period of suspension, catches the weight again on only the outside hind leg. The entire swivel block thus constantly performs a movement similar to the whipping of a scale bar. If the rider closely follows this rhythm, his upper body will perform a movement that oscillates back and forth from the vertical position

and his arms and hands will do the same. At the movement at which the hindquarters are lowered, the hands and arms will move back automatically so that the half-halt is produced automatically. The rider's legs, however, are slightly pushed away from the horse's body when the latter is pushed together the most, that is in the period of suspension, and drop back against it again when it is stretched out. This results automatically in the rider's natural, cadenced leg aids. (Hans von Heydebreck)

8 Even though particular attention must be paid to working the inside hind leg during the first collection of the canter, so as to cause the leg to step underneath the weight and prevent it from escaping toward the inside, the outside hind leg has the main task in the collected canter. It must not only, as indicated above, catch the weight but must also bend under it and spring off again elastically by softly catching the entire load with loose joints and pushing it off again with liveliness, thus ensuring softness as well as impulsion of movement. (Hans von Heydebreck)

9 The disadvantageous consequences of such attempts at forcing the hind legs to bend are manifest in jerky movements in which the hocks try to free themselves of this forced-on load by short jerks. Not infrequently this results in the so-called stringhalt or even spavin or other diseases of the hocks and fetlock joints. (Hans von Heydebreck)

10 This is recommended primarily to overcome crookedness in the counter-canter. (Hans von Heydebreck)

11 The travers-canter should be demanded only with a slight lateral deviation but in good collection which must be characterized primarily by softly pushed-together hindquarters that are supple and resilient in their upper joints. The hands should be limited to slight, cadenced half-halts, while the rider's legs, also vibrating in cadence, ask the hind legs to jump under in a lively manner. The rider must feel as if he had the major portion of the horse's body in front of him. (Hans von Heydebreck)

12 The three-beat will become a four-beat already with the development of the dressage canter, but this phenomenon must not be discernible with the naked eye since it otherwise would indicate that the movement has become dragging. (Hans von Heydebreck)

13 The opinion represented here that the pirouette is more beautiful the fewer strides the horse requires for the entire turn does not correspond to the principles of classical equitation. The latter does not evaluate the performance of all turns about the hindquarters by their speed and also not by the number of strides they require, but according to whether the rhythm of the strides and the horse's balanced position remain exactly the same during the entire revolution as they were immediately before. The horse must continue to canter or redopp, must not become faster or fall sideways, and, after completion of the turn, must continue at once to canter straight on the track on which the turn was initiated. (Hans von Heydebreck)

[14] In an underestimation of the importance of this exercise for practical use, the earlier editions only indicated the development of the flying change and gave the advice not to make this change the subject of a special exercise but to wait until, in the course of the work, the horse would perform its changes with increasing skill and reliability, which would automatically bring about the flying change after a while. This neither corresponds to facts nor the practical significance of this exercise. It has therefore been necessary to discuss this subject in greater detail, particularly also in view of the fact that in recent times the flying change is required in almost all dressage tests and is often performed incorrectly. (Hans von Heydebreck)

[15] Fillis, who unquestionably was a master in the performance of the flying change and was the first who performed changes every stride to perfection, initially used this method, but then practiced it mainly on a straight line. (Hans von Heydebreck)

D. School Movements

1. Lower-Level Movements

School movements differ from balanced movements by their more elevated performance, by their greater impulsion, and by the decreased amount of ground covered in each stride. They require greater flexibility of the haunches, in other words collection, and thus a greater weight transfer to the hindquarters. The school exercises are grouped into lower-level and upper-level dressage movements. Lower-level dressage includes the collected paces of the three basic gaits that are performed with increased bending of the haunches and lateral movements that are ridden with a greater deviation. Before we turn our attention to these dressage movements, however, it appears advisable to briefly review the section of training that lies behind us, in the course of which we repeatedly entered the border regions between training for general riding and upper-level dressage.

In the chapters about balance and obtaining an artificial carriage, the rider's task in such training was defined as to enable the horse to carry itself in the manner required for mounted service and to maintain this carriage as long as its rider desired it. It was noted that the horse's forehand by nature carries a greater load than its hindquarters, which impairs the security of its movements, not in freedom, but under the rider. To overcome this drawback, we attempted to gradually relieve the forehand by moving more weight onto the hindquarters so that all four legs carried the same weight. We called the carriage of the horse's body produced in that way the "balanced carriage." This displacement of the weight toward the back was attempted by lowering the hindquarters from which then, when the weight was removed from it, the forehand was elevated automatically. This in turn gave us the means, due to the weight being moved backward, to temporarily compress the joints of the hindquarters, which had been pulled forward underneath the load. From this state we developed the forces inherent in the hindquarters, the thrust and carrying force, to such an extent that we were able to precisely determine the degree of their action.

Prerequisite for this working of the hindquarters to produce the horse's balanced carriage was the loosening of all of the muscles of the motion mechanism, the removal of any tension. This was accomplished by bending work which simultaneously enabled us to set the horse straight. We never lost sight of the important axiom that the success of any working of the horse was dependent on it remaining sensitive to the driving aids, that is, moving forward.

The bending work was done on straight and curved lines and on one and two tracks. It was intended to put the horse into longitudinal flexion and thus initially ask the individual hind leg to step forward toward the line of the center of gravity and cause it to relax and become flexible. This was accomplished particularly on the circle where the natural tendency of the horse's body toward the inside enabled the inside hind leg to carry more of the load and to spring back elastically. With the gradually increasing relaxation of the entire body of the horse, the horse's throughness improved as well and enabled us, through emphatic cooperation between driving and restraining aids, to temporarily engage the horse more, that is, collect it, and improve its balanced carriage.

The lateral movements, in particular, contributed significantly to perfecting the horse's balance. They produced the fine lateral balancing of the horse's body not only by the interaction of aids on the inside and outside, but also by the leg and rein aids that acted diagonally. The hind legs were thus pushed closer to the forelegs, and the resulting greater collection enabled us to shorten the tempo in all gaits.

In the chapter on the lateral movements it has already been pointed out that in training for general riding these movements must be practiced only with a slight lateral deviation; that one must be satisfied with the trot position in the shoulder-in and with the canter position in the travers; that this collection, which has been increased only until the horse attains the balanced carriage, is not sufficient for the proper performance of perfected lateral movements; and that, if one wishes to move to school movements, it is necessary to first increase the collection to such an extent that the lateral movements can be practiced in a truly perfect configuration, which necessitates further shortening of the tempo. In this way, one arrives at the tempi that are performed with increased flexion of the haunches and are called the school walk, the school trot, and the school canter.

These paces were mentioned only in passing in the preceding chapters. But their correct performance is a primary prerequisite for our turning to school movements without qualms. We will therefore briefly touch on these three movements and clarify what they look like, what is their purpose, and how we develop them.

The *school walk* is the improved collected walk of the general riding school. The horse appears more engaged and elevated, its steps are livelier and raised higher and therefore cover less ground than the working walk. The attained increase in collection also makes the horse more willing to obey any request from its rider without hesitation; it obeys within seconds. For that reason, all transitions into a faster gait or into a shorter gait and to the halt will take place promptly and softly and in perfect carriage, with the aids being hardly visible. The horse's agility is increased to such an extent that turns about the hindquarters from the walk can be performed fluidly without losing the cadence and sequence of footfalls of the walk. This immeasurably perfects the horse's understanding for these shorter turns in place and serves as a successful preparation for their performance at the canter, including the pirouette.

The school walk can be developed only in stages and in short sessions that are based on the correctly taught working walk. The reason that its development has not been discussed in greater detail in the preceding chapters is initially that, because of its lack of impulsion, the walk plays only a limited role in the early training of the horse. It has therefore been mentioned mainly when the establishment of an understanding between rider and horse was involved, that is, during the introductory phases. The rider must initially take up the walk and ride it in the form that the horse offers to him by nature. Any attempt to develop it more at this point fails due to its lack of impulsion, and results in irregularities in the sequence of footfalls that we have an opportunity to observe so frequently. It can be developed only with progressive dressage training hand in hand with the perfection of the gaits; it nourishes itself from the impulsion developed in the other gaits which it utilizes.

In the first stage of training the walk is only ridden on a long rein, must be free and natural, and serves primarily to rest the horse. However, the rider can always use the way the horse behaves in these walk intervals to determine whether his previous work was correct. Unrest, head-shaking, or boring into the ground indicate that errors have been made, particularly by the hands.

Only if the horse has a secure contact at the trot and, concomitant with it, self-carriage and throughness, can the rider attempt to influence the performance of the walk. Initially it will be his task to use his driving aids to cause the horse to stretch more and take longer steps, and then, immediately after a successful trot session in which the horse has performed the transitions between collected and free trot and vice versa fluently and in a good carriage, will he attempt to maintain this good carriage also for a few walk steps before he yields with his reins. This procedure is now repeated and will ultimately bring the result that the progress in throughness and self-carriage obtained in the trot work enables the rider to collect the walk as well for short periods of time.

Progressing systematically in this way it is possible, particularly with the perfection of transitions from all gaits into the walk and the halt, to produce the collected walk for general riding which, as indicated above, is the unavoidable basis for the school walk.

The development of this movement may begin when the horse can be collected with light aids from the working walk and remains very light on the bit, straight, and in good carriage. First the rider must shorten the walk by repeated light half-halts and attempt to refine the obedience to these shortening rein aids. If the horse willingly responds to these requests for shortening the tempo, the rider must use his legs to urge the horse's hind legs to step forward lively. Restraining and driving aids must not be given simultaneously, however, they must instead be given clearly separated from one another in such a way that the driving leg aids always are applied only after the horse has promptly obeyed the half-halt. In this way the school walk is created which must be distinguished by lively and raised steps in good elevation. These exercises must initially be performed only in short sessions and must be interrupted by rest periods in which the horse is urged to walk freely in ground-covering, quiet steps with a clear sequence of footfalls.

The school trot should initially be identified by the same, outstanding characteristics as the school walk, namely great collection and elevation, as well as diligent, raised, cadenced steps that do not cover much ground. But added to this as the most important feature must be impulsion which is lacking in the school walk. The school trot is also developed on the basis of the correctly collected trot in the balanced carriage. Only if the horse exhibits complete throughness and self-carriage in that gait, may it be asked to temporarily perform the more distinct, elevated steps while maintaining rhythm and collection.

The school trot should initially always be developed from the impulsive medium trot by way of the collected, shortened trot, with particular attention being paid to maintaining diligent, rhythmical, fluid steps. Otherwise it is easy for a faulty, dragging movement to develop in which the horse tenses its back and takes slow, suspended steps. Such suspended steps often lead inexperienced young riders to believe incorrectly that they can now turn to passage work, and they further the suspended steps instead of suppressing them. This faulty pace is usually produced by too much pressure from the rider's legs, causing his hands in turn to take forceful action in order to be able to master the suddenly developing thrust. It is therefore necessary to give the required aids to the hind legs with a light and lively acting leg which may be supported to advantage by a skillfully applied whip. The hands must also always be skillful in letting the step come out and must attempt to maintain the collection, not by steadily holding back, but by repeated, light halts.

If the hands hold back with too much force and if thus the hindquarters receive too much weight, impulsion is suffocated since the hind legs are no longer able to elastically push off the load that they have been asked to carry. This then results in another faulty movement in which the forelegs exhibit a stabbing, flinging action, while the hind legs follow weakly in a stalking fashion.

Since all upper-level dressage is based on the correct performance of the school trot, in the development of this school trot the rider must be able, as in all school movements, to finely adjust the driving and restraining aids relative to one another. He must avoid any harshness or force. Only then will he be able to maintain the horse's throughness which is his only guarantee for lively, fluid and elevated, cadenced working of the horse's limbs, an absolute prerequisites for the school trot.

If the school trot has progressed to this degree of perfection, the riding of lateral movements, while gradually increasing the lateral position and collection, will further improve the classical dressage carriage of the horse to such an extent that the rider need have no qualms about developing the actual school movements.

The canter has already been discussed in such detail in the preceding chapter devoted to this gait, and its step-wise perfection has been continued to the highest stage of completion, that detailed discussion of the *school canter* should really not be necessary. However, one special circumstance has only been hinted at, namely the change in footfalls that occurs. Although it has been mentioned that the perfection of the travers-canter and the renvers-canter gradually changes the gait from a three-beat to a four-beat canter, with the collection of the canter progressing to the canter in place. In a footnote it has already been additionally pointed out that this changed sequence of footfalls already occurs in the school canter on one track but must be almost imperceptible to the eye or the ear. To provide absolute clarity about this process and enable you to draw the conclusions required for giving the aids, we now want to examine the sequence of movement in somewhat more detail.

The school canter, like the school walk and the school trot, should be distinguished by impulsion, softness, and liveliness and therefore the four hoofbeats must occur lightly, quickly, and with the same loudness, in pairs, first the hind legs, then the forelegs, shortly after one another at equal intervals. As already mentioned in connection with the collection of the working canter, the outside hind leg here performs the main task of catching the load with softly resilient joints and then elastically pushing it off again Consequently, the outside hind leg must be asked to spring off more, swing forward, and bend; only then will the necessary flexion in the haunches and the rib cage result.

It then follows for the aids that the outside leg and rein must be predominant in the development of the school canter, while the rider's inside leg has more the task of preventing the hind leg on the same side from escaping, and he must maintain the flexion of the forehand with the inside rein. Here again, it will be decisive for success that the rider, with fine equestrian feeling, detects the proper moment for giving the various aids and, as in the development of the school walk and trot, matches them finely to one another. The instructions given for developing these school movements must be carefully adhered to in the development of the school canter. This gait will then also contribute considerably to the preparation of the actual school movements, although the school walk and trot, since they are closely related to the piaffe and passage, constitute the actual basis for the haute école.

In addition to these preparatory lower-level movements, the old masters used two other lessons as touchstones for whether their horses were ready for the upper levels, namely the halt and the subsequent holding of the horse in a collected position and the rein-back. And indeed the ease with which the horse is able to perform this movement properly may serve us as another yardstick for how much it is prepared for the following, longer movements involving increased bending of both haunches. The halt is the more perfect the more weight the horse puts on the hind legs, which are well pushed under and bent, while the horse is in light contact with the reins in a perfectly elevated position of head and neck, lightly on the bit, and the longer the rider is able to hold it in this position.

Accordingly, it should be clear that the halt in its perfection can be performed only by the fully trained dressage horse, while in the stage of dressage training under discussion, which relates only to the transition to movements with greater flexion of both haunches, we must still be satisfied with a less perfect performance of the halt. It will come closer to the perfect halt the more carefully the horse has been prepared in movements on curved lines and the finer the rider is able to set the ratio of restraining aids to driving aids in order to bring bending of the haunches, elevation, and on-the-bit carriage into full harmony with one another. From the feeling of contact, the rider will have an infallible yardstick for the evaluation of his halt; if he pushed the hind legs too far under, he will be unable to hold the horse on the bit; if he did not engage them enough, the horse will not be elevated sufficiently and the hands will have to carry some of the weight of the forehand.

Aside from the fact that the necessary driving and restraining aids must be adjusted finely relative to one another, the halt can be successful only if the rider, due to his fine equestrian tact, is able to hit the correct moments for his aids, that is, if he is able, through fine spur aids in the rhythm of the movement, to ask the hind legs, when they rise during the last steps or strides, to step further forward and, once they are set down, to give well-measured, through-going half-halts. Such a perfectly performed halt to stop the horse presupposes that the horse is completely through and willingly obeys the simultaneous aids from both reins because that is the characteristic of the full halt; not the fact that the horse stops.

The opinions heard today with respect to the difference between half-halts and full halts, which are that the full halt stops the horse while the half-halt only causes it to shorten its pace or to engage more, that is, collect itself, must therefore by examined and corrected.

[249]

In the young, green horse, there can be no mention of halts; one can only let it slow down, which one does with repeated, indicative rein signals. Only if a secure contact has been obtained from riding forward, and the impulsion generated by the lively stepping hind legs travels through the back and neck to the poll and the mouth and has caused the horse to push away from the bit, will the hands be able to give an aid that goes through to the rear since only then does the horse's body constitute a closed unit. Yet both reins will still not be able to act simultaneously because of unilateral resistances caused or augmented by the horse's tendency to carry itself crooked; each rein can only act by itself.

The lateral flexion achieved by the bending work to relax the muscles on one side and make them yielding here serves as the means, in unilateral cooperation of the rider's seat, weight, leg, and hand, to act through the entire horse and bring each hind leg forward individually, put weight on it, and bend it. That is the half-halt or half-arrêt! It explains the thorough effect of the shoulder-in-like half-halts which were discussed in the chapter devoted to this lateral movement. If the horse has been made uniformly through on both sides by these half-halts, the simultaneous pressure of both reins will be able to travel to the hindquarters without interference to put equal weight on both hind legs and flex them. Until this effect is so secure that the horse will stop immediately in perfect carriage, the horse must still pass through a further phase of training and the rider will first have to teach it that, if it receives a halt signal, it should initially only collect itself, shorten the tempo, or go to a lower gait. The halt exercises will also not reside in immediately bringing the horse to a complete stop through a halt aid but in repeating the halt aids again and again and, if resistance occurs on one side, supporting it by half-halts. The horse should stop only if the rider feels that both hind legs can be held underneath his seat.

The more perfect these halts become due to the increasing flexibility of the haunches, the more the horse will be able to step back properly once it has gained understanding from a preparatory procedure for this movement that is against its nature. The preparatory teaching will occur in that the horse, which must first be well on the bit when it stops on all four legs, is pushed back step by step with restraining hands. The rider's legs must only be in readiness to restrain in order to prevent lateral deviations of the hind legs. In the beginning the rider must not sit too heavily, particularly not on horses that have a long, soft back and soft hind legs. After each step, a short pause must be made and the horse must be praised. Only if it performs each step willingly on the bit, without rushing back, is it in order to ask for several steps in succession. Care must be taken that the horse continues to perform each step as a result of the alternating pressure of the hands, in the proper rhythm, on the bit, with one diagonal pair of legs after the other. The hind legs must stay close together, and the horse must always be willing to immediately step forward from the rein-back. For a perfect movement the hind legs must spring off the ground from lowered hindquarters, the forelegs from an elevated forehand; they must not creep.

Only if our work leads us to being able to ask our horse, in any one of the gaits that we have practiced so far, to come to a halt in good carriage with weight on the haunches, to remain a moment in the halt position, and to properly step backward a few steps, may we assume that it is sufficiently prepared for the school movements that require increased flexion of both haunches.

ENDNOTES

[1] See Endnote 8 on page 241.

[2] The position taken in earlier editions that the halts, the holding of the halt, and the rein-back are to be considered only as a touchstone as to how far the flexibility of the hind legs has progressed, but that there is no need to make them the object of a special exercise, does not do justice to these important exercises. I consider it already a deficiency that the preceding chapters did not discuss the half-halt, the halt-arrêt, in more detail. Although they are being mentioned several times and various mentions are made of through-going rein aids, the manner of giving these aids, the interaction of the various aids required, are not described in greater detail. And yet, the correct performance of the half-halts and the halts are extremely important. The older masters gave these important lessons much more space, and we find with them different, finely graduated terms, depending on the type of the desired effect. They mention not only half-halts and full halts, but also quarter-halts and light halts. Seeger, Steinbrecht's mentor, discussed this subject in the most detail and is also the only writer who, in contrast to the still generally represented view that the half-halt must be performed with the same but somewhat weaker aids as the full halt and that this causes the horse to stop, makes a significant distinction between the two exercises.
Seeger demonstrates that the aids for the half-halts are different than for the full halt and that the horse must first learn the half-halt and then the full halt. He says the half-halt must be performed from the unilateral, active action of the rider's leg, hand, and weight so that each hind leg is driven forward, loaded and bent individually. The rider should initially drive forward one hind leg with his leg on the same side, hold back the same hind leg with the

rein on the same side and load it with his weight, and then do the same thing with the other hind leg. Only one hind leg at a time is held back which gradually produces the full halt in which both reins act simultaneously and both hind legs are held back. This interpretation of the term "halt" by Seeger, which can also be found already in the works of his mentor, Weyrother, unquestionably also goes to the core of this so immensely important exercise which is so difficult to master for the young rider. (Hans von Heydebreck)

2. Movements of the Haute École

(a) Piaffe and Passage

In the haute école one distinguishes between *trot-like movements,* namely *piaffe* and *passage,* and *jump-like movements* or *airs above the ground.* Generally a distinction is made between natural and artificial movements of the horse and the just mentioned movements belong to the artificial group. This conventional distinction often leads to the opinion that these so-called artificial movements of the horse are unnatural movements. Observing the horse in its free state shows us that this assumption is erroneous. The noble, strong horse, in the fullest enjoyment of its freedom and strength, performs the piaffe and passage on its own volition, as well as all airs above the ground, and thus furnishes proof of the naturalness of these movements. It is a characteristic of the genuine art of riding and distinguishes the true classical school from the caricature shown to the public by the circus rider. The former desires nothing other than to develop the horse's natural gifts to perfection and make them subject to the human will. In the circus, however, the horse is presented in trained-on positions, movements and tricks which lie entirely outside of its natural talents and in no way make it more qualified for its actual purpose, its use as a riding horse.

In the correct knowledge that the driving forces for all performances of the horse lie in its hindquarters, dressage has no other ultimate purpose than to develop them, strengthen them, and bring them under the absolute control of the rider. All its movements serve this ultimate purpose since none strives to achieve anything other than making the hindquarters flexible and elastic. The trainer of classical dressage finds the means to accomplish this only in the correct distribution of the weights and uses no other tools to accomplish this than his seat and legs together with spurs and reins. If he is given the time necessary to proceed systematically, he will be able to teach every horse to the perfection of training that is commensurate with its talents. If he uses auxiliary means, such as lunge line, whip, or pillars, to facilitate his work or for the sake of the horse, their use is based on the same principle which guides all work in the saddle, namely to correctly distribute the weights by appropriate interaction of restraining and driving aids.

In the course of this book it has been attempted to explain that the

[253]

entire training of the horse, its schooling, is a logically ordered system of horse gymnastics. Readers who have followed with benevolence to this point will hopefully have gained the same conviction, unless they had it before. In this connection it must be taken into consideration that the particular talent of a horse may permit deviations in the sequence of the exercises, or may often even demand such deviations. It is the task of the experienced trainer to detect and determine the specific sequence suitable for each individual horse and that deviations from this sequence are not permitted since they may cause damage. In contrast, the circus trainer, who does not use gymnastic exercises but essentially acts only on the horse's senses, randomly picks out each one of his tricks and teaches it to his student. If he is able to teach the Spanish walk and other, so-called high school movements even to a green horse, because it need perform this trick neither on the bit nor with flexed haunches, we can gladly let him have this honor if we realize that the purposes he strives for are completely different from ours. He merely wants to please the public while we want to prepare our horses for use.

For that reason the classical dressage trainer will not practice exercises that require greater, simultaneous flexion of both haunches until he has set his horse's forehand so that he can use his hands to transfer its weight to the hindquarters and has made both hind legs flexible individually. For the trot-like movements of the haute école, the piaffe and passage, it will be sufficient to accomplish this preparation at the trot, while for the airs above the ground the preparation must also have taken place in the jump-like gait of the canter.

As mentioned in the chapter on the canter, the old masters often trained their horses at the trot up to the piaffe before they began to canter. This manner of proceeding is certainly correct and proper according to classical dressage if one has unlimited time. Since today, however, we are usually rather limited in this respect and a certain development of the canter is absolutely necessary for everyday use, we will generally use this gait before we turn to a higher development of the trot. The necessary degree of canter training will generally be considered to have been attained when we have brought our horse to the point that it is able to perform the counter-canter and have developed this sufficiently to perfect the gait.

This would perhaps be the chapter in which, for the sake of clarity, we should divide what should be considered a logical unit into two parts, namely in the canter draw a line between lower- and upper-level movements. Once we reach this stage, we would perfect the canter by exercises on two tracks up to the turns on the hindquarters to finally be able to perhaps crown our work with the jump-like airs above the ground.

Although in practice the canter work discussed in Chapter 7 will not always be accomplished continuously from beginning to end since its second part already belongs to the haute école which would best be started with the trot-like movements of piaffe and passage, it did appear to be advantageous to discuss the development of the canter to its utmost perfection without interruption in order not to blur the logical relationships if possible.

Turning now in greater detail to the *piaffe* and *passage*, it will initially be necessary to understand the ideal picture of these movements. What I already emphasized for the canter applies here perhaps even to a greater degree; namely that only individual, extraordinarily talented horses are normally able to learn such beautiful movements in the normal way in the hands of an experienced and skilled trainer and only very few come even close to the ideal. Nevertheless it is necessary for the trainer to always have this ideal picture before his eyes during his work so that he does not ultimately create a caricature.

As anyone knows, the piaffe is a trot-like movement in place with raised steps in a sustained cadence in which the legs, bending in their joints, work straight up and down. Since the horse is able to perform this movement correctly only if the major portion of the total weight is carried by the hind legs so that the forelegs need only lightly support it, with the forehand raised and elevated, the croup is lowered due to the intense flexion of all joints of the hindquarters. The back muscles that constitute the connection between the forehand and the hindquarters are elastically tensioned because of the intense flexion of the hind legs so that the loin region is curved upward and becomes noticeable. The more energetically the horse's legs spring off from the ground under a horse in such a carriage and the higher they are raised and the less body movement there is, the more perfect is the piaffe because it gives proof of the flexibility and elasticity of the joints of the hindquarters.

In the absolutely ideal piaffe the horse raises its foreleg so high that the forearm is horizontal and it raises the hind leg to the point that its hoof reaches half the height of the splint bone hollow of the resting leg, with the body performing only a soft, yet strong up and down movement.

[255]

Every step the horse must chew on the bit, with its neck well elevated and its poll yielding. In spite of its visible desire to move forward a slight pressure on the bit must hold it in place.

As mentioned already in the chapter on the seat, the old masters used to begin their riding lessons by putting their student on a horse that was able to piaffe well between the pillars, without giving him the reins. They would now ask him to follow the horse's movements softly and without constraints with his arms supported on his hips. Indeed there is no better, more natural way than to teach the young student this supple, sensitive seat, which is the basis of all good, natural riding, early on. The up and down movements of a well piaffing horse are so soft in spite of all its energy that the connection between the seat and the saddle or the pad is never loosened at any moment. Every time one hind leg is put down and the hip on the same side is consequently lowered, the rider's hip on the same side is lowered as well and lets the naturally hanging leg fall softly against the horse's belly. The student's upper body will then lean softly backward to correspond to the weight distribution of the horse. On a well piaffing horse, the relaxed student will very soon submit automatically to these effects of the movement and the resulting carriage of his body and will feel well. This of course will happen to a lesser degree, the less perfect the piaffe.

The most common deficiencies arise from incorrect weight on the hindquarters, which may either be loaded too heavily or not enough. If the load on the hindquarters is too heavy, that is, if the flexion of the joints is exaggerated and the hind legs have stepped too far underneath the load, they will no longer be able to energetically push away from the ground because the elasticity of the hind legs is suppressed by the overload, just as any mechanical spring will lose its elasticity if it is stressed too much.

Although a horse trained in this way may perhaps raise its forelegs high, the movements of his hind legs will make the spectator think that the hooves are sticking to the ground or are mired in deep mud from which they are unable to free themselves. In such a faulty piaffe the rider feels a weak, slack sensation underneath his seat bones. The reader will now understand what is meant by the statement that the movements of the body must be soft but still strong. This overloading of the hind legs will be a tendency of particularly those horses which have naturally flexible hindquarters but innate or trained-on difficulties in the forehand, particularly those that tend to present a false elevation with the lower neck pushed out and the poll tight. Since such a piaffe completely misses the purpose of this movement and, if used continuously, fails to strengthen the springs of the hindquarters, the engines of all movement, which the piaffe is intended to do, but instead decisively weakens them, the understanding trainer will attempt to prevent this evil or, if he notices that his horse has a tendency toward it, will try energetically to keep it from developing.

The means for this are easy to find in theory, although their use in practice often encounters great difficulties. Obviously it can only be accomplished by setting head and neck lower and moving the hind legs away from the center of gravity so that they are relieved of some of the weight. The same procedure will be used here that was mentioned repeatedly in connection with the collection of the canter, namely to try to prevent any incorrect load on the hindquarters, which is always expressed by an error in contact - in this case by the horse not being on the bit but above the bit - by energetically driving the horse forward onto the bit. In our case it will be advisable, as soon as we notice that the discussed fault is evident, to ride relentlessly forward, with legs and spurs asking the horse to push off from the restraining hands in order to re-establish the correct contact and, by initiating thrust, revive the suppressed springs of the hindquarters.

If one then collects his horse again for the piaffe the above experience will have taught us that care must be taken right from the start to keep the horse well on the bit. For this purpose we will not permit it to step completely in place, which a horse having such tendencies will always be glad to do, but to continuously drive it into the hands and forward during the piaffe. If this is unsuccessful, the piaffe must be interrupted and the legs and spurs must push the horse energetically forward to bring it into the hands. Once the horse is able to perform its piaffe on the bit, the overload on the hindquarters and the suppression of its springs will be overcome. But to even further improve the spring action of the hind legs, the rider's weight must temporarily move forward some more and the hind legs must be stimulated by lively, fine spur aids, supported by the whip. In this case as always, the most important thing is again the correct distribution of the weight or, in other words: the carriage of the skeleton to meet the intended purpose is the basis on which the correct activity of the entire muscular structure is based. However, the only means for distributing the weight as required by the intended purpose reside in the correct interaction of the driving and restraining aids.

When working a horse between the *pillars*, which we will also discuss in this chapter, all success evolves from the correct weight distribution. Therefore, if we note the above-described fault when working our horse between the pillars, a correction will also be possible by means that set head and neck lower and thus move the hind legs away from the center of gravity. We will thus tie the horse a little lower and attach the reins leading to the pillars somewhat lower so that the horse is forced to chew on the bit in its halter during the piaffe and does not have enough room to perform its piaffe above the bit. We will then have to apply encouraging aids with the short and long whip in such a way that the hind legs are not caused to step under further but instead are prevented from doing so and are only asked to spring off in a lively fashion. The whip must therefore not approach the hindquarters from the back to the front but from the front to the back, or it must be applied to the bottom of the belly. The main thing in connection with this work is and always will be that the horse performs its piaffe on the bit.

The opposite fault occurs if the hindquarters do not carry enough weight in the piaffe and thus are free enough to use their strength in an uncontrolled and rough manner. The hind legs, whose joints are then insufficiently bent, push off from the ground in an inelastic way so that the croup, which in the correct piaffe performs only soft, barely noticeable up and down movements, is caused to oscillate violently, giving the rider harsh shocks that fling him forward. In this faulty movement in which the carrying forces of the hindquarters are used insufficiently, the forehand is not relieved enough. The forelegs are therefore unable to perform elevated steps since they must catch the load that is thrown to them by the hindquarters and they are unable to work freely and without constraint. In this case as always, the faults of the gait will become evident through deficiencies in contact.

A horse performing the piaffe in this way with stiff and high hindquarters will piaffe on its shoulders, will be behind the bit because it correctly and naturally feels that if it were to go on the bit it would soon be unable to stiffen its hindquarters. Such a faulty piaffe can be corrected simply by establishing the correct contact through correct forward work. Here again the understanding trainer, if he works his horse only under saddle, will for the time being completely cease any work in place as soon as he feels a tendency to slow down and will drive the horse into his hands or even onto his hands by quite energetic means, if necessary with a long whip in the hands of an understanding assistant. Generally the horse, once it has decided to move forward from such a piaffe, will throw all of its weight onto the rider's hands in a corresponding type of passage or a suspended trot movement to retain the ability of preventing flexion of the hindquarters by stiffening them. Initially the rider should not interfere with this behavior because it gives him an opportunity to gradually bend the horse's hind legs after all through repeated half-halts. However, this must occur very gradually since the forward drive must be maintained in force during all of this work in order not to immediately jeopardize any success.

If one carefully considers this main principle, it will be possible after a while to transfer the weight of the forehand to the hindquarters by through-going half-halts and thus flex the hind legs which must always be asked to step forward lively. This more and more relieves the rider's hands which had been carrying the weight of the entire body mass and gradually establishes the correct contact with the bit. Even after this has been accomplished, it will be prudent to keep the horse going forward during the piaffe work for a long time and to arrive at the true piaffe in place only very gradually and only after a contact based on the drive forward has been established very securely. The more carefully the horse has previously been worked in the trot exercises and in increased flexion of the haunches by movements on two tracks, the more reliably and earlier will it arrive at a proper piaffe with the correct contact even if it has initially fallen into the above-described errors due to its reluctance toward the new task and an instinctive resistance that is inherent in any creature. It will therefore be prudent to constantly reconfirm the basis for all further training, the trot exercises.

In the work between the pillars it is obvious that the correction of the described faulty piaffe can also be accomplished only by driving the horse forward against the halter. Since, however, the main difficulty of this work, as of any work not under saddle, lies in the fact that our own feeling cannot help us here, it is not easy in this specific case to measure our aids correctly if it appears necessary to proceed energetically, on the one hand, and to practice moderation, on the other hand. Since work between the pillars should be alternated with work under saddle, it will be possible, should this difficulty arise, to support the work between the pillars by appropriate procedures under saddle.

Now that we have discussed the two most frequently occurring faults in piaffe work, which are based on incorrect weight distribution, we want to also mention those deviations from the norm that are best known to circus spectators and may also occur with a correct distribution of the weight to forehand and hindquarters. If the otherwise well trained horse wants to avoid full flexion of the hindquarters in the piaffe it has a means available for this purpose that we have become aware of more than we liked in the course of our previous work, namely to *escape to the side* with its hind legs. If one understands how much strength the entire motion mechanism must have to perform a correct piaffe since, in spite of energetic activity of the legs, the body performs only very slight up and down movements, one must not be surprised if a horse that is not very strong or not yet thoroughly flexed throughout tries to make such work easier for itself. It is obvious that movement in place is much easier if it is possible for the horse to put its body into regular pendulum oscillations and thus relieve its legs of a large portion of their work which involves starting up the machine and keeping it going.

The pendulum oscillations of the body are of course obtainable only by the hind legs escaping to the sides. Thus the horse kills two birds with one stone in that it not only facilitates the movement but in addition also does not require the haunches to bend fully. Such pendulum oscillations of the body can be accomplished only in two ways, namely that either the raised hind leg or the hind leg being put down onto the ground escapes toward the side. Both types do indeed occur. Most frequent is the first type in which the raised hind leg, instead of being pulled straight up, performs a sideways movement toward the outside which throws the body over to the other side, thus producing the mentioned, regular pendulum oscillations of the body whenever the legs change. It is not too disadvantageous since the hind leg being put down onto the ground still bends slightly under the load although the fact that the load does not come straight but at an angle makes the bend not quite clean. The sideways movement saves the raised leg a good portion of the bending of its joints. Horses with not much courage and particularly those having a certain weakness in their backs and hindquarters will usually tend to perform such a rocking piaffe. The less their strength, the less is, of course, the chance of teaching them a perfect piaffe movement. The gradual strengthening of their muscles attained by constant gymnastic exercises and a very quiet seat in which no alternating leg aids are given at all while through-going half-halts and lively aids with both legs and spurs are given simultaneously, supported by the whip to refresh and maintain the movement, must contribute to eradicating this fault as much as possible.

The other type of piaffe that swings back and forth, in which the leg coming down to the ground is set off to the side, is the greatest fault of all that can occur in this exercise. There then no longer is any flexion of the haunches because the foot that is set down no longer steps underneath the load but to the side of it. In connection with it, this faulty piaffe usually shows that the rising hind leg touches the ground once more shortly afterwards because the other hind leg to be put down next steps too far to the side of the load that it is unable to provide sufficient support. Horses which by nature show such unpleasant, dragging, staggering, and weak movements of the hindquarters will have a particular tendency for such a poor piaffe, and any corrective procedures will always have only limited success against such natural deficiencies.

Hardly anything can be done between free-standing pillars to overcome this fault. It is recommended to use a single pillar standard near the wall and tie the horse to it alternatingly from one side and the other. When the respective inside hind leg is put down it must be driven toward the outside hind leg which in turn is held by the wall. Most effectively this fault will be overcome by work under saddle in which the horse is asked to piaffe along the wall in a half-shoulder-in position. Before the inside hind leg is put down onto the ground, with the weight correspondingly distributed toward the inside, the inside spur drives it underneath the load and toward the outside hind leg that is being held by the wall. Of course, care must be taken when working on faults that are based on physical imperfections of the horse. Gradual progression is necessary so that the horse is not invited to become resistant if its natural limitations are exceeded.

In the described deviations from the piaffe, the forelegs will, of course, also perform the rocking movement of the entire body and will step in such a mixed-up way that the soundness of the bones is endangered to the utmost degree. If, nevertheless, trick riders not only love to accept such a rocking piaffe from the horse but even develop it further by throwing their own weight to and fro and giving very noticeable, alternating leg aids, the reason for this is that such a movement is not only much easier for the horse - albeit at the expense of its limbs - but is also fascinating for the layman's eye because it seems to develop a great amount of energetic and fiery activity. In any case, there is no doubt that even the best dressage horse under a thoroughly skilled rider would hardly enthuse circus spectators with his correctly performed movements. There is a certain justification for the circus school, but it is thoroughly different from the true dressage school which desires nothing other than the utmost development of flexion in the haunches for a horse that is on the bit under all circumstances. Circus riding is based on Baucher-like training tricks, the classical school on a system of gymnastic exercises that are gleaned from nature.

The ideal picture of a passage and the most common deviations from it evolve almost automatically from the above statements if we realize that this movement is created from the piaffe by precisely controlled procedures. These precisely controlled procedures are very important because the difference between the two movements is that in the piaffe the hindquarters develop carrying and spring forces, in the passage they additionally develop thrust. The developing thrust makes the transition from the piaffe to the passage clearly noticeable to the sensitive rider no matter how fluently the perfectly trained dressage horse performs it. There is a great difference between a piaffe in which I let the horse step forward a little to make it easier for the horse or for other reasons, and the passage. In the passage the forward movement is produced by controlled action of the thrust while in the piaffe it results only from the fact that the carrying force is not yet fully and completely utilized. In a good passage the horse will traverse one side of the arena almost always with the same number of strides once a certain tempo has been established, while in the piaffe this is not possible with the same certainty. The rider's aids which evolve from the oscillations imparted to him through the horse's movements are also changed immeasurably by the inclusion of thrust.

In the piaffe the rider's legs contact the horse's body because the horse's hip on the same side is lowered at the moment at which the associated hind leg is put down so that the spur gives it the aid to spring off again. It is held in its flexion under the load by restraining aids from the hands. When thrust begins, the hip of this side is raised due to the expansion of the joints required to move the body mass forward. This gives the rider an increased inclination toward the other side at that moment which brings his leg on that side in greater contact with the horse's body. At this moment, however, the non-pushing hind leg has been raised off the ground and, in the passage as in any other progressive movement, receives the aid for further forward and underneath movement from the rider's leg on the same side. In the piaffe the rider's leg is thus in contact with the horse's belly when the horse's hind leg on the same side is put down, in the passage when that same leg is raised.

Just as in the ordinary trot, the horse is able to perform the most varied graduations from the collected school trot to the extended trot, without the fully trained horse, whose contact is controlled precisely, changing its cadence, this must also be the case in the suspended trot. The better the horse carries itself in the forehand so that any rein aids travel all the way to the hindquarters with the intended effect, the more skillful and willing the hindquarters have become through careful gymnastic exercises to enable them to arbitrarily pick up the weight or push it forward. In other words: the more the rider is enabled, because of the perfect training of his horse, to regulate and measure thrust and carrying force of the hindquarters as precisely as he desires, the more accurately he will be able to give the passage any desired tempo, to shorten it all the way to the piaffe if he so desires or to extend it to a just as free, suspended trot which makes the horse appear to fly over the ground. Always, however, even in the freest tempo of the passage, the pace must retain its suspended expression, which is possible only with a certain elastic tension of the back muscles. Once this disappears, and with it the suspended pace, the horse no longer performs a passage but an ordinary trot.

The passage is thus a trot-like, suspended movement which is the more perfect and beautiful, the stronger and more energetic the horse springs off the ground, the higher it raises its legs, the more securely it maintains cadence and regularity of its strides, the more accurately its legs move up and down because it is set straight and the body does not swing sideways the slightest bit. The term "suspended pace" must be taken literally for the passage because between each one of the horse's strides there is a short moment, discernible to the practiced eye, in which the two supporting diagonal legs have just pushed the body off the ground while the other raised diagonal remains up in the air more or less high so that for a short time no foot is supported on the ground. This movement gives the pace its fiery and energetic character that must distinguish a good passage, as it does the good collected canter. This moment is therefore particularly suitable for illustration in pictures, and there would be a certain justification to call the passage a trot-like movement above the ground.

In the passage as well, carriage and position of the horse will depend on the degree of collection and the amount of ground covered by the horse. The shorter the pace, the more the carrying force of the hindquarters is utilized and the less its thrust; the more elevated the forehand becomes, the lower the croup, the more the joints of the hind legs will have to be bent and pushed underneath the load. The freer the passage, the more thrust and less carrying force are active, the more the skeleton must take on the balanced carriage. If a certain elastic tension of the back muscles is required for the suspended movement, as mentioned earlier, as it can also be noticed in the upward curving of the piaffing horse's kidney section, this must in no way lead to the conclusion that the passage is a gait in which the horse stiffens and tightens itself in some way. If you observe a horse performing a good passage, you must have the impression that the muscles are completely relaxed in this movement and work without tension and all of the horse's joints have so much elastic resiliency that in every stride the impulsion of the hind legs travels from the pasterns through the hindquarters, the back, and neck into the poll and the mouth and is audibly demonstrated by rhythmical chewing. That is also the reason why the movement feels particularly soft, elastic, and pleasant to the rider so that the passage as well as the piaffe are excellently suited to teach the student a soft, supple seat and thus also the correct feeling for the horse's movements.

Since we have now painted the ideal picture of the passage, let us again turn to the deviations of it that occur most frequently in practice. We can do this briefly because most of these deviations are related to the faulty types of the piaffe and develop from them quite consequently.

From the piaffe in which the horse is unable to take its hind feet off the ground because the hindquarters are overloaded results a passage in which the suppressed springs of the hindquarters do not work so that the horse, instead of springing off the ground with its hind legs, makes striding movements. In this deviation of the passage the rider no longer has the feeling of a trot-like movement produced specifically by the spring-off of the hindquarters. In the correct movement this occurs energetically but softly and elastically so that the rider's seat must never come loose in the saddle, not even the slightest little bit. The striding passage, similarly to the same type of piaffe, will always result in faults in contact. The horse will generally not perform this movement on the bit, that is, it will not move forward correctly. Just as in the piaffe, the fault can here be overcome only by energetic forward riding, with the spurs forcing the horse to push off from the restraining hands.

In the passage in which the horse moves forward, this will be much easier to accomplish than in the piaffe. The latter would have to be relinquished altogether for a while to regulate the contact first by riding forward and revive the springs of the hindquarters by developing thrust. Here, however, we do not need to completely interrupt our training, we must merely appropriately increase its tempo. If now the freer tempo naturally converts the striding movements of the hindquarters into trot-like movements, this alone in no way eradicates the fault. The important thing is to transfer the resilient movements of the hind legs from the freer passage to the shortened passage. This can of course be accomplished only very gradually and after longer confirmation at a freer tempo. Prerequisite for attaining the goal is always that the horse works correctly on the bit. As always, the correct contact gives us the limit as to how far we may go in collecting the horse.

In the second discussed deviation of the piaffe the horse, due to insufficient weight on the hindquarters, performs steps behind the bit with little action of the forelegs and insufficiently bent hind legs, giving the rider hard shocks that throw him forward. As already discussed, this results in a passage in which the horse looks to the reins for support for the still unflexed hindquarters. This faulty phenomenon is much less dangerous and more easily corrected than the previously discussed problem since the horse itself gives the rider the means for correction.

The *rocking piaffe* of both kinds also produces a similar movement in the passage. We can take care of it here very briefly since it must be corrected quite similarly to the piaffe and refer to the statements made there since its use for the forward movement of the passage requires no further discussion.

Since, however, the rocking passage is shown to us in the circus under the name of "*Spanish Walk*," we want to expend a few words to discuss this incorrect movement. The trick rider loves to accept it from the horse, the same as the corresponding piaffe, and makes it even more striking by his aids. It fools the inexperienced observer who perceives it as a greater performance of artistry and strength, although in truth, as discussed in connection with the piaffe, the pendulum oscillations make it half as difficult for the horse.

Such a rocking passage, however, is not yet sufficient for the trick rider to earn the full applause from his public. He makes it that much more dazzling by continuing to use his whip to ask the foreleg which, in the correct movement, rises with all its joints bent, to stretch out. The layman, who does not know the natural movements of the horse and therefore has no eye for what is unnatural, then sees quite a lively picture.

The trick rider requires such means to entertain his public and is therefore entirely justified to use them. He is truly appreciative of true dressage and merely provides some embellishments that he thinks are absolutely necessary to the products of dressage so that they become more noticeable to the layman. More understanding circus directors will always be very happy if they find a trainer who is schooled in classical dressage and is able to give their school horses the basics of correct dressage. It is then an easy task for the experienced trick trainer to provide the obligatory curlicues. In this way a presentation is developed which finds the applause of the layman as well as the acknowledgment of the expert. This must really be appreciated by any kind of artist. Where, however, dressage work is completely absent and the school horses are trained only according to the Baucher methods, that is, the "Spanish Walk" is developed only from the so-called march, we see the known caricatures of school horses who perform their lessons above or behind the bit while the hindquarters drag behind in irregular, slack movements.

Finally, we want to mention another incorrect movement that often gives the trainer a lot of trouble during the passage work, namely hindquarters *that hop* instead of stepping regularly as some horses do once in a while to make their work easier. Similarly to the rocking piaffe where the supporting hind legs are set sideways and are helped by another short step of the rising hind leg, they will also easily tend in the passage to distribute the work asked of one hind leg in each stride to both hind legs and in some strides to support the load not only by two but by three legs. For this purpose their hindquarters perform a movement similar to a short canter stride, with the one leg, that should actually be supporting, stepping forward somewhat. This very ugly fault will appear particularly in horses that harbor a certain weakness or sensitivity of the hindquarters particularly if the pace is shortened too much. It can therefore be eradicated only by selecting a free tempo with good contact with the bit. To increase the degree of collection in such horses will be possible not at all or only after the muscles have been strengthened sufficiently by longer gymnastic exercises. However, this fault also occurs in horses that have sufficiently strong hindquarters. It then develops from negligence and inertia or from over-zealousness. With lazy horses the spurs must ask the hind legs to step under more energetically, with impetuous horses only a very quiet seat and gentle careful aids are able to overcome the problem.

By completing the description of the ideal picture of the piaffe and passage and the most frequently occurring deviations, we now turn to the training of the horse in these movements. However, first we must once more emphasize very strongly the principle that in truly systematic gymnastic work, which is what we consider proper dressage to be from its first beginnings to its highest perfection, each exercise must be prepared; the horse must know it already when we begin with it.

Just like this axiom was appropriate for the lower-level movements, it must remain applicable also for those of the haute école. If a horse is truly carefully and conscientiously worked thoroughly according to the correct principles in all trot movements up to the school trot, one can confidently state: it knows how to passage. Unless nature has completely denied it the ability to perform such an act of strength, it will inevitably offer some suspended steps with gradually increasing collection, and these can be developed gradually with continued practice into an orderly passage.

A horse whose passage has been developed to the utmost perfection actually is also able to do the piaffe - always under the above-made presumption regarding its natural talents - because the continued collection of the passage leads to the rider's ability to finally hold the horse in place for a few steps, from which then with increasing practice, the piaffe gradually results. Whoever is able, in a soft, totally unconstrained balanced seat, to feel every movement of his horse and to smoothly follow it, if he clearly understands the term of a yielding poll and in connection with it the correct contact which gives him the lever to distribute the weights as he desires, and whoever finally has penetrated into the simple secret of the bent-straight carriage of the horse on which all movements on two tracks are based, will in a way receive the haute école movements, if his work is patient and enduring, as a reward for his diligence, at least from a naturally strong and agile horse. Whoever has moreover attentively read the chapters about bending the horse and about the movements on two tracks, particularly the shoulder-in, and understands their meaning and essence, requires hardly any further instruction about passage and piaffe. Careful work in the sense of the principles developed there quite reliably leads to a passage whose development in a way comes automatically and which in turn contains the seeds of the piaffe.

If now the collection of the trot obtained on the immovable basis of correct contact and perfect, pure, rib cage flexion inevitably leads to suspended steps, I would like to warn most emphatically against premature acceptance of such steps. Almost nothing else becomes so annoying for overall dressage training as suspended steps the horse has prematurely been permitted to perform or that have even been favored. There are a large number of horses, particularly those that have a certain stiffness in their backs, which in the course of collection work will very soon offer suspended steps and which one can ask with the greatest of ease to present a sort of passage. Yet these are the horses that must not be permitted to perform this movement, or at least only as late as possible. The older, experienced trainer who has learned to see that the true value of the art of riding does not lie in artificial gaits but in the pleasant experience of the horse in practical use and who has strengthened his character through long, conscientious practice of his profession so that vanity will no longer divert him from his path leading to the true final goal of dressage, will easily be able to avert the just mentioned danger. The young beginner, however, requires the most emphatic warning in this respect so that he will not sometimes be tempted. He should remember: the more distrustful he is of suspended steps occasionally offered by the horse and the longer he postpones their acceptance, the more reliably will he arrive at the true passage which then not only will not adversely affect the overall training but, to the contrary, will also significantly enhance it.

The true moment for beginning passage work has come if the horse is able to move fluently and in a clear rhythm in a highly collected trot according to its own particularities, that is, in the school trot, on one as well as two tracks, in any desired bend, and offers, when the collection is further increased, suspended steps on a straight line. Only a horse that performs its trot lessons perfectly securely and without constraints is sufficiently prepared for the passage and can be worked to advantage in this movement. The steps which it then offers if even more collection is asked are free of painful tension and may be accepted without qualms. But those steps that it shows from time to time during the trot work, before the exercises at this gait are firmly established, have significance only to the extent that they demonstrate the horse's ability to perform suspended steps. They are produced only because the horse is still stiff somewhere, usually in the back or the hindquarters, and always involve some holding back; they must be suppressed under all circumstances. Since these tense steps furnish proof that collection was increased at the expense of suppleness, their eradication and the re-establishment of the pure pace can occur only by loosening the horse completely through correct forward riding. On this basis collection can then be reintroduced but more gradually than before. The purity of the trot exercises always remains a yardstick for the correctness of the passage work. Therefore, even if the work was begun with full justification, it must be suppressed immediately in the manner indicated as soon as tense steps creep in which interrupt the regular trot tempo. Only after the school trot has become fluid and free of tension may one start again with the passage.

An aversion to the passage, which one frequently encounters from very understanding, practical riders and which they justify by saying that this movement is a restrained movement through which the horse forgets to willingly yield and go forward, is not justified if this beautiful movement is begun only after the correct preparation and is used with wise precaution and moderation. Since, however, this is unfortunately rarely the case and instead the horse is usually permitted to perform suspended steps too early, or they are even taught and are then used much too frequently and in an unsuitable way, it can regrettably not be denied that the opponents of the passage are usually correct in practice. It is possible to teach almost any horse a type of passage in a relatively very short time and not according to the Baucher methods but by work in the saddle. This requires nothing other than feeling and equestrian tact in addition to the ability of setting the horse's forehand in such a way, if necessary by artificial auxiliary means, that the rein aids go through to the hindquarters which are always very carefully asked to follow the forehand, presuming of course that one is not afraid of hard work, and the horse is not completely green or entirely disobedient. Yes, there may even be cases - we will revert to them in the course of this chapter - in which it is quite appropriate to use the passage relatively early as an artificial means for developing more energy and regularity in the trot movements, for example, for older horses whose lack of dressage training is to be supplemented where possible. For the young, not yet ruined horse, for which proper dressage training according to the system developed in this book is still possible without restrictions, the conscientious trainer will initiate passage work in very rare cases already in the second year, usually in the third year, and for a goodly number of horses not until the fourth year or later.

Those readers who, due to practical experience, have been able to follow the preceding statements will find no exaggeration in this principle and will have understanding for the requirement of the old masters that the completion of a dressage horse requires a period of five years, which most present-day riders consider most ridiculous.

No one who is able to correctly understand this movement will doubt that the passage, after proper preparation and applied in the correct way, may be a significant advantage in the training of the horse. The passage not only strengthens the muscles of the horse's back and hindquarters and makes them supple, the carriage of the forehand is also immensely perfected and strengthened by this work. In addition, obedience and attention to the aids must of necessity grow from the passage; all advantages that are of decisive significance for practical use. I cannot repeat it often enough that all lessons taught in the equestrian art, piaffe and passage as well as the movements on two tracks, are not intended to be anything other than means for training the horse to enable us to ride it with pleasure and to advantage in our practical lives. An exception is the school horse for which the movements are the ultimate goal as it is to be the teacher for the young trainer-to-be, to give him an idea of the ideal picture of the various movements, to give him the correct feeling for these movements and the soft, supple seat he needs, while familiarizing him with precise, fine balancing of his aids.

If we now turn to passage work, we must recall once more that, as agreed upon, we cannot begin the passage until the horse, after a session of movements on curved lines in a collected trot and set straight, offers a few suspended steps with even more collection. These initially only very few suspended steps now obviously constitute the basis on which an orderly passage must be built up quite naturally through continued practice and by no other means than with a soft balanced seat and the correct evaluation of the performance capability of the horse. Such a seat is the main and basic condition without which no dressage work is possible and particularly no such cadenced paces as the passage and piaffe, whose rhythm is so easily interfered with by any incorrect movement from the rider.

A horse that literally floats in passage and piaffe must be compared with a gold-weighing scale which works so accurately that its balance can

[270]

be disturbed by the weight of a hair. The only way not to interfere with such a finely balanced pace is therefore that the rider completely and intimately follows the horse's movements so that no part of the contacting surfaces between rider and horse, particularly the seat, comes loose at any moment. This cannot be accomplished by tightly clamping but only by soft resting. From this soft, intimate contact the aids that maintain the pace evolve quite automatically in that every time a hind leg springs off, the rider's leg on the same side drops against the horse's belly. If this alternating contact of the leg resulting from the horse's movement asks the respective hind leg to spring off at the proper time and in a lively fashion, stepping under as far as possible, the alternating rein aids, which are also given in the rhythm of the pace, will alternatingly load the hindquarters when the hind legs are put down, compress their joints, and ask them to again step off lively, simultaneously making the forehand freer and more elevated in its movements. Although the rider will obviously have to depart from this passive behavior on a horse that does not yet perform the passage securely and change to more active aids, this must always occur only on the basis of a soft, balanced seat and at the moments indicated by the movement. The weight imparting rein aid must be reinforced if necessary, and the alternating contact of the rider's legs must be accompanied by somewhat more pressure or also by a light touch with the spur.

Although these are the mechanical means which, in the normal course of events, create the passage from suspended steps joined together in careful trot work, they would not be of much value without special consideration and understanding. It is of primary importance here that the performance capability of the horse at that time is understood correctly and that the demands made on the horse are carefully adapted to it. As everywhere in dressage, it cannot be stated emphatically enough that moderation is necessary since nothing adversely affects success as much as overwork which creates insensitivity and dislike.

To obtain increased performances from the horse it is absolutely necessary for the rider to give his aids with a certain amount of energy, but these aids should be more of a psychological nature than physical. It is by no means the intensity of the aids that increases performance but, as already stated elsewhere, their correct interaction at the right moment. A pair of rough spurs awake fear in the horse and might perhaps cause it to temporarily put forth more effort. But since they interrupt the rhythm, this effort in no way benefits the pace. A fine spur aid, however, given at the moment at which the horse is ready to raise its hind leg, enhances its lively spring action without interrupting the pace. Because of the increased load, a half-halt following thereafter also causes the hind leg to bend in its joints again when it is put down, while it simultaneously increases the elevation of the raised foreleg because the weight has been removed from it. Yet, it does not interrupt the orderly sequence of the footfalls of the pace. Instead it makes the pace more expressive and cadenced.

If the forehand is pulled back harshly, however, the horse might temporarily engage its hindquarters, but since this hurts its hind legs, it will naturally subsequently try to protect them. Strong pressure from the rider's legs pressing the horse's ribs together will only bring it into forced, unnatural positions and movements with its tail pulled in, while the soft application of the leg with a threatening spur carriage causes a horse that knows the spur and obeys it to willingly and elastically use its strength.

A hand holding the horse with all the strength inherent in the rider's arm may perhaps keep the horse on the bit, but it will tighten its poll and cause it to lean on the bit with a dead mouth. A hand acting softly and without the exertion of force, however, in harmonious cooperation with seat and legs, will cause the horse to chew on the bit and willingly yield its poll. There is no denying that working the horse sometimes requires the rider to exert certain physical forces and this has been mentioned occasionally in this book. But a horse that has reached the stage of training that we are discussing right now no longer needs such exertions of force. It is a thoroughly unjustified opinion, albeit quite widespread, that elevated steps can be pushed out by strong pressure from the rider's legs.

Although, thanks to the nature of the horse, superior physical strength, which not everyone is blessed with, is in no way necessary for training a horse while the correct feeling that is based on a soft, good seat and can be acquired to a certain degree plays a much more important role, it is still a correct understanding for the mental characteristics and manifestations of the horse and, based on them, the appropriate reaction to them that is absolutely necessary. This is more true the farther we progress in our training. The correct evaluation of the horse's temperament and a clear understanding of its character are just as indispensable for success as the correct evaluation of its physical characteristics.

All such general comments are fully justified at any time in a book about training a horse for dressage, especially if a horse is involved that has reached a higher level of dressage training and stands before the development of haute école movements. Particularly for the development of the passage, it is of special importance to correctly evaluate the horse's temperament because the work with the horse depends considerably on it. The passage must be used with extreme caution for horses that have a suspicious or reticent temperament. Such horses, which are generally willing to perform shortened paces very quickly, will often use the passage from suspicion as soon as they have become acquainted with it - particularly if a stiff back makes it easy for them to perform suspended steps - in that they try to stay behind or above the bit with a tight back.

With such horses, even the beginning of passage work will have to be postponed considerably since they will have a tendency to interrupt a supple shortened trot which, if they are to work honestly in it, is very uncomfortable for them, with such suspended steps. To counteract this, any unintended suspended step must be suppressed at once by very energetically driving the horse forward in order to regulate the contact. Here more than in any other case, it is important that the lively flowing trot in all tempi does not suffer from the passage. It must therefore be practiced again and again with particular diligence and care, before the beginning of passage work as well as during it. The passage itself must be performed on such horses in a way that they are unable to protect themselves. They must be asked by all means available to work this exercise with full strength and energy.

The statements made about the use of psychological influences must here be applied especially because it is much less the intensity of the aids than their irresistible liveliness, in a way the superior energy of the rider, which urges such horses to honestly use their strength fully and completely.

The initial tempo selected for the passage will be more decisive and free and the horse will be asked to go in the correct and definite contact under all circumstances. If the horse tends to go above the bit, it must be made to push away from the bit by pressure from the spurs if necessary. If it likes to creep behind the bit, short jabs with the spurs, the whip, and possibly even the long whip must be used to bring it into the hands, even though the use of such means might temporarily interrupt the tempo of the pace. Once contact is established, the half-halts resulting from the movement must be given a little stronger than usual while the driving aids for maintaining the pace constantly take care that the half-halts go through the entire horse and flex the joints of the hindquarters to massage the back, so to speak, and soften it.

The above statements indicate that passage sessions, once the introductory period is over, will be a bit longer than for a talented horse because the desired success cannot be achieved in a few strides. If the work is to be useful, the rider must feel a completely relaxed back. Used in such a way, the passage will be of particularly extraordinary use in the overall training specifically for this type of horse for which it can be extremely deleterious if performed incorrectly. The usefulness of the passage will best become evident when, after a successful passage session, the horse will be more willing than before to move in a flowing collected trot.

Next to the reticent horse, the impetuous temperament requires special consideration in passage work. If the horse is treated appropriately, this movement can also be used to advantage for both types. If for the suspicious horse the beginning of work had to be postponed for a while, it will conversely sometimes be advisable to introduce the passage earlier than usual to the impetuous horse because the rhythmical and sustained tempo of this movement will moderate the impetuosity and bring the horse into patient submission. The work itself is in no way made more difficult by the impetuosity but, to the contrary, is facilitated since in this case the temperament drives the horse forward and onto the bit, saving the rider very many driving aids and permitting him to start relatively early with through-going half-halts which, if used correctly, will soon bring the horse into suspension.

As already discussed in the chapter on the canter, impetuosity is not always exclusively a matter of temperament. Liveliness is often augmented to impetuosity as the result of unfavorable conformation. Especially a soft back and then a strongly developed lower neck with broad jowls and, most of all, the all too frequent coincidence of these two evils often have the above-mentioned influence on the horse's temperament. Although the passage can also be used to advantage for this type of impetuous horse, particular care must be taken to maintain the appropriate carriage of head and neck. Only if the nose is set relatively low, making the top of the neck long and the lower neck disappear, will such a horse truly relax in the poll, and only in this position is it possible to use through-going half-halts, on which the development of the passage is primarily based, without doing damage in such cases. As soon as the nose is held too high, a soft back will be pushed down too much by such rein aids, a naturally heavily developed lower neck will be sculpted out even more, thus further constricting the space for the jowls so that the resulting pain will not reduce the impetuosity but increase it.

Since the passage is to be used in impetuous horses to calm them down, it is necessary, once the introductory period has been completed, to ride it in longer sessions, selecting the most collected and expressive tempo. Work should actually be facilitated by an impetuous temperament because the spirit of the impetuous horse will always keep awake its forward drive. It is therefore possible to shorten the pace considerably without having to fear that it becomes weak and lax, or without requiring strong aids that interrupt the cadence in order to freshen it. Here more than anywhere a soft, supple seat will be appropriate, with the aids resulting from the movement being entirely sufficient to keep the pace energetic. The rider can then direct his attention to light guidance to enable him to shorten the tempo by gradually taking the horse up with soft hands to the extent permitted by the physical performance capability of the horse. Contact and regularity of the steps are always an infallible yardstick in this respect.

The passage can be used to quite special advantage for those types of impetuous horses which, due to their temperament, perhaps in conjunction with an unfavorable conformation, tend to take rushing, jigging steps. Such horses frequently can perform a quiet, regular trot only through the passage. These are then the cases in which a relatively early use of this movement, as indicated earlier, is recommended. Since, however, in such horses, the suspended steps cannot result from the greater collection of the trot, a very special introductory procedure is necessary here which we should discuss in greater detail particularly since it may immensely facilitate and accelerate the development of the passage in all cases and can therefore be used whenever one has come to the conclusion after conscientious examination that the horse is ready for an introduction to passage work.

I have postponed the discussion of this method until now because the normal picture of the degree of dressage training as developed above, in which the passage is developed only by collecting the trot which is absolutely appropriate for well trained, strong horses with a good temperament that are worked systematically, as long as the necessary time is

[275]

available. Since, however, the just mentioned conditions are met only in the rarest of cases, but the work in haute école movements, conducted under the considerations and contemplations discussed so far may be of extraordinary value for the overall training of the horse, I recommend the *introductory method* to be discussed here which brings results in the majority of all horses suitable for riding and this without having to use anything other than *reins, legs,* and the *correct weight distribution.*

This method is essentially based on the horse being put into a trot-like movement in which it covers very little ground, with his hindquarters engaged well and taking short, springy steps. In this movement, which we want to call the *piaffe walk,* and which we practice continuously, gradually increasing the aids so that the steps become more elevated, energetic, and expressive until the horse, experiencing suspension, shows the first passage-like steps. The task of putting a horse into this piaffe walk is again one of those which can be accomplished much less by physical force than by liveliness and spiritual energy. The piaffe walk, if performed correctly, must in a way already contain the passage in that the well engaged hind legs spring off the ground with such force and liveliness that, in the highest perfection of this movement, the impression is created as if the horse, if it were given a bit more freedom, would go into suspended steps to lighten itself. This piaffe walk therefore, although it is not being used as a means for developing the passage, is in itself a very useful exercise and will be used to extraordinary advantage all over the large section of dressage training concerned with bending the haunches during the intervals between other exercises, for example between the trot exercises on two tracks or the exercises for collecting the canter. Later, when the time for beginning the passage work has come, it will no longer be necessary to develop this pace but the horse need merely be permitted to use it.

To get a horse to perform this piaffe walk, it should be put against the wall, at the walk, in a half-shoulder-in position, so that the outside hind leg is held by the wall, the inside hind leg by the shoulder-in position. In this position the horse is asked by half-halts in short succession, whose number and intensity must depend on the horse's temperament, to strongly engage the hindquarters. In horses of the type we discussed as the basis of this method, that is the impetuous horses with quick, hasty movements, it will only be necessary to briefly sit down while softly holding back with the hands to attain the intended result. The less sensitive and more phlegmatic the horse and the longer and more dragging his movements are by nature, the stronger, more intensively and more frequently must the aids be applied before the hindquarters step briefly under in the desired fashion. In no way must one expect to achieve the intended purpose by strong leg pressure or rough jabs with the spurs and forcefully pulling back the forehand. This would perhaps cause the hindquarters to temporarily creep underneath, but not create the desired lively, almost tripping stepping-under in which the springs of the hindquarters are not suppressed but only compressed to the extent that they have the strong desire to open again. Instead, success is realized by frequent repetition of short lively aids from hands and legs, with spurs and crop, with an open seat, and the upper body leaning back slightly so that the horse is, in a way, pushed between the rider's open knees, while the half-halts from the hands are not given with a tight rein but with loose but short reins and a light hand so that the horse chews busily on the bit.

The more the horse has been familiarized with the greater engagement of the hindquarters through work on curved lines, the more willing it will be to assume this introductory collection and will present these tripping, short steps of the hind legs that much earlier. The less prepared horse will often respond to these aids for a long time only by taking irregular strides in which it tries to escape flexing the hind legs either by flicking them out toward the back or by escaping to the interior of the arena. By the way, in this introductory work at collection care must be taken that the forward drive is always kept awake because only on such a basis is collection possible at all. As soon as the horse willingly responds to these brief, collecting aids by responding with short, lively steps, with the hindquarters pushed under well, it should be made to advance somewhat from this collection in the same short, lively steps. In that case the rider's upper body should lean forward slightly to somewhat relieve the hindquarters and should follow the movement in a soft, loose seat. Driving aids from legs and spurs and soft half-halts applied in the rhythm of the steps and carefully adapted in their intensity to the characteristic of the particular horse maintain the movement.

As with everything new to the horse that it should learn, nothing is more helpful in making it understand than frequent repetitions in short sessions which do not exceed the horse's attention span and good will. For that reason it will be advisable in this exercise as well to be satisfied with a few steps performed happily and willingly from the introductory

[277]

collection and to show the horse, by stopping and praising it, that it has done what was requested to then, and, after a pause, begin with a new attempt at collection. If this exercise is repeated no more than three or four times in succession in the pauses between other movements and if the rider is initially satisfied primarily with a willing response to the request, after a few days the horse will respond willingly and attentively to the aids for collection and present a few short, springy steps in good humor.

If one has thus gotten the first few steps out of the horse, their series must be extended until orderly piaffe walk sessions result whose length is determined by the fact that liveliness and elasticity of the horse must not be suffocated by overwork and they must always conclude with the best possible, lively steps. Although it will be advisable to accomplish this by still making the sessions rather short, it will not be possible to avoid that, on occasion, when the demands are increased, the rider feels that liveliness and energy of the steps falter. In that case, one must not hesitate to interrupt the pace at once by energetic collection and, once the hindquarters have been actively engaged again, to terminate the session with a few good steps.

In these exercises it is initially less important that the steps are in perfect cadence and rhythm but that they are thoroughly energetic and springy. Only if this elasticity has gradually become strong enough from continued practice that the steps begin to become suspended due to the connected elastic tensioning of the back muscles, a certain rhythm of the pace will develop. At this moment, the rider, who previously had to give very active hand and leg aids, must immediately change to a more passive behavior in which the movement then maintains itself and indicates the aids automatically. However, as soon as the pace ceases to be suspended because the steps are no longer springy enough, he must immediately fall back to his active aids.

Although this moment at which the steps begin to become suspended occurs very early with some horses and very late with others, a longer period of patient practice will be necessary in any case. One must not try to force success, which will be forthcoming; one must be patient and wait. The most important thing remains to correctly feel the described moment at which the horse attains the required tensioning of its back muscles. At that point the rider must immediately yield to the movement in a soft, supple seat. The session is then terminated after two or three suspended steps, the horse is praised and then, after a renewed introduction of collection, the horse is put back into the piaffe walk from which it then again must produce a few suspended steps. If one alternates these exercises with trot movements, always in the correct ratio, attempting primarily to correctly maintain contact and a yielding poll through proper forward riding, the horse will show more clearly with every day that it has understood what is wanted and will respond more and more willingly. The introductory session in the piaffe walk will become shorter on its own, the number of suspended steps greater until the horse responds to the request for collection by immediately presenting passage-like steps.

It should not require any detailed explanation that this success will arrive earlier, more securely and easily the more careful was the *preparation*, the more confirmed the only suitable carriage of the forehand, and the more lasting the thus created lever for bending the haunches was employed. A horse systematically prepared up to the passage, as already discussed earlier, is able to perform and will perform the passage in a surprising manner as soon as the rider informs it of his will in the described way. The less thorough the preparation, the earlier passage work is introduced for special reasons, the more the horse will fight it; it will be the more stubborn and fight longer the more energy in its character and the more tautness in its basic fiber.

When working against resistances that then develop, the rider must always remember our well-known main principle: "Ride your horse forward and set it straight!" Following it offers the means for breaking off the tip of all resistances and for ultimately subjecting the horse to the rider's will.

If you have read the first chapters of this book attentively, you will sufficiently understand the meaning of this principle whose use must be once again called to the attention of all readers: any collection is based on the proper forward drive being reliably established in the horse; and the hindquarters must under all circumstances cleanly follow the forehand. Whenever there are ever so irregular strides - which, by the way, as long as they are directed forward only, do no harm whatsoever - the skilled trainer must know how to set the hindquarters to follow the forehand or the forehand ahead of the hindquarters by means of appropriate rein and leg aids and primarily by means of the correct distribution of his weight so that at any time the strength coming from the hindquarters acts directly and unweakened against the rider's hands and thus enables them to let the weight of the forehand be transferred to the hindquarters.

[279]

Let us now turn to the question of how these passage-like steps - be they developed properly in the classical way solely by collecting the trot or with the aid of the just described method - can be developed further and utilized. In this connection it will initially be necessary to determine the suitable tempo for each horse, its working tempo so to speak, namely the tempo at which it is able to carry itself with the least amount of aids. At this tempo it must be strengthened gradually through patient practice to the extent that it becomes able, without significant effort and supported only by the rider's aids resulting from its movement, to perform longer periods of passage in a thoroughly relaxed manner. If this is possible with sufficient reliability along the wall in both directions, the next step is to accomplish the same on the circle.

Working on the circle, almost every horse will initially be more or less insecure because the absence of the wall and the curved track make the task more difficult. The rider must therefore direct his main attention toward keeping the horse straight and bent on the circular line of the circle. As soon as the hindquarters fall out, the suspended movement ceases and can be recovered only by several half-halts and setting the hindquarters in the direction of the movement. In addition, this passage work on the circle is a matter of quiet practice and contributes extraordinarily to increasing the security of the pace and to grind away small, still existing unevennesses to make the movement more pleasing to the eye and more comfortable.

If now the horse has reached the point where it is able to perform continuous longer sessions in its, so to speak, natural passage tempo along the whole arena, on the circle, and in simple changing lines which will be no problem whatsoever after the work on the circle, the rider may begin to think about perfecting the movement as much as possible, that is, making the steps higher, more cadenced, and stronger. To accomplish this, the rider should initially change from the natural tempo of the passage to a freer tempo to then develop and perfect as much as possible the forceful springing of the hindquarters and the elevated forward steps of the forehand. This free passage, in which the horse literally floats above the ground, seemingly without practically any contact with it, if the horse is to perform it truly with the expenditure of all its strength - naturally under consideration of its temperament - requires energetic aids from the rider, mainly lively spur aids in constant alternation with through-going half-halts. However, no aids must interrupt the cadence of this finely balanced pace; they must instead make it more impulsive and expressive and be given at precisely the correct instants of the movement. This is possible with the necessary infallible reliability only if the rider sits in a soft, quiet, supple seat.

Just as it was necessary in the development of the ordinary trot to first teach the horse to fully develop its thrust in a free tempo and thus get it to freely step forward from its shoulders before it was possible to collect the trot to advantage, just so the flying passage must serve as a means for collecting the pace to the limits of the horse's abilities without losing elasticity and expression of the steps. It must enable the rider to utilize the impulsion developed in it to shorten the tempo by way of repeated, through-going half-halts and yet obtain the most beautiful steps the horse is able to produce.

In these exercises for perfecting the passage one should never forget how strenuous they are for the horse and should therefore be moderate in their use. Exaggerated requirements will produce exactly the opposite from what is intended. The horse, instead of becoming more attentive, forceful, and fiery, will conversely become duller and more leathery. If instead, under careful consideration of the horse's capabilities, one uses these exercises only sparingly, they will gradually exert their perfecting influence also on the natural tempo of the passage in which of course the major work must be performed.

Consequently, exercises on two tracks will here, like in the working paces, be the next and most reliable means for furthering perfect flexion of the haunches and increasing the collection in an unconstrained way up to the piaffe. The principles for this work and the inner relationships between the individual lessons involved have been described in such detail in the chapter relating to them that we may be satisfied here with a short mention that the system of working on two tracks developed there is fully valid for the passage as well as for all other paces. The main difficulty of using these exercises in the passage and in work on the circle is that the horse is unable to maintain the suspension as soon as the hindquarters no longer act in the direction of the movement. Since this, however, is a very considerable difficulty, it would obviously be foolish to intend to use movements on two tracks in the passage before the pace has been confirmed to such an extent that the rider can direct his whole attention toward maintaining the bent-straight carriage of his horse. Even then, this task still requires the horse to be extremely obedient to the rein, leg, spur and weight aids and the rider to be absolutely secure in his soft, supple seat and, based on it, to have a perfect feeling for every movement of the horse. Even if these conditions are fully met, the task still remains very difficult because it will initially happen very often that the horse gives up the suspended pace. It is then best to ride the horse on one track and re-establish the suspension through the above-mentioned aids before the lateral pace is resumed. The greater the direction on two tracks, the greater is, of course, the danger that the hindquarters fall out and thus interrupt the suspended movement.

The more reliable the horse gradually becomes when doing the passage on two tracks and the more successful the exercises in collecting the passage from the free tempo have been, the more it will be possible to shorten the pace without damaging its cadence and expression until finally the horse can be held in place for a few steps in increased collection on a straight line and thus the transition to the piaffe has been found.

It really does not require any further description of how from these first steps of piaffe proper repetitions of the piaffe develop gradually in that the introductory passage becomes shorter and shorter and the number of piaffe steps increases. This process differs in no way from our method employed everywhere else which is based on a quite gradual increase of the demands and frequent repetitions in short sessions, adhering to the principle that the work must always end with a good impression and praise for the horse. One consideration, however, must not be forgotten at this stage of collection, not even for a moment, namely that the piaffe is useful for the overall training of the horse only if it is performed entirely on the bit and with a decisive forward drive; even a slight yielding of the hands must be sufficient to produce the appropriate forward movement. With horses that tend to hold back their strength the danger is only too obvious that, once they have understood the piaffe, they will utilize this movement to work behind or above the bit. This usually also has the deleterious consequences for the expression of the movement discussed at the beginning of this chapter. It is advisable, when practicing the piaffe, not only during the introductory period but also later when the horse has become somewhat secure in it, to let it piaffe forward for a few steps from time and time and to absolutely take care that there is good contact. With horses that have a reticent character, one must be particularly careful, and it will be good to keep moving forward a bit for quite some time when practicing the piaffe and even later always work in place only for a few steps and with extreme alertness.

At first, in developing the piaffe, as was done earlier for the passage, one will take advantage of the wall to hold the outside hind leg, since for this movement as well the rule applies that the movement can be strong and regular only if the hindquarters follow the forehand precisely. One should therefore not practice on the centerline until the movement is no longer difficult for the horse and should always let it move forward a little. If the horse has gradually learned to piaffe down the centerline, straight and well on the bit, it can be asked to perform a few steps in place and then gradually to repeat the movement in place several times. This now brings us to a stage of training which, utilized appropriately, ensures a high degree of comfort in use. This movement is possible only if, on the one hand, the forehand is set straight so perfectly that the slightest pull on the reins travels, like an electric current, through the entire horse into the lowermost joint of the hindquarters and, on the other hand, the spring action of the haunches is perfected to the highest degree and the flexible hindquarters are completely under the rider's control.

Thus, as we have seen, the collection of the passage will gradually lead to the piaffe in the normal course of dressage training. But, just like the passage, this movement can also be used to advantage much earlier than would be possible in this normal way. Specifically, the piaffe will be extremely useful for horses with a lazy temperament and dragging movements. For them one can often obtain diligent trot steps and a flowing canter only after they have been enlivened and made more agile through piaffe exercises. For such cases, the old masters left us an invention which, when applied appropriately, can be extremely useful, namely the *pillars*.

In recent times, another way of working the horse without a rider has become popular. It is not only simpler and less dangerous for the horse's temperament and skeleton than work between the pillars but also prepares for it most effectively, namely the "collecting work in hand."

For this work the horse is put into side reins, preferably in the side reins that have already been described briefly in the chapter about working on the lunge. The length of the side reins should be such that the horse is easily able to go on the bit, but they must initially not be too short. Just as for work on the lunge, the correct length of the reins can be determined only gradually, particularly since it must be carefully adapted to the individuality and the degree of dressage training of each horse. Moreover, the horse is put into a cavesson to which a lead rein is attached. The work in hand serves the same purposes as work between the pillars, namely to awaken an understanding in the horse for the collecting aids, initially without a rider; the horse should learn to engage its hind legs more, flex the hindquarters, carry more weight with them, and then push it off again. However, this type of work can begin much earlier than work between the pillars because it takes place while moving forward and therefore allows the rider to eliminate all possibly occurring difficulties, such as creeping back or pushing toward the side, by increasing the forward movement. Moreover, work in hand also has a very favorable educational effect since the horse becomes more familiar with the human being and thus more intelligent and sensitive. In addition, if handled correctly, such work has a very advantageous influence on the horse's temperament; impetuous and sensitive horses calm down, phlegmatic and lazy horses become livelier.

Work in hand must begin only after the horse reliably follows leg and rein aids and can already be collected at the trot and walk; no earlier than in the second year of training.

Only those horses should be worked in hand that have completed systematic training on the lunge and are completely familiar with cavesson, side reins, and lunge whip. It is usually advisable to first lunge the horse for a while as a loosening preparation for the work in hand in order to eliminate barn freshness and tension.

For working the horse in hand, one takes it along the wall, preferably starting on the left hand. The rider faces the horse, approximately at the level of its shoulder and holds the lead rein short in his left hand, the pillar whip or a long riding whip in the right hand. In addition to the lead rein, he may also grip the inside snaffle rein to support the aids from the lead rein. This will be advisable particularly at the beginning of training and for very temperamental horses.

First the horse must be fully acquainted with the whip; it must not be afraid of it, nor should it learn to consider the whip as merely a driving aid. For this purpose one takes the whip, before the actual work begins, and moves it repeatedly lightly over the horse's croup and hindquarters, down to the hocks, taps the saddle with it, initially very softly, gradually a little harder, to take away any fear of the whip.

Then the horse is asked by a light aid from the whip supported by the voice or a tongue click, to move forward, the trainer himself always going along, or one takes the horse slightly forward through a slight suggestion with the reins. If the horse willingly obeys the driving aids, work must be interrupted repeatedly by halts, for which the horse must stand very quietly, whereupon it is effusively awarded by praise and patting. The halt to stop the horse may also be supported to advantage by the voice as this is a particularly important aid in any case just as in the work between the pillars to be described later for impetuous as well as phlegmatic horses. Only if the horse starts forward willingly in response to whip and voice and promptly obeys the halt aids - which will occur the sooner the more careful the lunge training has been - the actual work may begin. Initially this should not take too long and care should be taken that it always ends on a good note. The slower one proceeds and the more all of the aids are adapted to temperament and individuality of the horse in question, the more reliable and better will be the success.

If obedience to the driving aids has been securely confirmed, the horse can be made more attentive to the restraining aids by asking it to step back a few steps - step by step - from the halt, before it is asked to go forward. This is advantageously done predominantly with the inside snaffle rein which pushes the horse back so to speak step for step with a short, light pressure. The whip must lie in readiness at the hind leg to nip in the bud any rushing back or crookedness. Whenever the horse is asked to back up, also for the rein-back under the rider, care must be taken that head and neck are in a position which ensures light, through-going action of the rein aids. In the beginning this introductory process for stepping back is concluded by a halt and praise; later the horse can be asked to step forward directly from the back-up movement by a short voice aid which is initially supported by a light, strong whip aid. The better the horse has stepped back and the more promptly it moves forward, the more lively and diligent will its first steps be, whereupon the horse is again asked to halt at once and is praised effusively.

In this way short trot steps will gradually be formed from which, if the session progresses quietly and expertly, piaffe-like movements will gradually evolve. Success depends first of all on the driving and restraining aids that act in coincidence as they do under the rider and are adapted to the individuality and behavior of the horse. Only calm, genuine horsemen who have gained an understanding of the horse's psyche will chose the correct manner of proceeding especially for this work. Only the person who has gained feeling and equestrian tact in the saddle will be able to

[285]

give his aids at the proper time, in the appropriate intensity and carefully matched to one another. Prerequisite is again that reins and whip are used with relaxed, resilient arm and hand joints. Both aids, the driving as well as the restraining aids, must be given with a soft hand. Most of all, the rein hand must never get stuck in pulling, or pull backwards; it must act just as for the half-halt, that is, it must close only temporarily and form the barrier from which the horse pushes off.

Right from the start the straight carriage must be given particular attention. On the left hand on which it is practical to remain until the horse has gained a certain understanding for the work in hand and works somewhat on its own, the tendency to become crooked or to escape inward with the hindquarters will successfully be counteracted by the wall which holds the right hind leg. Much more care must be taken to prevent the left shoulder from pushing into the arena. This is accomplished best by the rein hand remaining close to the horse's head and acting as little as possible to the side. It may also be useful to tie the right side rein shorter. Most of all, as soon as the horse tries to go crooked, the restraining aids must be limited and forward movement must be emphasized. The horse should not be asked to step completely in place until it is able to make pure, cadenced piaffe steps and keeps its two hind legs close together. This must also be demanded only temporarily; in between times the movement should always be left out again at the front.

On the right hand the work will usually be more difficult at first, but now it will be possible to eliminate the crookedness completely because now the whip can ask the right hind leg to become more active and step straight underneath the load. Just like under the rider, a slight shoulder-in position will be the best way to control this leg as it allows the whip to hold the hind legs together and to suppress any deviation of the right hind leg before it develops. In order not to be forced to act too much with the rein hand, it may be advisable, under certain circumstances, to give the horse's head on this hand a slight position to the inside by way of the side rein. With progressing work, as soon as the horse is definitely securely set straight, impulsion and expression of the piaffe steps will usually be better on the right hand than on the left.

The deficiencies and faults already mentioned in connection with the description of the piaffe work will of course also appear during the work in hand. With respect to corrective methods reference should be made here quite generally to the suggestions given there as well as for work between the pillars. However, the following points should be emphasized once more: The most important thing remains always that the horse keeps moving, for which the hind legs must work with liveliness. Whoever has sharpened his feeling and eye for detecting an impulsive pace, which must always be the nucleus of any successful training of the horse, will have no doubt whether this condition has been met and will find the means for eliminating deficiencies in this respect.

Impulsion is generated by the elastic activity of the hind legs and is propagated though the back to the entire body of the horse which is thus caused to move in soft movements that swing up and down. One should therefore primarily observe the back and the hindquarters and not only the forehand!

Two deviations from the ideal picture of the piaffe described at the beginning of this chapter must be detected and properly eliminated. Either the work of the hind legs is so weak that they appear to be sticking to the ground and the body appears immobile, or the hindquarters are convulsively pushed up so that the entire body moves in a restless, forward flinging manner. The first-mentioned fault usually appears in horses that have a soft back and hind legs, the other in horses that have a rigid back and inflexible hindquarters. Just as under the rider, the weak movement can be eliminated only by forward work, the painfully tense movement only by repeated half-halts, in which case the rein hand is carried somewhat higher.

Now let us briefly refer to temperament-caused deviations in the course of the movement. The same way as under the rider, phlegmatic and impetuous horses will show different, unchanging typical movements in hand as well; the phlegmatic horse becomes too slow, the impetuous horse begins to rush. These deficiencies will also have to be eliminated similarly to those under the rider. Therefore, phlegmatic horses must be worked only in short, lively sessions, in which they are encouraged by whip and voice, while the impetuous horses, unless they become unnaturally excited, must be worked in longer sessions in which they are repeatedly calmed down by the insertion of pauses and praise. One should attempt to dampen their over-eagerness with a soothing voice and light half-halts. They then calm down on their own and will gradually find the correct, cadenced steps.

Regarding the manner of giving all of the aids, one should again follow the advice given for work between the pillars. I mention here only that even with very lazy horses it is not the frequency and intensity of the driving aids that ensure success but the lively, encouraging, in a way electrifying manner in which they are applied.

If the horse has been given the preliminary instruction in hand to the point that it takes regular piaffe steps, work under the rider may also begin. Likewise, as soon as the horse is able to perform a few steps of piaffe in place, well on the bit, it can also be put between the pillars without too many misgivings.

It is not assumed that this book will be read by people who need an explanation of the pillars, and I therefore assume that their use is known. Although the reader may have become convinced in the course of our discussions that correct, orderly dressage training generally uses no other means than available to the rider in the saddle, an exception can be made for the pillars. For certain cases they may even be recommended.

Horses that work reliably between the pillars may be of considerable use particularly in the training of young riders. Of course one must not falsely hope that a horse could be fully worked between the pillars because such work requires forward movement under all circumstances. Used with expertise, the pillars may support and further proper dressage work in the saddle. Any professional rider can only be advised to consider work between the pillars already in his younger years in order to acquire a certain mastery of them. Whoever is able to correctly use the collecting work in hand and the work between the pillars and has a soft, supple seat, will be able to work in our profession up to a high age without having to seek refuge in overchecks and dumb jockeys which, as already mentioned elsewhere, are damaging and against nature.

Since the actual working of the horse between the pillars occurs exclusively from the rear, this work, although it takes place without moving forward, may nevertheless further develop and enhance the drive forward, the basis of all dressage. The cooperation of driving and restraining aids, on which any true schooling of the horse is based, can be accomplished more perfectly between the pillars than in running gear because the driving aids can be given with far greater accuracy and restraining takes place, although in the most definitive manner, but with a tool that neither mistreats the horse's mouth nor its nose.

In any case, overcheck and dumb jockey destroy many more horses than the pillars. Instinctively even the inexperienced person will be less likely to decide on the use of the pillars than these training aids; but if he does, he will probably very quickly come to the end of his rope so that he cannot do too much damage! However, the pillars also permit rough mistreatment of the horse; yet, it takes so much brutality to vent one's anger on a tied, defenseless creature that such horrible aberrations should be counted among the exceptions. In running gear it may happen, however, that an ignorant person lets his poor horse run around in an unnatural, forced elevation for such a long time that it is robbed of all its natural strength without the person having the slightest knowledge of what he is doing.

To turn now to the actual *work between the pillars* and initially only to the extent that it relates to the production of a proper piaffe, we want to point out beforehand which degree of dressage training a horse must have reached to be put between the pillars to its advantage. In answering this question consideration must be given to the fact that the horse works between the pillars without the weight of the rider and that its dressage training therefore need not have progressed to the level required for any work in place under the rider, particularly for the piaffe. Nevertheless, it is not recommended to put a young horse between the pillars to keep its still soft bones from being damaged in any way. It is also not advisable to use the pillars for a green horse that is neither through in the poll nor has received any instruction in bending its haunches. Obviously, success between the pillars will occur the faster and more reliably the further the horse has already progressed in dressage training, the more it has learned to engage in response to the interaction of driving and restraining aids. However, it would be urgently desirable for the horse to have learned already to respond to the first collecting aids by engaging its hindquarters and elevating its forehand.

The theory on which work between the pillars is based is very simple. For the horse to learn to trot in place, which it of course would not do if it were simply driven forward into the halter by a whip, one attempts initially to utilize the change in place possible between the pillars to get the horse to move. The horse, however, that is tied to the pillar reins is able to change its place only by moving its hindquarters to the right or left, while its forelegs participate in this movement almost entirely in place. One now tries to regulate this back and forth movement of the hindquarters, which the horse will easily agree to, in that one attempts to make these regular, first striding and later trot-like steps extend the same distance to both sides, trying constantly to keep the horse on the pillar reins by light driving aids and engaging its hindquarters. The respective inside hind leg in particular must be asked by timely contact with the whip to regularly step over the outside hind leg. The more this back and forth movement gradually becomes regular as a result of patient practice, the more the horse becomes engaged and the more correct the steps become, the more the arcs of the hindquarters are reduced under the constantly driving aids until they finally disappear altogether and the horse steps in place. This in a way concludes the introductory period and the actual gymnastic exercise begins, by means of which the still inexpressive trot steps in place must gradually be perfected into the piaffe.

As easy as this work appears to be in theory, the difficulties encountered in practice are multitudinous. To give rules of behavior for every possible occurrence is completely impossible. It must be left mainly to the observation and inventiveness of the individual to take the necessary steps to help out if necessary. Only the most important principles and rules can be discussed which everyone who intends to work a horse to advantage between the pillars must observe under all circumstances.

First and foremost I ask everyone who undertakes this type of work to think himself deeply into the soul of the poor creature that is tied between two posts, sees a human being standing there, armed with two whips, is unable to follow its forward drive and ignorant of what it is supposed to do. Whoever is able to clearly see the animal's situation will certainly avoid the main errors that are usually made and will practice patience and indulgence. Added here should be the repeatedly stated admonition to use only very short sessions for any instruction of the horse, sessions that end with good impressions and praise, and not to intend to force success but wait patiently and be surprised by it when it comes about. If success does occur, don't reap it immediately to the extreme but do the horse a favor and terminate the work! Be generous using your voice and try to keep the horse always in a comfortable mood!

Just as nothing is lost during the work under saddle as long as it is possible to keep the horse moving forward, it remains the main axiom for work between the pillars: under no circumstances let the forward movement stop! As long as the horse moves, there is a chance that the movement will become regular. The situation becomes problematic only if it sets itself down and lurks or lets anything happen to it. A great help is an understanding assistant who, with the lunge line attached to the cavesson in hand, stands in front of the horse, particularly at the beginning, to render extraordinary support. In general it is a great calming factor for a horse, a consolation in fact, to see a human being in front of it, and it will therefore be willing to obey his aids. However, such aids will essentially be limited to pulling the horse forward softly against the reins if necessary and, during the to and fro movement, moving the forehand, to the extent permitted by the contact with the pillar reins, in the opposite direction from the direction in which the hindquarters are to move. Just as it is of the utmost importance for any dressage training outside of the saddle to correctly utilize the horse's eyes and ears for its instruction, the assistant can also be of great use in this respect during the entire work session, assuming that he himself is interested in the matter and gets along with the trainer who carries the whips and therefore is situated behind the horse.

As under the rider, the only work between the pillars that is of true value for dressage is the work that the horse performs with the correct contact, here with the halter, a principle that one cannot call to mind often enough. The machine-like stomping behind the pillar reins that one sees so frequently is not only of no use it is also damaging because it easily becomes a vice which the horse also uses under saddle if it wants to creep behind the bit. It is just as wrong, although less objectionable at the beginning, if the horse pushes itself into the pillar reins with all its might. This fault must gradually disappear the easier it becomes for the horse to engage its haunches. In such a case it is sometimes quite appropriate to connect the pillar reins to the snaffle rings instead of the halter.

Initially the pillar reins should be attached in such a way that the horse, when it steps toward the pillars, does not come any closer than that its shoulders reach the level of the pillar stands. It then finds less room for resistance. Later, as soon as the introductory period is over and the actual work begins, it is advisable to gradually let the pillar reins become longer so that the horse has more freedom to elevate its forehand. The height at which the reins are attached to the pillars must of course depend on the size and conformation of the horse and also on whether one wants to act more toward elevation or bringing the horse on the bit. Since the horse steps toward the pillar reins, they are the only effective reins during the work. It is actually superfluous to attach any reins to the horse's girth or saddle. Nevertheless this is advisable because it makes the horse more attentive and it will sooner be willing to collect. If overchecks are employed for horses that tighten their backs for resistance, this must be done under the consideration that elevation must develop gradually from flexion of the haunches; these reins must therefore be attached long enough that they merely indicate the downward limit that the horse must not exceed.

For the whip aids the same should be repeated that has already been said for the rider's aids, namely that their successful action depends in no way on the intensity of their use but that instead fine, timely applied aids are by far the most effective. The right moment for the whip aid is the moment at which the respective leg is raised.

It is possible to extraordinarily refine the horse's attention to the whip aids during work between the pillars but one can also dull the horse against it until it loses sensitivity. Therefore it is advisable to be extremely sparing with true lashes even for very phlegmatic horses and instead revive their temperament by loud shouts and the stimulating type of aids.

After these few explanatory words about the pillars everyone intending to tackle this difficult job is aware in advance that he will very often encounter difficulties and that true mastery can be obtained only through long experience. Whoever is not aware that he must be able to control himself under all circumstances and does not have sufficient patience should not even dare to undertake it! Love for the horse, incessant observation of its moods, and thoughts about it must be the major contributors. In any case, one should always follow the principle: Better too little and too slow than too much and too fast!

If now the horse that has been prepared for the piaffe by work in hand or between the pillars is to be taught the piaffe under the rider and in response to his aids, it is best for this purpose to place a sensitive, supple young rider on the horse while it is being worked in hand or between the pillars and make it work only in response to the whip aids. Likewise, when the trainer first mounts the horse himself, it is best to initially have an assistant with a whip as reinforcement. However, these auxiliary means must gradually disappear and the trainer's own aids must become effective, with the skillfully employed spurs and the lively supporting whip playing an important role. To actually work the horse in the piaffe, one should then go to the wall and there use the method described at the beginning of this chapter.

After we have thus thoroughly worked our horse in the piaffe, be it only in the saddle with gradually increasing collection, be it without the rider working it in hand or between the pillars, we will be ready to crown our work with turns on the haunches from the passage, the so-called "doublés," for which the horse must not only have learned to step over in the passage but also to be completely balanced between the rider's legs in the piaffe. Only if the horse is completely secure in these movements and its obedience to hands and legs is very refined is a "doublé" conceivable at all. If these conditions are met, however, we arrive at what applies more and more the farther we progress in dressage training, namely that the preparation was long and difficult, but the movement itself becomes more a matter of quiet teaching and practice. Regarding the performance of doublés, which can ultimately be increased to half and whole pirouettes, it should still be mentioned that, upon approaching the intended turning point, the passage should be collected to become a piaffe and in this piaffe the forehand must move around the hindquarters step by step. Success depends primarily on the control of the outside hind leg which therefore must be watched closely by the outside spur. As soon as the outside hind leg is able to fall out, the suspended steps definitely cease.

At the conclusion of this chapter I want to point out once more with emphasis that it is possible to bring almost any horse to perform some type of passage and perhaps even the piaffe, but that only very few horses are born that are able to learn to perform these beautiful movements in such a perfect, classical manner as they are expected of the dressage horse. Always, however, if these two movements are to be considered true dressage, impulsion, a straight carriage, and throughness must be their clearly noticeable features.

ENDNOTES

[1] This thesis cannot be proven. The rider's leg is always pushed away from the horse's body when the hind leg on the same side swings forward due to the thus produced tension of the belly muscles on that side and drops back against the horse's body as soon as these muscles are relaxed again when the hind leg is stretched. If the rider's leg then acts with more pressure, the hind leg will push harder; if it acts only in brief taps, the hind leg will spring off earlier and in a more lively fashion. (Hans von Heydebreck)

[2] Experience has shown that the striding passage can rarely be improved by merely increasing its tempo. Generally one will be forced to stop with the passage and develop, through very energetically driving aids, a trot that is so impulsive that the springs of the hind legs begin working again with force. Frequent changes between free and collected tempo, again and again going into the extended trot to then reduce the tempo again by good half-halts so that the full impulsion remains effective in the collection usually are the quickest

way to reach the intended goal. (Hans von Heydebreck)

3 More often than believed, the horse's crookedness is here again the actual reason or at least makes the eradication of this ugly fault more difficult. Therefore any bending work for setting the horse straight will be the best way to correct it in this case as well. (Hans von Heydebreck)

4 For any true expert these views about the time it takes to correctly train a horse up to the haute école are in no way exaggerated. To the contrary, it appears to be advisable to establish the principle that passage work should never be begun at all before the third year of training. (Hans von Heydebreck)

5 As useful and successful as this piaffe walk may be for the preparation of passage, experience has shown that, if used in exaggeration or incorrectly, it harbors many dangers and drawbacks. In particular, it often damages the pure sequence of the steps in the walk which thus becomes irregular and pacing. It is therefore necessary to observe the admonition about development of the walk given in the previous chapter on the lower-level movements and not to begin the piaffe walk until the school walk is well confirmed in the horse. (Hans von Heydebreck)

6 If here and at other locations the position of the hindquarters following the forehand is emphasized as a prerequisite for suspended steps, this must be understood with a certain reservation. Although the suspension ceases as soon as the hindquarters no longer act in the direction of movement, anyone who has worked many horses in the passage will have noted that the natural crookedness of the horse, even if it appeared to have been overcome in the natural paces, reappears in the development of suspended steps and that it is easier for a horse for a long time, if not always, to find the push for the suspension in a crooked carriage rather than in the bent-straight carriage. The true straightness of the horse in passage and piaffe is therefore one of the most difficult tasks of dressage training and a correct shoulder-in to the right and travers to the left in these movements is a performance most worthy of recognition in the art of riding. Generally the rider will be forced for a long time, if not always, to sacrifice more or less of the impulsion for the sake of a straight carriage or more or less of the horse's straight carriage for the sake of impulsion.* Passage and piaffe in a correct bent-straight carriage can be accomplished only by long, patient work and then only by strong horses with harmonious conformation. However, the value of these movements should not be underestimated, even if they cannot be developed to the peak of perfection, since they quite extraordinarily enhance the development of a swinging back which is the ultimate soul of riding. (Paul Plinzner)

* Although certain minor concessions can be made with respect to straightness at first, during the introductory period, it cannot be emphasized strongly enough that passage and piaffe should not be practiced continuously in a crooked carriage. Rather the renewed occurrence of crookedness that appeared to have been eradicated during the training for general riding should cause the rider to most emphatically attack this problem through proper bending

work on one and two tracks in the basic paces. Otherwise the horse will only learn from the dressage training to escape the rider's will by way of false, suspended steps. I can therefore only recommend with the utmost urgency to pay the greatest attention to setting the horse straight during passage and piaffe work as well and to interrupt it immediately with energetic forward riding as soon as the horse tries to escape the rider in some way by carrying its body crooked. Yes, impulsion is the soul of riding, but it can be fully developed only in a horse that is in balance because it is set straight. Only then is it possible to obtain a clear, regular sequence of footfalls and only then is the pure, impulsive pace ensured. (Hans von Heydebreck)

⁷ The now following statement by the author about work between the pillars as a training aid is given too much emphasis. As is evident from later publications by Plinzner about the working methods of his mentor, Steinbrecht did not use the pillars, nor did his mentor Seeger. Other masters of the art of riding and particularly the few schools where haute école training has been practiced to the present on the basis of classical dressage, primarily the Spanish Riding School in Vienna, employ the pillars only very sparingly. The trainers of that school employ them practically not at all in the training of their school horses but use them mainly only for seat exercises for their young human students, a method that they took over from the old masters and that Steinbrecht, in his chapter about the "seat," acknowledges as being particularly useful.

In the Spanish Riding School the horses are put between the pillars only after they have been firmly confirmed in the basic haute école lesson, the piaffe. As a preparation for classical dressage work under saddle, the trainers of that institute employ a different, extremely useful training aid, namely the collecting work in hand. In an earlier footnote (see Endnote 3 on page 28) I have already called attention to this work and recommended it briefly. The advantage of this method is primarily that it makes it much easier to follow the two basic principles to which Steinbrecht admonishes us at the beginning of this book, namely "forward" and "setting straight," that does work between the pillars. This collecting work has spread out from Vienna and has pushed work between the pillars more and more into the background even at locations where it had very recently been practiced. Everything said in the next paragraphs in praise of work between the pillars applies to these methods to a much greater degree. In particular, the advice given there to every expert rider to "become familiar with the work between the pillars as early as possible," can be applied with much greater justification for the collecting work in hand which has the additional great advantage that the trainer-to-be is able to obtain a finer feeling in his hands which is impossible in work between the pillars.

If in spite of these limiting objections to work between the pillars, much space was given to it here, this is done from reverence for the author and also because there is presently hardly a work on riding in which this training aid is discussed in an expert manner. I have preceded the description of the work between the pillars with a short description of "collecting work in hand" since this training aid is not only easier and more useful but also the best preparation that can be given a horse before it is put between the pillars. (Hans von Heydebreck)

8 Under certain circumstances, one may omit the cavesson completely later on when the horse has become somewhat secure in the piaffe in hand and give the half-halts only with the snaffle rein, so that the latter can be brought more easily into harmony with the driving whip aids and can be adjusted more finely. (Hans von Heydebreck)

9 All of these prerequisites are ensured under all circumstances if the horse has learned through proper collecting work in hand while going forward to collect itself up to the piaffe. (Hans von Heydebreck)

10 The horse thus performs the same movements as in the turn about the forehand. (Hans von Heydebreck)

11 This fault is eliminated more easily and lastingly if the halter reins are attached higher up on the pillars. Then the horse's mouth remains unhurt under all circumstances. (Hans von Heydebreck)

12 This must not be considered a contradiction of the fact that in the piaffe under the rider the hind leg receives its aid from the rider's leg when it is set down. By slightly leaning backwards with his upper body the rider keeps the hind legs of the piaffing horse underneath the load, while the rein aids, by compressing the springs of the haunches and thus keeping alive their urge to expand again, put weight on the hind legs by their restraining effect. Between the pillars, where both these aids are absent, the whip must ask the hind legs to step underneath the load.* (Paul Plinzner)

* With respect to the described procedure for the natural leg aid resulting from the movement, I would like to note the following: The leg always approaches the horse's body more as soon as the hind leg on the same side is set down and exerts its influence until it springs off. The more lively and earlier the leg acts before this moment, the more lively and earlier will the hind leg on the same side spring off again. The rider's leg is pushed away as soon as the hind leg on the same side swings forward. The important part in the forward stepping of the hind legs is not how far forward they step but primarily that the stifle and hock joints do not hang out behind because the hooves stay on the ground too long. (Hans von Heydebreck)

(b) Haute École Lifts and Airs Above the Ground

Now that we have schooled our horse in the piaffe with increased flexion of both haunches, ameliorated, however, by the fact that they alternated in picking up and pushing off the load and were lightly supported in this work by the front legs - although the hind legs had to perform the major portion of the work - we may consequently turn now to those movements in which both haunches carry all of the weight completely simultaneously and uniformly and must be able to push it off together. These movements are generally called the *airs above the ground* and constitute the highest perfection of dressage. It is impossible to move the center of gravity further back than is required for these movements, otherwise the horse would fall over backwards. Just as the natural jump of a horse is best developed from the canter, which itself is a series of jumps, the jump-like haute école movements are developed from the perfected canter performed with increased weight on the haunches.

After having perfected the bending of the haunches at the canter through movements on two tracks so that it became a redopp in which all of the weight is already carried solely by the haunches for brief movements, we have entered the path to the airs above the ground. But before we depart on it, we must understand what performance we are asking from the horse and we must determine whether nature has blessed it with the strength necessary to perform them so that we do not jeopardize the success of long, careful work by undertaking the impossible.

For this purpose we will initially have to determine again the picture of the perfect movements which most of us have seen on old paintings but few of us have seen performed in reality. Every jump, be it a natural jump performed by the horse to overcome an obstacle, be it the dressage leap that arises from the most perfect flexion of the haunches, naturally begins by raising the forehand on hind legs that have been pushed underneath the load. In the natural jump this raising of the forehand, the subsequent stretching during the jump, and finally the landing flow into one another in such a way that it will be difficult to separate them visually. In the dressage leap, however, which is a well cadenced movement, they are clearly distinguished from one another. This lifting of the forehand for the dressage leap constitutes in itself a particular movement called the *pesade* or *levade*.

In this movement the hind legs, whose joints, particularly the stifle joints, are flexed greatly and whose hooves must therefore have stepped forward underneath the center of gravity, carry the entire load of horse and rider. The horse raises the forehand so that its body describes an angle of about 30° to 45° with the ground while it is securely on the bit with light contact. The forelegs, in order not to increase the weight in front, are naturally bent at the elbow joints, the splint bones are placed against the forearms.

Depending on its natural conformation, the strength of its hindquarters, and its training, the horse will be able to hold this position for a longer or shorter period of time to softly put down the forelegs again as soon as the rider's hands yield. The horse's ability to perform the levade is based primarily on the *flexibility of its haunches in stifle and hock* and their complete control by the rider. Only by intensive flexion of the haunches in the stifle and hock joints is it possible at all to hold the pesade. Without this flexion of both joints, for example with only the hocks flexed, it is impossible to obtain the necessary lowering of the croup. Only if the croup is lowered completely does the center of gravity drop back far enough that the horse is able to balance itself on its hind legs for longer periods of time, and only by properly sitting on the intensely flexed haunches does the horse have the mechanical security to do this.

Because of this great flexion of the stifle joint, the hip joint protrudes more to the rear and this pointed appearance of the croup - in old pictures this is always very distinct and is always pointed out emphatically in the descriptions passed on to us by the old masters - is the particular characteristic of the raised forehand in the haute école. The back which, due to the intensive flexion of the hindquarters, will naturally be slightly humped in the loins, will become somewhat hollow in front of the loins due to the raising of the forehand, and thus give the rider a secure and comfortable seat.

This seat is determined by the consideration that the rider must give to adapting it precisely to the horse in balance which, as emphasized repeatedly before, will be the case if the gravity lines of both coincide. Although on a rearing horse the rider lowers the forehand by increasing the weight in front and leaning forward, the same position would make it impossible for the horse to balance itself on the hindquarters in the levade. Instead, the rider will have to lean his upper body back slightly in order to bring his weight distribution in harmony with that of the horse. In the levade as in all true haute école movements, it will be confirmed that the thoroughly trained horse itself gives the relaxed rider the correct position, with the trainer contributing, through his own correct weight distribution, to the same in the horse.

Just like the weight distribution, the reins also require attention and precision in the levade. The horse must be on the bit in the levade as well. It must not look for the missing support of the forehand by leaning on the bit and much less creep behind the bit. If the rider wants to make his horse perform an haute école lift, he will use his legs and spurs to stimulate the hind legs into stepping forward, will lean slightly back, and, in the true sense of the word, raise the weight of the forehand by the resulting slightly rearward directed rein aid to transfer the weight to the bending hind legs. If thus the rider's hands carry the weight of the forelegs when they are lifted, the rider's hands will be relieved the more the horse approaches the balanced position of the levade in which the hands need only maintain a slight contact with the horse's mouth as long as the horse balances itself. He will help the horse with his hands as soon as the horse begins to lose its balance by picking up the reins if the weight in front becomes too heavy or by yielding with a slightly driving pressure from his legs, if the weight on the hindquarters becomes too heavy. These last mentioned aids also produce the lowering of the forehand after the levade. This is accomplished softly and gradually in that the hands watch the horse's balance carefully, holding back with the weight at any moment.

The characteristic of a levade performed correctly on the bit is the horse's willingness to immediately move forward afterwards in a collected carriage, which would not be the case if the movement had been performed behind the bit. Such a lift behind the bit, the greatest fault that can possibly occur, is the particular tendency of horses that have a reticent temperament. Just as any collected work had to be performed with greater caution than usual with such horses, it will be necessary to be particularly careful during the lifts of the forehand that it is done well on the bit. Otherwise the horse would easily use it to creep behind the bit and hold back. Any tendency toward this must immediately be counter-acted emphatically through energetic driving aids, and such a horse, after it has performed a lift with good contact and well on the bit, must be asked to move forward in piaffe steps. This method can be used to advantage for any horse to check or correct its contact, for as soon as there is any reticence in the horse, this is when it will appear as the horse will try to escape moving forward in the piaffe by raising its forehand behind the bit. Lively forward driving leg aids, if necessary forcefully supported by spurs and whip, must energetically suppress this tendency.

That is a reason why horses having a reticent temperament are not suitable as true school horses although movements of the haute école can be used to thoroughly train them if they are physically able to perform such movements. They will never be able to do without strong, and therefore more or less visible, aids which under all circumstances interfere considerably with the impression of a classical presentation.

Horses with an impetuous temperament, unless this is based primarily on a physical imperfection, can be used much more likely for the haute école. The security, quietness, and softness of the rider's seat and the resulting fineness of the guidance are means for presenting them in the proper manner. For the schooling of young trainer aspirants, however, reticent horses can also be used to great advantage because they never do more than they can get away with and force the rider, particularly in movements that require great collection, to recognize the necessity of correct contact.

The classical lift of the forehand now produces the air above the ground when the horse is asked by lively aids from spurs, short or long whip, to use the elasticity of its hind legs to push the entire weight resting on its bent haunches off from the ground to thus rise "above the ground" with all four legs, well on the bit. Depending on the strength and courage inherent in the horse, the action of the hindquarters in the air above the ground will turn out differently. If the horse raises the hind legs only slightly above the ground, we get the *courbette*; if it is able to push the load away so forcefully that croup and back approach the horizontal, we get the *croupade*, which is the more perfect the more precisely horizontal the horse's body floats above the ground. If finally we believe our horse to be able to even greater exertion of strength, we ask it by way of the short or long whip or the spur to strike out with its hind legs while it is in the horizontal leap. If the horse does not think it has the strength to perform this movement and responds to the request for striking out only to the extent that it shows its shoes we have the *ballotade*. If, however, it does strike out perfectly, this is the *capriole*, the most difficult and most perfect of all airs above the ground, the crown of the haute école.

From all these leaps the horse should initially touch down first with the hind legs, with the haunches receiving the load with elastic resiliency;

immediately afterwards the forelegs must support the forehand to impart the next following movement whatever it might be. If one wanted to push the development of the airs above the ground even further, the next step would be that the horse no longer needs its forelegs to support the load or to transfer it to the hindquarters for the next movement. We would then arrive at making our horses perform a series of stepping, canter-like or finally jump-like movements in which it would balance itself only on the hindquarters. I don't know though whether this would not go beyond the limits of what is natural because nature has intended the forelegs to support the forehand in every movement - whatever this might be - or to transfer the load back to the hindquarters. In some horses that are constructed in perfect symmetry, have great courage, and extraordinarily strong hindquarters it is possible, however, to produce such movements strictly on the hindquarters, for example, a pirouette in several strides or even a few courbettes in succession without touching the ground with the forelegs in either movement. However, the desire for such movements would make us shoot beyond our goal. Therefore we do not want to include them in our considerations but return to the airs above the ground as they develop from the description above.

The horizontal carriage of the body, which gives the good haute école leap, if it goes beyond a courbette, its finely defined character, will of course be obtained with greater ease the less high was the introductory lifting of the forehand. The higher therefore the leap, with the body in a horizontal carriage, the more perfect a leap it is and the more it demonstrates the strength and energy of the horse. Although it is up to the rider to control things in that he gives the aids earlier or later at his discretion and, on the other hand, is able to moderate or stimulate the raising of the hindquarters by the greater or lesser intensity of the aids, he must nevertheless leave it in part to the horse's instinct to select the height of the leap according to its own performance capability. The more a movement consumes the full strength and energy of the horse, the more carefully the rider must avoid going too far in his demands. In any case, the rider must not give the aid for a leap as long as the hand still carries the weight of the forehand. He must wait for the moment when the contact becomes lighter because the horse begins to approach the balanced carriage in his levade.

Just as the raising of the forehand can be called classical dressage only if it is performed in perfect carriage and well on the bit, these conditions

[301]

must be met no less stringently for the airs above the ground. Although the danger of remaining behind the bit is probably overcome by the energetic jumping movement, it is possible that the horse might lose its carriage when it tries to support the lifting of the hindquarters by a certain upward tossing of head and neck. During the introductory period in which the horse still expends more effort than necessary because of its unfamiliarity, the trainer will hardly be able to counteract this phenomenon. With increasing security, however, he will be able to suppress it more and more in the correctly flexed and set horse. However, the correct contact during the leap will depend primarily on whether the elasticity of the hindquarters acts straight and unweakened against the load and thus against the hands. The foundation for the correct effect of the elasticity must be laid already during the introductory raising of the forehand. As soon as one leg steps farther forward and is thus given more weight than the other during this period, it is impossible for the springs to act in unison. A leap introduced in such a way will become crooked and thus of necessity interfere with contact, aside from the fact that it will be impossible for the horse to deploy all of its forces because they are not given the proper direction.

Already in the levade this problem will become apparent. Since only very few horses have hind legs that are completely equally developed, most of them will tend to protect the weaker one and put more weight on the stronger leg by putting it further forward. Only if this unequal aptitude was detected right at the start and has been considered during all of the preceding training in that the weaker limb was gradually strengthened through appropriate exercises, will it be possible over time to satisfactorily eliminate this fault, although it will, under all circumstances, reappear at the beginning of the airs above the ground. Spur, long and short whip must ask the held-back hind leg to take over its portion of the load.

The main difficulty of the airs above the ground is that both haunches must act simultaneously and in entirely the same way, supporting as well as springing. Even in highly talented horses this difficulty and the faults resulting from it, namely lack of balance in the levade and crooked direction of the leaps, will be around for a shorter or longer time until the horse, with decreasing timidity and increasing understanding of what it is supposed to do, instinctively, and through the aids from its trainer, learns to use its limbs in the appropriate way, that is, in complete synchronism. The irregular development of the two hind legs is also the reason why among the actually very small number of horses whose temperament, physical symmetry, and the elasticity of their back and especially their hindquarters make them appear suitable for the airs above the ground only a disappearingly small number remain who progress to the point that they can perform their airs above the ground truly according to classical dressage and completely on the aids. Yet, it may be possible to get many a horse to perform some sort of air above the ground.

The old masters were particularly concerned that their haute école jumpers bend their forelegs nicely in their pastern and fetlock joints. Indeed, this bending of the foreleg which the horse takes over from the classical raising of the forehand into the leap is a characteristic, just as in the piaffe and passage, of the ease and relaxation with which the horse performs its movement. However, the tucking up of the cannon bones which, as mentioned above, enhances the rearward placement of the weight, will in most horses, once they are asked to perform the airs, be attainable only with the aid of the whip.

For that reason an assistant cannot be dispensed with for this purpose during work under saddle. The more the horse understands what it is to do and the more willingly and easily it rises, the more it will be possible for it to bend its forelegs on its own which is a prerequisite for the proper balance of the levade.

The smaller the distance between the spots where the hind legs take off and where they land, the more perfect is the air above the ground. The straighter upward the leap is directed, the more perfectly the elasticity of the hind legs is able to act; the more forward ground the hind legs cover the less elasticity there is and the more thrust.

When horses jump naturally, thrust always is a participant although the jump is primarily based on the elasticity of the hindquarters. The farther and the less high the horse jumps, the more thrust it needs. Even if it jumps straight up, thrust must not be completely absent. Consequently, the leap produced from the classically raised forehand will be that much easier for the horse the more it is permitted to use thrust to support the elasticity of the haunches, the more the horse is allowed, through yielding of the rider's hands, to leap forward. Although during work between the pillars the leap must be in place in any case, this is much easier because of the absence of the rider's weight and also because of the firm support that the horse is able to take from the halter. When working in the saddle, one will of course begin with the easier task and initially allow the horse to leap somewhat more forward. Only if the leap is straight and well on the bit can one begin to attempt to change the direction to more upward so as to gradually arrive at developing nothing but elasticity.

When training a horse in the airs above the ground, we must counter the assumption that it should be possible to teach every horse a certain, predetermined type of airs above the ground. A horse that is able to do a horizontal air can be trained in such a leap and also perhaps in the courbette; but the type of leap must essentially be left to the horse's talents, as it must be left to the horse in any case to perform a natural jump over an obstacle as it deems it proper.

In the course of the work, be this under saddle or between the pillars, it will sometimes happen, before one even thinks about airs above the ground, that the horse, if it is held back in front and asked by the spurs or whip to exert all its strength in collected paces, tries to somehow vent its excitement or displeasure before it decides to fully exert itself, either because of a certain resistance to the rider's demands or because it does not completely understand the rider, by performing a more upward leap if it is able at all to accomplish such a feat. Such moments give the trainer the best indication for the evaluation of his horse. If the horse repeats this manner of venting its excitement and if a certain sameness or similarity is noted in these leaps, these exertions of strength and energy prove not only that the horse is an haute école jumper but they also indicate with more or less clarity for what type of leap the horse has talent. Finally, observing the horse at such occasions gives a better clue as to what can be made of it than a careful examination according to the teachings of anatomy. In any case, it is never as easy in practice as it is in theory to determine reliably what type of leap this is, since the types of leaps the eye sees often blend into one another.

In the course of dressage training, the leap often changes completely, and a horse that initially performed a croupade may end up becoming a capriole horse, while another horse that in its excitement at the beginning of work struck out behind, may later on reliably perform only the ballotade or even only the croupade. The main thing is initially to produce a horizontal leap. The trainer must accept it in the form the horse offers and can only gradually polish it and try to perfect it. This can be done only with increasing security and relaxation of the horse, if the activity of both haunches is uniform, the forehand carried appropriately, and, connected with it, there is reliable contact with the bit.

Finally, we want to determine once more the stage of training that the horse must have reached before one can think about developing the levade and from it an air above the ground. Initially the jump-like gait, the canter, must have reached the degree of perfection we described in the respective chapter. It must have become so elevated from the various exercises described there that it became a redopp and that the horse, discernible to the observer's eyes and senses, rested for a brief moment only on its hindquarters in every canter stride. Another absolute requirement is that the horse is perfectly secure in the piaffe. If this stage of training has been reached, the rider will have so much control over the haunches that he will be able at any time to hold the canter almost in place for a few strides. Of course this is possible only from a truly well collected canter in which the horse trills as mentioned before on the most energetically engaged hind legs.

To produce these leaps in place, the spurs must stimulate the hind legs with suitable liveliness. For this cantering in place, the end of a short, quite lively session will be particularly suitable because for the last stride it will then be possible without significant difficulties to move the forehand, on well stimulated hindquarters, somewhat higher than usual to perform the so-called *falcade* which then constitutes the transition to the later raising of the forehand according to the haute école. The more willingly the horse can be collected from the canter to perform these leaps in place and the final falcade, the more we will be able to gradually shorten the introductory canter session until we are able to ask the horse to perform a few canter strides in place from the halt, with the last stride being a falcade.

In this exercise we will gradually reduce the lateral bend and increase the straight carriage. In addition we will simultaneously enliven both hind legs to get the horse to jump under the same distance with both hind legs and correspondingly to raise and put down the forelegs in the same manner. The flat, lively strides resulting in this way, which are very characteristically called *terre à terre*, now give us, if they are orderly, that is, performed between hands and legs in spite of all their liveliness, a reliable way to the airs above the ground. Initially this will only be the levade since a series of such leaps need be concluded only with a greater elevation of the forehand to obtain the beginnings of this movement. If then, with increasing security, the number of terre-à-terre leaps is reduced and they are used only to give the haunches the required flexion in an easy, unconstrained way and to bring the hind legs more underneath the center of gravity, the forehand can gradually be lifted higher and the horse can be held a bit longer in it.

In this phase of training, the presence of an understanding assistant will be of great value. He carries a short whip in one hand and a dressage whip in the other so that he can contribute not only to the control of the inside hind leg - the outside hind leg being controlled by the wall where, of course, these first exercises must take place - but also with suitable whip aids and the correct use of his voice to the enhancement of the lifting of the forehand, its holding in the raised position, and the correct bending of the forelegs. Of course, these exercises must be performed alternatingly on the right hand and on the left in order to prevent any irregularities in the activity of the haunches. During the time of this instruction, all customary rules must be observed, primarily the rule of short sessions, a good end, frequent rest intervals, and effusive praise.

Most horses suitable for this movement, as soon as they understand what they are to do, will appear quite willing to lift the forehand. But this must give us cause to proceed with great care so that the matter does not become a problem. From now on no unintentional raising of the forehand must be allowed. Instead, as soon as the horse appears to want to rise on its own, it must immediately be driven forward onto the bit and must be asked to perform energetic forward piaffe steps.

In the pauses between the levade exercises a few piaffe steps will be a very beneficial influence because they strengthen contact and obedience and keep the haunches supple. Such exercises should be continued until the trainer is certain that the horse understands him completely. Then he can begin to completely omit the introductory terre-à-terre leaps and to ask the horse to do the levade directly from the halt after the hind legs have first been put underneath the load. Only then will the levade be developed fully in that now the horse rises calmly and consciously. This makes it easier for the horse to find its balanced position and it will learn to maintain it for a longer period of time.

Before a horse is able to perform the levade reliably along the wall on both hands with calmness and security and can be held in the levade, one must not go into the center of the arena for this purpose. In the center of the arena the main difficulty is that the horse, no longer having the support of the wall, will exhibit a certain timidity and will tend to escape to the side with its hind legs. This can best be prevented by first performing a few piaffe steps at the point where the levade is to be performed in order to ensure obedience to the spurs and to stimulate the uniform activity of both haunches.

To produce a good haute école jumper, the development of a levade that is perfect in every respect cannot be stressed highly enough. Only from a correct levade and, most of all, a straight lifting of the forehand, can a straight, good leap result. One should therefore by no means try to develop the leap from the levade too early. First the horse should be confirmed in the levade as much as possible, along the wall as well as at any other location in the arena. Only after the horse performs its levade completely securely on the bit and balanced between the two spurs as if between two weights can one hope to produce a good leap.

It is probably unnecessary and fruitless to discuss the development of the airs above the ground in any more detail. It just appeared to be desirable to demonstrate once more how consequential progress on a path adapted to nature will finally lead to the highest peak of dressage in a natural, logical way, presuming that the horse in question has the natural physical and mental qualities that are absolutely necessary to accomplish it. Whoever proceeds systematically according to natural principles in the schooling of his horse without, in impatient haste, skipping steps of the ladder to be climbed will certainly be told by the horse itself up to what degree of training it can be brought according to its natural talents in that, if it is sufficiently prepared, it will always at least give a hint of the next following exercise if it is asked. If someone has the rare fortune of getting a horse whose talents prove to be sufficient for the highest stages of dressage training, he will not need at those levels a more precise guideline than has been attempted to provide here. He will have refined his own feeling and the sensitivity of the horse and will have produced such a degree of harmony between himself and the horse that he actually need only carefully listen to his student's nature to ascertain that it is willing and able to obey him, or at least willing to try.

ENDNOTES

[1] Since the horse does not leave the ground with all four legs, the pesade, or levade, is actually only a preliminary movement for the airs above the ground and, in addition, the most perfect exercise for the simultaneous flexing of the hind legs. It is, therefore, considered to belong to the movements that serve to make both hind legs flexible simultaneously, that is, primarily the halts, and is thus a perfect school halt. (Hans von Heydebreck)

[2] If hereafter we speak, for the sake of simplicity, only of the horizontal carriage of the body in the higher leaps of the haute école, this should be understood only as a definite approach to the horizontal. Only the capriole will generally be truly horizontal when the impulsion of the striking-out raises the croup. (Paul Plinzner)

[3] In the Spanish Riding School in Vienna the levade is always developed from the piaffe. Seeger, Steinbrecht's mentor, also initiated it that way. (Hans von Heydebreck)

E. Epilogue

In the "Conclusion" appended to the earlier editions it was summarized once more that the training of the horse from beginning to end occurs according to the same irrevocable rules, and therefore the opinion that the hunter, the horse for general riding, and the dressage horse must be worked according to quite different, mutually exclusive principles was based on a misunderstanding of the nature of horse training. Any working of the horse for the purpose of schooling it for any type of practical use, be it on the steeplechase track, in the hunt field, in military service at the front, or in a carrousel must begin with "being able to give oneself a secure lever by suitably shaping head and neck so that it is possible to reliably influence the forward urging body mass." It was stated that there is no use of the horse in which this principle of all dressage was not required.

Today probably all knowledgeable and experienced riders are convinced that systematic gymnastic exercises are indispensable for any riding horse no matter what its intended later use. And this use today is very varied and multifaceted because, aside from the above-mentioned uses, the development of equestrian competitions has placed other, higher, and varied demands on the utility horse in which only solid, expert training promises success. Jumping and cross-country riding now demand performances which were considered impossible in the past. The training required for this purpose, necessitating special, systematic familiarization and schooling of the horse for these purposes, gave rise to the thought that dressage training is not only superfluous but even detrimental for the jumper and cross-country horse. The reason for such phenomena is not only the erroneous understanding of the term "dressage training," but also the errors made and in part caused in the training regime by ever increasing demands in competition dressage tests.

The working method employed today by many trainers, however, often evidences a lack of the necessary understanding of the true meaning of the art of riding. If you have carefully read the two chapters of this book, combined under the heading, "Purpose of Dressage," and have entered into Steinbrecht's mind, you will have no doubt that dressage has the purpose of enabling the horse's muscles through systematically ordered gymnastic exercises to enable its skeleton to carry itself as required for service under saddle, a carriage that enables it to always be in balance, that is, to go in self-carriage. This extremely important characteristic of the riding horse, which is decisive for its successful use in any practical application, is unfortunately absent in many of our so-called "dressage horses."

In his "Conclusion," the publisher of the first edition laid down the principle that any work on the horse must "begin with the suitable shaping of head and neck," with the "perpendicular nose" being mentioned as an external characteristic of this desirable shape. Such a requirement may easily lead to misinterpretations. From the beginning it directs the trainer's attention toward shaping the forehand although the shape of the forehand is actually always a function of the suitable development and shaping of the hindquarters which must be enabled through gymnastic exercises to relieve the forehand. This then produces the proper carriage of the forehand automatically.

Steinbrecht's bending work shows us the way on which we can reliably reach this goal and, by loosening all muscles and joints, leads us to the re-established natural self-carriage which had been innate in the horse but was initially interfered with by the weight of the rider. In this natural self-carriage the horse finds its natural way of going for its utility self-carriage in which impulsive paces, throughness, obedience, and balance are ensured. *In the training of a utility horse it is never important which lessons it is taught but that it acquires these characteristics.*

To do this, the horse will have to pass through the training stages clearly developed by Steinbrecht. First, once it has gained confidence in its rider, it must go forward in response to driving aids and must learn to stretch into the bit, thus enabling the reins to exert whatever influence is desired. Through bending exercises the horse must be made to relax and set straight to then transfer the impulsion generated by the hind legs forward into the poll to cause it to yield. Finally, through the interaction of the rider's legs, weight, and hands, the horse must carry more weight on its hindquarters, must energetically push off with them and receive some of the impulsion generated in this way. This impulsion is then returned by means of the rider's hands through poll, neck, and back to the horse's hind legs that are carried forward underneath the load to thus relieve the forehand when required.

Which exercises should be used for this purpose depends on the horse's conformation, its individual talents, and finally on its intended use; they are never an end in themselves, always only a means to an end!

However, this gymnastic training must always go hand in hand with careful familiarization work and special schooling and preparation for the later intended use. Expediently all of this work will have to take place out in the open, preferably in the open country, particularly for horses that are destined for performance tests cross-country and in the jumper ring, where the self-carriage established in the riding arena or in a dressage ring must then be checked and confirmed.

If our so-called good dressage horses then lose their self-carriage, this is not the fault of "dressage" per se but of "false dressage training." Correct, truly gymnastic dressage training can never unfavorably influence the performance of a horse cross-country.

Such errors in dressage training became evident even in Steinbrecht's times. In his chapter on the "Purpose of Dressage" he repeatedly refers to this problem and finds the reason for such occurrences in the noticeable lack of understanding and skillful trainers. The publisher of the first editions of the "Gymnasium" also mentions this fact repeatedly and recommends in the chapter on "Piaffe and Passage" and in the "Conclusion" the re-establishment or new establishment of academic riding schools at the princely stables for the training of good professional riders. In view of the fact that such stables no longer exist here in Germany at present I have omitted the respective statements in that chapter. However, because of the extreme importance that I see in this subject of the preservation of the true equestrian art I do want to discuss the value and significance of such riding colleges in this summarizing epilogue and explain the need for them.

No art, no science, no craft, no trade, not even agriculture is able to continue in existence without the knowledge gained through scientific research and practical experience being laid down, evaluated, and made available for use in practice. State-run schools of higher education under the direction of experts must serve this purpose. They provide the necessary instructor personnel and educational materials and thus permit even those without means, if they are able to demonstrate the talent and education required for their subject, to gain the knowledge and skills needed for their occupation. In particular, these schools must train the instructors. Only the equestrian art does not have such schools!

Certainly, at present we still have the Cavalry School at Hanover with its dressage and jumper stable which has a fertilizing influence on all equestrian life. But its effective range is limited and naturally extends primarily to military riders who, due to their short periods of service and the increasing motorization, will become a smaller and smaller group. It does not look promising for any truly expertly trained riding instructors and understanding trainers to come from the military. And the equestrian art cannot be maintained solely by holding horse shows, much less can it be brought to a higher stage that way.

Due to the fact that, as already mentioned, the number and difficulty of the movements to be ridden in dressage tests keeps going higher and higher, we have arrived at the point where decent riding suffers. In the equestrian competitions at the Olympics, haute école movements are already required in dressage although the majority of the riders and horses are not fully capable of even meeting the requirements for general riding. What is shown then is no longer equestrian art but tricks!

Just as other arts, such as painting or music, cannot be nurtured and maintained solely by public exhibitions or events, but must be provided with schools that are maintained for just that purpose where young artists can be trained, the disciples of the equestrian art must be given an opportunity to delve into the essence of their art to acquire the necessary scientific education and equestrian skills. This can be accomplished only by a state-supported school of higher education that is equipped with the best instructors and instructional materials, and particularly with excellently trained horses! Only such a school can cultivate and maintain the true equestrian art - yes, riding is an art and not a craft and also not only a sport. A private school is not able to accomplish this since it will always be guided by commercial concerns instead of subject-oriented, scientific, artistic, and cultural concerns.

Although the attentive reader, having followed to the end Steinbrecht's teachings and principles as reflected in this work, will have no doubt that riding is truly an art and a science and that only the most diligent study and long years of practice and experience will bring forth the knowledge and abilities required in this field, I would like to take the liberty of illuminating this subject once more and explain to the outsider as well the necessity for the establishment of such state-run colleges of equestrian education.

Whoever is familiar with the history of the art of riding knows that at all times there were only a few true masters of equitation and that these in turn produced only a few first-class students who were able to work successfully as instructors. Probably no other art has produced so few significant masters as the art of riding. And why? Because no art had to struggle with such a multitude of different and complicated difficulties as the art of riding. It places particularly multifaceted demands not only on the person practicing the art, that is, the rider, but also on the instrument he uses, the horse, and in addition it must overcome many inhibitions in the teaching of its subjects.

To justify this claim, I want to compare the art of riding with other arts and follow the line of thought once developed by a famous French master of equitation who to this day is still considered a recognized equestrian authority in France, General l'Hotte.

First there is the person interested in the art, the student! He must combine in himself so many different characteristics, physical, temperamental, and mental, as nature only rarely gives to an individual person, and as no other art requires of its student to such an extent. For the rider of classical equitation it is not sufficient to have physical traits, like the painter, sculptor or musician who needs favorably constructed arms and hands to practice his art, the rider's whole body must have favorable proportions since all its parts, limbs, and muscles must cooperate during a ride.

Added to this must also be quite specific character traits, namely calmness paired with energy, an even temper without weakness, firmness without roughness. Moreover, the rider must be able to control himself so that he always remains master of his emotions and is able to counter impatience with patience, impetuosity with calmness, laziness and disobedience with decisiveness. Free of conceit, his love for the art must be based on a certain moral fortitude so that no disappointment will shatter him, no difficulty can make him falter; perseverance must distinguish the classical rider more than any other practicing artist.

These physical and character traits must be supplemented by a full mastery of the scientific principles of equitation so that the rider is accountable for all occurrences during his riding and is able to draw knowledge from them to utilize when he himself is in the saddle and in his role as instructor.

But even if these so extensive and necessary prerequisites are met, the most important factor must still be added, namely the proper feeling, the fine "equestrian tact." Steinbrecht has the particular distinction of consistently referring emphatically to this basic requirement for good riding, and he demands that the foundation for such equestrian tact must already be laid during the student's first seat exercises and never be disregarded in the further course of his training.

This fine feeling, however, if a seed for it is present - as has been emphasized at every opportunity in the preceding chapters - can be acquired only on truly well trained horses. And this leads us to the instrument the rider uses to practice his art, the horse.

Every horse combines in itself - as does every human being - certain individual physical, temperamental, and mental traits, and its schooling therefore requires the corresponding individual training and treatment that are adapted to these traits.

If one considers the green horse as the raw material from which the work of art is to be created, one can clearly see how great the difficulties are that the rider practicing the art will encounter in his work. The sculptor forms his work of art from an inanimate raw material that is always the same, be it marble, clay, or wax. The trainer, however, must change a living being with its innate special characteristics into a work of art. No horse is like another and each individual horse requires a working method that is adapted especially for it. And sometimes the trainer learns only during his work, although he may have extensive practice and experience, the particularities and the intrinsic virtue of the material with which he is working. He continues to encounter new difficulties and obstacles. After truly successful work days come new surprises and disappointments. Although other artists also have some days on which their creative work is not as successful as on others, they are never exposed to the type of disappointments encountered by a horse trainer.

But even assuming that after long, careful work the job is completed, a work of art in the form of a perfectly trained dressage horse has been created. Now the artist must play this instrument according to his art. How much easier and simpler is this, for example, for the musician. Although the violinist will have to tune his violin before he actually plays it, that is hardly a problem for the practiced ear and requires no special skill. And once this has been done, the instrument will always produce the same sound if the same touch and bow-stroke are used.

The tuning and handling of the living instrument, the horse, by a rider is quite different. Even the preparation each time requires his fullest artistry and - aside from the artistic perception - it requires not only skilled arms and hands; all the limbs and organs of his body participate. In addition he needs not only the proper hearing and musical interpretation like the violin player but also a sensitivity that has been refined to the utmost, equestrian tact. The vitality inherent in the animal, its will, the independent impulses of its temperament constantly give the rider, and particularly the less experienced rider, a plethora of complicated difficulties that he can overcome only if he has already acquired the secure fine feeling of equestrian tact. Moreover, the slightest error in the aids - like, for example, a wrong touch or bow-stroke by the musician creates the wrong tone - detunes the instrument again. The horse is no machine, its rideability no permanent state; it cannot be wound up for use when desired, ridden poorly for days, and then put back into the corner. No, it must be schooled in gymnastic exercises every day, its body must be made supple, its attentiveness and obedience must be awakened and checked.

Consequently, any possibly established equestrian college, may it have the best possible dressage horses, would always have to take scrupulous care that their rideability is maintained. These horses cannot go day by day under several half-finished riders without their level of training suffering unless they are always subsequently worked again by classically educated trainers. A private school will of course be reluctant to take such a measure since commercial considerations for running the business must be a determining factor in this respect as well. Therefore such a private institution will never be able to truly use all their resources to supply a new generation of expertly educated trainers to whom one can entrust young horses for training without worry and to provide qualified riding instructors who are able to give truly expert riding lessons. Already the acquisition of school horses that are truly suitable for all teaching purposes, their keep and replacement require expenditures which such a business cannot afford because the income from lesson fees is too low.

The short lifetime of the works of art created by the artistic trainer will make the availability of a sufficient supply of teaching material with which the student can train and perfect his eye and feeling always more difficult than in any other field of the arts. A substitute can also not be produced as quickly as in other arts. Even the expert riding master requires a period from four to six years to train a dressage horse and there are then still doubts whether this new work of art will be a full substitute for the old one. That depends not only on the skill of the master but also on the natural characteristics of the raw material whose true quality will ultimately become evident only while it is being worked on.

The unforeseen loss of a horse will always have to be counted on - aside from the fact that the short life span of a horse already greatly limits its use as a teaching horse - and the inhibitions and difficulties produced by such a loss can be overcome only by a state-run institution which systematically takes care that there is a new supply of suitable young horses in training for replacements. These horses still in training, however, can also be used to great advantage in the development of young trainers and instructors so that they may get a glimpse of the phases of training of the horse and its step-wise development, enabling them to acquire the necessary scientific knowledge and practical skills in breaking and training young horses. In this way they receive not only a view of the character, conformation, and activity of the horse's limbs and organs, they also learn how the special traits and characteristics naturally inherent in every creature must be considered during training. Only then can they become true "horsemen" which is just as urgently necessary for the classically trained equestrian expert as his equestrian techniques and mastery of the principles of the system of the true equestrian art based on natural laws as described in such a clear and convincing manner in the present work by master Steinbrecht.

The multitude of demands placed on the general riding horse of today, which have been discussed before, will make it necessary that such a college is not limited to the training of dressage horses that are educated to the highest perfection but also caters to distinctly practical utility riding. It should also include jumping and cross-country riding and one of its most important tasks must be to prove that dressage is never an end in itself but that its systematically ordered exercises give the horse's body and its limbs the agility and strength required for service under saddle, whatever type this might be.

Most of all, such an equestrian college must produce true riding masters who, through their expertise in the saddle and their complete, scientific equestrian education, are able to act as exemplary teachers and develop proficient teaching personnel. Only the person who has undergone such a thorough, systematic preliminary education and has demonstrated in a test that he is able to become a riding instructor should in the future be licensed to work as a stable director or riding teacher.

Finally, such an institution would serve the purpose of keeping the equestrian art pure and protect it against aberrations as they are so easily introduced by modern innovators and false prophets. In this respect the German equestrian world has had a lot of experiences. A college at which Steinbrecht's teachings, developed so clearly and irrefutably in this book, are used as the guideline and applied in practice will always be the most reliable fortress against such dangerous modernization attempts. An example is here the Spanish Riding School in Vienna which is the only place in the world at present that still adheres to the academic art of riding. The best judge of the Austro-Hungarian art of riding and the greatest equestrian expert of the old Austro-Hungarian army alive, General von Josipovich, attests that "to this day, the Spanish Riding School has been able to continue to adhere to the old, proven, good principles and has fought off all attempts at reducing the true art to the profane by attempts at modernization or the introduction of promotional riding tricks."

In connection with this I as well as the publisher of the earlier editions want to dedicate a few words to the haute école horse which is disappearing more and more from the earth. I hope that the attentive reader will have no doubt about the value of the haute école and the school horses trained according to its principles and about its value for practical use. It is obvious to fear that the many phenomena appearing in dressage riding, briefly mentioned at the beginning of this chapter, in which movements of the haute école are required within a program for general riding, damage the reputation of the haute école. The performances shown there suffer not only from considerable shortcomings with respect to the execution of these movements and include even very basic faults, but they also create the appearance that haute école work is damaging for practical everyday riding.

The majority of horses do not have the foundation that is absolutely necessary for military riding, namely self-carriage and a pure, impulsive way of going in the basic gaits. Thus the haute école is reduced to trick riding, its so-called movements become circus tricks because the horses do not display the major characteristic of any true haute école movement: flexion of the haunches as a result of gradually increased collection. Thus the haute école loses its connection to the military school for which it should not only be the crowning end but also make available the means to overcome difficulties that occur in the course of training and to eliminate faults that have inadvertently crept in.

General von Josipovich, whom I want to quote again here, characterizes the essence of the haute école very effectively as follows: "The purpose of the classical training of the horse is not to show it in parades, its purpose is to loosen its joints, to give them agility and especially the ease of movement in a position of balance in which they are able to move for a long time, much longer than untrained horses, with little expenditure of strength.... In the classically trained military horse, collection is sometimes demanded to a greater degree, but then only temporarily in dressage movements or for purposes of correction. In the haute école horse, however, it is demanded for the duration of the riding program to be performed.... The means of the haute école can be used to train even much more difficult and complicated individuals than those of the military school.... The methods employed by the haute école also belong to those used to improve the horse in cases where inadequacies in conformation and temperament made it unsuitable for military purposes. Naturally in that case it is important for the rider to use these means with a particularly fine equestrian tact, with patient and methodical endurance, and to let them be effective only - not until this horse is able to perform all movements of the haute école - but until it is possible to overcome the conformation and temperament flaws of this horse through the gymnastic means of the haute école and to make it usable for military service. Things are different if the purpose is to train a horse in the haute école for breeding and show purposes, as this is done at the Spanish Riding School in Vienna, or for competition in shows. Such purposes require that the completely trained horse be able to move for longer periods of time in the utmost collection inherent in these movements and with full impulsion without tiring itself or the rider."

Diverse and extensive are the tasks that would have to be performed by a state-supported equestrian college, immense, however, would also be the value for all German riders and thus for the German horse breeding industry. If we had such an institution, the differences of opinion that still emerge in practice about equestrian subjects would disappear and all equestrian performances would be judged uniformly. Such a college should be based on the old proven principles but should also scientifically examine new problems that arise through advances in stop-action photography or from new discoveries about the activity of the organs and forces moving the horse's limbs. It should make these results available to the entire German equestrian world.

Steinbrecht's teachings will then always be the soundest and most reliable foundation because he builds on the laws of nature on which any true art must be based.

We still feed on the heritage of earlier times in which there were not only numerous experienced and systematically schooled riders that came from the military riding schools but primarily also professional stable directors that were scientifically trained at academic riding schools. Today hardly any of them are left. If we do not create an institution that trains us new masters, the art of riding will imperceptibly but certainly be lost.

[1] Translator's note: A carrousel is a military tournament showpiece involving two parties. It was first introduced in France at the end of the 16th century to take the place of jousting.

Lightning Source UK Ltd.
Milton Keynes UK
UKOW04f1919050814

236402UK00017B/123/P